BEHAVIOUR ANALYSIS IN THEORY AND PRACTICE
Contributions and Controversies

edited by

D.E. Blackman

University of Wales, College of Cardiff, U.K.

H. Lejeune

University of Liège, Belgium

Routledge
Taylor & Francis Group
LONDON AND NEW YORK

First published 1990 by Lawrence Erlbaum Associates Ltd.

Published 2019 by Routledge
2 Park Square, Milton Park, Abingdon, Oxon, OX14 4RN
52 Vanderbilt Avenue, New York, NY 10017

First issued in paperback 2019

Routledge is an imprint of the Taylor & Francis Group, an informa business

British Library Cataloguing in Publication Data
Behaviour analysis in theory and practice : contributions
and controversies.
1. Behaviour analysis
I. Blackman, D. E. (Derek E.) II. Lejeune, H. (Helga)
150

Typeset by Acorn Bookwork, Salisbury, Wilts

ISBN 13: 978-1-138-87694-1 (pbk)
ISBN 13: 978-0-86377-144-6 (hbk)

Contents

PART V CONCLUSION

List of Contributors

G. Ádám Department of Comparative Physiology and Psychophysiology, Hungarian Academy of Science, University of Budapest, Budapest, Hungary.

J. Aschoff Max-Planck-Institut für Verhaltensphysiologie, 8138 Andechs and Institut für medizinische Psychologie der Universität München, München, Federal Republic of Germany.

L. Balázs Department of Comparative Physiology and Psychophysiology, Hungarian Academy of Science, University of Budapest, Budapest, Hungary.

G. Bárdos Department of Comparative Physiology and Psychophysiology, Hungarian Academy of Science, University of Budapest, Budapest, Hungary.

R. Bayés Universidad Autonoma de Barcelona, 08193 Bellaterra, Barcelona, Spain.

J.P. Bronckart Faculté de Psychologie et des Sciences de l'Education, Université de Geneve, 24 rue General-Dufour, 1211 Geneve 4, Switzerland.

A.C. Catania Department of Psychology, University of Maryland Baltimore County, Catonsville, Maryland 21228, U.S.A.

N. Dugdale Department of Psychology, University College of North Wales, Bangor, Gwynedd LL57 2DG, U.K.

G. Hall Department of Psychology, University of York, York YO1 5DD, U.K.

M.M. Iwata Mammatech Corporation, Gainesville, Florida, U.S.A.

J.-L. Lambert Institut de Pedagogie Curative, Université de Fribourg, CH-1700 Fribourg, Switzerland.

E. Láng Department of Comparative Physiology and Psychophysiology, Hungarian Academy of Science, University of Budapest, Budapest, Hungary.

H. Lejeune Laboratory of Experimental Psychology, University of Liège, Sart-Tilman, B-4000 Liège, Belgium.

C.F. Lowe Department of Psychology, University College of North Wales, Bangor, Gwynedd LL57 2DG, U.K.

B.A. Matthews Department of Sociology, University of Maryland Baltimore County, Catonsville, Maryland 21228, U.S.A.

H.S. Pennypacker Department of Psychology, University of Florida and Mammatech Corporation, Gainesville, Florida 32611, U.S.A.

V. Pouthas Laboratoire de Psycho-Biologie de l'Enfant, EPHE, CNRS, 41 rue Gay-Lussac, 75005 Paris, France.

M.N. Richelle Laboratory of Experimental Psychology, University of Liège, Sart-Tilman, B-4000 Liège, Belgium.

A. Rivière Universidad Autonoma de Madrid, Madrid, Spain.

E.H. Shimoff Department of Psychology, University of Maryland Baltimore County, Catonsville, Maryland 21228, U.S.A.

M. Sidman New England Center for Autism, 33 Turn Pyke Road, Southborough, Massachusetts 01772, U.S.A.

J. Weisz Department of Comparative Physiology and Psychophysiology, Hungarian Academy of Science, University of Budapest, Budapest, Hungary.

Preface

The contributions to this book are derived from invited plenary addresses that were given to the Second European Meeting on the Experimental Analysis of Behaviour, held at the University of Liège, Belgium in July 1988. At that time, 5 years had elapsed since the First European Meeting, held in 1983 at the same venue, the invited addresses to which formed the basis of the book *Behaviour analysis and contemporary psychology*, edited by C.F. Lowe, M.N. Richelle, D.E. Blackman and C.M. Bradshaw (Lawrence Erlbaum Ltd, 1985).

Both these meetings were by any standards very successful. In addition to the invited addresses at the Second Meeting, more than 50 submitted papers were included in the programme, based on the general themes of timing, language, variability of behaviour, human operant behaviour, conceptual and epistemological problems, psychopharmacology and psychophysiology, rational thinking, and the schedule control of behaviour. In addition, over 100 posters were presented at the conference. More than 250 people attended, drawn mainly from the countries of Western Europe, but also in a few cases from Eastern Europe, and from North, Central and South America. The unusually friendly atmosphere at the conference was based on the engaging enthusiasm of the participants, but it was also facilitated by the excellent local administrative arrangements, made by members of the University of Liège under the guidance of Professor Marc Richelle, as in 1983.

The success of the conferences, and the nature of the resulting books, also derives from some principles that were fundamental to the International Scientific Committees who organised the programmes, and which should be emphasised here. The phrase *the experimental analysis of behaviour* has, and was intended here to have, connotations of contemporary behaviourism based on Skinnerian principles, but the phrase is also open of course to a more literal interpretation as any experimental investigation within psychology. The Second Meeting was overtly designed to provide a forum for interaction between those who would happily describe their theoretical orientation as that of contemporary behaviourism and others who might have rather different theoretical orientations but whose research interests are in phenomena of relevance to contemporary behaviourism. Hence arose the themes of the plenary symposia, which provide the sections of the present book, namely chronobiology, behavioural analysis and the emergence of rational thinking, behavioural analysis and language, and behavioural medicine. A second principle favoured by the organising committee (as for the First European Meeting) was that the conference should be designed to have an international and a predominantly European base. This is not to say that active participation from other parts of the world was not encouraged or welcomed, but steps were taken to encourage psychologists and behavioural scientists from a large number of countries in Europe to participate. With respect to the invited addresses that form the contributions to this book, contributors were drawn from Belgium, the Federal Republic of Germany, Hungary, France, Spain, Switzerland, the U.K., and from the U.S.A. The cultural as well as the theoretical diversity of these contributors should be recognised.

Behaviourism as such has not played as predominant a role in European psychology as it has in North American (see Richelle, Chapter 14). This book is intended to reflect the contributions made by the authors to the success of a conference that was carefully designed to address aspects of interest to contemporary behaviourism in a European context and in a relaxed manner which happily accepted theoretical and cultural diversity. As editors of the present book, we are grateful to the authors of the chapters for their patience and kindness in dealing with our requests. We are also grateful to the Scientific Organising Committee of the conference for giving us this opportunity to co-ordinate the permanent record of an important aspect of the Meeting.

D.E. Blackman
H. Lejeune

I

CHRONOBIOLOGY: ETHOLOGICAL AND BEHAVIOURAL PERSPECTIVES

1 Circadian Temporal Orientation

Jürgen Aschoff
Max-Planck-Institut für Verhaltensphysiologie, 8138 Andechs and Institut für medizinische Psychologie der Universität München, München, Federal Republic of Germany

This chapter is based on a lecture that I gave in Liège, and therefore I think it appropriate to commence with reference to one of the famous sons of that town, George Simenon, the creator of Detective Inspector Maigret. In his novel *Les anneaux de Bicêtre*, Simenon (1963) tells the story of René Maugras, a man hospitalised because of a severe stroke. Maugras is paralysed and cannot speak, but, more importantly, he has lost his sense of time. To a large extent, the novel deals with Maugras' experiences as he regains his temporal orientation. On the very first page we learn that "to Maugras there is neither day nor hour". He hears the chimes that strike the hour but he does not try to count them. On the very next morning, he is uncertain whether days or weeks have passed, and he still is not interested in the precise time of day. However, a short time later, having realised that he has awakened just before 06:00 two days running, he begins to wonder whether it was by chance or whether it was due to some mechanical intervention of his unconscious.

In another of Simenon's books, *Dimanche* (1959), he characterises Emile by his awakening: "He never had needed an alarm clock. Already some time he lay awake. The day had dawned. He had known it before he had opened his eyes, even before he noticed that the sun had risen." Evidently, Simenon is occupied with two major aspects of temporal orientation: the recognition of the time of day, and the perception of the passage of time.

Present address: Jacobistrasse 29, D-7800 Freiburg, Federal Republic of Germany.

This paper is dedicated to H.-J. Staudinger on the occasion of his 75th birthday in November 1989.

He also alludes to the precision of waking, and the peculiar role it plays within the 24-hour cycle. All three are related to the circadian clock, as I will show later.

PRINCIPLES OF CIRCADIAN ORGANISATION

Entrainment of Free-running Rhythms

By evolutionary adaptation to the regular changes in environmental conditions between night and day, eukaryotes have acquired a temporal programme which matches the 24-hour day. The periodic processes on which this programme rests have the property of self-sustaining oscillations. This is demonstrated by the observation that, under constant conditions, the periodicity persists with a cycle that deviates slightly from 24 hours. Hence, we speak of free-running "circadian" rhythms—derived from the Latin *circa* (about) and *dies* (day) (Halberg, 1959). Circadian rhythms are controlled by central pacemakers, two of which have been located in the nucleus suprachiasmaticus (the prime pacemaker in mammals) and the pineal organ (mainly controlling rhythms in birds and reptiles). The pacemaker can be entrained (synchronised) by periodic signals from the environment, designated as *zeitgebers*. The most important zeitgeber is provided by the cycle of light and dark. However, other periodic factors (e.g. cycles of low and high temperature and social cues) are also effective in some organisms.

To illustrate the entrainment of a free-running rhythm, the locomotor activity of a pig-tailed macaque (*Macaca nemestrina*), kept in continuous illumination and exposed alternately to constant and daily ambient temperatures, is shown in Fig. 1.1. Under constant conditions, the onset of activity occurred earlier on consecutive days, indicating a circadian period (τ) shorter than 24 hours. Under ambient conditions, when the temperature alternated between 12 hours at 17°C and 12 hours at 32°C, the rhythm became entrained to 24 hours. After a forward shift of the temperature cycle by 8 hours (day 48), the rhythm (due to its inertia) did not follow immediately, but after a series of transient cycles. Stable entrainment is characterised by a distinct phase-relationship between rhythm and zeitgeber (in Fig. 1.1 the onset of activity precedes the rise in temperature by about 3 hours). In chronobiology, this "anticipation" of the entraining signals is called a positive phase–angle difference.

The phase–angle difference established during entrainment depends on the period of the free-running rhythm (τ) and the period of the entraining zeitgeber (T). The second of these is shown in Fig. 1.2 by actograms of a blowfly (*Phormia terraenovae*) entrained by cycles of light and dark with T = 22 and 27 hours, respectively. An activity rhythm whose τ is longer

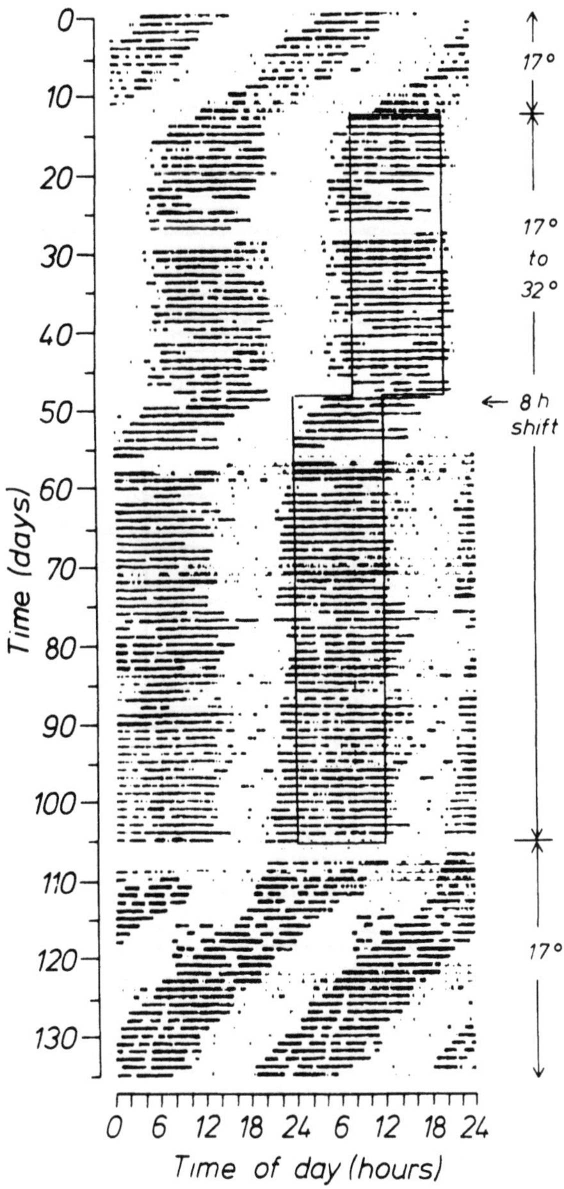

FIG. 1.1. Activity rhythm of a pig-tailed macaque kept in continuous illumination and exposed alternately to constant and daily ambient temperatures (high temperatures within rectangles). At day 48, the temperature cycle was shifted by 8 hours. Ambient temperatures (in °C) indicated at the right margin. Black marks and horizontal bars represent activity. Daily recordings are pasted beneath each other on a chart, and the whole record is then plotted twice along the abscissa (from Tokura & Aschoff, 1983). Reproduced with the permission of the American Physiological Society.

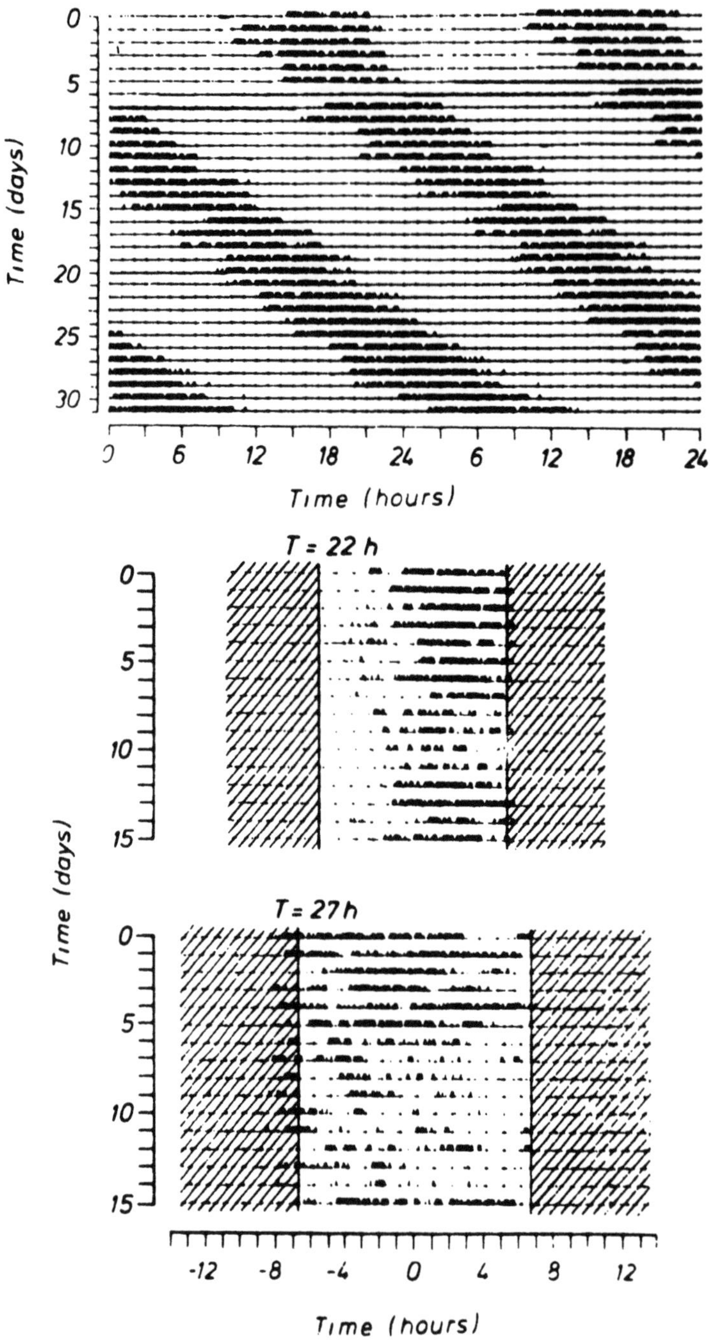

FIG. 1.2. Records of wheel running activity in a blowfly kept either in constant illumination (above) or in light–dark cycles with $T = 22$ hours (middle) and 27 hours (below), respectively. Activity represented by black marks and bars; uppermost record plotted twice along the abscissa. White area: 400 lux; shaded area: 2 lux (from Aschoff & von Saint-Paul, unpublished).

than 24 hours under constant conditions, assumes a negative phase–angle difference with a short *T*, and a positive one with a long *T*.

When entrained to the 24-hour day, the circadian system can be used as a clock to serve a variety of purposes, such as the co-ordination of activity and rest to the hours of light and darkness, the synchronisation of activity among individuals and the sexes, and the adjustment of certain activities to specific environmental conditions. More specifically, the clock can be used to recognise the time of day and to measure time intervals (a detailed discussion of these aspects of temporal orientation can be found in Aschoff, 1984). In this chapter, I will confine myself to a few topics which will illustrate the complexity of the circadian system.

One of the remarkable examples of temporal orientation is provided by the time sense of honey bees. As was first documented by Beling (1929), bees can be trained to come to a feeding place at the same time each day, where sugar water is offered for a short period of time. The proposition that this capacity is based on an internal clock (von Stein-Beling, 1935) is now generally accepted (cf. the critical survey by Brady, 1987). However, it still needs to be explained how bees "learn" to remember the exact time that the food is offered. It should be noted that in training experiments, the bees usually arrived at the feeding place prior to the time that the sugar water was available. Such anticipation could be expected if the schedule of periodic feeding acts as an entraining zeitgeber on a circadian rhythm, the period of which is shorter than 24 hours. Furthermore, if this concept is accepted, one should expect that the duration of anticipation depends on the interval between consecutive feedings.

To test this hypothesis, we recorded the activity rhythms in colonies of the South African race *Apis mellifera capensis*, kept in a continuously illuminated flight room and fed either *ad libitum* or for 2 hours per day only. The inter-feeding interval (*T*) was varied from 22 to 25 hours (Frisch & Aschoff, 1987). The results from two such experiments (Fig. 1.3) demonstrate that periodic feeding entrains the free-running rhythm, and that the duration of anticipatory activity is long when T = 25 hours and short when T = 22 hours. In other words, the phase–angle difference between the onset of anticipatory activity and the onset of feeding depends on *T*, as one would expect from an entrained circadian system.

A Separate Food-entrainable Oscillator?

In contrast to its effectiveness in bees, periodic restricted feeding (RF) fails to entrain the circadian pacemaker in mammals (e.g. the rat: Boulous, Rosenwasser, & Terman, 1980; Inouye, 1982; Stephan, Swann, & Sisk, 1979; and the squirrel monkey (*Saimiri sciureus*): Aschoff & von Goetz, 1986). In the rat, the free-running activity rhythm is not altered when *ad libitum* feeding is replaced by RF (Fig. 1.4). Instead, the feeding schedule

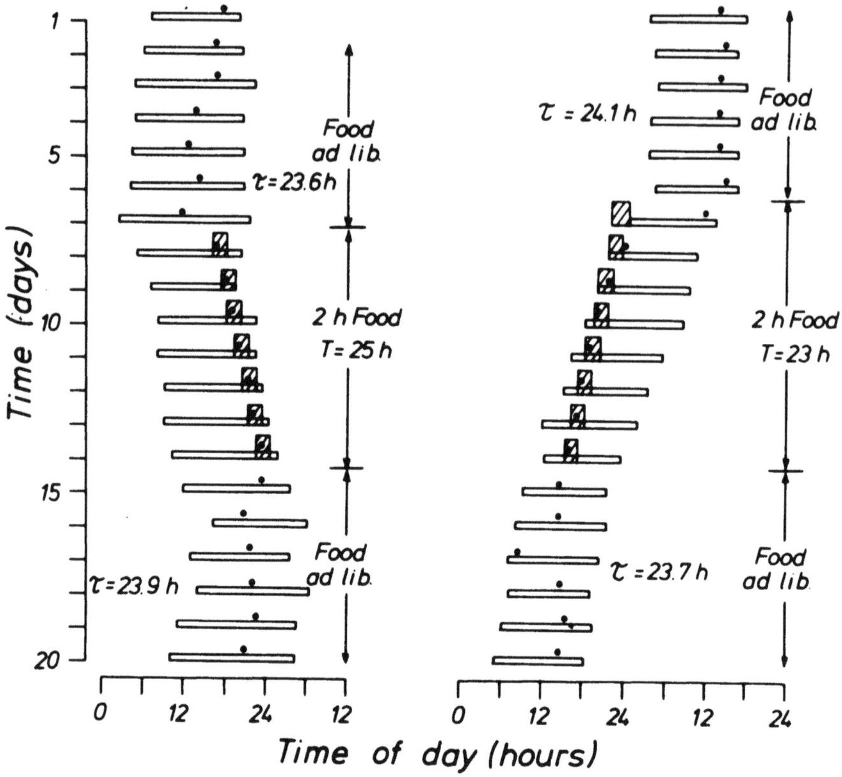

FIG. 1.3. Circadian activity rhythms in two colonies of honey bees kept in continuous illumination and fed either *ad libitum* or for 2 hours per day. $T = 25$ hours (left) and 23 hours (right). Horizontal bars, main activity time (= activity above the circadian mean); dots above bars, peak activity; hatched areas, feeding time. τ = circadian period (from Aschoff, 1986). Reproduced with the permission of the *Italian Journal of Zoology*.

uncouples from the main activity band an activity component which anticipates the feeding time, and which persists for a few cycles after the termination of RF, indicating an oscillatory process.

The duration of anticipator activity (AA) depends on the inter-feeding interval T, in accordance with the rules of entrainment (Fig. 1.5). Hence, it is appropriate to express anticipation in terms of phase–angle differences between an oscillator and the feeding time as the entraining signal (this is shown in Fig. 1.6 for a variety of functions). In Fig. 1.6, all of the curves show the same dependence of AA on T. Figure 1.6 includes data from animals which have been made arrhythmic by lesions of the suprachiasmatic nuclei; they demonstrate that rats do not need the circadian pacemaker to anticipate feeding time.

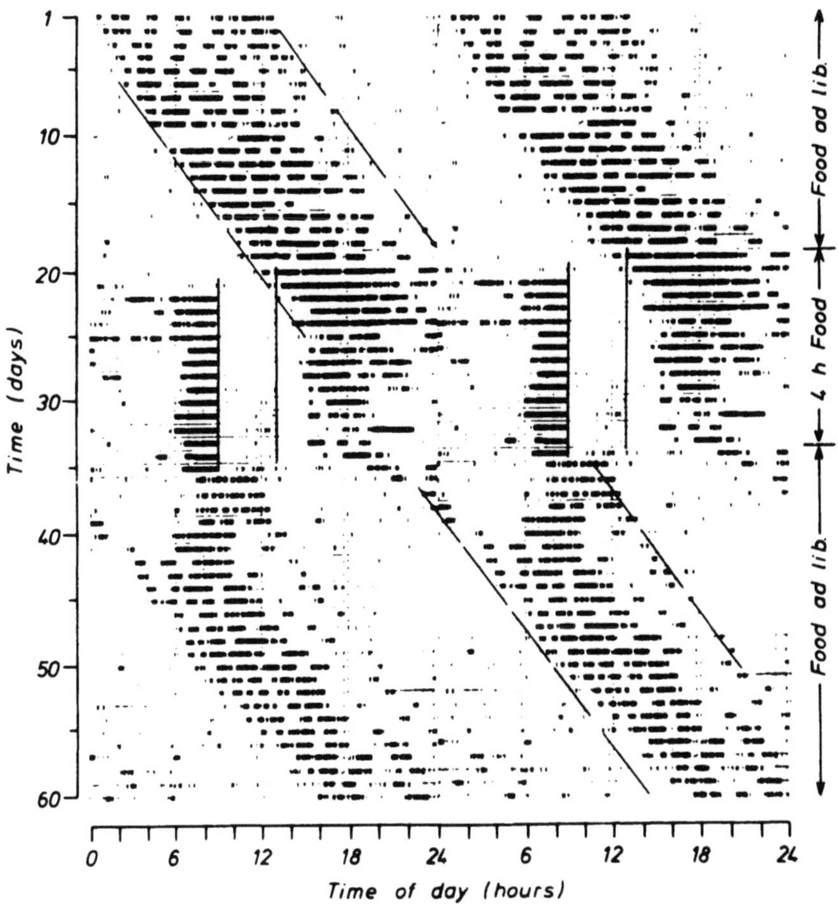

FIG. 1.4 Wheel running activity (black marks and bars) of a rat kept in continuous dim illumination and fed either *ad libitum* or for 4 hours per day only. The original record is plotted twice along the abscissa. Feeding time between the two vertical lines. Dashed lines represent the regressions through onsets and ends of activity in the pre- and post-schedule steady state (from Aschoff, 1987a). Reproduced with the permission of Hokkaido University Press.

From the dependence of AA on T, and from the slopes shown by the curves in Fig. 1.6, it cannot be concluded with certainty that anticipation is based on an oscillatory process. Similar dependencies and slopes could result from a system that represents an hourglass (interval timer). There are, however, three observations which support the notion of a food-entrainable oscillator (Stephan, 1986): the persistence of the meal-associated band of activity after the termination of RF (see Fig. 1.4; cf. Coleman, Harper, Clarke & Armstrong, 1982); the limited range of T

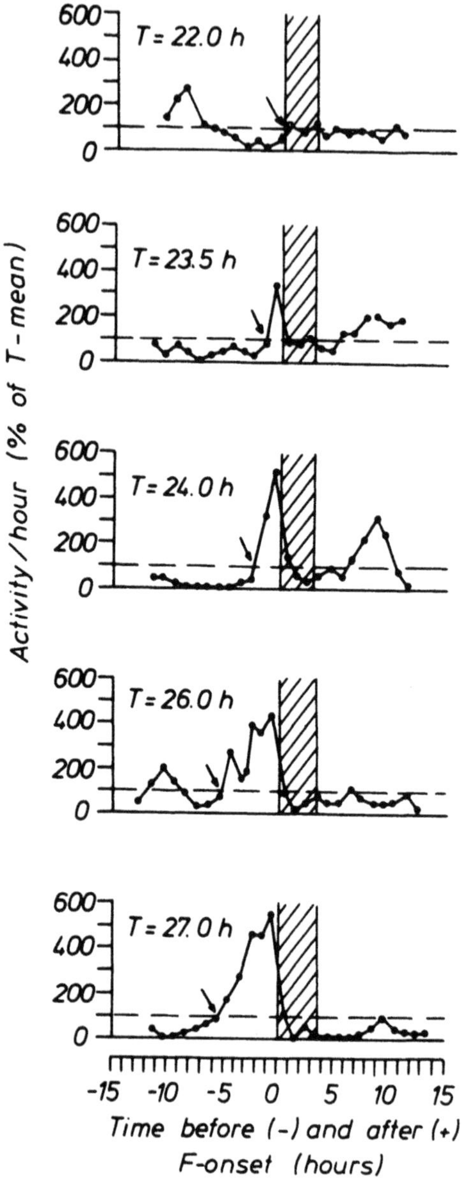

FIG. 1.5. Patterns of wheel running activity in rats during the last days of a schedule with daily restricted feeding. Hourly values expressed as a percentage of the hourly mean recorded during the full circadian cycle. Data averaged over 9–12 rats kept in schedules with inter-feeding intervals (*T*) varying from 22 hours (uppermost diagram) to 27 hours (lowermost diagram). Shaded areas = feeding time. Arrows indicate the time at which the anticipatory activity surpasses the *T*-mean of activity (from Aschoff, 1987a). Reproduced with the permission of Hokkaido University Press.

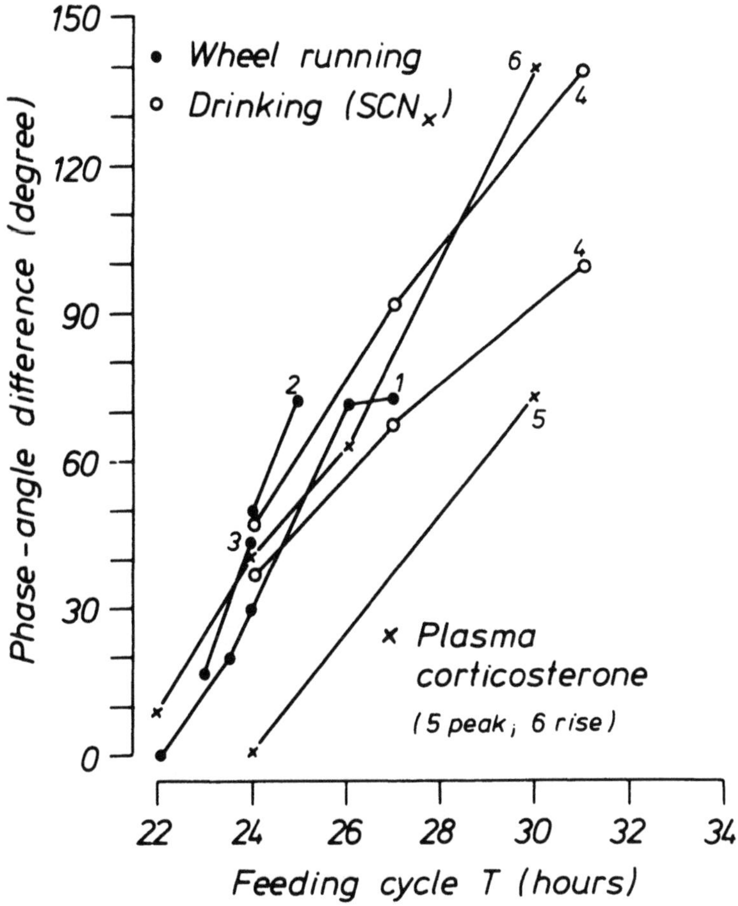

FIG. 1.6. Phase–angle differences (expressed as degree of the full circadian cycle) between onset of anticipatory activity and onset of feeding time, measured in rats in constant conditions under the influence of various schedules of restricted feeding and drawn as a function of the inter-feeding interval *T*. *SCN*$_x$, suprachiasmatic nuclei lesioned. Sources of data: 1, Aschoff, von Goetz, and Honma (1983); 2, Edmonds and Adler (1977); 3, Stephan *et al.* (1979); 4, Stephan (1981); 5, Saito and Kato (1985); 6, Honma, von Goetz, and Aschoff (1983). (From Aschoff, 1987a.) Reproduced with the permission of Hokkaido University Press.

values within which AA can be seen (Boulos et al., 1980; Stephan, 1981); and the occurrence of transients in AA after a shift in the feeding time (Stephan, 1984). These three features provide useful tools in the attempt to differentiate between oscillators and interval timers that may interact with each other when a feeding schedule is complemented by other cueing signals (Terman, Gibbon, Fairhurst, & Waring, 1984), or in the control of reproductive processes (Silver & Bittman, 1984). The principles mentioned can be applied to other time domains as well, e.g. in the analysis of responses to short-term fixed-interval schedules (Richelle & Lejeune, 1980).

Two conclusions may be drawn from the findings so far:

1. The circadian system includes, in addition to the main pacemaker which is entrainable by light, oscillating units which respond to food (and other non-visual signals?) as the entraining signal, and which may be controlled by separate, subordinate pacemakers. The whole system represents itself as a hierarchy of driving and driven oscillators. How these interact is an issue of debate (Aschoff, 1987a; Rusak, 1989).
2. The anticipation of a signal as a part of the capacity to remember a certain time of day can result from the entrainment either of the main or a subordinate circadian oscillator. A distinction has to be made between such a clock-regulated process and mechanisms which involve an interval timer.

THE HUMAN CIRCADIAN SYSTEM

Synchronised and Desynchronised Rhythms

Within the human organism, almost every function undergoes a regular 24-hour modulation. Figure 1.7 shows the circadian rhythms for rectal temperature and three performance measurements—estimation of time, speed of tapping and grip strength—recorded throughout 3 days in seven subjects who slept from 23:00 to 07:00 on the first and third days, and who were kept awake during day 2. It is obvious that, during daytime, subjective time passes more quickly, and performance is better than at night. The data further demonstrate that the rhythms persist during sleep deprivation, and hence are not caused by the sleep–wake cycle, but are under the direct control of the circadian clock.

In similar experiments with prolonged sleep deprivation, reductions have been found in the amplitude of some rhythms (cf. the data on time estimation in Fig. 1.7), indicating an amplifying effect of the sleep–wake cycle. These "masking" effects can obscure the shape of a rhythm (its phase) as controlled by the pacemaker, but they also contribute to the stabilisation of the circadian system (Aschoff, 1981; Wever, 1985).

By means of artificial zeitgebers, human circadian rhythms can be entrained, within certain limits, to periods of T which deviate from 24 hours. Figure 1.8 presents the results of an experiment that took place in a sound-proofed isolation unit, and in which the zeitgeber was provided by a light–dark cycle that was controlled from outside the unit and comple-

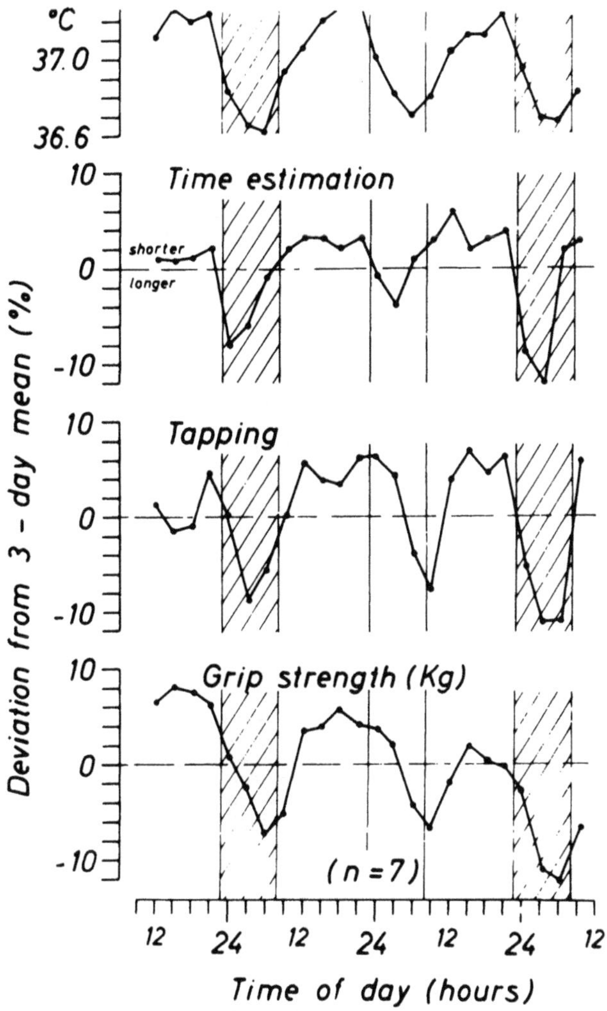

FIG. 1.7. Circadian rhythms of rectal temperature, estimation of time (10 sec), tapping speed (at maximum possible rate) and grip strength (kg). Means derived from seven subjects who were deprived of sleep during the second day of the experiment. The performance data are expressed as percentage deviations from each individual's 3-day mean. Hatched areas = sleep in darkness. The subjects were awakened twice for the tests (from Aschoff, Giedke, Pöppel, & Wever, 1972). Reproduced with the permission of English Universities Press.

mented by regular gong signals. In addition, small reading lamps were provided allowing the subject some independence from the main light–dark cycle. In accordance with one of the rules of entrainment (cf. Fig. 1.2), the subject who was a "late riser" when $T = 24$ hours, became an "early riser" when T was lengthened to 26.7 hours. At the end of the experiment, when T was shortened to 22.7 hours, the sleep–wake cycle and the rhythm

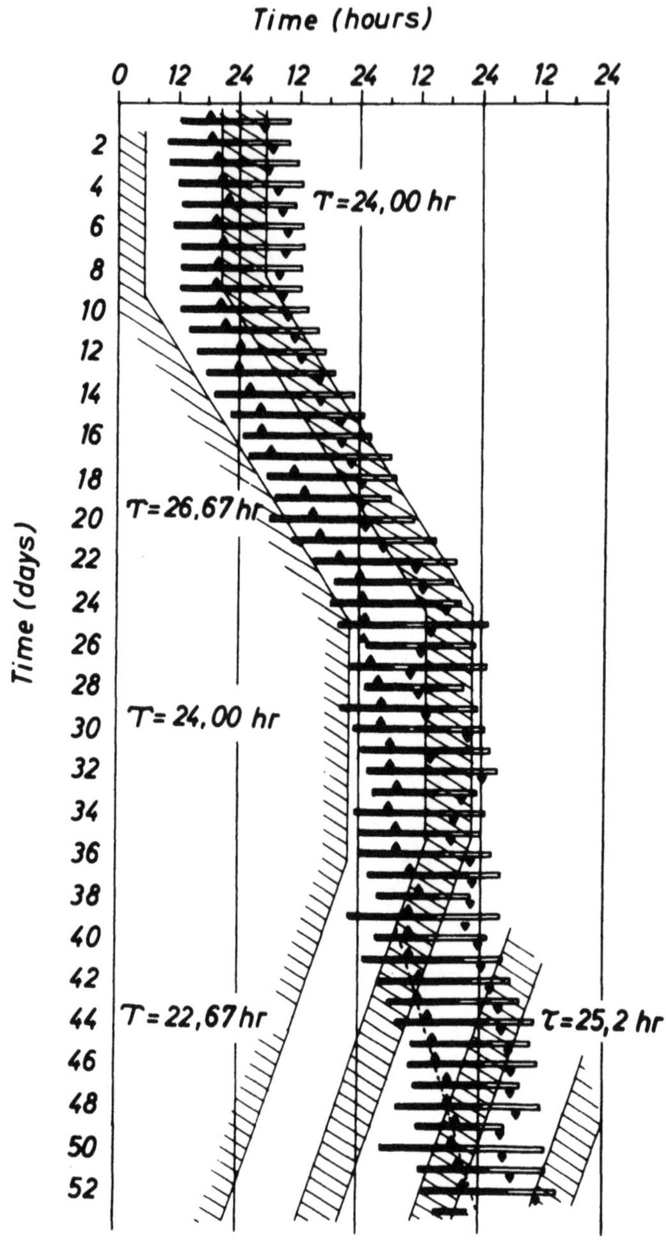

FIG. 1.8. Circadian rhythms of wakefulness and sleep (black and white bars) and rectal temperature (triangles above and below bars for maxima and minima, respectively), recorded in a subject who was living in an isolation unit under the influence of an artificial light–dark cycle complemented by regular gong signals, with reading lamps available. Shaded areas = darkness; *T*, zeitgeber period; *τ*, mean circadian period (from Aschoff, Pöppel, & Wever, 1969). Reproduced with the permission of Springer-Verlag.

of rectal temperature were no longer entrained and free-ran with a circadian period τ of 25.2 hours.

A series of similar experiments revealed that the limits of entrainment by such a "weak" zeitgeber were reached when T was less than 23 hours or greater than 27 hours. Furthermore, it should be noted that when T changed from 24 to 26.7 hours (see Fig. 1.8), the rhythm of rectal temperature changed its phase-relationship to the sleep–wake cycle: the maximum temperature occurred at the end of wakefulness when T = 24 hours, but shortly after awakening when T = 26.7 hours. These findings again indicate that the rhythm of rectal temperature is not strictly coupled to the sleep–wake cycle, and suggest that both rhythms may be controlled by different oscillators.

A complete separation of the rhythm in rectal temperature from the sleep–wake cycle can be achieved with subjects who are exposed to an artificial light–dark cycle without access to a reading lamp. Under these conditions, subjects are behaviourally forced to rest during the dark time of the zeitgeber. Consequently, the sleep–wake cycle can be extended to periods outside the normal range of entrainment. The results of two such experiments are presented in Figure 1.9. In both cases, the rhythm of rectal temperature became uncoupled from the sleep–wake cycle and began to free-run when T reached 22.3 and 26.5 hours, respectively. This splitting of the circadian system into two components—one entrained to the zeitgeber and the other one free-running—has been called "forced internal desynchronisation" (Wever, 1979).

Subjects who live in an isolation unit under constant conditions, i.e. without any external time cues, usually develop free-running rhythms with periods close to 25 hours. In a sample of 27 subjects, a mean period (± S.D.) of 25.02 ± 0.56 hours was found (Wever, 1984). From this tendency of the human circadian clock to be slow, it follows that daily forward corrections are necessary to synchronise it with the 24-hour day, and that the jet-lag syndrome is usually less severe after a westbound than after an eastbound flight. The intra-individual variability in the onset of wakefulness was 2.16 hours, compared to 2.93 hours in the onset of sleep. This means that, similar to what is known from animals (Aschoff et al., 1971), the time of waking represents an especially precise marker of the circadian cycle. Furthermore, it is noteworthy that the durations of wakefulness and sleep in consecutive cycles were negatively correlated with each other, a finding which somehow disagrees with the interpretation of sleep as a "restoring" process. Finally, a significant difference was found between the sexes for some of the parameters of free-running rhythms: females had a circadian period of 24.75 ± 0.48 hours, and their sleep lasted for 9.75 ± 1.16 hours; males had a circadian period of 25.22 ± 0.56 hours, and their sleep lasted for 8.40 ± 0.92 hours (Wever, 1984). These data, which are

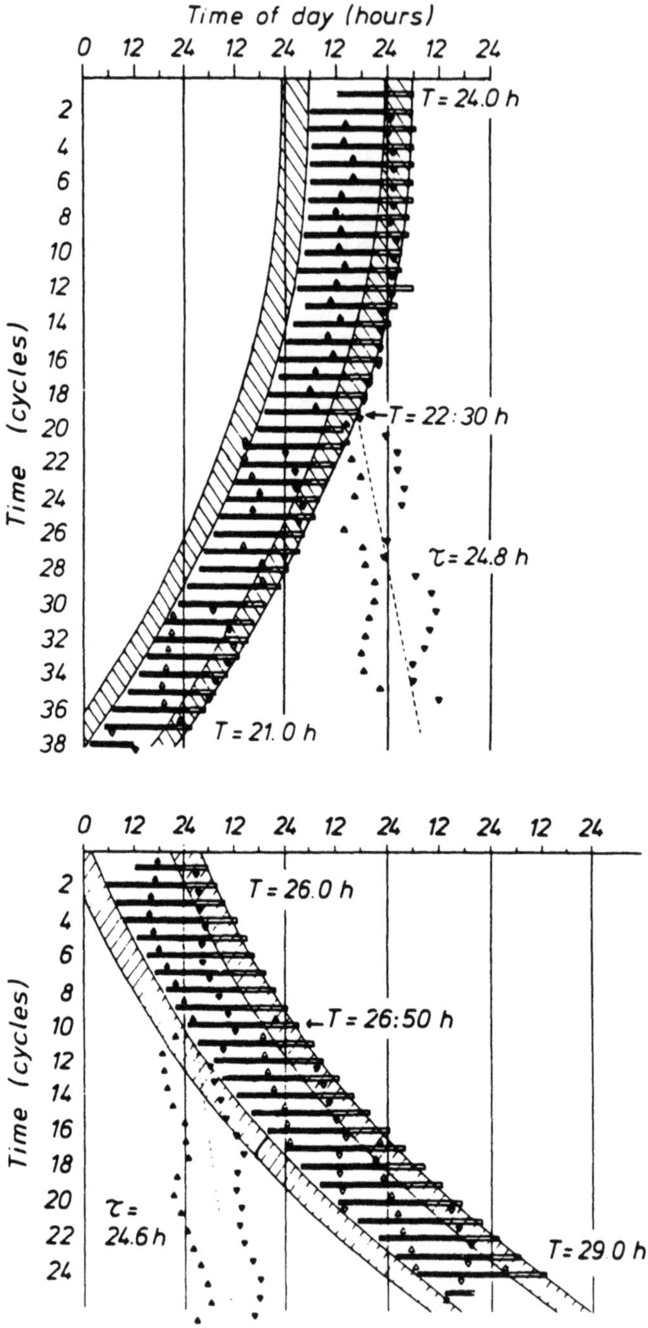

FIG. 1.9. Circadian rhythms of wakefulness and sleep (black and white bars) and rectal temperature (triangles above and below bars for maxima and minima, respectively), recorded in two subjects who were living in an isolation unit under the influence of a light–dark cycle without access to reading lamps. Shaded areas = darkness; T, zeitgeber period; τ, mean circadian period (from Wever, 1983). Reproduced with the permission of Springer-Verlag.

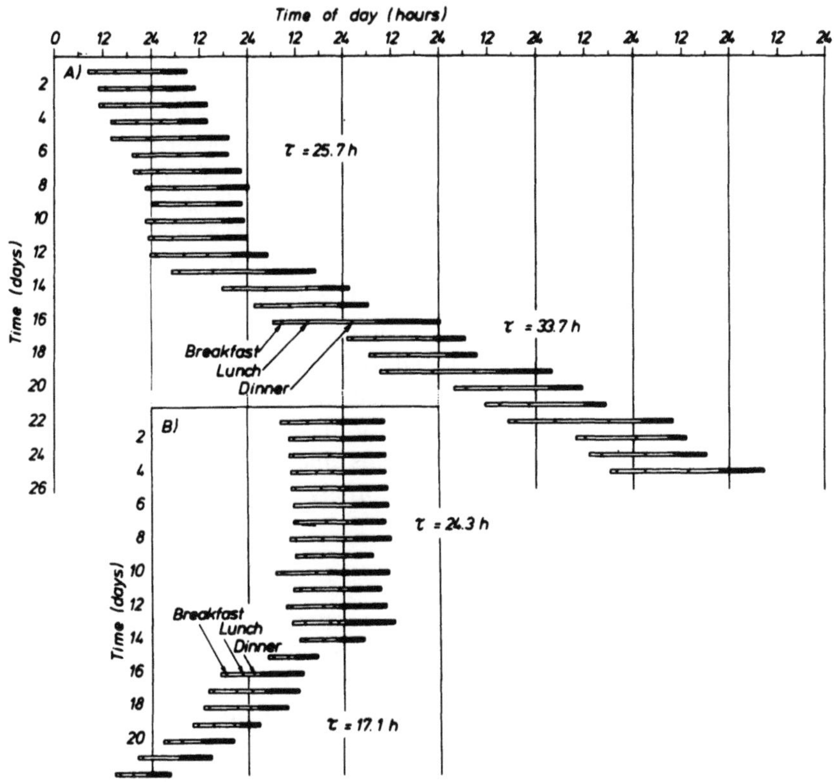

FIG. 1.10. Circadian rhythms of wakefulness and sleep (white and black bars), recorded in two subjects who were living singly in an isolation unit under constant conditions. The two records exemplify the occurrence of internal desynchronisation due to either a sudden lengthening (A) or shortening (B) of the sleep–wake cycle. During desynchronisation, the rhythm of rectal temperature (not shown) is uncoupled from the sleep–wake cycle and free-runs with a period of about 25 hours. τ = circadian period (from Aschoff *et al.*, 1986). Reproduced with the permission of the Guilford Press.

based on an average of 26.9 cycles per experiment, indicate, among other things, a fair degree of stability in the human circadian system. On the other hand, drastic changes in the state of a free-running rhythm can occur. Sometimes the sleep–wake cycle is lengthened to 30 hours or more, or is shortened to less than 22 hours. In such instances, the rhythm of rectal temperature (as that of other autonomic functions) continues to free-run with a circadian period close to 25 hours. In contrast to forced internal desynchronisation (cf. Fig. 1.8), these splittings of free-running rhythms are called "spontaneous internal desynchronisation". Figure 1.10 illustrates (without indicating the temperature rhythm) "long desynchronisation" by a lengthening (above), and "short desynchronisation" by a shortening (below), of the sleep–wake cycle.

The occurrence of internal desynchronisation has given rise to the hypothesis that the human circadian system consists of at least two oscillators, one controlling the sleep–wake cycle and the other controlling autonomic functions (Wever, 1979). The two oscillators interact, and are usually coupled to each other. Desynchronisation occurs when the coupling forces, for whatever reason, become too weak. During desynchronisation, the two oscillators still influence each other. This is shown by regular modulations of the amplitude in the rhythm of rectal temperature (Aschoff, Gerecke, & Wever, 1967) as well as of the duration of sleep (Zulley, Wever, & Aschoff, 1981), depending on whether the rhythms are in phase or out of phase with each other. Various mathematical two-oscillator models have been developed to describe these features (Moore-Ede & Czeisler, 1984). It must be noted, however, that a more recent model which postulates only one oscillator in combination with two clock-controlled thresholds for sleep, also seems able to simulate all the phenomena mentioned (Daan, Beersma, & Borbély, 1984).

The Passage of Time in Isolation

In April 1961, soon after commencing our experiments in an isolation unit, we could make two general observations (Aschoff & Wever, 1962):

1. To live in a monotonous environment without time cues had no harmful effects. On the contrary, most subjects emphasised that they had felt quite comfortable, and agreed to be available a second time.
2. To not know what time it is, could be irritating during the first few days, but interest in real time was soon lost. One subject, who had a circadian period of 25.9 hours, noted on the 13th day that:

> It was only during the first two or three days that I had the somewhat embarrassing feeling to be without time . . . now each day runs along evenly and I do not mind lacking any knowledge of the time of day.

As the experiments progressed, it became increasingly clear that the subjects were generally unaware of the fact that their body clocks were running slow, and that their days were unusually long. At the end of the experiment, many of the subjects expressed their belief to have lived on a more or less regular 24-hour schedule. This is the more surprising as about 33% of the subjects underwent either long or short internal desynchronisation. How can it be that extreme long or short days are perceived as being equal to 24 hours?

To try and answer this question, we asked our subjects to press a button whenever they thought that 1 hour had elapsed. Such 1-hour estimates had to be made as long as the subject was awake, throughout the whole experiment. In addition, some of the subjects had to estimate, just before or after each 1-hour estimate, one or two short time intervals. The subjects had to press another button for the duration of what they thought was 10, 20, 30, 60 or 120 sec. The subjects were not instructed how to carry out the test, e.g. by counting each second. At that time, we only knew that short time estimates were modulated in a circadian fashion (cf. Fig. 1.7), an observation that gives no clue to the processes involved, and next to nothing was known about long time estimates (MacLeod & Roff, 1936). It also wasn't clear whether short and long time estimates are both related to the circadian clock or based on different mechanisms, a question which remained unanswered until recently:

> It is impossible at the present stage to claim wide validity for a model based on the assumption that temporal regulations for short intervals are strictly distinct from biological periodicities such as circadian rhythms. (Richelle, Lejeune, Perikel, & Fery, 1985, p. 96)

Altogether, 42 volunteers participated in the time-estimation study, 9 females and 32 males. In all of the experiments, the subjects steadily adhered to the task of producing 1-hour estimates. Short time estimates were made by 30 subjects, of whom 15 had to estimate two different intervals. To illustrate the database on which the subsequent analysis rests, Fig. 1.11 presents consecutive 1-hour estimates and 10-sec estimates made by two subjects in the course of 5 days. The long time estimates were almost without exception longer than 1 hour, and they show a considerable within-cycle as well as cycle-to-cycle variability. The 10-sec estimates were either consistenty too long (S 31) or a little too short (S 39). Intra-individual variability seemed to be smaller with the 10-sec than with the 1-hour estimates.

A closer inspection of Fig. 1.11 prompts one to consider whether variations in the duration of wakefulness (empty spaces between the black bars) might be reflected in variations of the means (cf. the dotted lines) of the 1-hour estimates but not the means of the 10-sec estimates. Support for this assumption is given by Fig. 1.12, which shows the consecutive "daily" means of the 10-sec and 1-hour estimates, together with the duration of wakefulness as measured in four subjects whose rhythms remained internally synchronised (left), and four subjects whose rhythms eventually became desynchronised by a lengthening of the sleep–wake cycle (right). The curves demonstrate (1) a moderate stability of individual means in internally synchronised rhythms, (2) the concurrent lengthening of wakefulness and 1-hour estimates after desynchronisation, and (3) the lack of any change in the 10-sec estimates due to desynchronisation.

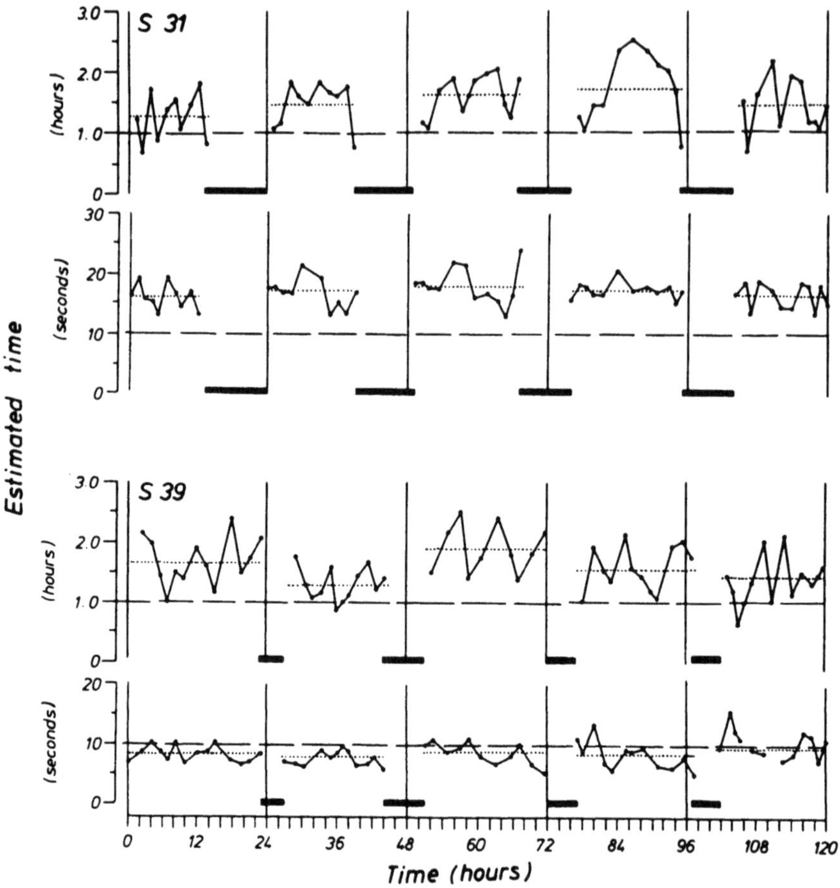

FIG. 1.11. Consecutive 1-hour and 10-sec estimates made by two subjects (S31 and S39) during 5 days of isolation without time cues. Horizontal black bars, sleep; dotted lines, means of estimates (from Aschoff, 1985b). Reproduced with the permission of Hokkaido University Press.

Apart from demonstrating independence on the state of the circadian system, the 10-sec estimates shown in Fig. 1.12 indicate a fair intra-individual stability as well as large inter-individual differences in the daily means. In essence, this holds for all short time estimates (Fig. 1.13). Only a few subjects suddenly switched from one to another level (e.g. S 42 in the 30-sec estimates) or changed their means slowly towards the end of the experiment despite remaining internally synchronised (e.g. S 14 in the 20-sec test, SS 33 and 35 in the 120-sec test, and S 39 in the 10-sec test). The intra-individual, day-to-day variability, expressed as a percentage of the mean, ranged from 5% with the 120-sec estimates to 14.4% with the 10-sec

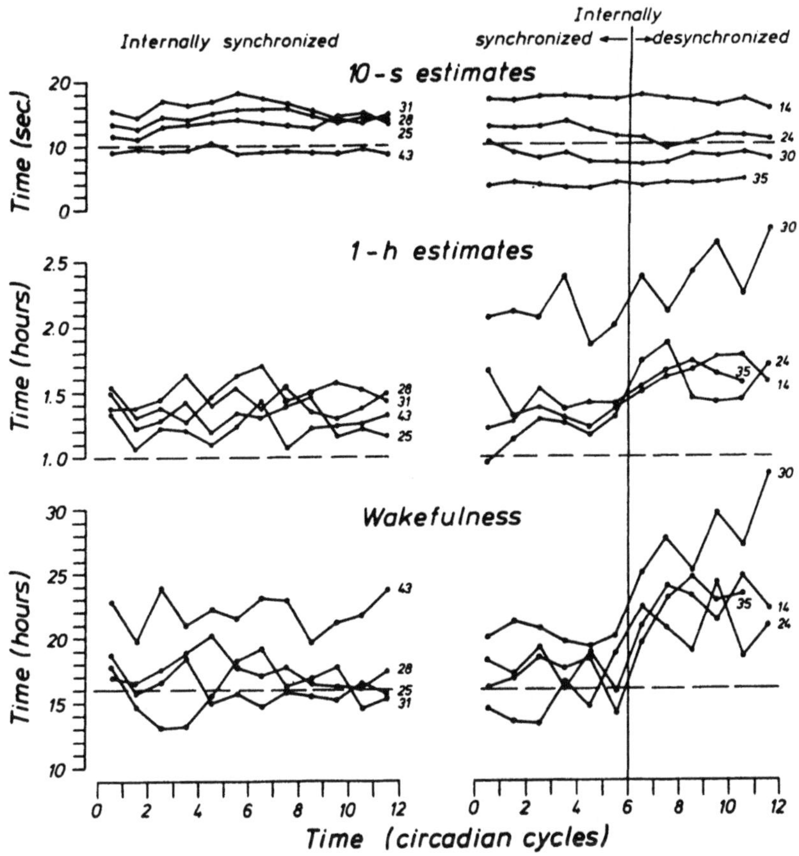

FIG. 1.12. "Daily" means of 10-sec and 1-hour estimates, and duration of wakefulness, measured during 12 consecutive circadian cycles in the isolation unit. (Left) Four subjects who remained internally synchronised. (Right) Four subjects whose rhythms became desynchronised by a lengthening of the sleep–wake cycle. Numbers at curves = codes of subjects (from Aschoff, 1985b). Reproduced with the permission of Hokkaido University Press.

estimates; this is much less than the inter-individual differences in the means (Fig. 1.13). Of the 15 subjects who had to estimate two different short intervals, 9 showed significant positive correlations between the two estimates (cf. Aschoff, 1985a, Fig. 16). These findings suggest a common process for all short time estimates, which may run slow or fast depending on the individual.

As can be derived from Fig. 1.10, internally synchronised, short desynchronised, and long desynchronised rhythms represent three distinctly different states of the circadian system. Hence, it seems meaningful to compute the mean values of all measurements made in a subject during

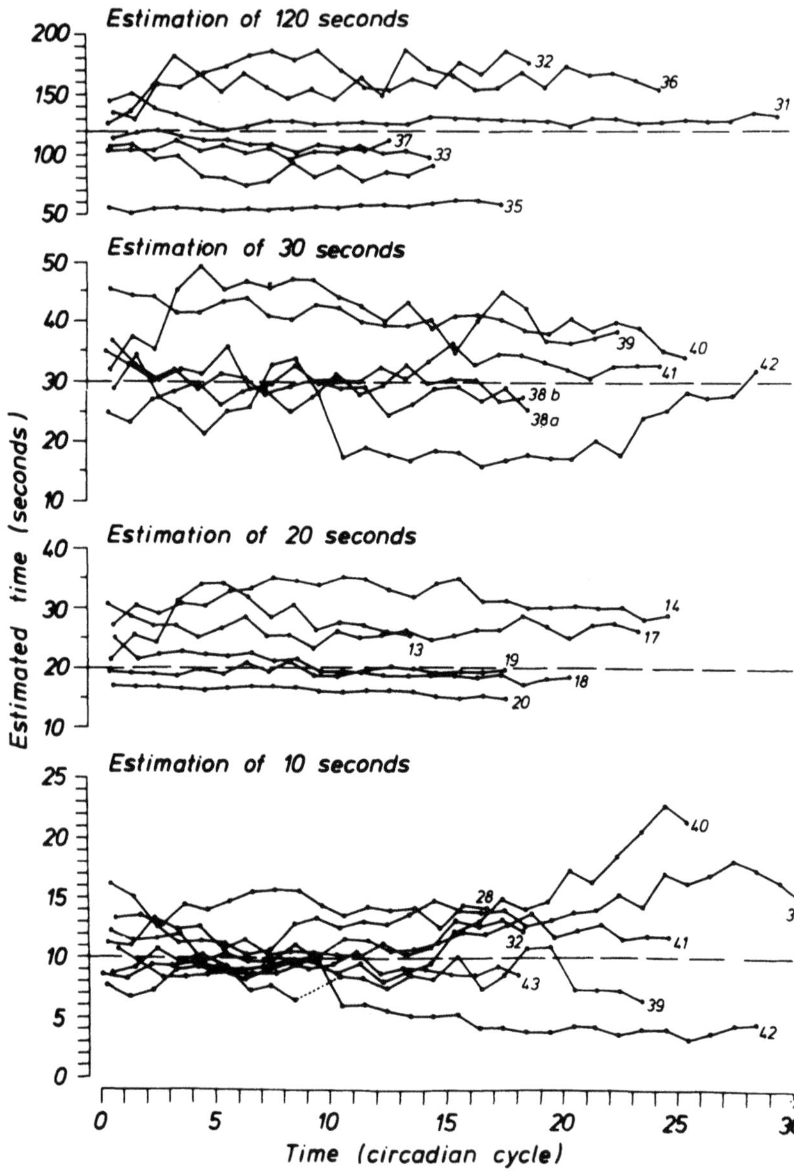

FIG. 1.13. Consecutive "daily" means of short time estimates made by subjects (numbers on curves) who lived in the isolation unit under constant conditions without time cues (from Aschoff, 1985a). Reproduced with the permission of Springer-Verlag.

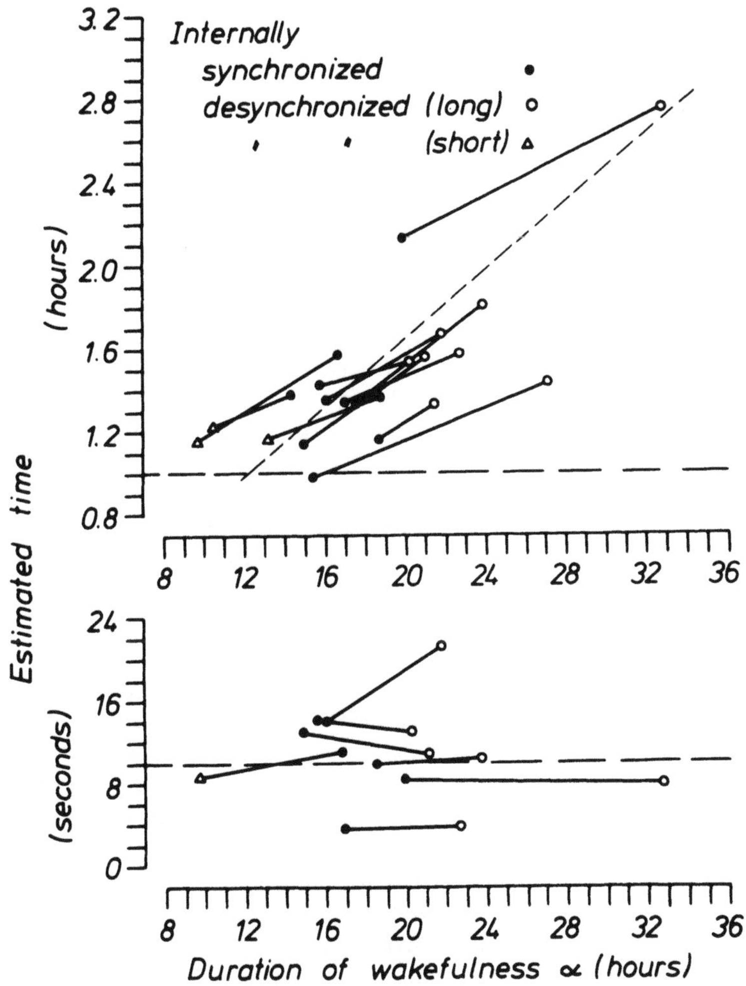

FIG. 1.14. Means of 1-hour (above) and 10-sec estimates (below) related to the duration of wakefulness. Data averaged intra-individually from all cycles of synchronised rhythms (●) and of desynchronised rhythms (○, △). Lines connect data from the same subject. In the upper diagram, the oblique dashed line represents proportionality between 1-hour estimates and wakefulness (from Aschoff, 1985b). Reproduced with the permission of Hokkaido University Press.

each of these states separately, and to relate them to the duration of wakefulness (α). The results of such computations (summarised in Fig. 1.14) demonstrate that a lengthening of α is always accompanied by a lengthening of the 1-hour estimates, and a shortening of α by a shortening of the 1-hour estimates. In contrast, the means of the 10-sec estimates were unaffected by desynchronisation in six out of seven subjects. From these results, two conclusions can be drawn:

1. The estimations of short and long time intervals must be based on different mechanisms.
2. Subjects are not even aware of drastic changes in the duration of wakefulness because they experience about the same number of "hours" on short as on long "days".

Whereas with the short time estimates the individually chosen intervals remained constant, the long time estimates were characterised by a constant number of estimates per subjective "day". If perfect, such a constant rate should result in proportionality between the 1-hour estimates and α. As can be seen from Fig. 1.14, this is not always achieved, because a subject may, after desynchronisation has occurred, switch to a somewhat lower or higher rate, e.g. from 12 to 13 estimates per "day" during long desynchronisation (cf. Aschoff, 1987b, fig. 10). The overall mean of the frequency of the 1-hour estimates was 11.5 per day during internal synchronisation ($n = 30$), 12.8 during long desynchronisation ($n = 12$) and 9.6 during short desynchronisation ($n = 3$) (Aschoff, 1985a).

The day-to-day variability of α and the means of the 1-hour estimates allows the computation of intra-individual coefficients of correlation between the two measures. Of 48 subjects, 47 revealed positive coefficients, 32 of which were significant (cf. Aschoff, 1985a, fig. 4). The males had a slightly lower mean coefficient (0.56, $n = 33$) than the females (0.71, $n = 9$). This difference is largely due to the fact that long desynchronisation (which improves the coefficients of correlation) occurred in only 18% of the males, but in 55% of the females. The mean duration of an estimated hour was 1.42 hours for subjects who had internally synchronised rhythms, 1.65 hours for long desynchronisation and 1.18 hours for short desynchronisation. The deviations in the individual means from these overall means were much larger than those found in the short time estimates. Within the group of subjects who remained internally synchronised, the smallest mean (± S.D.) was 1.11 ± 0.08 hours, and the largest mean was 2.06 ± 0.40 hours. In summary, then, it can be concluded that (a) in temporal isolation the passage of time is consistently underestimated, and (b) each individual has a "personal speed" of passing time, which between individuals can differ by more than 100%. Such inter-individual differences in "personal time" may also become apparent in everyday life, as was pointed out by Proust (1954, p. 314): "Il faut cependant faire cette réserve que les mésures du temps lui-même peuvent être pour certaine personne accélérées ou ralenties."

During internal desynchronisation, a subject may be awake for 30 hours or more, or for less than 12 hours. The question then arises of how meals are organised under such conditions. Because we usually become hungry again 4–5 hours after having last eaten, it could be assumed that a subject who is awake for 32 hours instead of the normal 16 hours—ingests three extra meals, and that a subject who is awake for only 12 hours skips one meal. As shown in Fig. 1.10, this did not happen in our experiments. Instead of altering the number of meals, the subjects adjusted the intervals between meals to the duration of α. According to the data for the two subjects presented in Fig. 1.15, a lengthening of α by 36% was matched by an equal lengthening of the intervals from breakfast to lunch and from lunch to dinner, as well as the 1-hour estimates.

Altogether, the records of meal times for 43 subjects could be analysed. The coefficients of correlation between intervals and α were 0.52 for wake-up time to breakfast, 0.908 for breakfast to lunch, 0.908 for lunch to dinner, and 0.869 for dinner to bedtime (cf. Aschoff, von Goetz, Wildgruber, & Wever, 1986, Fig. 7). Somehow, this dependence on α is least expected for the interval from waking to breakfast, because one might assume that breakfast is taken within a relatively short "standardised" time after awakening, according to personal habits. But even this first interval of a day's routine is closely related to α. It seems as if the organism already "knows" at the time of waking, for how long wakefulness will last that particular day.

A further point of interest concerns problems of metabolism. If, during desynchronisation, the inter-meal intervals become twice as long, or two-thirds as long—as they are during ordinary life—one should expect changes either in the amount of food eaten or in bodyweight. Neither of these assumptions was confirmed from our studies. In the meantime, results from similar experiments have been published which show that the caloric content of meals is the same in synchronised and desynchronised subjects, and that bodyweight remains fairly stable (Green, Pollack, & Smith, 1987). These observations give support to the hypothesis that metabolic rate is related to the duration of the sleep–wake cycle (Aschoff, 1985b).

Apart from judging time intervals, a few subjects have tried, at certain times of their sojourn in isolation, to estimate the real time of day. Such data are available from P. DeCoursey, who served as the second volunteer in our isolation unit, and from M. Siffre, who spent 58 days in a cave (Siffre, 1971). From the very beginning, both subjects had circadian periods considerably longer than 24 hours; hence, their estimates fell increasingly behind real time (Fig. 1.16). The estimates made during the first 4 days can be approximated well using straight lines; they reveal a mean period of 28.0 hours for DeCoursey and of 28.5 hours for Siffre. Data after 4 days are available only from Siffre; however, they are limited to a few days separated by many days when notes were not kept. Interpola-

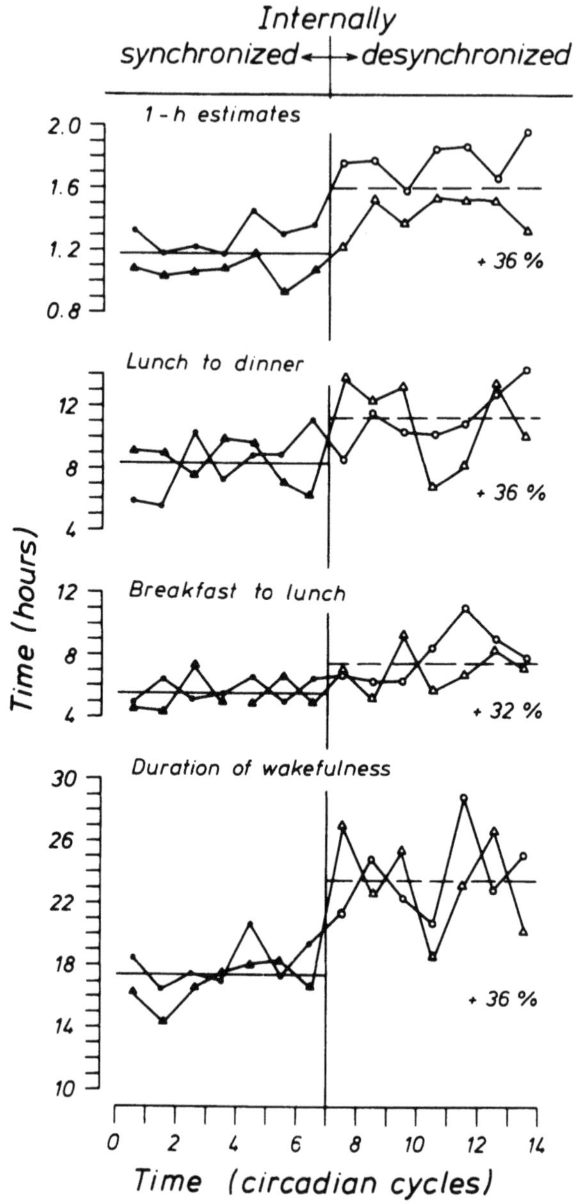

FIG. 1.15. Duration of wakefulness and of the intervals between meals, together with the "daily" means of 1-hour estimates, recorded in the isolation unit in two subjects whose rhythms became long desynchronised. Horizontal lines: means before and after desynchronisation, averaged from both subjects. Numbers give the percentage increase due to desynchronisation (from Aschoff, 1987b). Reproduced with the permission of Verlag für Psychologie.

tions between these data points indicate that Siffre's clock was increasingly slowed down, eventually reaching a circa-bi-dian period of 49.5 hours. It is due to these long circadian periods that Siffre considered the 58 days of his stay in the cave to have lasted for only 33 days.

In the course of discussing data from two cave experiments which were presented by Fraisse, Siffre, Oleron, & Zuili (1968), Richelle pointed out that in explaining the errors made by a subject in isolation, a distinction has to be made between the estimation of time intervals and the construction of a calender by counting awakenings:

> Le dérèglement du calendrier des sujets isolés ne parait ainsi nullement s'expliquer par un trouble dans l'estimation du temps; elle s'explique par une impossibilité du prendre conscience correctement d'une durée biologique particulière, la durée du sommeil. (Richelle, 1968, p. 310)

It is probably more difficult to estimate the duration of sleep than that of any time interval experienced during wakefulness. Hence, larger errors might be expected when the time of day is estimated immediately after waking up, as compared to estimates made later on during the day. It is therefore surprising to note that the estimates made at waking (Fig. 1.16, ●)

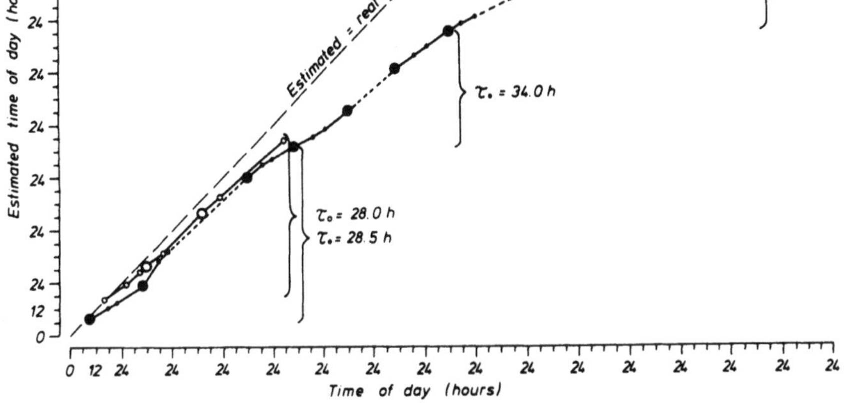

FIG. 1.16. Estimates of the time of day, made by two subjects who lived in an isolation unit (DeCoursey) and in a cave (Siffre), respectively. ●, estimates made after awakening.

do not deviate from the general trend of data points more than the other estimates do. Apparently, the precision of waking time mentioned above is also reflected in the process of temporal orientation at that time, despite the inability to estimate the duration of sleep. The information comes from the circadian clock, the "unconscious" upon which René Maugras was pondering, and from which Emile derived the certainty that the day had dawned.

CONCLUDING REMARKS

There seems to be general agreement that the experience of duration depends on how much information is processed in a given interval:

> If one is in a situation with low informational content (if one is bored), time appears to slow down; if mental content is high because of a lot of interesting information, time appears to pass quickly (Pöppel, 1987, p. 1215).

At first glance, this interpretation seems to fit the data obtained in isolation: The situation is of low informational content, and hence the apparent passage of time is slowed down. However, this slowing down—as indicated by the 1-hour estimates—is *not experienced* by the subjects: They are not "bored", and the passage of time appears to them unchanged. This suggests that the apparent duration of time depends on informational content only as long as there is a reference system with which the experienced time can be compared; it applies to subjects who are entrained to 24 hours and know the time of day. In the isolation unit, such a reference system is not present, because there are no external time cues, and the internal reference system as possibly represented by the circadian pacemaker is either slowed down as well (during internal synchronisation) or of no use any more (during internal desynchronisation, i.e. when the phase-relationship between the pacemaker and the sleep–wake cycle changes continuously).

One final aspect of temporal orientation ought to be mentioned. It has often been noted that time seems to pass more quickly as we get older. It is not unreasonable to relate this phenomenon to age-dependent changes in the circadian system. If with increasing age the period of the clock lengthens, the entrained system will lag increasingly behind the zeitgeber, and will thus give the impression that the external day has sped up. Data to support or contradict such a concept are scarce. It has been claimed that in rodents, τ becomes shorter (Pittendrigh & Daan, 1974), whereas in insects no effects of age could be found (Aschoff & von Saint-Paul, 1982). In humans the τ of the free-running rhythm in body temperature does not seem to depend on age, but the frequency of internal desynchronisation is higher in subjects older than 40 (70%) than in a group of younger subjects (22%) (Wever, 1979). Because long desynchronisation prevails by far over short desynchronisation, it could well be that, in older subjects, this tendency results in a phase lag during entrainment. Of course, such a biological approach to explain the apparent acceleration in the passage of subjective time does not contradict psychological interpretations (e.g. Schopenhauer, 1851, in his essay "Vom Unterschiede der Lebensalter"). According to Schopenhauer's reasoning, the estimated duration of a year is inversely related to the quotient which results from dividing a year by our age. Whatever the real basis of the phenomenon may be, its general knowledge once inspired Agatha Christie to turn the argument around. In *The Clocks*, a murder riddle eventually solved by Maigret's colleague Hercule Poirot, a 50-year-old witness explains to Detective Inspector Hardcastle: "Time goes so fast. I suppose that one tends to think it's less than it is because it makes you yourself feel younger." (Christie, 1963, p. 149)

REFERENCES

Aschoff, J. (1981). Circadian rhythms: Interference with and dependence on work–rest schedules. In L. C. Johnson, D. I. Tepas, W. P. Colquhoun, & M. J. Colligan (Eds), *Biological rhythms, sleep and shift work*. Jamaica: Spectrum.

Aschoff, J. (1984). Tages- und Jahresuhren zur Orientierung in Raum und Zeit. *Nova Acta Leopoldina, N.F., 258*, 9–36.

Aschoff, J. (1985a). On the perception of time during prolonged temporal isolation. *Human Neurobiology, 4*, 41–52.

Aschoff, J. (1985b). Time perception and timing of meals during temporal isolation. In T. Hiroshige & K. Honma (Eds), *Circadian clocks and zeitgebers*. Sapporo: Hokkaido University Press.

Aschoff, J. (1986). Anticipation of a daily meal: A process of "learning" due to entrainment. *Monitore Zoologico Italiano (N.S.), 20*, 195–219.

Aschoff, J. (1987a). Effects of periodic availability of food on circadian rhythms. In T. Hiroshige & K. Honma (Eds), *Comparative aspects of circadian clocks*. Sapporo: Hokkaido University Press.

Aschoff, J. (1987b). Circadian Zeitordnung und Zeitwahrnehmung beim Menschen. In M. Amelang (Ed.), *Bericht über den 35. Kongress der Deutschen Gesellschaft für Psychologie in Heidelberg 1986*, Vol. 2. Göttingen: Verlag für Psychologie.

Aschoff, J. & von Goetz, Chr. (1986). Effects of feeding cycles on circadian rhythms in squirrel monkeys *Saimiri sciureus*. *Journal of Biological Rhythms, 1*, 267–276.

Aschoff, J. & von Saint-Paul, U. (1982). Circadian rhythms in the blowfly, *Phormia terraenovae*: The period in constant light. *Physiological Entomology, 7*, 365–370.

Aschoff, J. & Wever, R. (1962). Spontanperiodik des Menschen bei Ausschluß aller Zeitgeber. *Naturwissenschaften, 49*, 337–342.

Aschoff, J., Gerecke, U., & Wever, R. (1967). Desynchronization of human circadian rhythms. *Japanese Journal of Physiology, 17*, 450–457.

Aschoff, J., Pöppel, E., & Wever, R. (1969). Circadian Periodik des Menschen unter dem Einfluß von Licht-Dunkel-Wechseln unterschiedlicher Periode. *Pflügers Archiv, 306*, 58–70.

Aschoff, J., Gerecke, U., Kurek, A., Pohl, H., Rieger, P., von Saint-Paul, U., & Wever, R. (1971). Interdependent parameters of circadian activity rhythms in birds and man. In M. Menaker (Ed.), *Biochronometry*. Washington, D.C.: National Academy of Sciences.

Aschoff, J., Giedke, H., Pöppel, E., & Wever, R. (1972). The influence of sleep-interruption and of sleep-deprivation on circadian rhythms in human performance. In W. P. Colquhoun (Ed.), *Aspects of human efficiency*. London: English Universities Press.

Aschoff, J., von Goetz, Chr., & Honma, K. (1983). Restricted feeding in rats: Effects of varying feeding cycles. *Zeitschrift für Tierpsychologie, 63*, 91–111.

Aschoff, J., von Goetz, Chr., Wildgruber, C., & Wever, R. (1986). Meal timing in humans during isolation without time cues. *Journal of Biological Rhythms, 1*, 151–162.

Beling, I. (1929). Über das Zeitgedächtnis der Bienen. *Zeitschrift für vergleichende Physiologie, 9*, 259–338.

Boulos, Z., Rosenwasser, A. M., & Terman, M. (1980). Feeding schedules and the circadian organization of behavior in the rat. *Behavioral Brain Research, 1*, 39–65.

Brady, J. (1987). Circadian rhythms—endogenous or exogenous? *Journal of Comparative Physiology, A161*, 711–714.

Christie, A. (1963). *The clocks*. London: Fontana (17th Impression 1977. Glasgow: Collins).

Coleman, G. J., Harper, S., Clarke, J. D., & Armstrong, S. (1982). Evidence for a separate meal-associated oscillator in the rat. *Physiology and Behavior, 29*, 107–115.

Daan, S., Beersma, D. G. M., & Borbély, S. A. (1984). Timing of human sleep: Recovery process gated by a circadian pacemaker. *American Journal of Physiology, 246*, R161–R178.

Edmonds, S. C. & Adler, N. T. (1977). The multiplicity of biological oscillators in the control of circadian running activity in the rat. *Physiology and Behavior, 18*, 921–930.

Fraisse, P., Siffre, M., Oleron, G., & Zuili, N. (1968). Le rythme veille-sommeil et l'estimation du temps. In J. de Ajuriaguerra (Ed.), *Cycles biologiques et psychiatrie*. Genève: Georg et Cie.

Frisch, B. & Aschoff, J. (1987). Circadian rhythms in honeybees: Entrainment by feeding cycles. *Physiological Entomology, 12*, 41–49.

Green, J., Pollack, C. P., & Smith, G. P. (1987). Meal size and intermeal interval in human subjects in time isolation. *Physiology and Behavior, 41*, 141–147.

Halberg, F. (1959). Physiologic 24-hour periodicity: General and procedural considerations with reference to the adrenal cycle. *Zeitschrift für Vitamin-, Hormon-, und Fermentforschung, 10*, 225–296.

Honma, K., von Goetz, Chr., & Aschoff, J. (1983). Effects of restricted daily feeding in freerunning circadian rhythms in rats. *Physiology and Behavior, 30*, 905–913.

Inouyé, S. T. (1982). Restricted daily feeding does not entrain circadian rhythms of the suprachiasmatic nucleus in the rat. *Brain Research, 232*, 194–199.

MacLeod, R. B. & Roff, M. F. (1936). An experiment in temporal orientation. *Acta Psychologica, 1*, 381–432.

Moore-Ede, M. C. & Czeisler, Ch. A. (Eds) (1984). *Mathematical model of the circadian sleep–wake cycle*. Pacific Grove: Boxwood Press.

Pittendrigh, C. S. & Daan, S. (1974). Circadian oscillations in rodents: A systematic increase of their frequency with age. *Science, 186*, 548–550.

Pöppel, E. (1987). Time perception. In G. Adelman (Ed.), *Encyclopedia of neuroscience*, Vol. II. Boston: Birkhäuser.

Proust, M. (1954). *A la recherche du temps perdu. VIII. Le temps retrouvé*. Paris: Gallimard.

Richelle, M. (1968). Discussion remark. In J. de Ajuriaguerra (Ed.), *Cycles biologiques et psychiatrie*. Genève: Georg et Cie.

Richelle, M. & Lejeune, H. (1980). *Time in animal behaviour*. Oxford: Pergamon Press.

Richelle, M., Lejeune, H., Perikel, J.-J., & Fery, P. (1985). From biotemporality to nootemporality: Toward an integrative and comparative view of time in behavior. In J. A. Michon & J. L. Jackson (Eds), *Time, mind and behavior*. Berlin: Springer-Verlag.

Rusak, B. (in press). The mammalian circadian system: Models and physiology. *Journal of Biological Rhythms, 4*.

Saito, M. & Kato, K. (1985). Circadian anticipatory response to food intake in behavioral and endocrine functions. In T. Hiroshige & K. Honma (Eds), *Circadian clocks and zeitgebers*. Sapporo: Hokkaido University Press.

Schopenhauer, A. (1851). *Parerga und Paralipomina*. Sämtliche Werke, Vol. IV: Aphorismen zur lebenswiesheit. Leipzig: Reclam.

Siffre, M. (1971). *Hors du temps*. Paris; Fayard.

Silver, R. & Bittman, E. L. (1984). Reproductive mechanisms: Interaction of circadian and interval timing. *Annals of the New York Academy of Sciences, 423*, 488–514.

Simenon, G. (1959). *Dimanche*. Paris: Presse de la Cité.

Simenon, G. (1963). *Le anneaux de Bicêtre*. Paris: Presse de la Cité.

Stephan, F. K. (1981). Limits of entrainment to periodic feeding in rats with suprachiasmatic lesions. *Journal of Comparative Physiology, A143*, 401–410.

Stephan, F. K. (1984). Phase shifts of circadian rhythms in activity entrained to food access. *Physiology and Behavior, 32*, 663–671.

Stephan, F. K. (1986). The role of period and phase in interactions between feeding- and light-entrainable circadian rhythms. *Physiology and Behavior, 36*, 151–158.

Stephan, F. K., Swann, J. M., & Sisk, Ch. L. (1979). Entrainment of circadian rhythms by feeding schedules in rats with suprachiasmatic lesions. *Behavioral and Neural Biology, 25*, 346–363.

Terman, M., Gibbon, J., Fairhurst, S., & Waring, A. (1984). Daily meal anticipation: Interaction of circadian and interval time. *Annals of the New York Academy of Sciences, 423*, 470–487.

Tokura, H. & Aschoff, J. (1983). Effects of temperature on the circadian rhythm of pig-tailed macaques *Macaca nemestrina*. *American Journal of Physiology, 245*, R800–R804.

von Stein-Beling, I. (1935). Über das Zeitgedächtnis bei Tieren. *Biological Reviews, 15*, 18–41.

Wever, R. A. (1979). *The circadian system of man*. New York: Springer-Verlag.

Wever, R. A. (1983). Fractional desynchronization of human circadian rhythms. *Pflügers Archiv. 396*, 128–137.

Wever, R. A. (1984). Properties of human sleep–wake cycles: Parameters of internally synchronized free-running rhythms. *Sleep, 71*, 27–51.

Wever, R. A. (1985). Internal interactions within the human circadian system: The masking effect. *Experientia*, 41, 332–342.

Zulley, J., Wever, R., & Aschoff, J. (1981). The dependence of onset and duration of sleep on the circadian rhythm of rectal temperature. *Pflügers Archiv, 391*, 314–318.

2 Temporal Regulation of Behaviour in Humans: A Developmental Approach

Viviane Pouthas
Laboratoire de Psycho-Biologie de l'Enfant, EPHE, CNRS, Paris, France

In lay and scientific circles alike, timing activities in human adults tend to be spontaneously associated with behaviours that are mediated by highly accurate systems of measurement, themselves based on elaborate concepts of time. In the human species, however, as in others, there are forms of adjustment to time which do not require these sophisticated cognitive tools. This chapter deals with early temporal regulations which are observable in the first weeks of life and even, for some, during the prenatal period. No review of the studies on the way(s) these regulations evolve or are acquired can hope to be exhaustive. For this reason, I have opted to focus on a certain number of examples in three distinct fields from a developmental perspective.

To follow a logical sequence, the first section is devoted to the ontogenesis of biological rhythms, which are defined as adaptations to the temporal regularities of the environment, both physical and social. Knowledge of the regularities of these biological rhythms allows child-minders to anticipate periods when young infants are awake and active. This is of prime importance in determining the "right" or "best" time for both child-minding and communcation. Therefore, current data on *the ontogeny of rest–activity cycles and sleep and wakefulness rhythms* will be reviewed. First, we will look at the ultradian and circadian oscillations of foetal motility, and then we will concentrate on the development of sleep–wake circadian rhythmicity in the infant.

Ultradian and circadian oscillators are not the only clocks which time the physiological functions and behaviours of the young human organism. *Cyclicity and rhythmicity in the motor activity of infants*, which have been argued to reflect the presence of endogenous high-frequency oscillators, will be considered next.

Finally, we will examine adjustments to arbitrary external durations. These *acquired timing activities* are the result of learning, in contrast to the temporal regulations analysed in the first two sections, which are either an emergent property of a genetically determined system (biological rhythms) or pre-established activities with endogenous time bases (cyclic and rhythmical behaviours), even if environmental factors may play some role in their development or evolution.

This descriptive review lays the groundwork for approaching a number of unresolved issues whose importance has been stressed over the last 20 years (Pouthas et al., 1986; Richelle, 1968; Richelle & Lejeune, 1979; Richelle, Lejeune, Perikel, & Fery, 1985); namely, is there a relationship or even a continuity between biological rhythms and learned adjustments to time? Are the early forms of temporal regulations the foundation for the development of the complex timing activities involving symbolic and cognitive processes found in adults?

ONTOGENY OF SLEEP AND WAKEFULNESS RHYTHMS IN INFANCY

Ultradian and Circadian Oscillators of Foetal Motility

There is considerable evidence that ultradian periodicities of motility emerge during the last third of foetal life: A regular alternation of active and quiet phases has been observed in the foetus (Junge, 1979; Timor Tritsch et al., 1978). The mean durations of these motility cycles, although variable, increase with age, from 12 min at 27 weeks to 60 min at birth (Dierker, Pillay, Sorokin, & Rosen, 1982). Some authors have suggested that the high motility phase may reflect a primitive form of active sleep (AS): (Sterman, 1967; Sterman & Hoppenbrowers, 1971). The presence of motility cycles during foetal life, as well as in premature infants (Karch et al., 1982; Parmelee, Bruck, & Bruck, 1962), together with data showing active sleep cycles in newborns (Prechtl, 1974) (although randomly organised during the first weeks of life), suggest that there is a continuity in the mechanism controlling this cyclicity from foetal life to the neonatal period (Harper et al., 1981).

It has been observed that foetal movement not only follows ultradian rhythms, but also obeys circadian ones. The peak value of motor activity generally occurs at the beginning of the night. Evidence for this circadian rhythmicity comes from observations by the mother herself (Birkenfield, Laufer, & Sadovsky, 1980; Minors & Waterhouse, 1979), as well as abdominal strain gauge recordings (Wood, Walters, & Trigg, 1977) and ultrasonic scanning techniques (Roberts, Little, & Campbell, 1978).

The ultradian and circadian periodicities observed in the human foetus do not necessarily imply that it possesses one or more biological clock(s). One possibility is that the circadian variation of motility is determined by the mother's alternation of sleep and activity (Mills, 1975) or, alternatively, by foetal–placental endocrine rhythms (Arduini et al., 1986), but for the moment these remain suppositions. In contrast to animal studies (Deguchi, 1975; Reppert & Schwartz, 1983), which have shown that there is a foetal biological clock in the suprachiasmatic nucleus synchronised by maternal rhythms, human data have yielded only indirect proof of the existence of circadian and/or ultradian oscillators during foetal life (Hallek & Reinberg, 1986).

Ullrier (1974) reports that heart rate and active sleep cycles follow circadian variations in premature infants (born after 33 weeks of gestation). Subsequently, 10 days after birth, ultradian periodicities replace the circadian periodicity, which does not reappear in the infant until several weeks later. Similarly, no circadian variation of physiological functions or sleep–wake cycles has been recorded in newborns. Although it is assumed that circadian rhythms are governed by an innate mechanism, they do not develop for several weeks.

The Development of Sleep–Wake Circadian Rhythmicity in the Infant

The distribution of sleep throughout the nyctihemeron changes dramatically over the first weeks of life (Minors & Waterhouse, 1979). At first, the newborn spends equal proportions of the day and night asleep; however, by the third week, the child stays awake slightly longer during the day. Then, by about 4–6 months, wakefulness is concentrated in the daytime and sleep at night (Hellbrugge, 1960; Hellbrugge, Ehrengut Lange, Rutenfranz, & Stehr, 1964). This is the general schema, but there is a wide variation in the age at which these changes take place, as confirmed by parents' reports and the experimental data summarised in Fig. 2.1 (Reinberg, Hallek, & Hellbrugge, 1987). Several studies have focused on the question of whether the development of circadian rhythms is genetically or environmentally determined. Although the findings tend to indicate that both are involved, more genetically oriented studies stress the influence of a spontaneous maturation process, whereas more environmentalist works emphasise the role of experiencing external synchronisers.

At birth, the human infant is suddenly exposed to an enormous variety of new sensory experiences. As Mills (1975) points out, these sensory experiences follow a pronounced nyctihemeral rhythm, the alternation of

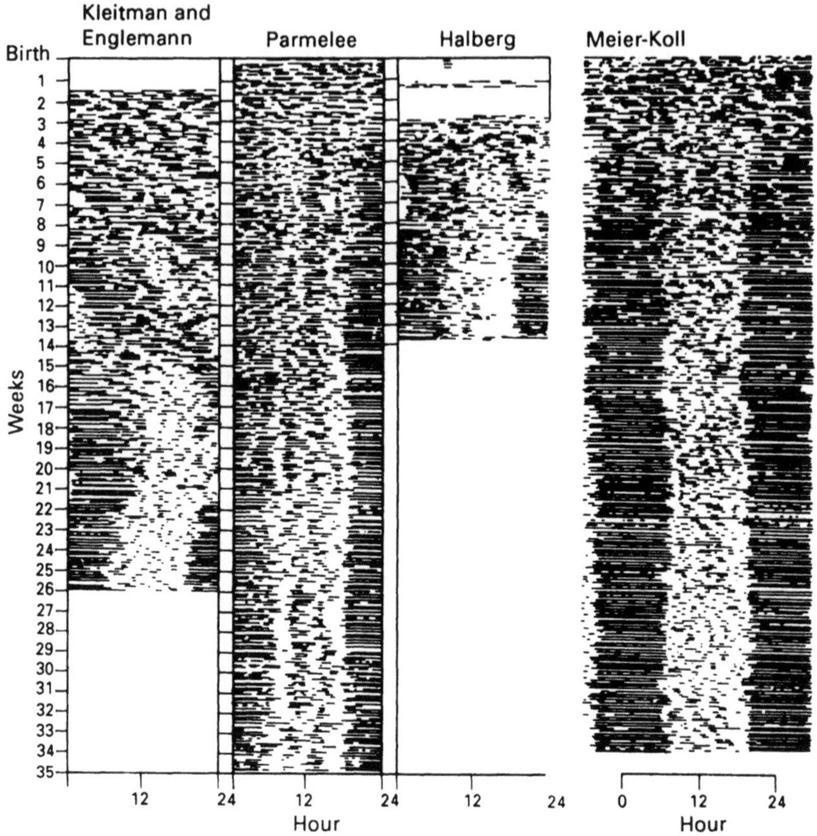

FIG. 2.1 Comparative development of sleep and wakefulness in four infants who were fed on demand. Observations by Kleitman and Engelmann (1953), Parmelee (1961), Halberg (1960) and Meier-Koll (1979). Distribution of sleep (black bars) and wakefulness (in white) over a 24-hour period (from Reinberg et al., 1987).

light and darkness probably being the most obvious of these external rhythms. However, data on an infant kept in continuous uniform illumination and fed on demand (Martin du Pan, 1970), suggests that a rhythmic environment is not a prerequisite for the development of circadian rhythmicity. Figure 2.2 shows that sleep and wakefulness in this infant were fairly random at first, but by days 60–65 a long sleep generally took place between 06:00 and 15:00, indicating that the infant had adopted a rhythmic pattern with a period of roughly 24 hours. When he was exposed to a normal light and dark cycle at 80 days of age, his endogenous rhythm changed to an external one, with greater amounts of nocturnal sleep and diurnal wakefulness. The observation by Kleitman and Engelmann (1953)

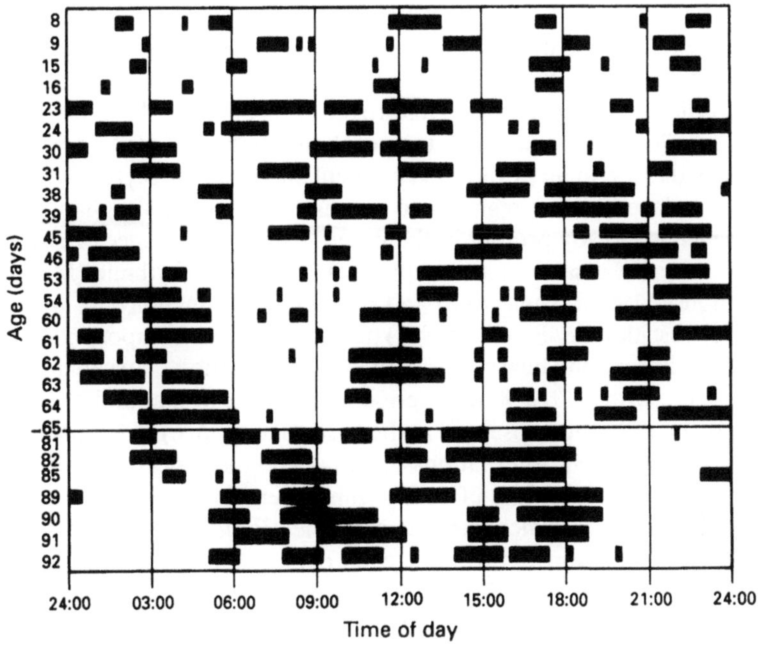

FIG. 2.2. Distribution of sleep (white) and wakefulness (black) in an infant who, from the eighth day of life, was kept in isolation in uniform illumination and fed on demand. After day 80 of life, the infant was exposed to normal alternation of light and dark. Note that the ordinate does not represent successive days. Data from Martin-du-Pan (1970) (from Minors & Waterhouse, 1981, Fig. 8.3).

that an infant who was also fed on demand but was raised in a light and dark cycle exhibited a "free-running" rhythm during weeks 9–15 (see Fig. 2.1), may indicate that the circadian clock matures before the child develops the ability to respond to external synchronisers (Minors & Waterhouse, 1981).

Thus, both maturation of circadian oscillators and maturation of systems of perception of synchronisers are involved in the ontogenesis of circadian rhythms in humans (Reinberg et al., 1987). During the first weeks of life, when oral activity and tactile information predominate, the periodic care given to the infant acts as a synchroniser (feeding, clothing, bathing, etc.). Circadian rhythmicity of the electric skin resistance develops first (Hellbrugge et al., 1964). By the second month, after the maturation of visual and auditory systems, other external factors become important, such as the alternation of dark and light. But because of the nocturnal sleepiness of an infant's caretakers, the periodicity in attention payed to him or her (personal contacts, face-to-face interactions, verbal behaviour, etc.) also plays a part. Martin du Pan's (1970) observations have pointed to the role of these external factors in synchronising infants' endogenous rhythms to that of the environment.

According to some authors (Hellbrugge, 1960; Sander, Stechler, Burns, & Julia, 1970), a systematically temporal distribution of feeding (e.g. a 4-hour schedule) enhances the development of circadian rhythmicity. This may take place because regimented care is similar to an ultradian component which is already present in the infant. Thus, the absence of circadian rhythms in newborns does not imply that they are arrhythmic (Minors & Waterhouse, 1981). Their sleep and physiological functions are timed by ultradian oscillators. Prechtl (1974) found ultradian components in the EEG, respiratory and heart rates, and in the alternation between quiet and active sleep, with a 30 to 90-min period comparable to that of the ultradian rhythmicity of motility observed in the foetus (see above). Kleitman (1963) argued that the cyclic alternations of active and quiet sleep seen in young infants were manifestations of a more fundamental biological rhythm than sleep–wakefulness, which he termed the *Basic Rest–Activity Cycle* (BRAC). In addition to the 50- to 60-min period of this fundamental rhythm, Kleitman noted a 3- to 4-hour periodicity in episodes of wakefulness. Reinberg et al. (1987, p. 344) present the sleep–wake and spontaneous feeding rhythms of a full-term infant, fed on demand. After an initially random distribution of activity, by the fourth week regular awakenings occurred every 4 hours, during which the infant was fed. This very stable ultradian phenomenon is probably not attributable to the periodic recurrence of hunger as Kleitman claims (Berg & Berg, 1987).

One major topic of debate is how the various oscillators interact to regulate rest and activity or sleep and wakefulness during development. Hellbrugge (1973; 1974) suggested that the circadian rhythms "grow out of" the ultradian ones. However, the mechanism whereby this occurs is unknown, and the assumption is open to two types of criticism (Minors & Waterhouse, 1981). First, Meier-Koll et al.'s (1978) and Morath's (1974) data suggest that the circadian rhythm is produced by the dropping out of ultradian cycles during the night rather than by the lengthening of periods. Secondly, ultradian periodicities do not disappear in the human adult, but can be found in the regular recurrence of REM periods during sleep, and in cycles of increased alertness or efficiency during wakefulness (Berg & Berg, 1987).

In summary, the most obvious manifestation of our biological rhythms is the alternation of sleep and wakefulness (Hallek & Reinberg, 1986). The studies reviewed here show that the development of sleep–wake circadian rhythmicity first arises from a spontaneous maturation process. But the adjustment of the clock depends on "the accumulation of experience"

(Mills, 1975) as well as synchronisers, especially social ones. Thus, "the manner in which regular circadian or ultradian patterns emerge may be a function of the degree to which caretakers and infants adapt to each others' rhythms" (Davis, 1981, p. 268). It is easier to see that a lack of circadian synchronisation (e.g. during long post-natal hospital treatment) can slow the development of temporal structures by the child and be detrimental to growth in general. Clinical studies on epileptic infants (Hallek, Reinberg, & Schmid, 1983) have revealed the consequences of malfunction in newborns' mechanisms of temporal adaptation. These infants suffer from complete desynchronisation of their activity and sleep rhythms. Because of their "slower chronobiological development", and the resulting desynchronisation, they are asleep when others are active and vice versa. Understanding how wakefulness or "alertness" is timed is of importance not only in pathological but also in normal contexts. The role these chronobiological variables may play for infants in learning situations (Koch, 1968), as well as for children (Koch, Montagner, & Soussignan, 1987), should not be underestimated.

CYCLICITY AND RHYTHMICITY IN INFANT MOTOR ACTIVITY

One of the benefits of the development of biological rhythms is the increase in the young infant's ability to meet the regular and consequently predictable changes in his or her physical and social environment (light *vs* dark, noise *vs* silence, attention *vs* lack of attention from caretakers, etc.). Low-frequency oscillators are not the only ones which control the temporal patterning of behaviours in young children. Periodicities at much higher frequencies, in the few seconds or few minutes range, have been reported in infants' motor activity. Recent work by Robertson (1982; 1985; 1987) has shown that the spontaneous motility of foetuses and neonates, which is generally considered to be random, in fact varies cyclically. In addition, a remarkable quantity and variety of rhythmical movements observed in the first year of life have been described. As Thelen (1981) has stressed, "the frequency and diversity of rhythmically repetitious movements are so great that the infant appeared to be following the dictum 'If you can move it at all, move it rhythmically'." These cyclic and rhythmic movements are often considered to play an important role in motor development. More precisely, the clocks which time them are viewed as possible precursors of timing mechanisms that control the temporal regulation of more complex motor acts later on in development. This hypothesis will be examined below in the light of experimental and observational data.

Cyclicity in Spontaneous Movement

Robertson (1982), using time-lapse photography, recorded the spontaneous movement of newborns in a waking state. Then, by means of Fourier analysis and spectral density functions, he obtained a measure of its cyclic organisation, which showed dominant rhythms between 0.24 and 1.86 cycles/min. This intrinsic temporal organisation of motor activity can be observed in the foetus after mid-gestation (Robertson, 1985), although parameters differ. According to Robertson (1987), this change may correspond to the functional significance of cyclic patterning of spontaneous motor activity before and after birth, but there are no data available to support this assumption. However, the regular alternation of periods of high and low levels of activity could facilitate the neuromotor development of the foetus by segregating in time the benefits of suprathreshold activity and quiescence. After birth, cyclic fluctuations might regulate infants' interactions with their physical and social environment, by facilitating attention to visual and auditory information during quiescence and by eliciting responses from adults during higher levels of activity. This does not imply that cyclic motor activity is the best source of regulation. However, it might serve a regulatory function in the first weeks of life before the emergence of more goal-directed behaviours (Hopkins & Prechtl, 1984; Wolff, 1984).

Rhythmical Stereotypies

Rhythmical stereotypies are also considered to represent one of the major stages of early motor development. Rhythmical stereotypies are defined as movements of a part or the whole body repeated at least three times at regular intervals of about 1 sec (Thelen, 1981). They emerge during the first days of life (Prechtl & Nolte, 1984), reach a maximum at 6 months, and then decline by the end of the first year.

The example described in greatest detail by Thelen (1981) is that of kicking (see Fig. 2.3). In all infants, a kick consists of a very rapid flexion (lasting 200–300 msec), a short but variable pause, and then an extension a little longer in duration than the flexion (300–600 msec), followed by a pause before the next flexion whose duration differs considerably from one infant to another (observational data range from 140 msec to 5 sec). Flexion and extension correspond to the swing phase of locomotion, and the interkick interval to the stance phase. Similarly, the speed of kicking and speed of locomotion increase when the duration of the interkick interval and the stance period decrease, the other phases remaining relatively constant. Thelen (1981) argues that kicking is the expression of a central motor programme used for locomotion later on in development.

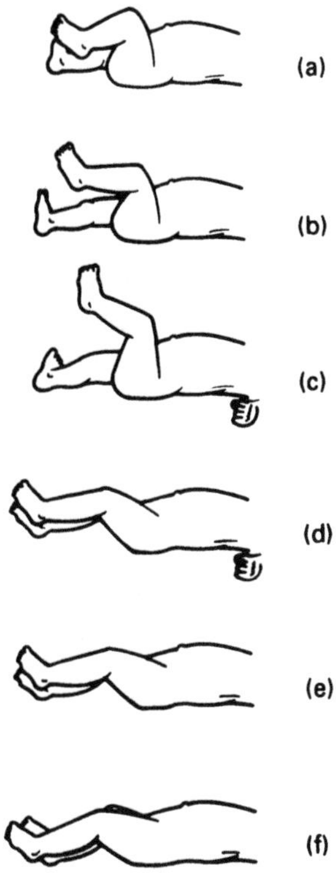

FIG. 2.3. Temporal parameters of an infant single-leg kick. (A, B) flexion phase; (C, D, E) extension phase; (F) interkick interval (redrawn from Thelen, 1981).

This hypothesis can be generalised to other infant rhythmicities, which similarly are simple co-ordinations forming a basis for more mature, skilled behaviour. According to Ashton (1976), these stereotypies may play an important role in the temporal regulation of the different subroutines of the mature motor act. He claims that the subroutine hypothesis proposed by Kay (1969) and Connolly (1970) to explain the acquisition of motor skills in children, is incomplete because it does not take the temporal dimension into account. Young children must not only select the most appropriate subroutines from their repertoire and decide on the order in which they should be performed, but they should also learn during training *when* to shift from one routine to another, *how long* to pause between each routine and *when* to stop. Connolly (1977) raises the question as to how this timing is accomplished. It is unlikely that the environment provides the "learner" with a high-frequency time base. Twenty years ago, Wolff (1967; 1968a; 1968b) proposed the idea—adopted by Ashton (1976) and Thelen (1981)—that the high-frequency rhythmical behaviours of infants, such as sucking and breathing as well as gross motor stereotypies, were controlled by an endogenous microrhythm that is the precursor of temporal substrata for later co-ordinated movement in older children and adults.

Despite their intrinsic pattern, there is no contradiction in assuming that rhythmical stereotypies can be controlled by environmental stimuli, because they are clearly not produced in a vacuum. Learning to catch a ball involves practising closing the hand at the right time; in other words, learning to extract temporal information from speed and distance. In addition, rhythmical behaviours can be used as instrumental behaviours, as demonstrated by Rovee-Collier and Gekoski's (1979) elegant experiments. According to Thelen (1981), young infants may "control" their spontaneous kicking by progressively adjusting the interval length between kicks. Practising how to modify the temporal parameters of pre-established rhythmical behaviours may provide young infants with the bases for the acquisition of more complex temporal regulations, such as learned adjustments to external arbitrary durations which do not correspond to biological oscillations and thus require the development of the ability to perceive and measure accurately the passage of time (Fitzgerald & Brackbill, 1976). Experimental support for this hypothesis will now be examined.

ACQUIRED TIMING BEHAVIOUR

Timing of Non-nutritive Sucking Activity in Very Young Infants

Recent works which have analysed how newborns and young infants learn to time non-nutritive sucking (De Casper & Fifer, 1980; De Casper & Sigafoos, 1983; Provasi, 1988) provide meaningful examples of "early acquisitions following immediately upon the training of hereditary wirings" (Piaget, 1952, p. 204). Non-nutritive sucking consists of an alternation of bursts of about 4–10 sucks (at a rate of 2–3 sec) and pauses of roughly 3–15 sec (Fig. 2.4A). De Casper and Fifer (1980) and De Casper and Sigafoos (1983), using the mother's voice or intra-uterine heartbeat as a reinforcer (Fig. 2.4B), showed conclusively that newborns (3 days old) were able to learn to shorten the duration of their pauses as compared to the median value obtained during a baseline phase. In contrast, increasing the duration of interburst intervals (IBI) seems difficult for the newborn. De Casper and Sigafoos (1983) stress the asymmetry of the two types of required modifications, i.e. shortening or lengthening the IBI: "the frequency of the shortest intervals increased most in the IBI $< t$ condition while the frequency of intervals just slightly greater than the minimum requirement increased most in the IBI $> t$ condition". Two factors may account for this. First, the motor programme which governs sucking activity in newborns is regulated

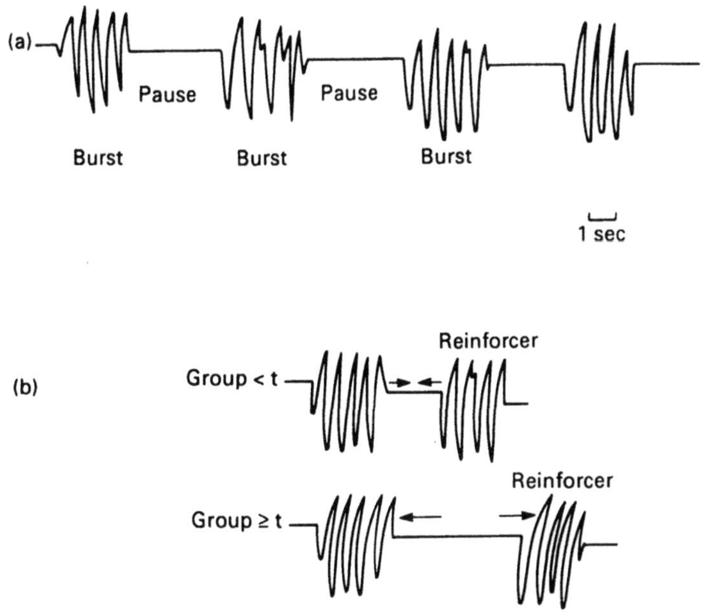

FIG. 2.4. (A) An example of a 4-day-old infant's non-nutritive sucking behaviour (redrawn from a polygraph recording). (B) Schema of the experimental procedure used by De Casper and Sigafoos (1983), t represents the reinforcement criterion imposed during the reinforcement phase. In group $< t$, a sucking burst produced the heartbeat sounds only if it followed an interburst interval (IBI) that was less than the 30th percentile of the baseline intervals. In group $> t$, a sucking burst produced the heartbeat sounds only if the preceding IBI was greater than the 70th percentile of the baseline intervals.

in such a way that lengthening the IBI above a certain threshold may result in a loss of the rhythmicity of sucking behaviour and finally in its cessation. On the other hand, it has been argued that very young infants have difficulty in inhibiting their behaviour (Hulsebus, 1973). On the assumption that developmental changes may intervene during the first months of life—i.e. less rigidity of sucking behaviour (Crook, 1979), more evolved inhibitory capacities (Hulsebus, 1973) and a decrease in infants' dependence on their own rhythm as they learn to integrate it to that of their caretaker (Ashton, 1976)—Provasi (1988) compared newborn's performances with those of 2-month-old infants using De Casper & Sigafoos' (1983) ingenious experimental procedure. Provasi's main finding was that newborns only exhibited temporal regulation of sucking activity when they had to shorten the duration of the pauses, a result consistent with De Casper's (De Casper & Fifer, 1980; De Casper & Sigafoos, 1983) data. In contrast, infants aged 2 months successfully learned to lengthen their IBI.

Nevertheless, learning to increase rest periods at the age of 2 months is still more difficult than learning to diminish them. In the group $< t$, the required temporal regulation was learned as of the first "trials", whereas the group $> t$ required the whole experimental phase for acquisition.

As a whole, these findings show first that non-nutritive sucking can become an instrumental behaviour affected by environmental stimuli, as demonstrated by Rovee-Collier and Gekoski (1979) for kicking. They are exemplary in that they prove that very young infants are able to learn to modify the temporal organisation of a pre-established rhythmic activity which has endogenous time bases. This strengthens the assumption that rhythmic wired-in behaviours can be used to construct complex temporal regulations later on in development.

Timing Behaviour in 1- to 7-year-old Children

To date, we lack conclusive evidence as to whether elaborate timing adjustments in adults are the outcome of a continuous evolution whose bases are found in more primitive behaviours (such as those described above), or whether they result from dramatic changes in the capacity to time behaviour connected to the acquisition of symbolic functions and complex cognitive processes (around 6–8 years of age). However, a number of developmental studies using operant conditioning methods have investigated young children's (in the 1- to 7-year age range) adjustments to arbitrary durations (e.g. Bentall, Lowe, & Beasty, 1985; Macar, 1988; Pouthas, 1985; Stein & Landis, 1978; Weisberg & Tragakis, 1967). Their data shed some light on the relationships between the precocious forms of temporal regulation observed in infants (sensorimotor regulations) and the more elaborate ones found in older children and adults.

In a task where subjects were required to space their own responses, i.e. Differential Reinforcement of Low Rates of Responding (DRL), Pouthas (1981) and Pouthas and Jacquet (1987) found a clear relationship between age and type of timing behaviour, reflecting continuous evolution of performance. The youngest children (10–24 months old) appear to depend on gross motor activities to learn to "wait" for a certain amount of time before making the operant response. The inter-response times they produced, which are often too long, are not adjusted to the required delay (Fig. 2.5). Following a systematic "route" around the experimental room, repeatedly turning over the building block used as a seat, or leaning to one side of the response device and then to the other, are examples of collateral activities which became systematic throughout training and differed for each subject. I have argued (Pouthas, 1985) that young children who establish a particular repetitive action scheme to "wait", are estimating a duration by relying upon a motor rhythm.

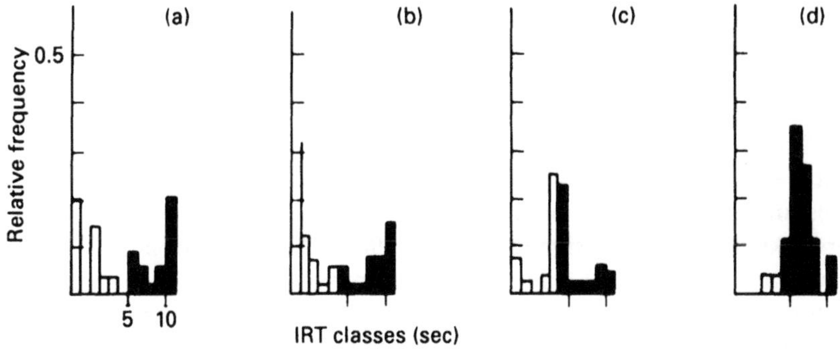

FIG. 2.5. Examples of individual inter-response time distributions at the end of a 5-sec DRL training for subjects of different ages: (A) 2 years; (B, C) 4½ years; (D) 7 years. Shaded columns indicate reinforced inter-response times.

Between the ages of 4 and 7, the capacity to acquire the precise temporal regulation of behaviour emerges in some children, whereas patterns of responding in others do not differ from patterns in younger subjects (Fig. 2.5B, C). At 7 years of age, the timing of responses is very efficient. Examination of 4½-year-olds' individual performances (Pouthas & Jacquet, 1987) show further that the evolution of DRL performance between 4 and 7 years of age not only depends on the capacity to delay responding, but also on the acquisition of the ability to represent reinforcement contingencies (i.e. the temporal parameters of the task) to oneself. This competence may be present in some 4½-year-old subjects and not in others. Informative instructions which bring the temporal characteristics of the task to the attention of subjects of this age enhance their performance. They may allow the children to represent the "solution" and give themselves rules for estimating the required waiting interval. However, two sets of data strongly suggest that this "cognitivist" explanation is not sufficient to account for how young children time their responses. First, in post-experimental interviews, neither 4½- or 7-year-olds, whose spacing of responses was accurate, reported using "chronometric counting" (e.g. 1 per sec). However, 9- and 11-year-olds consistently did so in another study (Pouthas, 1985). The former tended to be inactive and to wait without apparent motor behaviour, except one 4½-year-old child who repeated the same movement of his thumb during the interval. Those 4½-year-olds whose performance was poor, developed non-systematic collateral behaviour.

The second argument against a purely "cognitivist" explanation stems from results obtained in a discrete-trial response duration task (Pouthas, Droit, Jacquet & Wearden, 1990). Uninstructed 4½-year-olds were able to time their responses accurately without having discovered the "solution to the game" and, consequently, without having given themselves rules for responding, compared to those elaborated by older children (11 years), as evidenced by post-trial probes.

What mechanisms are involved? Do these processes rely on mechanisms that are established earlier in ontogenesis? The possible control by endogenous time bases remains an unresolved issue. Recently, however, visuomotor tasks have been designed (Macar, 1988; Macar & Grondin, 1988) to probe the hypothetical role of proprioceptive feedback in the timing of motor responses. These experiments required that a rubber bulb be pressed for a specific period of time, so that visual reinforcers could be obtained. In the first study (Macar, 1988), rhythmical oscillations in pressure, ranging from 0.4 to 2 Hz in frequency, were observed in 3- to 5-year-olds on certain trials. Macar suggests that such oscillations might constitute periodic cues which aid timing performance. The results from a second study (Macar & Grondin, 1988), using a more refined analysis on 5-year-olds, indicates a low probability of occurrence of rhythmical pressure oscillations, and no consistent relationship between muscular parameters and the accuracy of temporal behaviour. One possible explanation for these "negative" results is that, at the age of 5, children have acquired a certain form of knowledge about duration and this cognitive tool is superimposed on time bases which were established and used at a younger age to control operant timing performance. This seems likely, because in order to make the task attractive to young children, subjects are given highly suggestive images of the passage of time during the learning phase. In addition, they are instructed *when* (a certain image corresponding to the "right time") to release the pressure on the bulb. Thus, the images associated with the verbal injunction may have provided the children with symbolic and cognitive means of measuring duration, which were both easy to use and sufficient for accurate temporal estimation.

There are obvious obstacles when designing experimental procedures for 3- to 8-year-olds which can disentangle the role of timing mechanisms established earlier in ontogenesis from the role of increasingly complex cognitive processes. Further research should attempt to go beyond this methodological limitation so as to analyse the evolution of the interactions between these two systems.

CONCLUSION

This chapter has examined several forms of adjustments to time in infants and young children in three distinct fields of research—chronobiology, psychobiology and learning. On a global level, the grouping of these three fields seems rather heterogeneous. However, what links them is the empirical data, which all attest to the remarkable capacity of young infants to time their behaviours precisely without the aid of means of measurement based on conceptual constructs about duration. Studying human subjects in a developmental perspective raises the basic issue of whether the idea of time and its measurement has its origin in the biological and behavioural rhythms which are functional early in ontogeny. The data presented here provide at least partial clues. However, there is much to be gained from a more integrated and synthetic approach to timing in young human subjects. This approach would incorporate often neglected chronobiological variables into the study of temporal learning, and would analyse interactions between early timing mechanisms and developing cognitive processes. As such, it might be in a position to provide a definitive response to the question of continuity from enacted to represented time, to use Piaget's (1946) terms.

ACKNOWLEDGEMENTS

I wish to thank Professor H. Bloch and Dr J. P. Lecanuet of the Laboratoire de Psycho-Biologie de l'Enfant for their relevant comments on the first draft of this chapter. Thanks should be extended to Connie Greenbaum for revision of the English version. I am also grateful to A. Y. Jacquet for her indispensable aid in preparing the manuscript.

REFERENCES

Arduini, D., Rizzo, G., Parlati, E., Giorlandino, C., Valensise, H., Dell'acqua, S., & Romanini, C. (1986). Modification of ultradian and circadian rhythms of fetal heart rate after fetal–maternal adrenal gland suppression: A double blind study. *Prenatal Diagnostics*, *6*, 407–417.

Ashton, R. (1976). Aspects of timing in child development. *Child Development, 47*, 622–626.

Bentall, R. P., Lowe, C. F., & Beasty, A. (1985). The role of verbal behavior in human learning: II. Developmental differences. *Journal of the Experimental Analysis of Behavior*, *43*, 165–181.

Berg, W. K. & Berg, K. M. (1987). Psychophysiological development in infancy: State, startle, and attention. In J. D. Osofsky (Ed.), *Handbook of infant development*, pp. 238–317. New York: John Wiley.

Birkenfield, A., Laufer, N., & Sadovsky, E. (1980). Diurnal variation of fetal activity. *Obstetrics and Gynecology*, *55*, 417–419.

Connolly, K. (1970). Response speed, temporal sequencing and information processing in children. In K. Connolly (Ed.), *Mechanisms of motor skill development*. London: Academic Press.

Connolly, K. (1977). The nature of motor skill development. *Journal of Human Movement Studies*, *3*, 128–143.

Crook, C. K. (1979). The organization and control of infant sucking. In H. W. Reese & L. P. Lipsitt (Eds), *Advances in child development and behavior*, Vol. 14, pp. 209–252. New York, London: Academic Press.

Davis, F. C. (1981). Ontogeny of circadian rhythms. In J. Aschoff (Ed.), *Handbook of behavioral neurobiology*, Vol. 4, pp. 257–274. New York: Plenum Press.

De Casper, A. J. & Fifer, W. P. (1980). Of human bonding: Newborns prefer their mothers' voices. *Science, 208*, 1174–1176.

De Casper, A. J. & Sigafoos, A. D. (1983). The intrauterine heartbeat: A potent reinforcer for newborns. *Infant Behavior and Development*, 6, 12–25.

Deguchi, T. (1975). Ontogenesis of biological clock for serotonin: Acetyl coenzyme a *N*-acetyltransferase in pineal gland of rat. *Proceedings of the National Academy of Sciences USA*, *72*, 2814–2818.

Dierker, L. J., Pillay, S. K., Sorokin, Y., & Rosen, M. G. (1982). Active and quiet periods in the preterm and term fetus. *Obstetrics and Gynecology, 60*, 65–70.

Fitzgerald, H. E. & Brackbill, Y. (1976). Classical conditioning in infancy: Development and constraints. *Psychological Bulletin*, *83*, 353–376.

Halberg, F. (1960). Temporal coordination of physiological functions. In Biological Clocks. *Cold Spring Harbor Symposium on Quantitative Biology*, *25*, 11.

Hallek, M. & Reinberg, A. (1986). Foetus et nouveau-nés ont-ils aussi des horloges biologiques? *La Recherche*, *17*, 851–852.

Hallek, M., Reinberg, A., & Schmid, R. (1983). Circadian and ultradian rhythms in behavior and seizures in children with petit mal epilepsy. *Chronobiologia*, *10*, 131.

Harper, R. M., Leake, B., Miyahara, L., Mason, J., Hoppenbrowers, T., Sterman, M. B., & Hodgman, J. (1981). Temporal sequencing in sleep and waking states during the first 6 months of life. *Experimental Neurology*, 72, 294–307.

Hellbrugge, T. (1960). The development of circadian rhythms in infants. *Cold Spring Harbor Symposium on Quantitative Biology*, *25*, 311–323.

Hellbrugge, T. (1973). Ultradian rhythms in childhood. *International Journal of Chronobiology*, *1*, 331.

Hellbrugge, T. (1974). The development of circadian and ultradian rhythms of premature and full-term infants. In L. E. Scheving, F. Halberg, & J. E. Pauly (Eds), *Chronobiology*, pp. 349–351. Tokyo: Igaku Shoin.

Hellbrugge, T., Ehrengut Lange, J., Rutenfranz, J., & Stehr, K. (1964). Circadian periodicity of physiological functions in different stages of infancy and childhood. *Annals of the New York Academy of Sciences*, *117*, 361–373.

Hopkins, B. & Prechtl, H. F. R. (1984). A qualitative approach to the development of movements during early infancy. In H. F. R. Prechtl (Ed.), *Continuity of neural functions from prenatal to postnatal life*, pp. 179–197. Philadelphia: SIMP.

Hulsebus, R. C. (1973). Operant conditioning of infant behavior: A review. In H. W. Reese (Ed.), *Advances in child development and behavior*, pp. 112–153. London: Academic Press.

Junge, H. D. (1979). Behavioral states and state related to heart and motor activity patterns in the newborn infant and the fetus ante partum. *Journal of Perinatal Medicine*, *7*, 134–138.

Karch, D., Rothe, R., Jurisch, R., Heldt-Hildebrandt, R., Lübbesmeier, A., & Lemburg, P. (1982). Behavioural changes and bioelectric brain maturation of preterm and fullterm newborn infants: A polygraphic study. *Developmental Medicine and Child Neurology*, *24*, 30–47.

Kay, H. (1969). The development of motor skills from birth to adolescence. In E. A. Bilodeau (Ed.), *Principles of skill acquisition*. London: Academic Press.

Kleitman, N. (1963). *Sleep and wakefulness*. Chicago: Chicago University Press.

Kleitman, N. & Engelmann, T. G. (1953). Sleep characteristics of infants. *Journal of Applied Physiology*, *6*, 269–282.

Koch, J. (1968). The change of conditioned orienting reactions in 5 month old infants through phase shift of partial biorhythms. *Human Development*, *11*, 124–137.

Koch, J., Montagner, H., & Soussignan, R. (1987). Variation of behavioral and physiological variables in children attending kindergarten and primary school. *Chronobiology International*, *4*, 525–535.

Macar, F. (1988). Temporal regulation in children of 3 to 5 years old. *Cahiers de Psychologie Cognitive*, *8*, 39–51.

Macar, F. & Grondin, S. (1988). Temporal regulation as a function of muscular parameters in 5-year-old children. *Journal of Experimental Child Psychology*, *45*, 159–174.

Martin du Pan, R. (1970). Le rôle du rythme circadien dans l'alimentation du nourrisson. *La Femme l'Enfant*, *4*, 23–30.

Meier-Koll, A. (1979). Interactions of endogenous rhythms during postnatal development: Observations of behaviour and polygraphic studies in one normal infant. *International Journal of Chronobiology*, *6*, 179–189.

Meier-Koll, A., Hall, U., Hellwig, U., Kott, G., & Meier-Koll, V. (1978). A biological oscillator system and the development of sleep–waking behavior during early infancy. *Chronobiologia*, *5*, 425–440.

Mills, J. N. (1975). Development of circadian rhythms in infancy. *Chronobiologia*. *2*, 363–371.

Minors, D. S. & Waterhouse, J. M. (1979). The effect of maternal posture, meals and time of day on fetal movements. *British Journal of Obstetrics and Gynaecology*, *86*, 717–723.

Minors, D. S. & Waterhouse, J. M. (1981). Rhythms in the infant and the aged. In D. S. Minors & J. M. Waterhouse (Eds), *Circadian rhythms and the human*, pp. 166–186. Bristol: Wright.

Morath, M. (1974). The four-hour feeding rhythm of the baby as a free running endogenously regulated rhythm. *International Journal of Chronobiology*, 2, 39–45.

Parmelee, A. H. (1961). A study of one infant from birth to eight months of age. *Acta Pediatrica*, *50*, 160.

Parmelee, A. H., Bruck, K., & Bruck, M. (1962). Activity and inactivity cycles during the sleep of premature infants exposed to neutral temperatures. *Biologia Neonatorum*, *4*, 317–339.

Parmelee, A. H., Stern, E., & Haber, A. (1973). Activity states in premature and term infants. *Developmental Psychobiology*, *6*, 209–215.

Piaget, J. (1946). *Le développement de la notion de temps*. Paris: Presses Universitaires de France.

Piaget, J. (1952). *La psychologie de l'intelligence*, 3rd edn. Paris: Armand Colin.

Pouthas, V. (1981). Adaptation à la durée chez l'enfant de 2 à 5 ans. *L'Année Psychologique*, *81*, 33–50.

Pouthas, V. (1985). Timing behavior in young children: A developmental approach to conditioned spaced responding. In J. Michon & J. Jackson (Eds), *Time, mind and behavior*, pp. 100–109. Berlin: Springer-Verlag.

Pouthas, V., Droit, S., Jacquet, A.-Y. & Wearden, J. H. (1990). Temporal differentiation of response duration in children of different ages: Developmental changes in relations between verbal and non-verbal behavior. *Journal of the Experimental Analysis of Behavior, 53*, 21–31.

Pouthas, V. & Jacquet, A.-Y. (1987). A developmental study of timing behavior in 4½- and 7-year-old children. *Journal of Experimental Child Psychology*, *43*, 282–299.

Pouthas, V., Macar, F., Lejeune, H., Richelle, M., & Jacquet, A.-Y. (1986). Les conduites temporelles chez le jeune enfant (lacunes et perspectives de recherche). *L'Année Psychologique*, *86*, 103–121.

Prechtl, H. F. R. (1974). The behavioural states of the newborn infant. *Brain Research*, *76*, 185–212.

Prechtl, H. F. R. & Nolte, R. (1984). Motor behaviour of preterm infants. In H. F. R.

Prechtl (Ed.), *Continuity of neural functions from prenatal to postnatal life*, pp. 79–92. Blackwell Scientific Publications Ltd. Oxford. Clinics in Developmental Medicine.
Provasi, J. (1988). Capacités et apprentissages de régulations temporelles chez le nourrisson dans l'activité de succion. Unpublished doctoral dissertation, Université René Descartes, Paris.
Reinberg, A., Hallek, M., & Hellbrugge, T. (1987). Rhythmes biologiques. In M. Manciaux, S. Lebovici, O. Jeanneret, E. A. Sand, & S. Tomkiewicz (Eds), *L'enfant et sa sante'*, pp. 337–360. Paris: Doin.
Reppert, S. M. & Schwartz, W. J. (1983). Maternal coordination of the fetal biological clock *in utero. Science*, *220*, 969.
Richelle, M. (1968). Notions modernes de rythmes biologiques et régulations temporelles acquises. In J. de Ajuriaguerra (Ed.), *Cycles biologiques et psychiatrie*, pp. 233–255. Paris: Masson.
Richelle, M. & Lejeune, H. (1979). *L'animal et le temps*. In *Du temps biologique au temps psychologique*, pp. 73–128. Paris: Presses Universitaires de France.
Richelle, M., Lejeune, H., Perikel, J., & Fery, P. (1985). From biotemporality to nootemporality: Toward an integrative and comparative view of time in behavior. In J. A. Michon & J. L. Jackson (Eds), *Time, mind and behavior*. Berlin: Springer-Verlag.
Roberts, A. B., Little, D., & Campbell, S. (1978). 24 hour studies of fetal respiratory movements and fetal body movements in normal and abnormal pregnancies. In R. W. Beard & S. Campbell (Eds), *Current status of fetal heart rate monitoring and ultrasound in obstetrics*, pp. 209–220. London: Royal College of Obstetricians and Gynaecologists.
Robertson, S. S. (1982). Intrinsic temporal patterning in the spontaneous movement of awake neonates. *Child Development*, *53*, 1016–1021.
Robertson, S. S. (1985). Cyclic motor activity in the human fetus after midgestation. *Developmental Psychobiology*, *18*, 411–419.
Robertson, S. S. (1987). Human cyclic motility: Fetal–newborn continuities and newborn state differences. *Developmental Psychobiology*, *20*, 405–442.
Rovee-Collier, C. K. & Gekoski, M. J. (1979). The economics of infancy: A review of conjugate reinforcement. *Advances in Child Development and Behavior*, *13*, 195–255.
Sander, L. W., Stechler, G., Burns, P., & Julia, H. L. (1970). Early mother–infant interaction and 24-hour patterns of activity and sleep. *Journal of American Academic Child Psychiatry*, *9*, 103–123.
Stein, N. & Landis, R. (1978). Effects of age and collateral behavior on temporally discriminated performance of children. *Perceptual and Motor Skills*, *47*, 87–94.
Sterman, M. B. (1967). Relationship of intrauterine fetal activity to maternal sleep stage. *Experimental Neurology*, *4* (suppl.), 98–106.
Sterman, M. B. & Hoppenbrowers, T. (1971). The development of sleep–waking and rest–activity patterns from fetus to adult in man. In M. B. Sterman, D. J. Mc Ginty, & A. M. Adinalfi (Eds), *Brain development and behavior*, pp. 203–228. London: Academic Press.
Thelen, E. (1981). Rhythmical behavior in infancy: An ethological perspective. *Developmental Psychology*, *17*, 237–257.
Timor-Tritsch, I. E., Dierker, L. J., Hertz, R. H., Deagan, N. C., & Rosen, M. G. (1978). Studies of antepartum behavioral state in the fetus at term. *American Journal of Obstetrics and Gynecology*, *4*, 524–528.
Ullrier, R. E. (1974). On the development of ultradian rhythms: The rapid eye movement activity in premature children. In L. E. Scheving, F. Halberg, & J. E. Pauly (Eds), *Chronobiology*, pp. 478–481. Tokyo: Igaku Shoin.
Weisberg, P. & Tragakis, C. J. (1967). Analyses of DRL behavior in young children. *Psychological Reports*, *21*, 709–715.
Wolff, P. H. (1967). The role of biological rhythms in early psychological development. *Bulletin of the Menninger Clinic*, *31*, 197–218.

Wolff, P. H. (1968a). The serial organization of sucking in the young infant. *Pediatrics*, *42*, 943–956.

Wolff, P. H. (1968b). Stereotype behavior and development. *Canadian Psychologist*, *9*, 474–484.

Wolff, P. H. (1984). Discontinuous changes in human wakefulness around the end of the second month of life: A developmental perspective. In H. F. R. Prechtl (Ed.), *Continuity of neural functions from prenatal to postnatal life*, pp. 144–158. Philadelphia: SIMP.

Wood, C., Walters, W. A. W., & Trigg, P. (1977). Methods of recording foetal movement. *British Journal of Obstetrics and Gynaecology*, *84*, 561–567.

3 Timing: Differences in Continuity or Generality Beyond Differences?

Helga Lejeune
Laboratory of Experimental Psychology, University of Liège, Liège, Belgium

Chronobiology deals with recurrent phenomena in living organisms. The so-called biological rhythms result from the evolutionary adaptation of organisms to regular changes in the environment. One of the most striking biological rhythms is the circadian rhythm of general activity (see Aschoff, this volume). Biological rhythms are, however, not limited to a 24-hour period. They range from a fraction of a second to several weeks, months or even years (migration of salmon or eels). They concern not only animals but also plants. They can also be found at the level of the organ, cell or cell component. Biological rhythms seem to be under the control of endogenous self-sustaining oscillating processes (the so-called biological clocks). They persist in constant environmental conditions where periodic stimulations or "Zeitgebers" are absent. Biological clocks can be considered as genetically built-in mechanisms: It has been shown, for example, that circadian activity persists in successive generations of mice raised in a constant environment.

The following paragraphs deal with another behavioural adaptation to time in animal subjects. This timing behaviour is selected by the environment during ontogeny and is extinguished if the critical selecting features of the environment are withdrawn. It does not seem to depend on built-in biological clocks and does not transmit from one generation to the next. Rather, it reflects functional properties of stopwatch-like processes that can be reset at any moment. It has so far been obtained or studied only for a limited range of durations (from a few seconds to a few minutes). The timing behaviour of concern here is typically obtained in artificial laboratory settings in which animal subjects are submitted to operant temporal differentiation or regulation schedules. Temporal differentiation schedules reinforce the temporal characteristics of the response, e.g. its duration (Differential Reinforcement of Response Duration, DRRD), latency (Differential Reinforcement of Long Latencies, DRLL), or inter-response time (Differential Reinforcement of Low rate, DRL). The Fixed Interval schedule (FI) cannot be classified as a temporal differentiation schedule because it does not reinforce the temporal characteristics of the response. This schedule reinforces the first response emitted after a specified delay has elapsed since the previous reinforcement. Responses emitted during the delay are without consequence. In this schedule, timing emerges with practice: a pause without a response follows reinforcement delivery. After this pause, the subject resumes its response and continues to respond at an accelerated rate until the next reinforcement. This schedule will be referred to as the "temporal regulation" schedule.

Animal subjects not only adapt to temporal schedule constraints, but they are also able to evaluate the duration of external events. In temporal discrimination experiments, animal subjects express their judgement about the duration of an external stimulus (light, sound) via an operant response. For example, pigeons in a two-key operant chamber will be reinforced to peck the left response key after the presentation of a long "standard" stimulus (10 sec of light) and to peck the right key after a short "comparison" stimulus (1 sec of light). After this easy discrimination has been learned, the duration of the short stimulus is increased stepwise on non-reinforced trials and the experimenter records the proportion of "long" responses (left key pecks) for each value of the comparison stimulus. These data can then be shown graphically, with the stimulus duration on the x-axis and a proportional scale (0.1–1.0) on the y-axis. This typical plot, the "psychometric function", is a S-shaped curve which makes it possible to compute the "point of subjective equality" (duration for which "short" and "long" responses are equiprobable), the "just noticeable difference" (the smallest difference in duration that is perceived with regard to a standard duration) and the "Weber fraction" (the ratio between the just noticeable difference and the value of the standard duration). In several (but not all) cases, the Weber fraction remains constant whatever the duration of the standard stimulus. The data thus confirm Weber's law according to which discriminability is proportional to the standard stimulus value.

We intend to review here some issues concerning the generality of results within temporal differentiation, regulation or discrimination data. The discussion will focus on animal subjects, though data from human subjects will also be considered. Recent experimental developments and theoretical speculations tend to indicate that timing behaviour is governed by rather general mechanisms, that lawful relationships do exist between physical and behavioural time, and that behavioural time itself obeys particular rules. The question behind the following paragraphs is: Does the huge diversity of experimental results fit within a general mould, or is it more straightforward to consider timing behaviour in a biological perspective that acknowledges the existence of differences within evolutionary continuity?

GENERALITY AND THE EXPERIMENTAL PROCEDURE

The data collected in temporal differentiation experiments can be presented in an orderly manner as distributions of response durations, latencies or inter-response times. These distributions of temporal estimates can be described by their central tendency and dispersion indices, e.g. the mean and the standard deviation. The ratio between the standard deviation and the mean, the coefficient of variation, is an index of the sensitivity of the organism to the temporal schedule requirement. Furthermore, relations between temporal estimates and schedule requirements can be described in terms of mathematical functions: the linear function ($M = bt + a$) and the power function ($M = kt^n$), in which M is the average performance measure, t is the parameter of the timing task, and b, a, k and n are fitted constants. These so-called scaling functions describe the relationship between dependent (average temporal estimates) and independent variables (schedule parameters). A third empirical relation which has been found in animal data conforms to Weber's law and follows the linear equation $s = cm + d$, in which s is the standard deviation, m the mean performance measure, and c and d fitted constants.

Weber's law has been integrated within a recent theoretical account of response timing in animal subjects, i.e. scalar timing theory (Gibbon, 1977). At the behavioural level, this theory has a double requirement. The first is constancy of the coefficient of variation: The standard deviation of the distribution of temporal estimates must be a constant fraction of the mean. This coefficient of variation can thus be considered analogous to the Weber fraction in temporal discrimination data. The second is mean accuracy: The mean of the distribution of temporal estimates must match with real time, i.e. with the temporal schedule parameter. For example, if the schedule reinforces response durations of 5 sec, the mean of the response durations emitted by the subject should match 5 sec. Thus, in the case of scalar timing, the relationships between mean estimates and temporal schedule parameters on the one hand, and means and standard deviations of the distributions of estimates on the other, can be fitted with linear functions.

Important sets of data are congruent with Weber's law and scalar timing (Gibbon, 1977). These data have been obtained from animal and human subjects. For example, mean response duration varies with real-time criteria, and coefficients of variation are approximately constant in human subjects on a short-duration (0.5–1.3 sec) production task (Wearden & McShane, 1988). However, Zeiler, Scott, and Hoyert (1987) do not confirm scalar timing in a similar experimental setting, but with a much wider range of temporal criteria (from 0.5 to 32 sec in geometric progression).

The cross-procedural generality of results has been discussed in several reports (Catania, 1970; Platt, 1979; Stubbs, 1979; Zeiler, 1986). It has been shown that, in many cases, true temporal control is obscured by additional non-temporal processes. As noticed by Zeiler (1985), Weber's law holds in temporal discrimination but to a lesser extent in temporal differentiation data, where sensitivity tends to differ according to the procedure. In temporal discrimination procedures, the response has no temporal character *per se*, and simply reflects the judgement of the subject with regard to an exteroceptive stimulus of a given duration. In temporal differentiation procedures which select temporal characteristics of a motor response, response durations, latencies or inter-response times may be affected by factors such as the level of motivation for food, the nature of the response or the adventitious strengthening of non-temporal aspects of the response. As a consequence, distributions of temporal estimates are often multimodal and reflect the interference between timing and non-timing processes. Furthermore, the critical duration that should control behaviour is derived from performance (functional time; Zeiler, 1983), instead of being presented to the subject, as is the case with temporal discrimination procedures.

If the cross-procedural generality of results depends upon the bias-free expression of central timing mechanisms, the alternative is, thus, to consider that temporal differentiation or regulation schedules are unsuitable for such an analysis or to overcome the difficulty by resorting to one of three possible strategies: building models of temporal differentiation or regulation behaviour which integrate timing and non-timing processes; designing bias-free procedures; or carefully selecting the data prior to analysis. These alternatives will be briefly commented upon.

Multiprocess Models

The integration of timing and non-timing processes within a model of temporal differentiation or regulation, and the computer simulation of such a model, may give indirect evidence of an "undercover" operation of pure timing under an "altered" overt behaviour. For example, Zeiler (1981) proposed a two-state model, according to which performance in temporal differentiation paradigms depends upon transitions between a timing state (i.e. a period in which accurate timing occurs) and a free response state that corresponds to the base duration of the operant (i.e. the duration of the operant in the absence of any timing requirement) (see also Zeiler, 1986). Computer simulation of this model for a range of timing requirements and base durations yielded a reasonable account of performance in temporal differentiation experiments, in terms of mean emitted response duration, value of the coefficient of variation, distribution of response durations, and percentage of reinforced responses. Another modelling attempt was made by Wearden (1985), who considers that FI pausing derives from a combination between scalar timing and a non-timing, random response process. Pause termination should be more dependent on the non-timing process at high interval values. This model offered an accurate description of behaviour. It was also successfully applied to response duration differentiation and to FI data from species other than the rat (Lejeune and Wearden, in press). However, the weakness of models that mix scalar timing and non-timing processes is obvious. They are difficult to test because different coefficients of variation might result from differences in the timing process, in the non-timing process or both processes. In other words, differences in temporal sensitivity cannot unambiguously be related to one or the other component of the model. Thus, different coefficients of variation may almost always be reconciled with an underlying scalar timer (Lejeune and Wearden, in press). Further insight into the hypothesized internal processes at play is needed before models can be valuably implemented.

Interference-free Procedures

In the last 10 years, there has been an emphasis on designing interference-free procedures, such as the peak procedure used by Roberts and Church (1978). This procedure can be traced back to Catania who, in 1970, presented the first data obtained in a similar design. Basically, this procedure is derived from FI and is very simple. Subjects are trained on a discrete-trial FI procedure, in which an exteroceptive stimulus is present during the intervals. Some of the intervals are longer than the basic duration and are not reinforced. After extensive training, response rate functions in these test intervals have a Gaussean-like shape. They make it possible to isolate two crucial variables: peak rate, i.e. the highest rate emitted at a given moment in the interval, and peak time, i.e. the precise moment at which peak rate occurs. Peak time is considered to be the estimate of the moment at which the reinforcer will be delivered. The data obtained with the peak procedure (see Fig. 3.1) are considered unbiased because peak rate can be altered without changing peak time (e.g. by changing the probability of food or the subject's motivation for food:

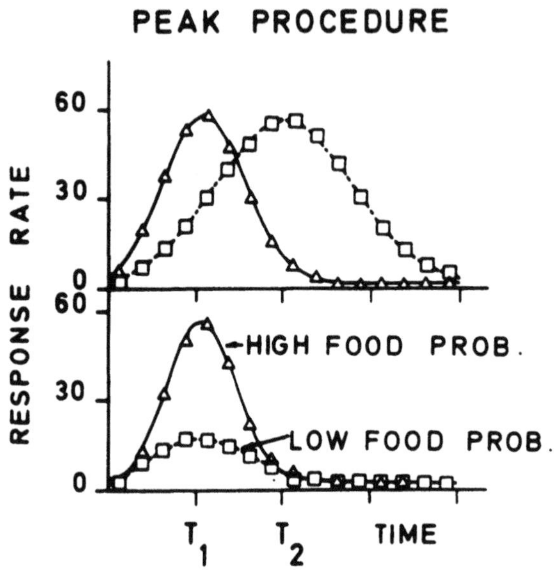

FIG. 3.1. Schematic diagram showing the independence between peak time and peak rate in the peak procedure. (Top) Change in the time of food (from T_1 to T_2) changes peak time without changing peak rate. (Bottom) Change in the probability of food changes peak rate without changing peak time (redrawn and modified from Roberts, 1981, Fig. 2, p. 245).

Roberts, 1983). They are also congruent with scalar timing theory. This procedure has so far only been used with adult rats and pigeons, but its apparent simplicity makes it a good candidate for further research with other species or ages.

The peak procedure is not the only procedure that has been designed to disentangle "pure timing" from confounding variables. An attempt was made with the two-lever FMI schedule as early as 1962, by Mechner and Guevrekian. The critical delay between A and B responses was considered to reflect timing, with the B/A interval under the control of motivational variables. Mechner and Guevrekian reinforced rats with water on a two-lever, 5-sec FMI schedule requiring a delay of at least 5 sec between the A and B responses. They showed that increased thirst did not alter the A/B inter-response time but shortened the non-critical B/A interval.

Data Selection

Data selection can be made either by discarding parts of the data that do not seem to be controlled by timing processes, or searching for rare bias-free cases among temporal differentiation data. A study by Zeiler (1985) illustrates the first alternative. In a two-component concurrent Random

Interval–Differential Reinforcement of Other behaviour schedule (RI-DRO), in which only one component was available at a time, pigeons could respond at any moment to the left switching key and choose one or the other schedule. After the presentation of food, or at the beginning of the session, the next reinforcer was assigned to one of the components via a probability gate. A second gate controlled the proportion of reinforcements in DRO (0.2, 0.5 or 0.8). Elapsed time was thus the only means by which the pigeons could test the situation and evaluate if a reinforcer was associated with the ongoing DRO component. The critical temporal data collected in the schedule were switching latencies from DRO, on non-reinforced trials. Temporal estimation was thus evaluated via a pause, and the switching response gave an estimate of the moment at which reinforcement should have occurred in DRO, as does the response rate function in the peak procedure. As is usual with other temporal differentiation procedures, the distributions of switching latencies were weighted both in the short and long latency ranges, which leads Zeiler to "comb" his data and to discard such noise before submitting it to analysis. After cleaning his data, Zeiler was able to show that linear functions related pause requirements and mean DRO switching times on the one hand, and standard deviations and means of the distributions of DRO switching times on the other, and that the data supported Weber's law, as do the temporal discrimination results.

Isolated cases from the classical temporal differentiation data seem, however, to be less contaminated by non-timing processes than the other results. As mentioned above, using human subjects, Wearden and McShane (1988) obtained duration production data that were congruent with scalar timing theory. Lejeune and Richelle (1982a) and Lejeune and Jasselette (1986) observed accurate DRRD and DRL performances in pigeons when a perching response was used, up to response durations or Inter-Response Times (IRTs) of 50 or even 70 sec (see Fig. 3.2). The unimodal response distributions that were obtained could be described as Gaussean functions with a peak location close to the schedule value and an almost stable coefficient of variation. Zeiler and Hoyert (1989) obtained conformity to Weber's law with a temporal reproduction procedure. Pigeons had to observe a duration of keylight (signal) and thereafter begin and complete a sequence of 15 pecks on another key, in a time window ranging from 100 to 150 percent of the duration of the signal. This procedure yielded unimodal ratio times and constant coefficients of variation, over a wide range of signal durations (4 to 29.8 seconds). The strongest control emerged with 8 or 10 different signal durations per session. Zeiler and Hoyert explain this lawful behaviour by the fact that the reproduction procedure reduces the difficulty of detecting target durations by providing unambiguous signals to the subjects. These results suggest that a reasonable

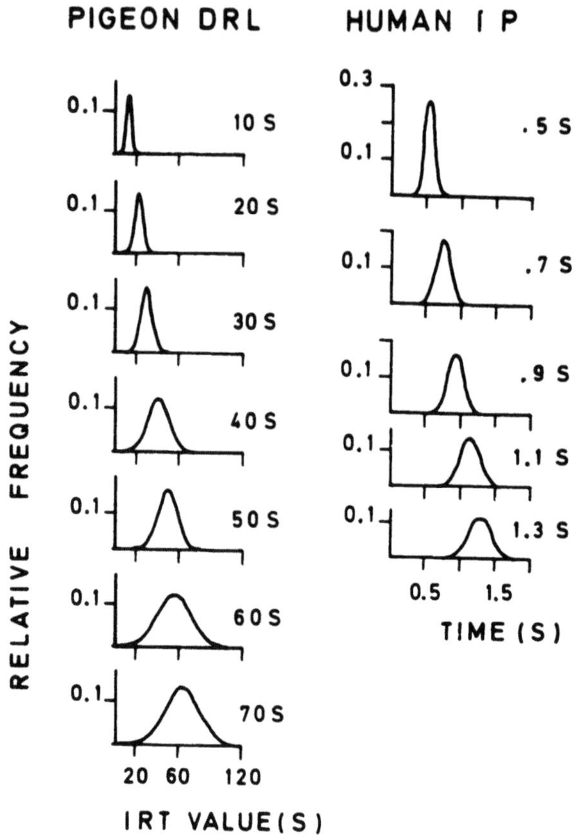

FIG. 3.2. Relative frequency distributions of times produced by human subjects on an interval production task (0.5, 0.7, 0.9, 1.1 and 1.3 sec), and of Inter-Response Times emitted by pigeons on a DRL task with perching responses (DRL 10, 20, 30, 40, 50, 60 and 70 sec) (redrawn and modified from Wearden & McShane, 1988, Fig. 2, p. 369 for the human subjects data).

degree of conformity with scalar timing theory can be obtained when an appropriate response or procedure is chosen.

Even if temporal discrimination procedures are seemingly free of interference, this does not mean that the conclusions drawn are not dependent on procedural characteristics. Linear and power functions each describe part of the huge amount of data collected in duration scaling experiments that study the relationship between objective and subjective time (Macar, 1985). Differential thresholds have been found to obey Weber's law in numerous human and animal experiments; however, such an analysis has been questioned in other studies. The issue was raised again in a recent paper by Chatlosh and Wasserman (1987), who ran a within-subjects comparison with pigeons on two temporal discrimination procedures. They found that the behaviour of their birds critically depended on procedural details, and that duration discrimination was also affected by variables that influence other stimulus discriminations. The authors caution that:

> failure to scrutinize procedural details when attempting to consolidate findings into a cohesive theory of temporal discrimination may result in misconceptions about animal timing processes, while preoccupation with a single procedure will most probably result in conclusions that do not generalize across other experimental paradigms (Chatlosh & Wasserman, 1987, p. 308).

The same could be said for temporal differentiation research, but it would probably be misleading to endow procedural details with excessive power and to overlook other meaningful variables, such as the species, as discussed below.

The preceding examples, particularly peak procedure and scalar timing, are convenient illustrations of a trend that emerged in recent research on animal timing, i.e. attempts at generalisation in a domain where exceptions to lawfulness are rather the rule (temporal regulation or differentiation of behaviour). These examples also show that temporal regulation or differentiation schedules have aroused tremendous interest since Catania's (1970) seminal paper, where he began to discuss the suitability of this type of data for an analysis in psychophysical terms. Many of the studies undertaken since then have tried, in different ways (three of these are described above), to disentangle pure timing from non-timing processes. However, after Platt (1979), Zeiler (1986) seems to consider that schedules of temporal differentiation are irrelevant to scaling, and that it is not worth only focusing on the part of the behaviour that seems to be under temporal control, because "behavior matches neither the time requirement nor mean reinforced duration" (Zeiler, 1986, p. 104. See however Zeiler and Hoyert, 1989). Zeiler considers that these schedules are not versions of the psychophysical procedures used in human subjects and, therefore, should not be treated as such. Zeiler (1986) and Zeiler et al. (1987) suggest instead a reinterpretation of temporal differentiation data within optimal foraging theory and consideration of experiments in terms of adaptation, with the assumption that the maximised factor is reinforcement frequency. As stated by Zeiler (1986, p. 111), "the application of optimal foraging theory to the standard differentiation tasks remains to be accomplished". Future work will thus have to assess the heuristic value of this proposition.

SOME ISSUES CONCERNING CROSS-SPECIES GENERALITY

Generality will be discussed here from two complementary viewpoints—across species and within species—especially with regard to the stimulus, response and reinforcer effects on timing performance. A previous review (Richelle & Lejeune, 1980) had shown that only a restricted number of species had been studied, mostly rats and pigeons. More recent research has not added many other species to this list. A first tentative classification showed that, in the basic FI or DRL schedules, mammals such as mice, rats, cats, monkeys or apes exhibit higher performance scores than birds, followed by reptiles or fish species. At first sight, such a classification, with all its shortcomings, seemed to support a hypothesis that relates the timing capacity of a species to its position on the phyletic tree. However, a closer look at the data and recent research, questions such an oversimplification.

Inter-species comparisons raise a classic problem for the domain of comparative psychology, i.e. the equivalence of the experimental settings to which the subjects are exposed. For example, does a leverpress have an identical status for a monkey, a rat, a pigeon or a fish? Are the exteroceptive stimuli to be discriminated equivalent for various species? Does a similar percentage of weight loss control an identical level of motivation for food and are pellet food or liquid reinforcers as potent for one species as for another? The arbitrariness of the operant (Skinner, 1956), as well as the status of the stimulus for different species, have been addressed in several experiments that were undertaken within the biological constraints framework (Breland & Breland, 1961; Hinde & Stevenson-Hinde, 1973; Seligman & Hager, 1972). Notions such as preparedness (Seligman & Hager, 1972) or Species-Specific Defence Reactions (Bolles, 1970) are no longer ignored, but research on the generality of timing or inter-species differences in timing has remained scarce, probably due to the difficulty of resolving the above problems.

Generality and the Response

The phylogenetic hypothesis was first questioned by data from experiments that compared closely related species. The fixed-interval performances of homing pigeons and turtle doves differed more than those of homing pigeons and albino rats (Lejeune & Richelle, 1982b). A further challenge to the phylogenetic hypothesis comes from studies where several responses have been compared for one species submitted to a temporal differentiation schedule. Platt (1984) provides an interesting example of an interaction between response and temporal performance. Rats were submitted to a percentile reinforcement schedule that provided similar pay-offs for different responses (lever pressing or "chimney" response, i.e. rearing on hind legs and insertion of the snout in a "chimney") or temporal response properties (latency, IRT, duration and changeover IRT), and which continuously updated the reinforcement criterion on the basis of the most recent performance. In such a setting, the asymptotic levels of performance differed greatly depending upon the operant or the temporal response property that was selected. For example, lever pressing yielded response durations that remained under 5 sec, whereas asymptotic "chimney" response durations were located between 10 and 20 sec. However, with an IRT property, lever and "chimney" performances were similar. The rather low asymptotic performance values that were reached with the different responses or temporal properties led Platt to consider that an incentive process favouring the immediacy of reinforcement and inducing a bias for short response values interferes with further progress in performance. Thus, temporal differentiation depends not only on the nature of the response or the temporal property that is selected, but also upon a process that counteracts the contingency effect.

It has also been shown that, to a large extent, the nature of the response controls the performance obtained with pigeons in DRL. Whereas pigeons fail to space keypecks efficiently beyond 20 sec or so, they are very accurate with a perching response, up to response durations or spacing requirements of 40–70 sec (Lejeune & Jasselette, 1986; Lejeune & Richelle, 1982a). Similar data were obtained with turtle doves (*Streptopelia rizoria*) (see Fig. 3.3). Hemmes (1975) has shown that a treadle-pressing response is more efficient than pecking in DRL, but it has been clearly demonstrated that the temporal differentiation obtained with the perching response depends upon accurate timing (with a small range of estimates around mean values), which is not the case with treadle-pressing or keypecking. Furthermore, temporal control of the perching response can hardly be explained in terms of mere base duration, as Zeiler (1986) suggested for keypecking and treadle-pressing in DRL. Recent reanalysis of the perching data as an analogue of peak procedure data has yielded mean temporal estimates and coefficients of variation that fit with scalar timing (Jasselette, Lejeune and Wearden, 1990). Responses do not seem to have the same status with regard to the expression of the temporal regulation capacities of a species. These results illustrate the difference between capacity and performance. The so-called "internal clock" is constrained by the species-specific behavioural repertoire.

However, the effect of the operant on timing also critically depends on the experimental procedure. The conclusions drawn from temporal differentiation data cannot be generalised to fixed interval performance, where spontaneous temporal regulation of the responses develops but is not

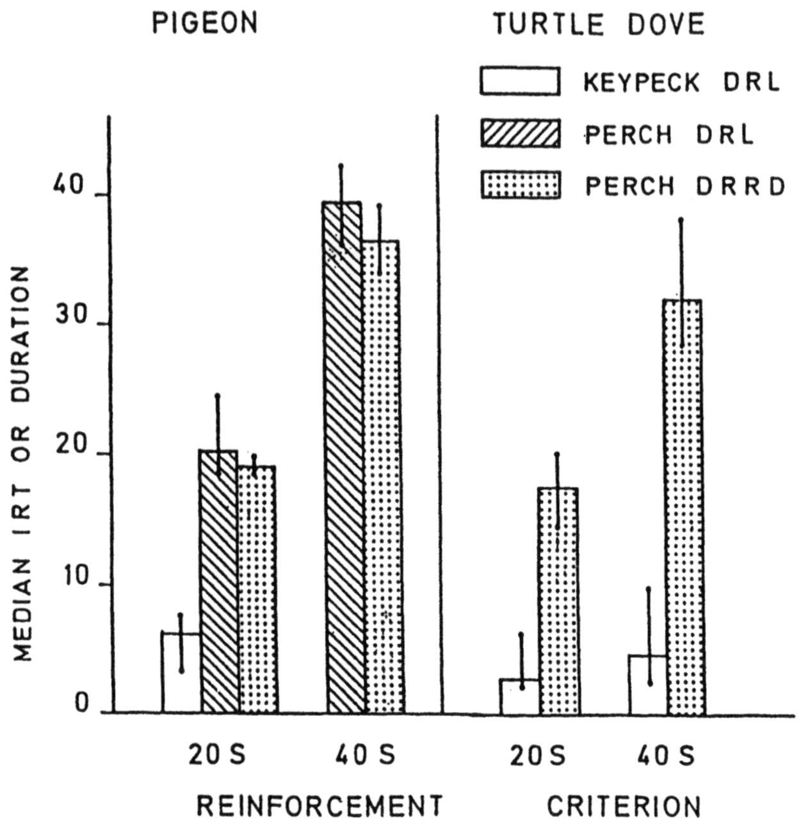

FIG. 3.3. Median IRT (DRL) or response duration (DRRD) for 20- or 40-sec reinforcement criteria in pigeons (left, $N = 3$) and turtle doves (right, $N = 4$), with a keypeck or a perching response. Thin vertical lines at the top of each column link extreme performance values for each condition. Data were computed from the last three or five sessions for each condition.

required for reinforcement to be delivered. Comparative studies have shown that FI keypecking and treadle-pressing in pigeons, or FI lever-pressing and running in rats, yield similar adjustment levels (Lejeune & Jasselette, 1985; Lejeune, Richelle, & Mantanus, 1980). Although the response rate depends upon the operant, the duration of the spontaneous post-reinforcement pause and the distribution of responses within the interval do not.

Generality and the Stimulus

Species-specific constraints have been described not only in instrumental or operant conditioning paradigms, but they have been observed in numerous other experimental settings such as classical conditioning and sign-tracking. These experiments have also shown that, for different species, a given Conditioned Stimulus (CS) is not equivalent. Whereas for a pigeon visual stimuli are more readily associated with food and more readily control behaviour than do olfactory stimuli, another ordering holds for mammals, such as dogs or cats (associative bias).

If a particular stimulus has gained a critical value with regard to survival for a given species, and can be more readily associated than another with an appetitive or a noxious stimulus, one can ask whether the discrimination of the duration of that stimulus would be influenced by its nature. This problem of cross-modal equivalence in duration discrimination has been addressed in humans, rats and pigeons. With rat subjects, experiments tend to show that the nature of the stimuli does not influence the discrimination of their duration and thus confirms cross-modal timing (Roberts, 1982). For example, psychometric functions derived from the bisection procedure indicate that, with light and sound, points of subjective equality are almost identical and close to the geometric mean of the extreme stimulus durations (see Meck, 1984). Data obtained with the peak procedure further show that stimuli from different modalities are timed by the same clock, that clock readings are stored in the same memory but that the clock nevertheless can distinguish between modalities (Roberts, 1982). As stated by Roberts (1983, p. 365), "non verbal animals can perform cross-modal abstractions that direct behavior": one quality of the stimulus, i.e. its modality, is ignored, while another quality, i.e. its duration is attended to.

Even if psychometric functions for different modalities are equivalent when modalities are tested over successive blocks of sessions or with different groups of rat subjects, this is no longer the case when procedures are modified in order to induce perceptual response biases. When, within a session, two stimulus modalities are used with an unbalanced probability (e.g. 80% of light signals vs 20% of sound signals), or when stimulus are miscued (when the duration to be timed is preceded by a fixed duration signal that can be from the same or from another [miscuing] modality), psychometric functions no longer match those obtained when a single pure modality is used (Meck, 1984).

Cross-modal data obtained from pigeons in duration discrimination or peak procedures differ from those described for rat subjects (Roberts, Cheng and Cohen, 1989). Pigeons are more accurate with light than with tone stimuli. With the peak procedure, species related differences do appear when light or tone stimuli are discontinued by a modality switch (light to tone or the reverse) or a time-out. Pigeons behave as if they did reset their internal clock upon stimulus change whereas rats would keep their clock running while timing a discontinuous or multimodal stimulus event. Rats just add together the stimulus durations preceding and following the time-out or the durations of the components of a complex stimulus.

Rats and pigeons thus seem to differ in their respective timing strategies. Such species-related differences might also be partly related to the attentional dominance of light over sound evidenced in pigeons (Kraemer and Roberts, 1985) or to procedural variables. Cheng and Roberts (1989) designed a procedure which forced pigeons to take into account the duration at the first component of a light-tone or tone-light complex, for predicting the moment of food occurrence. They obtained mixed results. Two birds out of five did time only the second component of the complex stimulus. Nevertheless, data from three other birds showed that pigeons are able to time multimodal events. These birds seem to follow a response rule indicating that the duration of the complex stimulus as well as the duration of the second component are taken into account. These data have been interpreted with regard to the information processing model of timing developed by Church and his associates (see, e.g. Church, 1984; Gibbon, Church and Meck, 1984). The six components of the model are: a pacemaker that emits pulses, a switch that conveys pulses to an accumulator that feeds a temporary working memory, a permanent reference memory that stores temporal information from past trials, and a comparator that controls the response on the basis of a decision rule that stems from the comparison between the values in working and reference memory (see Fig. 3.4). Within this frame, Cheng and Roberts (1989) consider that rats and pigeons share similarities in keeping their internal clocks running during a complex stimulus. However, whereas rats use a single clock and a unique reference memory, pigeons seem to use a single clock with two reference memories, one related to the duration of the complex stimulus event, the other to the duration of the last component of this event. Birds would follow a response criterion resulting from the weighted average of the durations stored in these memories. In other words, inter-species differences might be accounted for in terms of the relative weight given to timing the complex stimulus versus only the second signal. Rats would favour the former strategy whereas pigeons would focus on the stimulus contiguous with food delivery.

It has also been shown that the intensity of the stimulus can interfere with temporal discrimination. When pigeons are trained on a bisection task, their performances are identical when dim or bright stimuli are not mixed within a session. However, when they are mixed, the birds are more likely to choose the "short" response alternative after longer durations of dim light, which implies that a dim visual stimulus is perceived as shorter than a bright stimulus of identical duration (Wilkie, 1987). Such data have also been interpreted with regard to the information processing model of timing developed by Church and his associates (see Fig. 3.4). Within this model, it has been speculated that the intensity of the visual stimulus may, via an arousal effect, change the rate of the pacemaker, as drugs or particular nutrients seem to do (e.g. Meck, 1986; Meck & Church, 1987).

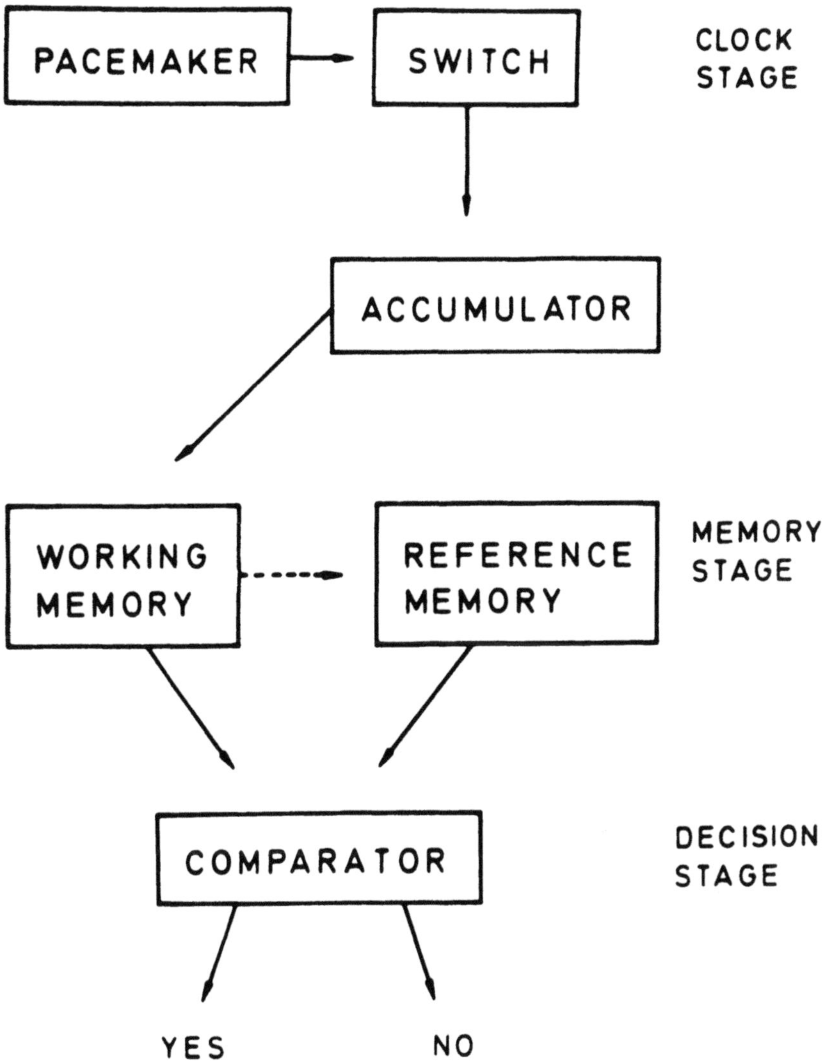

FIG. 3.4. Information processing model for the internal timing mechanism (redrawn and modified from Gibbon et al., 1984, Fig. 2, p. 54).

Generality and the Reinforcer

The reinforcer is the third relevant variable in a learning paradigm. The effect of this variable on temporal regulation or discrmination can be analysed along two lines: the quality of performance on the one hand, and the precise topography of the response on the other. The reinforcer itself can be characterised by its magnitude (amount or duration) or its nature (food, Intra-Cerebral self-Stimulation or ICS, shock). Several studies have demonstrated that in FI the magnitude of the reinforcer has an impact on the quality of steady-state operant performance if various magnitudes are contrasted within an experimental session (as just discussed for stimulus modality and intensity). The effects are much less evident if magnitudes are tested over successive blocks of sessions. These classical data have been confirmed and refined in more recent experiments, such as those by Howerton and Meltzer (1983) and Hatten and Shull (1983). Furthermore, it has been shown that magnitude effects depend upon the specific behaviour under study and cannot be explained via a general incentive or unconditional inhibitory mechanism (Reed & Wright, 1988; Richelle & Lejeune, 1980). In temporal discrimination settings, where the response has no temporal character *per se*, fluctuations in the motivational state of the subjects produced by the manipulation of the reinforcer, may induce response biases or failures when attending to the stimulus before making a judgement about its duration. Such bias effects have been shown to depend upon the relative reinforcement rate for correct responses (e.g. Davison & McCarthy, 1987).

The data described above demonstrate that timing performances can be influenced by the magnitude of the reinforcer. However, do they also depend on its nature? The scarcity of reports addressing this question makes it impossible to offer a definitive answer. Few studies have provided a real within-experiment comparison (see Richelle & Lejeune, 1980) and the problem is further complicated by the fact that reinforcers also differ in the locus and intensity of their effects (e.g. food *vs* ICS).

Finally, the nature of the reinforcer may also influence response timing via its effect on response topography. Numerous reports have shown that the nature of the food reinforcer (solid or liquid) modulates the topography of the keypeck response in pigeons. Birds reinforced with water tend to "slurp" the key with a closed beak, whereas grain-reinforced subjects strike the key with an open beak, whose gape is precisely adjusted to the size of the reinforcing kernels (LaMon & Zeigler, 1984; 1988). Similarly, rats exposed to autoshaping procedures, have been shown to display gnawing or licking motions toward the lever according to their reinforcement history with solid or liquid reinforcers (Davey et al., 1984). Besides challenging the arbitrariness of the response, these findings have strengthened the case for the interference between species-specific constraints and schedule control. They have further stressed the fact that the keypecking response in particular is not free from the constraints linked with the feeding or drinking habits of a species. Keypecking behaviour has been described as "impulsive" and under the control of Pavlovian factors. Pigeons lose "self-control" and systematically choose a small but immediate reinforcer over a large but delayed one, as opposed to rats (see, e.g. Logue, 1988; Logue, Chavarro, Rachlin, & Reeder, 1988; Van Haaren,

Van Hest, & Vandepoll, 1988). The similarity between the keypeck and the consummatory response has cast some doubt on the validity of such an operant for the expression of timing capacities—similar conclusions can be reached for the licking response in rats (Welzl, 1976) and non-nutritive sucking in infants (De Casper & Sigafoos, 1983; Provasi, 1988). However, it has long been demonstrated that keypecking (as well as non-nutritive sucking) is sensitive to response duration or spacing requirements, but within limits that cannot be overthrown (Provasi, 1988; Zeiler, Davis, & De Casper, 1980).

CHRONOBIOLOGY AND THE TEMPORAL REGULATION OF BEHAVIOUR

The relationship between chronobiology and the temporal regulation of behaviour concerns the generality issue, as far as it is hypothesised that a link may exist between these timing mechanisms. For example, it has been speculated that the degree of freedom of a species with regard to its innate biological clocks is a direct function of its position on the phyletic tree (Richelle, Lejeune, Perikel & Fery, 1985). The comparison between data from restricted feeding experiments (see Aschoff, this volume) and Fixed-Interval schedules reveals analogies for which straightforward explanations are lacking. However, they offer a glimpse of the ties that may exist between both types of adaptation to time.

In 1922, Richter showed that periodic feeding influences the activity of rats in laboratory settings. If food was made available for 25 min every 24 hours, they developed an activity pattern that strictly anticipated the limited access to food. This activity started 2–3 hours before the food was presented. More recent research has shown that the free-running activity of rats in constant environmental conditions can be dissociated from activity bouts that anticipate the periodic presentation of a limited duration of access to food. Anticipatory activity adjusts strictly to the period of the feeding rhythm, whereas general activity recorded over successive 24-hour cycles maintains a free-running circadian course. Anticipatory activity has also been recorded if food access is made dependent upon an operant response (Bolles & Stokes, 1965; Boulos, Rosenwasser, & Terman, 1980; Terman, Gibbon, Fairhust, & Waring, 1984). The anticipation of food is comparable to operant activity in the fixed interval schedule. The analogy is the more striking for data recorded with long Fixed-Interval schedules. Whereas Dews (1965) described typical FI keypecking behaviour in pigeons over FI values ranging from 500 to 100,000 sec (i.e. about 28 hours), anticipation of the restricted food access breaks down if the periodicity of feeding departs from approximately 24 hours (see Fig. 3.5). Similar behavioural outcomes do not seem to obey identical rules or mechanisms.

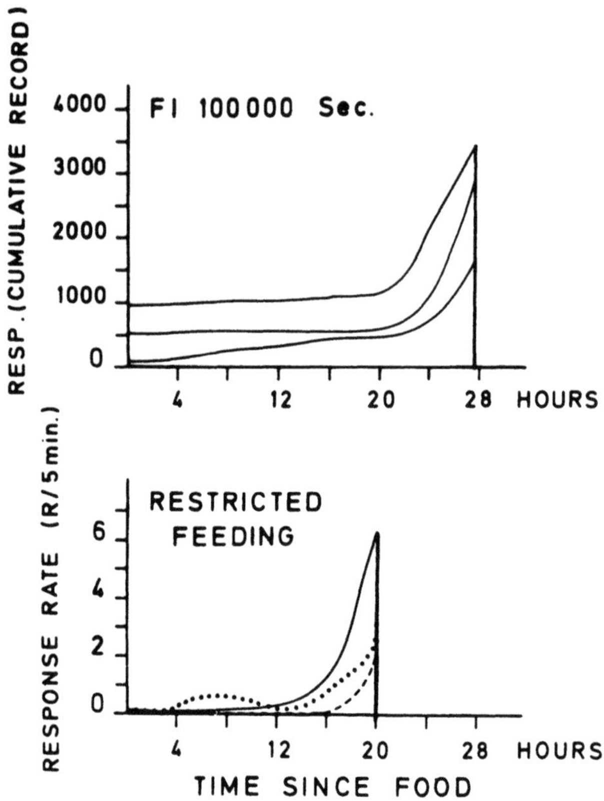

FIG. 3.5. (Top) Cumulative records of keypecking in three consecutive 100,000-sec FI intervals in a pigeon (redrawn and modified from Dews, 1965, Fig. 7, p. 434). (Bottom) Schematic representation of response rates (responses/5 min) in rats on a restricted feeding paradigm where food is available (via a lever-press response) for 4 hours every 20 hours (x-axis: time elapsed since the end of the last food availability). Unbroken line: anticipatory lever pressing with free-run activity in approximate phase-coincidence with meal-time. Dotted line: anticipatory lever pressing with free-run activity and meal-time in phase opposition (free-run peaks 5–9 hours after meal-time). Broken line: anticipatory lever pressing with cues added prior to food access (redrawn and modified from Terman et al., 1984, Fig. 2, p. 475).

The analogy between anticipatory responses with interval timing and restricted feeding led Terman et al. (1984) to study the interaction between both mechanisms. They first added auditory cues predictive of meal-time to a restricted feeding procedure in which food was contingent on lever pressing (these cues lasted for 4 hours, 2 hours, 6 min or 3 min, in different experimental conditions). It was thought that such cues would suppress the need for anticipatory responses, and start an interval timer that controlled a progressive acceleration of response rates up to meal-time. These cues might be considered analogous to discriminative stimuli in discrete-trial timing procedures, or to conditioned stimuli in Pavlovian delay conditioning. Without cues, anticipatory activity was increased when the free-running activity and meal-time were in phase coincidence. Cues in the hour range did not suppress activity prior to their onset, which reveals the operation of a circadian anticipation timer. These cues, however, suppressed or lowered activity at their onset, which indicates a cue-supported relief from the need to anticipate meal-times, as well as cue timing. Response suppression at the onset of the 4-hour cue was more than twice that of the 2-hour cue, which shows that the duration of suppression does not obey a simple proportional rule. Cues in the minute range induced no response suppression. They were preceded by several hours of anticipatory activity and were linked to the largest increase in response rate before meal-time. Furthermore, response rate patterns within these short cues revealed the operation of a scalar interval timer. Transitions from short to long cues were associated with transient peaks in response rate, appropriate to the discontinued cue duration.

Terman et al. (1984) also scheduled food omission on some days, which renders the experimental setting analogous to a giant 24-hour peak procedure. In these food omission probes, Terman et al. aimed at tracking the subjective "anchor point" or timing peak which, in interval timing, coincides with the delivery of the reinforcer and is necessary for the continuous estimation of time left to reinforcement. Their results indicate that higher response rates were obtained at the time of food omission than during anticipation. In the case of access to food for 4 hours, rates increased progressively during the food omission period. The anchor point was thus located at the end of the food omission period. It was followed by a sharp decline in response rates, which reflects an estimation of the duration after which food can no longer be obtained. These data thus suggest that rats estimate precisely the duration of food availability. If the duration of food access is abruptly shortened from 4 to 0.5 hours, with the meal onset unchanged, a double peak in activity emerges on omission trials: one at the end of the new 0.5-hour meal-time, and another (that eventually might disappear) at the end of the previous 4-hour meal-time (see Fig. 3.6).

Taken together, these data suggest that the anticipation pattern in restricted feeding situations results from the interaction of three clock systems: a circadian free-running timer which influences the level of anticipatory activity rather than the accuracy of meal-time estimation; a circadian anticipation timer which dissociates from the free-running clock under restricted feeding situations; and a cue-supported interval timer that can be arbitrarily reset and which is able to time multiple intervals concurrently, as upon transition from a short to a long pre-meal cue.

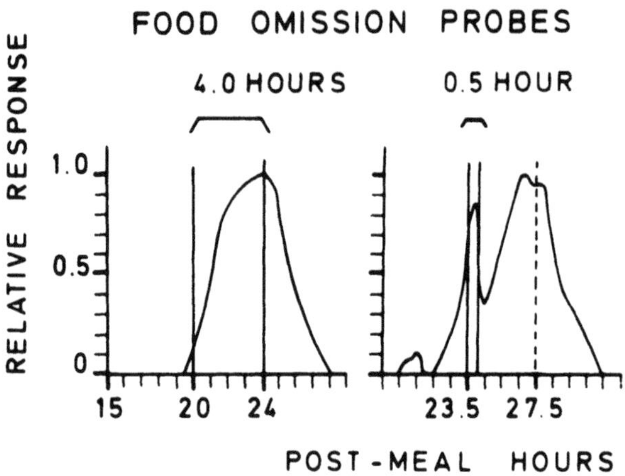

FIG. 3.6. Response gradients of rats averaged over food omission probe days. (Left) Omission probe after a 4-hour meal-time. (Right) Omission probe after a shortening of meal-time (from 4 to 0.5 hours) with meal-time onset unchanged (broken line: end of the previous 4-hour meal-time). Response gradients peak towards the end of the food omission probes and decrease abruptly thereafter (redrawn and modified from Terman et al., 1984, Fig. 7, p. 484).

Brain lesion studies support the existence of separate endogenous light- and food-entrainable oscillators. The suprachiasmatic nucleus controls free-running activity, whereas the hypothalamic areas are involved in food anticipation (Inouye, 1982; Phillips & Milkulka, 1979; Stephan, 1981). Most interestingly, suprachiasmatic lesions preserve food anticipation and fixed-interval behaviour as well (Innis & Vanderwolf, 1981), which further underscores the fact that ties may exist between both adaptations to time, as suggested by Terman et al. (1984).

Other recent experiments on meal anticipation have focused on the manipulation of phase and period relationships between food-entrainable and light-entrainable activity rhythms. They tend to show that these rhythms are mediated via separate, weakly coupled but interactive pacemakers (Rosenwasser, Pelchat, & Adler, 1984; Stephan, 1986; Stephan & Becker, 1989), and therefore confirm that the mechanisms controlling food anticipation are distinct from those underlying free-running activity, at least in rats. However, field-oriented studies concerned with the relationship between prey (or food) availability and predator activity, have underscored the adaptive value of such a synchronisation (Daan & Aschoff, 1982; Daan & Slopsema, 1978), and suggest that the degree of dependence between food-entrainable and light-entrainable activities has to be evaluated with regard to the species-specific feeding patterns. The concern with adaptation is further stressed by the fact that anticipatory activity may be suppressed in small carnivores (minks and weasels) in the case of food abundancy, and appears only in the case of food scarcity (Zielinski, 1986). Similarly, anticipatory activity disappears when rats are returned to ad libitum feeding (Rosenwasser et al., 1984; Ruis, Talamini, Buis and Rietveld, 1989). However, Stephan and Becker (1989) did show that severe deprivation is not requested for anticipatory activity to show up. It clearly develops with long-duration food access (10 hours), which tends to indicate that the food signal is more potent than homeostatic demand. Rosenwasser et al. (1984) suggest that under *ad libitum* feeding, the food-entrainable oscillator becomes coupled to the light-entrainable oscillator and phase-shifts or free-runs parallel to it. Such a flexible coupling might allow animals to synchronise their foraging activity with predictable (feeding schedule) or unpredictable food availability. Rosenwasser et al. (1984) also consider that the suppression of food anticipation under *ad libitum* conditions might be due either to an extinction process (food availability being no longer phase-bound to the 24-hour cycle—see also Ruis et al., 1989) or to a drop in the motivation for food, due to the restoration of normal bodyweight. The choice of the species and the knowledge of its feeding habits should thus be considered critical variables for further research on the relationship between circadian and interval timing.

Related studies that address optimal foraging behaviour have evaluated the time horizon in animal subjects. An important set of data has been collected on bird species, such as Great Tits (see Krebs & Kacelnik, 1984, for a review and discussion). Time horizon problems can be tackled in the laboratory by manipulating the time interval between two "feeding patches"—one mimicking a depleting patch (Progressive Ratio schedule, PR), the other a rich patch (Continuous Reinforcement schedule, CRF) that is made available after a specified delay to the beginning of a session. In such experimental designs, rats can anticipate a rich patch (CRF) up to 1 hour distant, but suppress feeding from the depleting patch (i.e. responding on the PR lever) only if the rich patch is 40 min or less away. Rats thus exhibit a time horizon of about 16 to 40 min (Timberlake, Gawley, & Lucas, 1987; 1988). Other data did show that the time horizon also depends on the procedure, the evaluation of food quality, the novelty of the test environment and the time elapsed between testing and post-session feeding (Lucas, Gawley and Timberlake, 1988). The temporal distance between daily foraging episodes plays a critical role that challenges classical optimal foraging theory according to which animal subjects act as "rational consumers" and have an infinite time horizon. Timberlake et al. (1987; 1988), as well as Krebs and Kacelnik (1984), consider that a limited time horizon makes sense for species that live in unpredictable environments (where a captured prey is preferable to a potential one), and advocate a flexible view about timing and timing horizons that may depend upon several mechanisms, among which is the circadian clock.

The above review of animal data has argued for the integration between laboratory and field studies. It has also illustrated the fact that relationships between circadian and interval timing, chronobiology and the temporal regulation of behaviour, have only begun to be identified (for data about other aspects of this relationship, see Groos & Daan, 1985; Richelle et al., 1985).

ANIMAL AND HUMAN TIMING

Generality in timing behaviour must also consider the relationship between animal and human data. From a comparative point of view, is it legitimate to consider that human capacities and achievements are rooted in more simple organisms' abilities? Stated in general terms: Do human subjects display, as a consequence of the specificity of their cognitive development and of their mastery of language, forms of adaptation that are radically different from those observed in non-verbal organisms, or do human beings progressively shift from animal-like behaviour to human (adult)-like achievements? In the case of such a transition, do adult forms of temporal skills eradicate the previous animal-like adaptations or do they only mask them without wiping them out? Do animal and human subjects share common timing mechanisms and does it make sense to raise the generality issue? Time is not a unitary concept for animal species, as the comparison between circadian and interval timing above tends to show (Roberts, 1983, p. 348, considers that two different "clocks" are operating in the rat: one that covers a range of about 0–5 min, and another whose range roughly covers 20–28 hours). Similarly, classical data on the psychology of time in human subjects distinguishes between short (≤ 2 sec) and longer durations, between perception and the estimation of time (Fraisse, 1957).

Difficulties in comparing animal and human timing arises from two sources, the methodology and the range of durations under study. Animal experiments mimic human ones in providing analogues of the classical discrimination, production and reproduction paradigms. However, these procedures far from match the level of sophistication and complexity of those currently used in human experiments (see, e.g. Allan, 1979, for a description of psychophysical methods). Instead of adapting sophisticated human psychophysical procedures to animal subjects, some recent experiments have submitted human subjects to the temporal regulation and differentiation schedules currently used with animals, and the quest for "pure" timing (discussed above within the context of animal experiments) has been transposed to human studies. The problem at stake could be stated as follows: How to get rid of parasitic influences introduced by man-made chronometric devices or cognitive "clocks", boredom and lack of motivation?

One of the ideas behind this quest (besides the legitimate concern for recording "noiseless" data) is that human performances would be "animal-like" if such confounding variables could be avoided. This hypothesis has recently been supported by Lowe, Beasty, & Bentall (1983), who showed that infants behave like animals in FI and switch to "adult-like" forms of behaviour (i.e. DRL- or Fixed-Ratio-like responding) when language enters the scene. Related developmental data have recently shown that the transition between infant and adult-like behaviour is progressive, and that language and the ability to formulate self-instructions play a major part in determining the pattern of FI behaviour in children and adult subjects (Bentall & Lowe, 1987; Pouthas & Droit, 1987). Furthermore, animal-like FI patterns can be obtained at will in adult subjects if reinforcement is made contingent on responding only in the last third of an interval (Wearden, personal communication) or upon aspects of behaviour of which subjects are unaware. Bailey and Lowe (1988) reinforced human adults with points for playing a computer game. These points were scheduled according to FI and were not contingent upon manipulating the computer, but upon the movements of the swivel chair on which the subject was sitting. In such an FI setting, performances (patterning of the movements of the chair) were similar to those of animal subjects. Furthermore, the subjects were unable to describe the contingencies in operation. If such results can be confirmed, they would demonstrate that contingency-shaped behaviour can still occur in adult subjects, and that the emergence of cognitive functions and language does not erase the more "primitive" forms of adaptation that human subjects seem to share with animals.

Another demonstration of similar forms of adaptation in animal and human subjects can be found in recent interval production experiments in which the range of durations under study were constrained in order to make counting or other verbal strategies inoperative. As mentioned above, Wearden and McShane (1988) have shown that, in a task where human adults must produce response durations ranging between 0.5 and 1.3 sec, the peak of the relative frequency distribution of durations matched target time, and the ratio between standard deviation and mean of the distribution (the coefficient of variation) remained approximately constant as target time changed. These and other results (Wearden, in press) again suggest that human subjects somehow share with animals a similar timing system. However, it would be premature, as noted by Wearden and McShane (1988), to conclude that human subjects possess a scalar timing system, because most of the human data do not obey scalar timing, because different procedures used to evaluate the same duration may have different outcomes (Fraisse, 1957) and, finally, because processes other than scalar timing might be found to fit with the data. Indeed, different processes might lead to identical behavioural outcomes.

It is tempting to draw a parallel between the FI and the duration production cases discussed above. One of the reasons that might explain the discrepancy between Wearden and McShane's (1988) and Zeiler et al.'s (1987) data, although they were obtained in similar experimental settings, is the range of durations under study: 0.5–1.3 sec *vs* 0.5–32 sec, respectively. It could be that, as in FI, human performance in duration production would be "animal-like" only if interfering noise (such as counting) could be avoided, i.e. with durations that do not exceed 1 or 2 sec. Following the same line, it could be speculated that, as in FI, infants and young children submitted to DRL would perform more accurately than older subjects. Developmental data with DRL does not, however, parallel FI data: DRL accuracy improves with age and animal-like DRL performances emerge only as children gain inhibitory control over their behaviour. Teaching young children to pay attention to the temporal requirements of the task greatly improves their performance (Pouthas & Jacquet, 1987). Developmental data from infants and children in FI or DRL are comparable with the developmental data collected from rats submitted to these schedules (these data and relationships will be discussed below).

Psychophysical procedures have produced numerous results that add to the complexity of comparing animal and human timing. The comparison of animal and human data, either for time discrimination or the temporal regulation of behaviour, leads one to define the capacity of an organism as relative to the particular situation under study. Attempts to generalise have been made. For example, Roberts (1983) considers that animal and human subjects share similarities at three levels: an internal pacemaker, cross-modal timing and a linear scale. However, generalisations seem daring given the intra-individual, inter-individual and inter-species differences that were described in several experimental settings. As stated by Macar (1985, p. 123), commenting on duration discrimination data:

> there seems to be a consensus about the necessity of admitting the involvement of several mechanisms, according to duration range, particular task requirements or individual strategies . . . the hiatus emphasized by Fraisse (1957) between the perception and the estimation of time, around 2 seconds, is partial evidence for such multiplicity of processes.

Macar (after Goody, 1958) advocates a "flexible clock system" that would be constructed as a function of each particular situation, and that would somehow be encoded with practice and deleted when no longer functional.

Recent data on timing in infants and children, as well as comparative studies that try to submit animal and human subjects to "identical" procedures, should not be considered as attempts to "reduce" human capacities to animal ones. Rather, they tend to confirm, as Fraisse (1948) and Piaget (1946) concluded from experiments that have nothing in common with operant conditioning, that the development of human knowledge and skills about time is deeply rooted in more basic and concrete forms of adjustment, and that a bridge between biotemporality and nootemporality does exist (Michon & Jackson, 1985; Richelle, 1968). Both human and animal data are valuable in their own right, and their comparison, in a developmental perspective, should help to set landmarks along the quest for determinants (innate or environmental) and for crucial differences that might show up. Ontogenetical studies of temporal adjustments in animals are thus an indispensable complement to human developmental data.

GENERALITY AND AGE OF SUBJECTS

Until recently, no systematic attempt had been made to study the effect of age on time-related performances in animals. The available data rarely specifically address this issue and, if they do, are often restricted to the simple quantification of response rates. A few reports have shown that the FI schedule can control operant behaviour in newly hatched chickens (Marley & Morse, 1966), ducklings (De Paulo & Hoffman, 1981), quails (Lejeune & Nagy, 1986) and rats (Delay, 1982). Other studies have focused on mature and senescent subjects (Campbell & Haroutunian, 1981; Goodrick, 1969; Hamm, Dixon, & Knisely, 1984; Harrison & Isaac, 1984). Some reports emphasise the similarity between age-related response patterns (Hamm et al., 1984; Marley & Morse, 1966), whereas others point towards age-related differences (Campbell & Haroutunian, 1981; Goodrick, 1969; Harisson & Isaac, 1984; Lejeune & Nagy, 1986). The sections that follow describe a systematic attempt to study behaviour controlled by three classical temporal regulation schedules (FI, DRL, DRRD) as a function of age. The subjects were albino rats.

A first set of data concerned the comparison of weanling, adult and senescent albino rats in the acquisition of temporal performances. Experiments undertaken with FI or DRL were limited to the acquisition of performance at one schedule value, i.e. 60 sec in FI and 20 sec in DRL (Lejeune, Jasselette, Nagy, & Perée, 1986; Lejeune & Jasselette, 1987a). For response duration reinforcement (DRRD), successive criteria (0.5, 1.0, 1.5, 2.0 and 2.5 sec) were associated with successive 2-day blocks (Lejeune & Jasselette, 1987b). The main results of these studies can be summarised as follows (see Fig. 3.7).

The quality of the temporal regulation of behaviour in acquisition depends upon the age of the subjects: with FI, the Curvature Index (Fry, Kelleher, & Cook, 1960) is inversely related to subject age. Weanling, adult

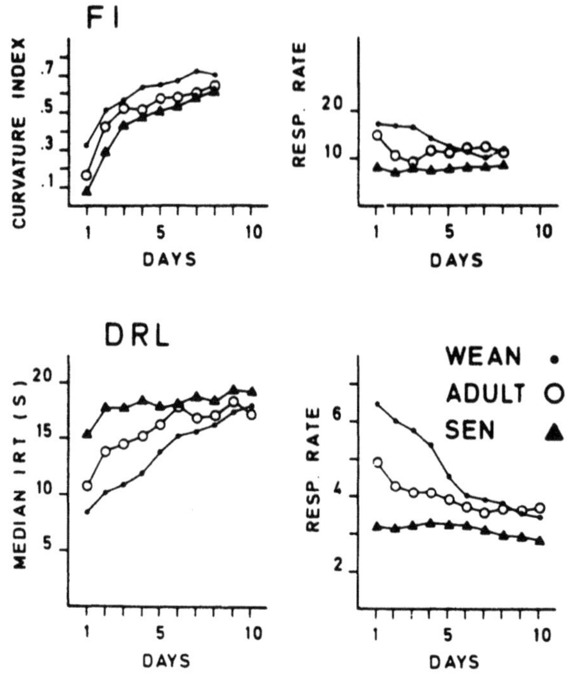

FIG. 3.7. (Top) Curvature Indices (left) and response rates (right) for weanling (●), adult (○) and senescent (▲) rats in the acquisition of a 60-sec FI performance. (Bottom) Median IRTs (left) and response rates (right) for weanling (●), adult (○) and senescent (▲) rats in the acquisition of a 20-sec DRL performance. x-axis, successive training days (redrawn and modified from Lejeune et al., 1986, Fig. 1, p. 338 and 2, p. 339; and Lejeune, 1989, Fig. 1, p. 323 and 3, p. 325).

and senescent rats rank in order, the youngest subjects earning the highest scores. In DRL and DRRD, the opposite picture emerges, i.e. median IRT or response durations are the lowest for weanling subjects, followed by adult and then senescent rats. The often noticed paradox between FI and DRL performance in adult subjects (Lejeune, 1978; Richelle & Lejeune, 1980) is not only present but even more clear-cut in young rats. Age-related differences could also be evidenced for response rates. In this case, the picture is identical whatever the reinforcement schedule: the rates are inversely related to subject age. Whereas rates from weanling subjects decrease over successive training days, those from senescent rats are less variable within-individuals and remain approximately constant over the length of the experiments. Adults occupy an intermediate position. The decrease in rate from the first to the last day of training is inversely related to the age of the subject.

In addition to these differences, there were also similarities. In the FI schedule, the post-reinforcement pause duration in weanling and older rats did not significantly differ (although it was on average higher in weanling subjects). In DRRD, transition data (i.e. the shifting from one reinforcement criterion to the next) showed that median response durations or efficiencies followed similar profiles in young and older subjects over the complete experiment. Weanling rats maintained in every case lower scores than adult subjects, but shifting from one criterion to the next was associated with identical trends in the evolution of the dependent variables. It is as if weanling and adult rats had a similar appraisal of the ratio between successive reinforcement criteria, but evaluated the critical durations with different time units.

These analogies led to speculation that the timing devices in weanling and older rats probably do not basically differ (which tends to support cross-age generality), and that the age-related differences described above could be due to more peripheral factors such as motivation for food or the age-specific level of general activity. The weanling rats emitted the highest response rates in DRRD, DRL and FI, especially over the first days of training, which can indeed be regarded as a consequence of high levels of hunger or general activity. However, neither motivation for food nor activity level can explain why these high response rates were linked to the highest Curvature Index values and long pauses in FI. This tends to indicate that inhibitory control of lever pressing exists in rats at weaning age and that general activity or hunger does not induce lever pressing in a non-specific way. Locomotion, exploration and manipulation may also provide material to build chains of collateral behaviour. Such chains may bridge the gap between successive lever presses in DRL or release the strain of forced immobility in DRRD. Paradoxically, what some authors consider as a behavioural index of the immaturity of inhibitory functions within the central nervous system (see, e.g. Bachevalier, 1976; Campbell, 1984; Campbell & Coulter, 1976), would help to inhibit operant behaviour. Chains of homogeneous collateral behaviour were observed both in FI and DRL in weanling rats (sleeping position, ano-genital grooming, or tail nibbling between responses or during the post-reinforcement pause). Such activities, which were centred on the subject and not directed towards items from the environment, were rare or absent in adult and senescent rats. At the end of the 8- or 10-day training period, age-related differences in the temporal regulation of behaviour that were highly significant early in acquisition faded away.

Even if the timing mechanisms proper do not basically differ in weanling (23–30 days), adult or senescent subjects, this does, however, not preclude the possibility that differences may be found in still younger subjects or in the retention of a learning episode. Forgetting may thus offer a clue to developmental differences that were no longer observable at the end of a 8- to 10-day training period. Subsequent experiments addressed both of these points.

They first confirmed the dissociation between response rate and temporal regulation of behaviour in FI. Two groups of weanling rats (weaned at 16 and 20 days of age, respectively) were submitted to a 60-sec FI schedule. The response rates followed a bitonic pattern (increase followed by decrease) in the precociously weaned rats (16 days), whereas they decreased regularly in the older subjects. Despite such a difference in the evolution of response rates, Curvature Indices and post-reinforcement pauses increased progressively with training and their values were similar across groups, i.e. precociously weaned rats were as accurate as rats weaned at 20 days of age. Secondly, age-specific differences in the retention of a DRL 20 sec performance after a 3-month rest were observed in an experiment comparing rats aged 23 days, 3, 7 or 24 months at the beginning of the training period (Lejeune, 1989). Whereas 3- and 7-month-old rats (adults) caught up and overshot training levels (they emitted longer IRTs and became more efficient), senescent and weanling rats remained less accurate and efficient than at the end of the training phase. Impairment of performance was particularly evident in the former weanling subjects. These results revealed age-related differences that were not visible at the end of the training period. They are congruent with reports on memory impairment in senescence (Campbell & Haroutunian, 1981; Craik, 1977) or infantile amnesia (Spear, 1979).

Whereas memory loss in senescence is probably a trivial correlate of ageing, impairment observed in the former weanling subjects can be tentatively interpreted along two lines. First, the same conditioning cubicles were used for training and retention testing, which led to a change of the ratio between body size and available space for the weanling rats that were tested as adults after a 3-month rest. The change in body size can be considered as a type of "internal" context change that is known to enhance forgetting. Furthermore, this change is probably also associated with an alteration in the perception of the environment, i.e. of the external context. The results can thus be interpreted within the framework of context effects on memory (see Balsam & Tomie, 1985; Spear, 1978).

The second line of interpretation arises from classical temporal regulation data. It is known from experiments on pigeons and rats that the transition from a large to a small cubicle, and vice versa, disrupts performance in FI and DRL (see Richelle & Lejeune, 1980). Frank and Staddon (1974) proposed the hypothesis according to which recovery under a new context depends upon the development of collateral behaviour adapted to the new situation. The weanling rat data tend to substantiate this hypothesis. As described above, most of the weanling rats (12 out of 14) systematically emitted chains of collateral behaviour in the second part of the training period. However, in retention testing, only 1 subject out of 12 displayed the collateral behaviour exhibited in training (i.e. tail nibbling). Collateral behaviour seemed to be forgotten in the remaining subjects, with consequent increased response rates and loss in timing accuracy and efficiency. Subsequent recovery of training levels was associated, in two subjects only, to the development, late in retention testing, of a new form of collateral activity. The presence of collateral behaviour in FI as well as DRL in weanling rats is congruent with the numerous reports on schedule-induced activities in FI or FT (Staddon, 1977), but challenges the hypothesis according to which such behaviour offers an outlet to inhibitory tension that develops specifically in temporal differentiation schedules (Richelle, 1972; Richelle & Lejeune, 1980), and orients future speculations toward a closer look at the interaction between temporal regulation and age-specific behaviour in a broad sense.

This very limited first set of data highlights the fact that, as in other learning situations, the temporal regulation of behaviour follows an age-specific evolution. This evolution may result from three sources that can interact:

1. An age-specific characteristic in the central timing mechanism *per se*. It could be speculated that, within the information processing model of timing (e.g. Gibbon et al., 1984) that views the central timing device as essentially being composed of a clock, a memory and a comparator, the pace of the clock or the memories of past temporal events change with ageing.

2. An age-specific characteristic at the level of the mechanism that translates timing into operant behaviour. It has, for example, been speculated that accurate response timing depends on response inhibition. This inhibitory mechanism, considerd here as a part of the transducer, would not be mature in young developing organisms. However, although behavioural inhibition has been demonstrated in classical Pavlovian paradigms (Pavlov, 1927), as well as in a few FI or DRL conditioning experiments (see Hemmes & Rubinsky, 1982; Richelle & Lejeune, 1980), the mechanism itself has until now remained elusive. Recent data with EEG recording in rats on FI tend to confirm that performance is underpinned by a release from behavioural inhibition (Lorig & Isaac, 1986).

3. Age-specific temporal adjustments may further depend on non-temporal or more "peripheral" factors such as motivation for food or exploration, and level of general activity, i.e. upon biologically constrained behaviours that are essential to the development and survival of the species. Research procedures are needed that allow the interactions between these factors to be disentangled. Peak procedure is one of them, and

the bulk of data collected over the last decade by Church, Roberts, Meck and their collaborators can be considered as a valuable contribution to that endeavour.

The relationship between developmental data in rats and those collected with human subjects can be commented upon as follows (see also Pouthas, this volume). First, age-specific data show that developmental variables seem to be at play in animal and human subjects.

Secondly, the comparison between FI and DRL data from infants or children on the one hand, and rats on the other, reveals analogies. FI seems to be well mastered by weanling rats and by human infants. However, DRL is not well mastered early in life, be it in rats or children. Young rats and young children (about 2 years old) emit high proportions of short IRTs (Lejeune & Jasselette, 1987a; Pouthas & Jacquet, 1983). Any verbal instructions given by the experimenter to wait, are not adhered to by children before the age of 3½, which suggests that young children are not sensitive to the temporal dimension of the DRL task or are unable to inhibit their responses (temporal abilities described in infants, or even in newborns, in other experimental settings tend, however, to demonstrate that the human species is "prepared" to cope with temporal constraints: see Pouthas, this volume). The DRL data for rats and children follow an evolution towards an improved accuracy of behaviour (Lejeune & Jasselette, 1987a; Pouthas & Jacquet, 1987).

Thirdly, the presence of non-operant behaviour, be it in children or in young rats, strengthens the generality of collateral behaviour across animal and human species. Young children have been described as engaging in gross motor activities of finer repetitive action patterns (e.g. grooming) between operant responses in DRL or during post-reinforcement pauses in FI, as if they would "estimate the duration by relying on a motor rhythm" (Pouthas, 1985, p. 105). Precise quantification and comparisons across ages and species are needed to further delineate the origin and functions of these behaviours in a developmental perspective.

The precocious ability to master FI in weanling rats and infants, the analogy betwen FI performance and the anticipation of the daily meal (restricted feeding experiments, see above), and the often noticed paradox between FI and DRL performance in animal subjects converge to assign a particular status to the FI schedule within the family of contingencies where forms of temporal regulation of behaviour are seen to develop. The early sensitivity of both animal and human subjects to the periodic delivery of the reinforcer underscores the fact that ties probably do exist between this schedule and biological rhythms, and suggests that FI performance, together with periodic meal anticipation, may be a link that bridges the gap between built-in biological periodicities and the adaptation to arbitrary temporal requirements; in other words, between species-specific behaviour in a natural setting and behaviour exhibited in the "artificially" constrained laboratory.

CONCLUSION

Generality and the quest for common timing mechanisms across procedures, species and ages has been the common thread running through this chapter. There is no doubt that lawful relationships between temporal estimates and real time do exist. They have been described within each category of temporal tasks, be it those concerned with the estimation of the duration of exteroceptive stimuli or those that deal with the temporal regulation of the subject's own behaviour (see, e.g. Catania, 1970; Macar, 1985; Platt, 1979). These relationships have opened the way for theorising about the mechanism and functioning of the hypothetical internal clock (see, e.g. Church, 1984; Gibbon, 1977; Killen aand Fetterman, 1988; Roberts, 1981). Scalar timing theory has been shown to fit with data collected in various but not all temporal tasks, and it can be considered an extension of Weber's law on the temporal regulation of behaviour. This theory is a sophisticated translation of the fact that animal or human subjects obey relative rather than absolute time. This level of sophistication and quantitative description, however, has its internal constraints that may limit the generality of the theory. Generality thus depends on the degree of resolution of the analysis. Qualitative descriptions of behaviour are less constrained and more general than are quantitative ones. Generality statements depend partly on the focal point of the experimenters and the attention they are willing to pay to data that do not fit with their hypothetical constructs. The focus on lawful data may overshadow concern about exceptions. These remain numerous.

Experiments have so far not been (or have rarely been) undertaken outside a limited range of species or durations (from a few seconds to a few minutes). Above critical durations of a few tens of seconds, scalar timing fails to fit the data. Room thus exists for alternative theories about the functioning of the internal timing mechanism(s) which, in the view advocated by Macar (1985), could be flexible devices constructed and deleted *ad hoc*. Generality in results has been questioned for cross-modal duration discrimination. It does not emerge from the comparison of different operants within a species or when a given operant is studied across species. The recent concern about "pure timing" is a tacit recognition of inter-species differences and of a dissociation between capacity and performance. Reinforcement magnitude effects are well documented. However, data about cross-reinforcement generality are scarce.

The comparison between daily meal anticipation in restricted feeding experiments and FI behaviour indicates that behavioural similarities do not necessarily result from a common mechanism. The generality of food anticipation seems to be restricted to the circadian range, whereas FI behaviour has been described in pigeons for a much wider range of durations. The precise nature of the underlying physiological substrates remains open to speculation.

Similar forms of adjustment have been described in adult animal and human subjects. This generality is, however, limited to particular experimental settings or conditions. Response timing is at the centre of a debate which opposes rule- and contingency-governed behaviour (Lowe, 1979; Wearden, 1988; see also Catania, this volume) and tries to delineate the specificity of human *vs* animal performances. Recent developmental data are very limited for animal species and the comparison of animal and human data obtained in similar experimental settings remains broadly speculative. These data, however, are promising steps that seem to point towards a continuity between animal and human timing performances; they open the way for an integrative and comparative view of time in behaviour, a view which articulates differences in continuity.

REFERENCES

Allan, L. G. (1979). The perception of time. *Perception and Psychophysics*, *26*, 340–354.

Bachevalier, J. (1976). Ontogenèse de l'apprentissage et de la mémoire chez le rat. *L'Année Psychologique*, *76*, 199–211.

Bailey, J. & Lowe, C. F. (1988). Contingency shaped responding in human adults. Paper presented at the Second European Meeting on the Experimental Analysis of Behavior, Liège, July.

Balsam, P. D. & Tomie, A. (Eds) (1985). *Context and learning*. Hillsdale, N.J.: Lawrence Erlbaum Associates Inc.

Bentall, R. P. & Lowe, C. F. (1987). The role of verbal behavior in human learning: III. Instructional effects in children. *Journal of the Experimental Analysis of Behavior*, *47*, 177–190.

Bolles, C. R. (1970). Species-specific defense reactions and avoidance behavior. *Psychological Review*, *77*, 32–48.

Bolles, R. C. & Stokes, L. W. (1965). Rats' anticipation of diurnal and a-diurnal feeding. *Journal of Comparative and Physiological Psychology*, 60, 290–294.

Boulos, E., Rosenwasser, A. M., & Terman, M. (1980). Feeding schedules and the circadian organization of behavior in the rat. *Behavioral and Brain Research*, *1*, 39–65.

Breland, K. & Breland, M. (1961). The misbehavior of organisms. *American Psychologist*, *16*, 661–664.

Campbell, B. A. (1964). Reflections on the ontogeny of learning and memory. In R. Kail & N. E. Spear (Eds), *Comparative perspectives on the development of memory*, pp. 23–35. Hillsdale, N.J.: Lawrence Erlbaum Associates Inc.

Campbell, B. A. & Coulter, X. (1976). Neural and psychological processes underlying the development of learning and memory. In T. J. Tighe & R. N. Leaton (Eds), *Habituation, perspectives from child development, animal behavior and neurophysiology*, pp. 129–157. Hillsdale, N.J.: Lawrence Erlbaum Associates Inc.

Campbell, B. A. & Haroutunian, V. (1981). Effects of age on long-term memory: Retention of fixed interval responding. *Journal of Gerontology*, *36*, 338–341.

Catania, A. C. (1970). Reinforcement schedules and psychophysical judgement: A study of some temperal properties of behavior. In W. N. Schoenfeld (Ed.), *The theory of reinforcement schedules*, pp. 1–42. New York: Appleton-Century-Crofts.

Chatlosh, D. L. & Wasserman, E. A. (1987). Delayed temporal discrimination in pigeons: A comparison of two procedures. *Journal of the Experimental Analysis of Behavior*, *47*, 299–309.

Cheng, K. & Roberts, W. A. (1989). Timing multimodal events in pigeons. *Journal of the Experimental Analysis of Behavior*, *52*, 363–376.

Church, R. M. (1984). Properties of the internal clock. In J. Gibbon & L. Allan (Eds), Timing and time perception. *Annals of the New York Academy of Sciences*, *423*, 566–582.

Craik, F. I. M. (1977). Age differences in human memory. In J. E. Birren & W. K. Schiae (Eds), *Handbook of the psychology of aging*. New York: Van Nostrand Reinhold.

Daan, S. & Aschoff, J. (1982). Circadian contributions to survival. In J. Aschoff, S. Daan, & G. A. Groos (Eds), *Vertebrate circadian systems: Structure and physiology*, pp. 305–321. Berlin: Springer Verlag.

Daan, S. & Slopsema, S. (1978). Short term rhythms in foraging behavior in the common vole *Microtus arvalis*. *Journal of Comparative Physiology*, *127*, 215–227.

Davey, G. C. L., Cleland, G. G., Oakley, D. A., & Jacobs, J. L. (1984). The effect of early feeding experience on signal-directed response topography in the rat. *Physiology and Behavior*, *32*, 11–15.

Davison, M. & McCarthy, D. (1987). The interaction of stimulus and reinforcer control in complex temporal discrimination. *Journal of the Experimental Analysis of Behavior*, *48*, 97–116.

De Casper, A. J. & Sigafoos, A. D. (1983). The intrauterine heartbeat: A potent reinforcer in newborns. *Infant Behavior and Development*, *6*, 12–25.

Delay, E. R. (1982). Age-related differences in the effects of *d*-amphetamine and illumination on fixed-interval responding of rats. *Psychopharmacology*, *78*, 298–299.

De Paulo, P. & Hoffman, H. S. (1981). Reinforcement by an imprinting stimulus versus water on simple schedules in ducklings. *Journal of the Experimental Analysis of Behavior*, *36*, 151–169.

Dews, P. B. (1965). The affect of multiple S^{Δ} periods on responding on a fixed-interval schedule: III. Effects of changes in pattern of interruption, parameters and stimuli. *Journal of the Experimental Analysis of Behavior*, *8*, 427–435.

Fraisse, P. (1948). Etude comparée de la perception et de l'estimation de la durée chez les enfants et les adultes. *Enfance*, *1*, 199–211.

Fraisse, P. (1957). *Psychologie du temps*. Paris: PUF. (*The psychology of time*. London: Eyre and Spottiswode, 1964.)

Frank, J. & Staddon, J. E. R. (1974). Effects of restraint on temporal discrimination behavior. *Psychological Record*, *24*, 123–130.

Fry, W., Kelleher, R. T., & Cook, L. (1960). A mathematical index of performance on fixed interval schedule of reinforcement. *Journal of the Experimental Analysis of Behavior*, *3*, 193–199.

Gibbon, J. (1977). Scalar expectancy and Weber's law in animal timing. *Psychological Review*, *84*, 279–325.

Gibbon, J., Church, R. M., & Meck, W. H. (1984). Scalar timing in memory. In J. Gibbon & L. Allan (Eds), Timing and time perception. *Annals of the New York Academy of Sciences*, *423*, 52–77.

Goodrick, C. L. (1969). Operant responding of non-deprived young and senescent male albino rats. *Journal of Genetic Psychology, 114*, 29–40.

Goody, W. (1958). Time and the nervous system. *Lancet, 7031*, 1139–1141.

Groos, G. & Daan, S. (1985). The use of the biological clock in time perception. In J. Michon & J. Jackson (Eds), *Time, mind and behavior*, pp. 65–74. Berlin: Springer-Verlag.

Hamm, R. J., Dixon, C. E., & Knisely, J. S. (1984). Long-term memory of a DRL task in mature and aged rats. *Experimental Aging Research, 10*, 39–42.

Harrison, D. W. & Isaac, W. (1984). Disruption and habituation of stable fixed-interval behavior in younger and older monkeys. *Physiology and Behavior, 32*, 341–344.

Hatten, J. L. & Shull, R. L. (1983). Pausing on fixed interval schedules: Effects of the prior feeder duration. *Behaviour Analysis Letters, 3*, 101–111.

Hemmes, N. S. (1975). Pigeons' performance under differential reinforcement of low rate schedule depends upon the operant. *Learning and Motivation, 6*, 344–357.

Hemmes, N. S. & Rubinsky, H. J. (1982). Conditional acceleration and external disinhibition of operant lever pressing by prereward stimuli, neutral and reinforcing stimuli. *Journal of the Experimental Analysis of Behavior, 38*, 157–168.

Hinde, R. A. & Stevenson-Hinde, J. (1973). *Constraints on learning*. London: Academic Press.

Howerton, L. & Meltzer, D. (1983). Pigeons' FI behavior following signaled reinforcement duration. *Bulletin of the Psychonomic Society, 21*, 161–163.

Innis, N. K. & Vanderwolf, C. H. (1981). Neural control of temporally organized behavior in rats: The suprachiasmatic nucleus. *Behaviour Analysis Letters, 1*, 53–62.

Inouye, S. I. T. (1982). Ventromedial hypothalamic lesions eliminate anticipatory activities of restricted daily feeding schedules in the rat. *Brain Research, 250*, 183–187.

Jasselette, J., Lejeune, H. & Wearden, J. (1990). The perching response and the laws of temporal differentiation. *Journal of Experimental Psychology: Animal Behavior Processes, 16*, 150–161.

Killeen, P. R. & Fetterman, J. G. (1988). A behavioral theory of timing. *Psychological Review, 95*, 274–295.

Kraemer, P. J. & Roberts, W. A. (1985). Short-term memory for simultaneously presented visual and auditory events. *Journal of Experimental Psychology: Animal Behavior Processes, 11*, 137–151.

Krebs, J. R. & Kacelnik, A. (1984). Time horizons of foraging animals. In J. Gibbon & L. Allan (Eds), Timing and time perception. *Annals of the New York Academy of Sciences, 423*, 278–291.

LaMon, B. C. & Zeigler, H. P. (1984). Grasping in the pigeon (*Columba livia*): Stimulus control during conditioned and consummatory responses. *Animal Learning and Behavior, 12*, 223–231.

LaMon, B. C. & Zeigler, H. P. (1988). Control of pecking response form in the pigeon: Topography of ingestive behaviors and conditioned keypecks with food and water reinforcers. *Animal Learning and Behavior, 16*, 256–267.

Lejeune, H. (1978). Sur un paradoxe dans l'estimation du temps chez l'animal. Revue critique. *L'Année Psychologique, 78*, 163–181.

Lejeune, H. (1989). Long-term memory for DRL: A comparison between weanling, adult and senescent rats. *Physiology and Behavior, 45*, 321–330.

Lejeune, H. & Jasselette, P. (1985). Fixed interval and fixed time treadle pressing in the pigeon: A comparison with FI and FT keypecking. *Behavioural Processes, 11*, 131–152.

Lejeune, H. & Jasselette, P. (1986). Accurate DRL performance in the pigeon: Comparison between perching and treadle pressing. *Animal Learning and Behavior, 14*, 205–211.

Lejeune, H. & Jasselette, P. (1987a). DRL performance in weanling rats: A comparison with adult subjects. *Physiology and Behavior, 40*, 271–278.

Lejeune, H. & Jasselette, P. (1987b). Differential reinforcement of response duration (DRRD) in weanling rats: A comparison with adult subjects. *Behavioural Processes*, *15*, 315–332.

Lejeune, H., Jasselette, P., Nagy, J., & Perée, F. (1986). Fixed interval performance in the weanling rat: A comparison with adult and senile subjects. *Physiology and Behavior*, *38*, 337–343.

Lejeune, H. & Nagy, J. (1986). Operant conditioning in the newly hatched quail: Fixed interval performance. *Behavioural Processes*, *12*, 317–326.

Lejeune, H. & Richelle, M. (1982a). Differential reinforcement of perching duration in the pigeon: A comparison with Differential-Reinforcement-of-Low-rate keypecking. *Behaviour Analysis Letters*, *2*, 49–57.

Lejeune, H. & Richelle, M. (1982b). Fixed interval performance in the turtle dove: A comparison with pigeons and rats. *Behaviour Analysis Letters*, *2*, 87–95.

Lejeune, H., Richelle, M., & Mantanus, H. (1980). Factors influencing temporal regulation. In M. Richelle & H. Lejeune (Eds), *Time in animal behaviour*, pp. 108–142. Oxford: Pergamon Press.

Lejeune, H. & Wearden, J. (1990). The comparative psychology of fixed-interval responding: Some quantitative analyses. *Learning and Motivation*, (in press).

Logue, W. (1988). Research on self-control: An integrating framework. *Behavioral and Brain Sciences*, *11*, 665–709.

Logue, A. W., Chavarro, A., Rachlin, H., & Reeder, R. W. (1988). Impulsiveness in the pigeon living in the experimental chamber. *Animal Learning and Behavior*, *16*, 31–39.

Lorig, T. S. & Isaac, W. (1986). EEG activity during fixed- and variable-interval responding. *Physiological Psychology*, *14*, 33–66.

Lowe, C. F. (1979). Determinants of human operant behavior. In M. D. Zeiler & P. Harzem (Eds), *Reinforcement and the organization of behavior*, pp. 159–192. Chichester: John Wiley.

Lowe, C. F., Beasty, A., & Bentall, R. P. (1983). The role of verbal behavior in human learning: Infant performance on fixed-interval schedules. *Journal of the Experimental Analysis of Behavior*, *39*, 157–164.

Lucas, G. A., Gawley, D. J. & Timberlake, W. (1988). Anticipatory contrast as a measure of time horizon in the rat: Some methodological determinants. *Animal Learning and Behavior*, *16*, 377–382.

Macar, F. (1985). Time psychophysics and related models. In J. Michon & J. Jackson (Eds), *Time, mind and behavior*, pp. 112–130. Berlin: Springer-Verlag.

Marley, E. & Morse, W. H. (1966). Operant conditioning in the newly hatched chicken. *Journal of the Experimental Analysis of Behavior*, *9*, 95–103.

Mechner, F. & Guevrekian, L. (1962). Effects of deprivation upon counting and timing in the rat. *Journal of the Experimental Analysis of Behavior*, *5*, 463–466.

Meck, W. H. (1984). Attentional bias between modalities: Effects on the internal clock, memory, and decision stages used in animal time discrimination. In J. Gibbon & L. Allan (Eds), Timing and time perception. *Annals of the New York Academy of Sciences*, *423*, 528–541.

Meck, W. H. (1986). Affinity for the dopamine D2 receptor predicts neuroleptic potency in decreasing the speed of an internal clock. *Pharmacology, Biochemistry and Behavior*, *25*, 1185–1189.

Meck, W. H. & Church, R. M. (1987). Nutrients that modify the speed of internal clock and memory storage processes. *Behavioural Neuroscience*, *101*, 465–475.

Michon, J. & Jackson, J. (Eds) (1985). *Time, mind and behavior*. Berlin: Springer-Verlag.

Pavlov, I. P. (1927). *Conditioned reflexes*. Oxford: Oxford University Press. (2nd edn: New York: Dover Publications, 1960.)

Phillips, J. L. M. & Milkulka, P. J. (1979). The effects of restricted food access upon locomotor activity in rats with suprachiasmatic lesions. *Physiology and Behavior*, *23*, 257–262.

Piaget, J. (1946). *Le développement de la notion de temps chez l'enfant*. Paris: PUF.

Platt, J. R. (1979). Temporal differentiation and the psychophysics of time. In M. D. Zeiler & P. Harzem (Eds), *Advances in analysis of behaviour, Vol. I: Reinforcement and the organization of behaviour*, pp. 1–30. Chichester: John Wiley.

Platt, J. R. (1984). Motivational and response factors in temporal differentiation. In J. Gibbon & L. Allan (Eds), Timing and time perception. *Annals of the New York Academy of Sciences*, *423*, 200–210.

Pouthas, V. (1985). Timing behavior in young children: A developmental approach to conditioned spaced responding. In J. A. Michon & J. L. Jackson (Eds), *Time, mind and behavior*, pp. 100–109. Berlin: Springer-Verlag.

Pouthas, V. & Droit, S. (1987). Temporal learning in four and a half year old children: Role of instructions and prior knowledge. Paper presented at the Experimental Analysis of Behaviour Group Meeting, Manchester, April (unpublished).

Pouthas, V. & Jacquet, A. Y. (1983). Attente et adaptation à la durée chez l'enfant. *Cahiers de Psychologie Cognitive*, *3*, 397–407.

Pouthas, V. & Jacquet, A. Y. (1987). Developmental studies of timing behavior in four and a half and seven year old children. *Journal of Experimental Child Psychology*, *43*, 282–299.

Provasi, J. (1988). Capacités et apprentissages de régulations temporelles acquises chez le nourrisson dans l'activité de succion. Unpublished doctoral thesis, Université René Descartes, Paris.

Reed, P. & Wright, J. E. (1988). Effects of magnitude of food reinforcement on free-operant response rates. *Journal of the Experimental Analysis of Behavior*, *49*, 75–85.

Richelle, M. (1968). Notions modernes de rythme biologique et régulations temporelles acquises. In J. de Ajuriaguerra (Ed.), *Cycles biologiques et psychiatrie*. Genève: Georg et Cie/Paris: Masson.

Richelle, M. (1972). Temporal regulation of behaviour and inhibition. In R. A. Boakes and M. S. Halliday (Eds), *Inhibition and learning*, pp. 229–251. London: Academic Press.

Richelle, M. & Lejeune, H. (Eds) (1980). Time in animal behaviour. Oxford: Pergamon Press.

Richelle, M., Lejeune, H., Perikel, J. J., & Fery, P. (1985). From biotemporality to nootemporality: Toward an integrative and comparative view of time in behavior. In J. Michon & J. Jackson (Eds), *Time, mind and behavior*, pp. 75–99. Berlin: Springer-Verlag.

Richter, C. P. (1922). A behavioristic study of the activity of the rat. *Comparative Psychology Monographs*, *1*, 1–55.

Roberts, S. (1981). Isolation of an internal clock. *Journal of Experimental Psychology: Animal Behavior Processes*, *7*, 242–268.

Roberts, S. (1982). Cross-modal use of an internal clock. *Journal of Experimental Psychology: Animal Behavior Processes*, *8*, 2–22.

Roberts, S. (1983). Properties and function of an internal clock. In R. L. Mellgren (Ed.), *Animal cognition and behavior*, pp. 345–397. Amsterdam: North-Holland Press.

Roberts, S. & Church, R. M. (1978). Control of an internal clock. *Journal of Experimental Psychology: Animal Behavior Processes*, *4*, 318–337.

Roberts, W., Cheng, K. & Cohen, J. S. (1989). Timing light and tone signals in pigeons. *Journal of Experimental Psychology: Animal Behavior Processes*, *15*, 23–35.

Rosenwaser, A. M., Pelchat, R. J., & Adler, N. T. (1984). Memory for feeding time: Possible dependence on coupled circadian oscillators. *Physiology and Behavior*, *32*, 25–30.

Ruis, J. F., Talamini, L. M., Buys, J. P., & Rietveld, W. J. (1989). Effects of time of feeding on recovery of food-entrained rhythms during subsequent fasting in SCN-lesioned rats. *Physiology and Behavior*, *46*, 857–866.

Seligman, M. E. P. & Hager, J. L. (Eds) (1972). *Biological boundaries of learning*. New York: Appleton-Century-Crofts.

Skinner, B. F. (1956). A case history in scientific method. In S. Koch (Ed.), *Psychology: A study of science*, Vol. 2, pp. 359–379. New York: McGraw-Hill.

Spear, N. E. (1978). *The processing of memories: Forgetting and retention*. Hillsdale, N.J.: Lawrence Erlbaum Associates Inc.

Spear, N. E. (1979). Memory storage factors leading to infantile amnesia. In G. Bower (Ed.), *The psychology of learning and motivation*, Vol. 13, pp. 91–154. London: Academic Press.

Staddon, J. E. R. (1977). Schedule-induced behavior. In W. K. Honig, & J. E. R. Staddon (Eds), *Handbook of operant behavior*, pp. 125–153. Englewood Cliffs, N.J.: Prentice-Hall.

Stephan, F. K. (1981). Limits of entrainment to periodic feeding in rats with suprachiasmatic lesions. *Journal of Comparative Physiology*, *143*, 401–410.

Stephan, F. K. (1986). Coupling between feeding- and light-entrainable circadian pacemakers in the rat. *Physiology and Behavior*, *38*, 537–544.

Stephan, F. K. & Becker, G. (1989). Entrainment of anticipatory activity to various durations of food access. *Physiology and behavior*, *46*, 731–741.

Stubbs, D. A. (1979). Temporal discrimination and psychophysics. In M. D. Zeiler & P. Harzem (Eds), *Advances in analysis of behaviour, Vol. I: Reinforcement and the organization of behaviour*, pp. 341–370. Chichester: John Wiley.

Terman, M., Gibbon, J., Fairhurst, S., & Waring, A. (1984). Daily meal anticipation: Interaction of circadian and interval timing. In J. Gibbon & L. Allan (Eds), Timing and time perception. *Annals of the New York Academy of Sciences*, *423*, 470–487.

Timberlake, W., Gawley, D. J., & Lucas, G. A. (1987). Time horizons in rats foraging for food in temporally separated patches. *Journal of Experimental Psychology: Animal Behavior Processes*, *13*, 302–309.

Timberlake, W., Gawley, D. J., & Lucas, G. A. (1988). Time horizons in rats: The effect of operant control of access to future food. *Journal of the Experimental Analysis of Behavior*, *50*, 405–417.

Van Haaren, F., Van Hest, A., & Vandepoll, N. (1988). Self control in male and female rats. *Journal of the Experimental Analysis of Behavior*, *49*, 201–211.

Wearden, J. H. (1985). The power law and Weber's law in fixed-interval post reinforcements pausing: A scalar timing model. *Quarterly Journal of Experimental Psychology*, *37B*, 191–212.

Wearden, J. (1988). Some neglected problems in the analysis of human operant behavior. In G. Davey & C. Cullen (Eds), *Human operant conditioning and behavior modification*, pp. 197–224. Chichester: John Wiley.

Wearden, J. (1990). Do humans possess an internal clock with scalar timing properties? *Learning and Motivation* (in press).

Wearden, J. & McShane, B. (1988). Interval production as an analogue of the peak procedure: Evidence for similarity of animal and human timing processes? *Quarterly Journal of Experimental Psychology*, *40B*, 363–375.

Welzl, H. (1976). Attempt to modify rate and duration of licking in rats by operant conditioning. *Behavioural Processes*, *1*, 319–326.

Wilkie, D. M. (1987). Stimulus intensity affects pigeons' timing behavior: Implications for an internal clock model. *Animal Learning and Behavior*, *15*, 35–39.

Zeiler, M. D. (1981). Model of temporal differentiation. In C. M. Bradshaw, E. Szabadi, &

C. F. Lowe (Eds), *Quantification of steady-state operant behaviour*, pp. 205–214. Amsterdam: Elsevier/North-Holland.

Zeiler, M. D. (1983). Integration of response timing: The functional time requirement. *Animal Learning and Behavior*, *11*, 237–246.

Zeiler, M. D. (1985). Pure timing in temporal differentiation. *Journal of the Experimental Analysis of Behavior*, *43*, 183–193.

Zeiler, M. D. (1986). Behavior units and optimality. In T. Thompson & M. D. Zeiler (Eds), *Analysis and integration of behavior units*, pp. 81–116. Hillsdale, N.J.: Lawrence Erlbaum Associates Inc.

Zeiler, M. D., Davis, E. R., & De Casper, A. J. (1980). Psychophysics of key-peck duration in the pigeon. *Journal of the Experimental Analysis of Behavior*, *34*, 23–33.

Zeiler, M. D. & Hoyert, M. S. (1989). Temporal reproduction. *Journal of the Experimental Analysis of Behavior*, *52*, 81–95.

Zeiler, M., Scott, G. K., & Hoyert, M. S. (1987). Optimal temporal differentiation. *Journal of the Experimental Analysis of Behavior*, *47*, 191–200.

Zielinski, W. J. (1986). Circadian rhythms of small carnivores and the effect of restricted feeding on daily activity. *Physiology and Behavior*, *38*, 613–620.

II BEHAVIOUR ANALYSIS AND THE EMERGENCE OF RATIONAL THINKING

4 Equivalence Relations: Where Do They Come From?

Murray Sidman
New England Center for Autism, Southborough, Massachusetts, U.S.A.

The topic of equivalence relations, sometimes referred to as stimulus equivalence or equivalence classes, is relatively new to behaviour analysis. There is reason to believe that the concept is important for our understanding of behaviour, but the term *equivalence* is occasionally beginning to be used somewhat more broadly than is perhaps useful. So I have chosen this occasion to go back over some of the basics and, at the same time, to discuss a fundamental and still unsolved problem: Where do equivalence relations come from?

THE BASIC EXPERIMENT

For those who are not familiar with the topic of equivalence, let me summarise the basic experiment (adapted from Sidman, 1971). Suppose we test a child on some conditional discriminations, a type often considered to indicate simple "reading comprehension". For example, the upper section of Fig. 4.1 is a diagram of a stimulus display on five keys. In the centre is a sample stimulus, i.e. a word, and in the outer keys are comparison stimuli, i.e. pictures. Given a word as the sample, will the child select the appropriate comparison picture? Will the child select the appropriate picture for each word in a list, say, of 20 words?

The lower section of Fig. 4.1 also shows a stimulus display, but with a picture as the sample and words as comparisons. Given a sample picture, will the subject select the appropriate word—again, for each of a set of 20 pictures?

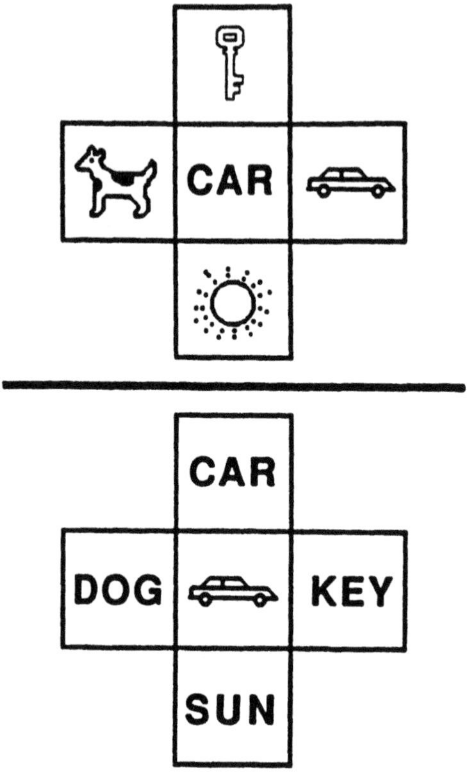

FIG. 4.1. Examples of stimulus displays on the five keys (not to scale). The centre keys contain sample stimuli, i.e. a word in the upper diagram, and a picture in the lower diagram. The four outer keys contain comparison stimuli, i.e. pictures in the upper diagram, and words in the lower. From trial to trial, the correct comparison is conditional on the sample.

These are, of course, simplified versions of standard reading comprehension tests. Children's understanding of textual material is routinely examined by asking them to match words and phrases to pictures, objects, and so on.

Let us start with a child who is unable to do either of these tasks, giving no evidence of reading comprehension. We could teach each performance directly, with standard conditional-discrimination procedures. But would the result be comprehension?

How about non-humans doing essentially the same thing? The stimuli usually differ from those in Fig. 4.1, but monkeys' or pigeons' performances are remarkably similar to children's. Can one say that the child is showing comprehension, but that the pigeon is just doing conditional

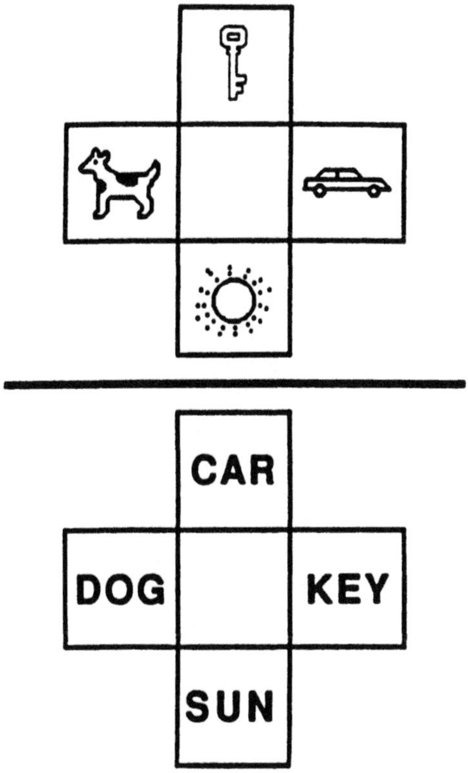

FIG. 4.2. Auditory–visual conditional discriminations. The comparison stimuli are visual (pictures or words), but the samples are now dictated words instead of printed words or pictures.

discriminations? How can we tell whether there is any difference between what the human and non-human is doing?

Here is a way to find out. Instead of teaching the visual word–picture relations directly, teach something else first. The upper display in Fig. 4.2 shows the same comparisons as Fig. 4.1, but now the centre key is blank. Instead of showing the child visual samples, we dictate a sample word, repeating the word so that the child does not have to remember it ("car, car . . ."). We deliver a reinforcer when the child selects the corresponding picture. After having learned to do this for a list of 20 dictated words, is the child showing auditory comprehension? Does the child understand the dictated words? At this point, we cannot know.

To set the stage for finding out, let us also teach a second task, illustrated in the lower section of Fig. 4.2. Now, with the same list of 20 dictated sample words, we teach the child to select the appropriate printed word. Having learned this, the child can relate each of the 20 dictated words to one of the 20 pictures or printed words.

When matching dictated words to pictures and printed words, is the child showing auditory comprehension? We can find out by retesting reading comprehension, giving the same tests the child had failed before (Fig. 4.1). Now, our subject does them perfectly, matching each of 20 printed words to its appropriate picture (upper display), and each of 20 pictures to its appropriate printed name (lower display).

New performances have emerged, without having been taught explicitly. After the child has learned to relate the dictated words to the pictures and to the printed words, the visual word–picture and picture–word performances are there, right away, often 100% correct on the first post-test.

This is a remarkable finding. We and others have repeated it many times, under a wide variety of conditions (e.g. Mackay & Sidman, 1984; McDonagh, McIlvane, & Stoddard 1984; Saunders, Wachter, & Spradlin, 1988; Sidman & Cresson, 1973; Sidman, Kirk, & Willson-Morris, 1985; Sidman & Tailby, 1982; Spradlin, Cotter, & Baxley, 1973; Stromer & Osborne, 1982; Wetherby, Karlan, & Spradlin, 1983). Each time it happens, it generates a kind of excitement that is matched only by one's first experience in shaping a new response topography. Here, having taught 20 relations between dictated words and pictures, and 20 more between dictated and printed words, we then found 40 new relations emerging, "free" so to speak. Those emergent relations between printed words and pictures indicated that our subject had acquired a 20-word vocabulary—both auditory and visual reading comprehension.

EQUIVALENCE

Clearly, when some subjects learn the two sets of auditory–visual conditional discriminations, something more is going on than we can see at the time. Whatever that "something" is, it sets the stage for the emergence of conditional discriminations that we have not explicitly taught. Here is where some simple-minded theory comes in—a guess about what else is going on.

The theory simply states that what is going on is the formation of equivalence relations, that the conditional relations between auditory samples and visual comparison stimuli are also equivalence relations. I call this a theory because all we can see directly are the conditional relations; we cannot see whether those conditional relations are also equivalence relations. But then, given the standard mathematical definition of equivalence relations, discussed later, we can test the theory. We shall see that if each directly taught conditional discrimination does give rise to equivalence relations, the new conditional discriminations *must* emerge.

In the context of our examples of dictated words, pictures and printed words, we can say that (1) if the dictated words were equivalent to their corresponding pictures and (2) if the dictated words were also equivalent to the corresponding printed words, then (3) the printed words and pictures would be equivalent to each other.

The formation of equivalence relations, and the emergence of the untaught conditional discriminations, provide a testable definition of "reading comprehension". It is possible to find out whether "understanding" is involved.

We can go a step further. In ordinary speech, people talk about the "meanings" of words. Sometimes they talk about dictionary meanings (a word and its synonym); sometimes they talk about a word and its referent (object, picture, quality, etc.); or they talk about symbol and substance (i.e. number and quantity). The second part of my theory states simply that in all of these instances—when people talk this way—the related items (word and synonym, word and referent, symbol and substance) will be found to be equivalent to each other. This is now a testable proposition.

What is Meant by Equivalence?

In order to generalise a bit from our first examples of words and pictures, let us look at equivalence in the context of some other stimuli, e.g. numbers, English number names and French number names. First, with a printed digit as the sample, the subject learns to choose the appropriate English digit name (Fig. 4.3a). The stimuli, of course, vary in sequence and position from trial to trial. Then, with a printed English digit name as the sample, the subject learns to choose the appropriate French name (Fig. 4.3b).

We may now ask some questions, for example: Are the digits the meanings of the words? Are the words the meaning of the digits? Do the English and French words have the same meanings?

Our simple theory leads us to rephrase these questions, and to ask, instead: Are the relations between digits and words equivalence relations? Is each digit equivalent to an English word, and is each English word equivalent to a French word? If these equivalences hold true, we will find that subjects will then be able to do something they were not able to do before, something we had never explicitly taught; they will be able to match each French word to the appropriate digit. Figure 4.3c shows some of the critical test trials.

In setting this test, we present baseline trials of the conditional discriminations we had explicitly taught the subject (Fig. 4.3a: digit samples and

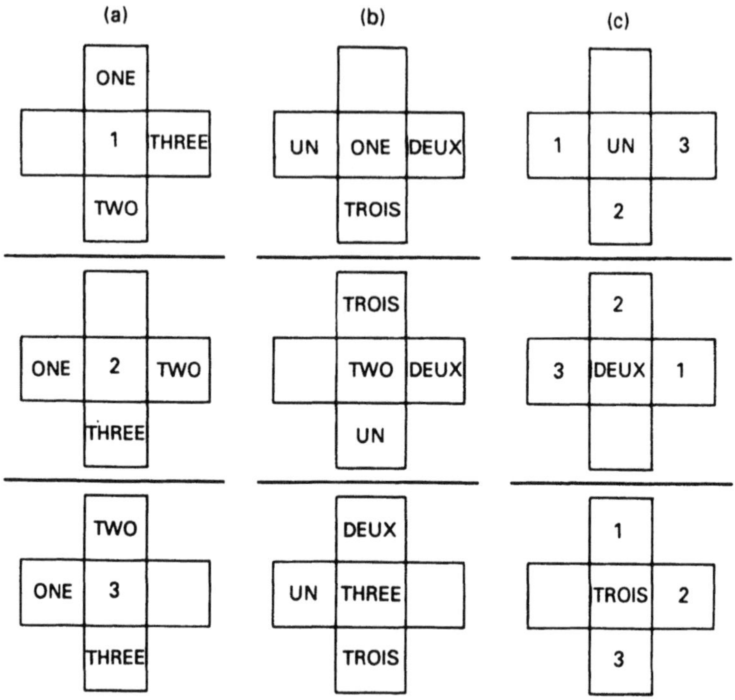

FIG. 4.3. Diagrams of three sets of conditional discriminations. (a) Digit samples and English digit–name comparisons. (b) The English digit names now serve as samples, with French digit names as comparisons. After being taught both of these sets of conditional discriminations, the subject is tested with the French digit names as samples and the digits as comparisons (c).

English word comparisons; Fig. 4.3b: English word samples and French comparisons). Among the baseline trials, we insert probes (Fig. 4.3c: French words as samples, and digits as comparisons). But now, we reinforce none of the subject's selections, thereby giving the subject no indication of what we expect. If the explicitly taught conditional relations are also equivalence relations, the subject will perform accurately on these new probe trials.

Figure 4.4 summarises what we have done. The stimuli presented as samples—one at a time—are shown in separate boxes; the stimuli presented as comparisons—three at a time—are all shown in the same box. The arrows point from samples to comparisons.

The subject learns to select an English word on the basis of the sample digit (indicated by the uppermost solid arrow), and a French word on the basis of the English sample (lower solid arrow). And then, in equivalence

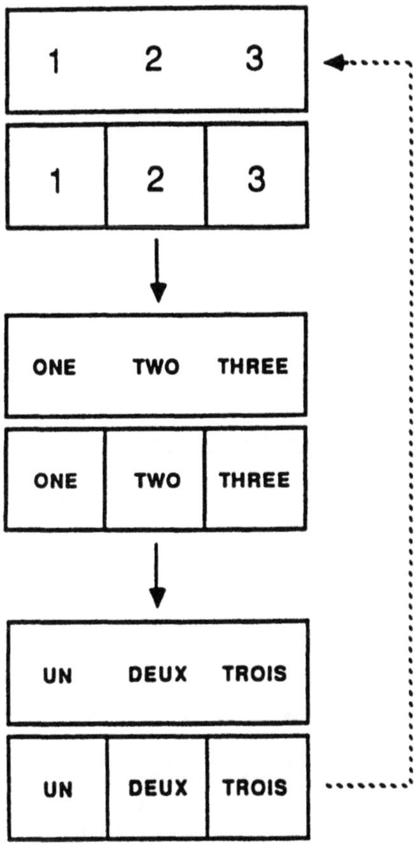

FIG. 4.4. The solid arrows in the centre indicate the two sets of conditional discriminations that were explicitly taught, i.e. digit samples (presented one at a time) with English-name comparisons (presented three at a time), and English-name samples with French-name comparisons. The dotted arrow to the right indicates the emergent conditional discriminations: French-name samples with digit comparisons.

test trials, with a French word as the sample, the subject proves able to select the appropriate digit from the three comparisons (indicated by the dotted arrow on the right-hand side).

How does equivalence make this possible? Why do I call this an equivalence test? The third part of the theory adapts the mathematical definition of equivalence relations, and recommends a behavioural test for each element of the definition. For behavioural analysis, one can, of course, define equivalence any way one wants; definitions stand or fall on the basis of their utility. But, so far, the proposed adaptation of the mathematical definition has turned out to be extremely useful: Any rela-

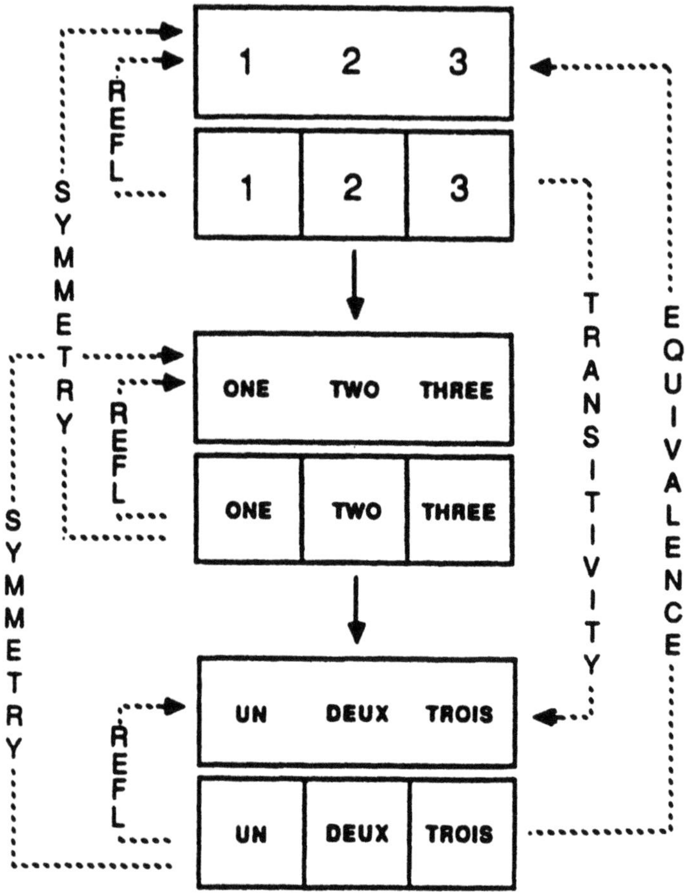

FIG. 4.5. Each arrow points from samples to comparisons. The solid arrows in the centre indicate the two sets of conditional discriminations that were explicitly taught. All of the dotted arrows indicate emergent conditional discriminations, not explicitly taught. The three tests for reflexivity (REFL), the two symmetry tests, the transitivity test and the equivalence test are illustrated here.

tion, to be classified as an equivalence relation, must meet each of three requirements—reflexivity, symmetry and transitivity. Here is a summary of how these mathematical concepts can be carried over into behaviour analysis.

Reflexivity. First, the relation must be reflexive, i.e. elements related to each other must show the same relation to themselves. For example, if the conditional relations between digits and English words are also reflexive, then each of these stimuli will bear the same conditional relation to themselves that they bear to each other, i.e. the subject will match digit to digit, and word to word. This is commonly called "identity matching", and brings the notion of sameness into the definition of equivalence. And so, the test for reflexivity is generalised identity matching, as shown in Fig. 4.5.

In Fig. 4.5, all of the arrows again go from sample to comparisons: the two solid arrows indicate the directly taught relations; the broken arrows indicate emergent, or derived relations.

The three reflexivity tests (labelled REFL on the left-hand side of Fig. 4.5) ask whether the subject will relate each stimulus to itself (digit to digit, English word to English word, and French word to French word). For exmple, given "3" as a sample in the uppermost test, will the subject select that same digit when given "1," "2" and "3" as comparisons? The subject must do this without explicit reinforcement; otherwise, one cannot be certain that the relation is generalised identity—something more than just this specific conditional discrimination.

Symmetry. The second requirement for equivalence is that the relation is symmetric, i.e. it must be reversible. If the relation between the sample and the comparison is symmetric, then the samples will function effectively as comparisons, and the comparisons as samples.

Each of the two explicitly taught relations can be tested for symmetry. The labelled arrows running from the samples to the comparisons on the left-hand side of Fig. 4.5 indicate the two symmetry tests. Having learned to relate sample digits to English-name comparisons, the subject must then be able to relate the names as samples to the digits as comparisons (the upper symmetry test in Fig. 4.5). Symmetry must also hold true for the English and French names (the lower symmetry test). If one is to be certain that the relations are truly symmetric, the reversed conditional relations must emerge without explicit reinforcement. Again, therefore, the tests are given in extinction.

Transitivity. Finally, the conditional relations must be transitive. In the general case, if A is related to B, and B to C, then transitivity will cause A to be related to C. A labelled arrow on the right-hand side of Fig. 4.5 denotes the transitivity test: Having learned to relate digits as samples to English names as comparisons, and English names as samples to French comparisons, the subject must then be able to relate digit samples to French comparisons. Again, the test consists of unreinforced trials.

The symmetry and transitivity tests yield derived relations, new in the subject's repertoire, but never explicitly taught; they are derived from the two sets of relations that were explicitly taught. (Reflexivity need not be derived from those relations.) Note that transitivity and symmetry, even though derived from the same relations, are independent of each other; each could emerge without the other. The subject could succeed on the transitivity test—relating digit samples to French comparisons—even while failing one or both symmetry tests—unable to relate French samples to English comparisons, or English samples to digit comparisons. Or the subject could fail to show transitivity while succeeding on one or both symmetry tests.

The Equivalence Test. The other labelled arrow on the right-hand side of Fig. 4.5 denotes what I have called an equivalence test. The subject proves able to relate French samples to digit comparisons. We are now in a position to see how the three properties of equivalence relations make this derived relation possible.

First, reflexivity makes each stimulus the same as itself, whether used as a sample or a comparison, regardless of its location, etc. Secondly, symmetry brings in the untaught relations between French samples and English comparisons, and between English samples and digit comparisons. Now, these two sets of derived relations that symmetry makes possible can themselves be tested for transitivity. If they are transitive, the subject will match French samples to digit comparisons.

However, I do not just call this final test a transitivity test; instead, I call it an equivalence test. It is actually a combined test for the three required properties of equivalence: reflexivity, symmetry and transitivity. We saw that subjects may be able to do the simple transitivity test (matching digit samples to French comparisons) even though they are unable to do the symmetry tests. There is, however, no way a subject could do the equivalence test (matching French samples to digit comparisons) without also being able to do both symmetry tests. Unlike simple transitivity, equivalence could not emerge unless both of the explicitly taught relations were symmetric, and the symmetric relations transitive. As measured in the equivalence test, transitivity is no longer independent of symmetry. A subject would therefore have no basis for doing the equivalence test unless both sets of directly taught relations possessed all three properties of equivalence relations.

Necessary Outcomes. The utility of our definition of equivalence depends on certain consistencies in the test results. If the directly taught relations are equivalence relations, then *all* derived relations *must* emerge. Certain necessities follow from this:

1. If the separate tests for reflexivity, symmetry and transitivity all prove positive, then the equivalence test *must* also prove positive. If a relation could possess all the properties of equivalence and still yield

a negative equivalence test, the proposed definition of equivalence would become useless.

2. If an equivalence test proves negative, tests for the defining properties of equivalence must show one or more to be absent; the subject must fail to show reflexivity or symmetry (at least one of the tests) or transitivity. A negative equivalence test, without at least one negative test for an individual property of equivalence, would make our definition of equivalence useless.
3. Given negative results for just one of the reflexivity, symmetry or transitivity tests, we must then attribute positive results on an equivalence test to some factor other than equivalence. Unless we can identify an artefact, we would have to conclude that our definition of equivalence is not useful.
4. Given a positive equivalence test, the subject must demonstrate all the relations that define equivalence. If a subject does the equivalence test but fails even one of the other tests, then one has to conclude that something besides equivalence was responsible for the subject's performance on the equivalence test; one must suspect the presence of artefacts or procedural inadequacies.

Let us summarise the particular example illustrated in Fig. 4.5. The end result is the establishment of three 3-member classes of equivalent stimuli. If we were to name these (in English), we might call them the "ones", the "twos" and the "threes". Within a class the digit, English name and French name can now be said to have the same meaning. It is under these circumstances—the formation of equivalence classes—that people say such things as, "words are symbols for numbers" and "two means deux", and as other stimuli become members of each class, "numbers are symbols for quantities", "objects are the referents of names", etc.

It is important to note that although I have made some theoretical statements, I have provided neither a model that requires equivalence relations to emerge from conditional discriminations, nor a theory that predicts when equivalence will or will not emerge. I have simply outlined a set of tests for equivalence classes. These tests have so far proved so consistent that the most fruitful response to seeming contradictions turns out to be a search for artefacts (e.g. Sidman, 1987). Equally important, the tests have proven useful for the analysis of an aspect of behaviour we cannot see directly unless we probe for it.

WHERE DOES EQUIVALENCE COME FROM?

So much for the basics. Now, how do we "explain" equivalence? That is to say, can we derive equivalence from more primitive behavioural functions, variables or processes?

Logic as the Source of Equivalence

Perhaps a good place to start is one of those seemingly obvious notions that turn out to be incorrect. It is tempting to say that equivalence is simply a matter of logic, that each of the derived relations (Fig. 4.5) is a logical necessity. But no such logical necessity exists.

Table 4.1 shows that we can find relations characterised by any possible combination of the three requirements for equivalence. Only relation 1 meets all the requirements. Here, we have a parallel relation between lines in a plane: line A is parallel to line B, and line B to line C. This relation is reflexive: each line is also parallel to itself. The relation is symmetric: line B is also parallel to line A, and line C to line B. And the relation is transitive: line A is also parallel to line C.

Relation 3, "greater than", is neither reflexive nor symmetric: a number cannot be greater than itself; and if A is greater than B, B cannot be greater than A. But if A is greater than B, and B is greater than C, A will also be greater than C, showing the relation to be transitive.

Relation 5 is symmetric, but neither reflexive nor transitive. Reflexivity would require A to live next door to herself. But the relation is symmetric: if A lives next door to B, then B also lives next door to A. If A lives next door to B, and B lives next door to C, transitivity would require A to live next door to C, but the relation does not permit that juxtaposition.

Given a relation between A and B, then, logic does not demand reflexivity: A being related to B does not require A to bear that same relation to itself; in relation 8, A may be one-half of B, but A cannot be one-half of itself. Nor does logic demand symmetry: A being related to B does not require that B bear the same relation to A; in relation 7, A being perfectly correlated with B does not require B to be perfectly correlated

TABLE 4.1
The Presence or Absence of the Defining Properties of Equivalence in Various Relations

Relations	*Reflexivity*	*Symmetry*	*Transitivity*
1. is parallel to (lines in plane)	+	+	+
2. is brother of (all males)	−	+	+
3. is greater than (whole numbers)	−	−	+
4. is greater than or equal to (whole numbers)	+	−	+
5. lives next door to (people)	−	+	−
6. has at least one point in common with (lines in plane)	+	+	−
7. is highly correlated with (events)	+	−	−
8. is half of	−	−	−

with A. And logic does not require transitivity: given that A is related to B, and B to C, A does not have to bear that same relation to C; in relation 6, line A may share one point in common with line B, and line B may share one point in common with line C, but line A may still not intersect with line C at all.

There is, therefore, no logical necessity for relations to be reflexive, symmetric or transitive. Conditional relations are completely indeterminate in this respect. Given "If A then B" and "if B then C", the conditional relations "if A then A", "if B then A" and "if A then C" need not follow. Logic does not demand that conditional relations be equivalence relations. None of the derived relations have to emerge from conditional discriminations. To reason, "If A is related to B, and B to C, then C must be related to A" is simply incorrect.

Table 4.1 is not a logical but a behavioural construction. Our experience with these and other relations tells us whether they possess the properties of equivalence relations. This is not a case in which logical derivations account for behaviour; rather, behavioural derivations justify the logic.

The relations emerging from the equivalence tests may even be regarded as a form of inductive inference; we might therefore entertain the possibility that equivalence is one of the behavioural processes that underlie inductive reasoning—but that is better saved for another occasion.

Verbal Behaviour as the Source of Equivalence

Experiments on equivalence relations often find the subjects naming the stimuli. Also, subjects are often able to state rules that describe the emergent performances. It has been suggested, therefore, that naming, verbal rules, or both, may be necessary for the emergence of equivalence relations (e.g. Devany, Hayes, & Nelson, 1986; Lowe, 1986).

Naming. Let us first look at the possibility that naming is critical for equivalence. It is not immediately clear what the function of the names might be. One possibility is that the same name assigned to several stimuli might mediate a common class membership for those stimuli. This was the hypothesised basis for the phenomenon of "mediated generalisation", studied classically by paired-associate techniques (e.g. Jenkins, 1963; 1965). Indeed, when subjects—even monkeys—are explicitly taught to respond in the same way to conditionally related stimuli, the relations characteristic of equivalence do seem to emerge (McIntire, Cleary, & Thompson, 1987). Definitive tests, however, remain to be carried out with non-humans. Common names can surely facilitate the formation of stimulus classes for humans, but whether the names are necessary for equivalence is not yet certain (Lazar, Davis-Lang, & Sanchez, 1984; Sidman, Cresson, & Willson-Morris, 1974; Sidman, Willson-Morris, & Kirk, 1986).

A common name for different stimuli does define a functional stimulus class, and I shall have more to say about the possible relation between functional classes and equivalence classes. But a significant problem arises when we do not explicitly teach the subject to give the same name to each stimulus that we are going to test for membership in an equivalence class. If the subject does give the same name to each class member, but without having been taught to do so, we then have to ask where the names came from. Under these circumstances, it is reasonable to suspect not that the common names gave rise to equivalence, but that equivalence gave rise to the common names.

Rules. A second possibility is that equivalence relations have to be rule-governed (Skinner, 1969), i.e. that the derived relations must be products of verbal rules. Some subjects are able to describe the network of directly taught and derived relations even in complex, interlocking sets of conditional discriminations (Bush, Sidman, & de Rose, 1989).

But once more, we must ask, "What comes first, the rules or the equivalence relations?" If the rule does come first, we must then ask where it came from. As we saw before, given a particular relation between A and B, and between B and C, there is no logical reason why that particular relation should also exist between C and A. Again, it is reasonable to suspect not that such rules give rise to equivalence, but that equivalence gives rise to the rules.

Skinner (1969) has stated that rules specify contingencies. The statement is surely true, but what is this process of "specification"? A behavioural interpretation has not been forthcoming. If equivalence gives rise to rules, then for a rule to specify a contingency may simply mean that the rule and the contingency are members of an equivalence class. This is a behaviourally precise—and testable—proposition.

As with naming, existing evidence on the role of rules in generating equivalence is not definitive. Perhaps the question of whether verbal behaviour (Skinner, 1957)—via naming, rules or some other route—is necessary for equivalence, will never be answered to everyone's satisfaction. It may not be possible to determine which is cause and which is effect. The question of verbal behaviour's primacy would be settled—with a negative answer—if equivalence relations could be demonstrated unequivocally with non-humans. It is important, therefore, to continue that search (D'Amato, Salmon, Loukas, & Tomie, 1985; Lipkens, Kop, & Matthijs, 1988; McIntire et al., 1987; Sidman et al., 1982; Vaughan, 1988).

I, personally, have been convinced by some relatively "soft" data. I have seen 4-member classes demonstrated by retarded subjects who did speak but only rarely, and then in utterances of only a few words, at most. Lengthy reasoning was not in their repertoires. They never performed long verbal chains like "A goes with B, and B goes with C; therefore, C must go with A". But this is difficult to prove—perhaps impossible. My observations will become accepted only when many other experimenters acknowledge having seen the same thing happen with comparable subjects. The evaluation of clinical judgements can take a long time.

Functional Classes and Equivalence

There are many different kinds of classes; stimuli can be related in other ways then equivalence. Goldiamond (1966) has defined a functional stimulus class as a group of discriminative stimuli all of which control the same behaviour (or, more precisely, the same two-term contingency). For example, a native English speaker will respond with the same name to a digit, to its written English name, and, when translating, to that digit name in any other language. With respect to the behaviour these stimuli control in common, they are substitutable for each other. Serving the same function, they form a functional class.

Are functional classes also equivalence classes? It is often assumed that they are the same, even though they are defined differently, and even though we test for their existence in different ways. Instead of asking whether they are the same, we might more productively ask if they are related and, if so, how? Here is one approach to these questions.

We started with a subject who had no concept of odd and even numbers. The first thing we did was to establish two functional classes, one containing odd and the other even numbers. (They were, of course, odd and even only to us, not to the subject.) As shown in the upper section of Fig. 4.6, one class that we taught had three odd numbers (1, 3 and 7) and the other had three even numbers (2, 4 and 8). The classes were established by a simple discrimination procedure. Trials consisted of the presentation of a pair of stimuli, one odd and one even. Nine different pairs were possible.

We started with the odd numbers positive and the even negative, as shown in the two columns in the upper left-hand part of Fig. 4.6 (trials were presented in mixed order). Selecting the odd member of the pair brought the subject a reinforcer. When he met a high accuracy criterion, we reversed the discrimination, making the even numbers positive and the odd negative (the two columns in the upper right-hand part of Fig. 4.6). We continued reversing and re-reversing the discrimination, the subject reaching a high accuracy criterion each time.

How do we know we established functional classes? Adapting a criterion that Vaughan (1988) used with pigeons, we continued reversing the discriminations until the subject made no more than one error at the beginning

REVERSAL TESTS FOR FUNCTIONAL CLASSES

ODD POSITIVE		EVEN POSITIVE	
POS.	NEG.	POS.	NEG.
1	2	2	1
1	4	4	1
1	8	8	1
3	2	2	3
3	4	4	3
3	8	8	3
7	2	2	7
7	4	4	7
7	8	8	7

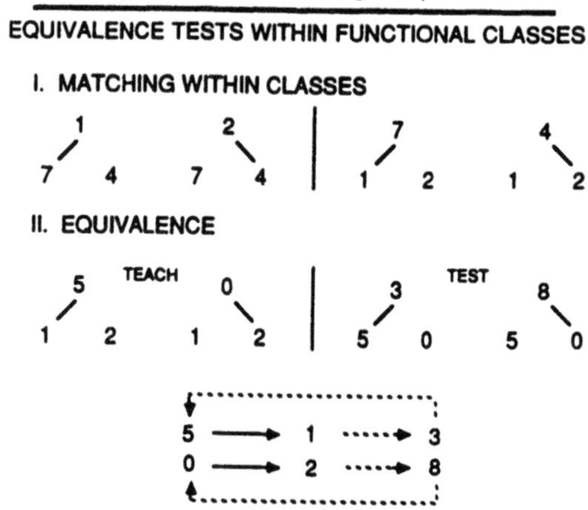

FIG. 4.6. The upper section shows the nine simple discrimination trials with odd numbers positive, and the nine with even numbers positive. Section I shows the sample and comparison stimuli in the tests for matching within the functional odd and even classes; a line connects each sample with its matching comparison, i.e. odd to odd and even to even. The left-hand side of Section II shows the new samples 5 and 0, that the subject was taught to relate to the functional class members 1 and 2, respectively. The right-hand side of Section II shows tests for the emergent conditional discriminations, with functional class members 3 and 8 as samples, and the new stimuli 5 and 0 as comparisons. In the diagram at the bottom, solid arrows indicate relations that were explicitly taught, and dotted arrows indicate emergent relations (see text).

of each reversal. After learning, say, to select odd numbers, the subject eventually made an error only on the first trial after the even numbers were made positive, and continued to select even numbers without a mistake on any of the remaining pairs. And he did the same when we again made the odd numbers positive. When a change in the contingencies for one pair of stimuli became sufficient to change the subject's response to all the other pairs, we knew we had two functional classes. We could then ask whether the subject would match class members to each other. By doing so, he would set the stage for equivalence tests.

Without going into the methodology, here are the first tests (done in extinction). As shown in Fig. 4.6 (I. Matching within classes), the subject was given trials with a sample (1 or 2) from either class, and comparisons (7 and 4) from both classes. By selecting the odd comparison when the sample was odd, and the even comparison when the sample was even, our subject showed conditional relations emerging between members of a functional class. He also demonstrated the symmetric relation (on the right-hand side of Fig. 4.6, I), continuing to match odd to odd, and even to even, when sample and comparison functions were switched—7 and 4 becoming the samples, and 1 and 2 the comparisons.

To test the relations for equivalence, we had to try to bring a new stimulus into each functional class. To do this, we taught the subject another conditional discrimination. With a new odd number, 5, as the sample, the subject learned to select an original odd class member, 1; and with a new even sample, 0, to select an original even class member, 2 (Fig. 4.6, II. Equivalence). The teaching was done with standard reinforcement procedures.

Having taught the new conditional discrimination, we probed the relation between the new stimuli, 5 and 0, and other original class members, 3 and 8 (on the right-hand side of Fig. 4.6, II). In this test (carried out in extinction), the subject selected 5 when 3 was the sample, and 0 when 8 was the sample.

Then, 5 and 0 were tested for functional class membership by including them in the simple discriminations (not shown, but adding seven new stimulus pairs to those at the top of Fig. 4.6). The subject always selected 5 when the odd stimuli were positive, and 0 when the even stimuli were positive. Teaching and testing the new conditional discriminations had brought the new stimuli into the functional classes.

The diagram at the bottom of Fig. 4.6 will help clarify how these results must have come about. We had explicitly taught the subject conditional relations between 5 and 1, and between 0 and 2 (shown by the solid arrows). Conditional relations between odd class members 1 and 3, and between even class members 2 and 8, had not been tested, but can be assumed on the basis of the positive within-class test (Fig. 4.6, I). Following the diagram: (1) If conditional relations exist between 1 and 3, and between 2 and 8, and (2) if those conditional relations are symmetric (reversing the direction of the dashed arrows), and (3) if the relations between 5 and 1, and between 0 and 2, are symmetric, and (4) if all of these relations are also transitive, then (5) the subject will select 5 when 3 is the sample, and 0 when 8 is the sample, thereby demonstrating equivalence.

Does this emergence of equivalence relations mean that the functional classes (that I have been calling "odd" and "even") were also equivalence classes? Such a conclusion is not yet justified. The reasons for this are as follows. Three things have happened here. First, teaching and reversing the simple discriminations established two functional classes. Secondly, teaching and testing the conditional discriminations established equivalence relations. And, thirdly, equivalence then made it possible to transfer new stimuli into the existing functional classes.

In our original experiments, the conditional discriminations did two things at once: They established classes (undefined, except that they were equivalence classes), and transferred the class membership to new stimuli. In this experiment, functional classes were established first, with relatively simple discrimination procedures. The conditional discriminations had only to transfer the class membership to new stimuli.

The establishment of equivalence relations by the conditional discriminations made it possible to enlarge the functional classes without requiring the new class members actually to participate in the defining contingency, but the functional classes themselves did not have to be equivalence classes. Bringing new members into already existing classes required only that the conditional relations be equivalence relations. Equivalence permitted the conditional relations to serve as transfer vehicles.

Therefore, we have no compelling reason to believe that functional classes must exist in order for equivalence classes to be established, or even that functional classes must also be equivalence classes. Interactions of the two do provide a powerful tool for potential application, and for gaining systematic information about the role of class concepts in behavioural analysis.

For example, our experience has already established a limitless number of functional classes for us: odd/even, numbers/letters, human/non-human, animal/vegetable/mineral, good/bad, large/small, many/few, first/second (important particularly for syntax), rich/poor, friend/enemy, words in English/Spanish/Chinese/etc., noun/verb/adjective/etc. We are always having to insert new elements into these classes, and we succeed in doing so without explicitly learning to relate the new elements to all of the already existing members of those classes.

A number of experiments have shown how equivalence relations permit this efficiency in the enlargement of existing functional classes (de Rose et al., 1988; Lazar, 1977; Lazar & Kotlarchyk, 1986; Silverman, Anderson, Marshall, & Baer, 1986). But functional equivalence and equivalence relations, although closely related, are not the same; nor does one explain the other.

Equivalence as a Fundamental Stimulus Function

If equivalence requires neither naming nor verbal reasoning, and is not derived from functional classes, the possibility remains that equivalence is a fundamental stimulus function. We have some reason for suspecting this to be so, quite independently of our current inability to derive equivalence from something more basic.

The diagram in the upper right-hand corner of Fig. 4.7 (within the box) shows a particular response (pressing a key) and no other producing a particular reinforcer (a coin). This is the reinforcement relation (Skinner, 1938), a two-term contingency between response and reinforcer.

Looking at the three right-hand columns in Fig. 4.7, we see instances in which the response produces its reinforcer (shown within the boxes) only in the presence of a particular stimulus (1, 2 or 3). This is the discrimination relation (Skinner, 1938; 1953), a three-term contingency that involves discriminative stimulus, response and reinforcer. We know, too, that the discriminative stimuli also become conditioned reinforcers.

Moving to the left, we see another set of stimuli—X, Y and Z. These determine which three-term contingency is in effect. This is the conditional discrimination relation (Cumming & Berryman, 1965), a four-term contingency that involves conditional stimulus, discriminative stimulus, response and consequence. We know, too, that the conditional stimulus may also enter into an equivalence class along with its related discriminative stimulus (X with 1, Y with 2, and Z with 3).

The conditional relations are not just larger discriminative relations. The three- and four-term contingencies are fundamentally different. In the three-term contingency, the discriminative stimulus requires a differential response to relate it to the consequence. In the four-term contingency, however, the conditional stimulus requires no such differential response to relate it to the discriminative stimulus. The subject has to do nothing special in the presence of X in order to produce stimulus 1, or in the presence of Y to produce 2, or in the presence of Z to produce 3.

The four-term relation, then, is different in kind from the three-term relation (Sidman, 1986). The three-term contingency is a stimulus–response–reinforcer relation, and the four-term contingency adds a stimulus–stimulus relation (Sidman, 1978).

Just as the conditioned reinforcement function appears at the level of the three-term contingency, equivalence relations appear at the level of the four-term contingency. And, just as the stimulus functions of reinforcement, discrimination, conditioned reinforcement and conditional discrimination represent unanalysable primitives in the description of behaviour, equivalence may represent yet another primitive.

It may well be that we simply have to accept equivalence relations as a given. I do not believe we can ignore that possibility. It is, of course, true that related conditional and discriminative stimuli do not always form equivalence classes. They may, however, always start that way, with differential experience being required to break equivalence down; equiva-

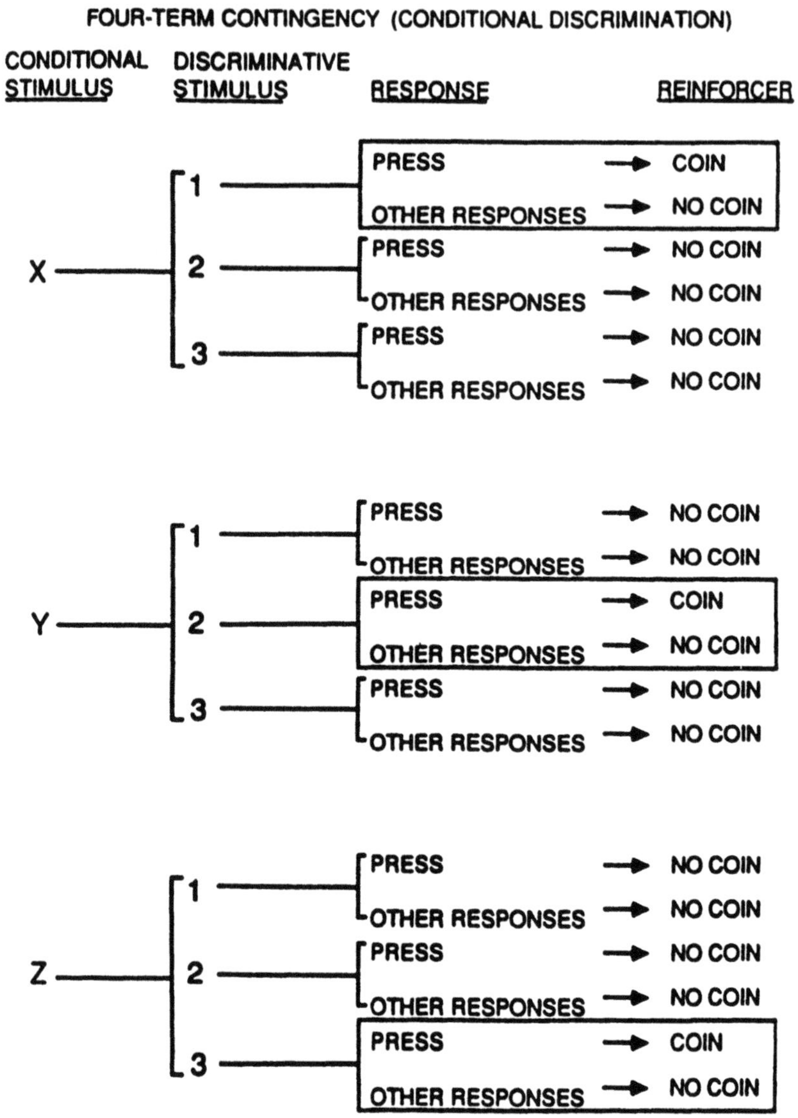

FIG. 4.7. Conditional discriminations with three samples (conditional stimuli: X, Y and Z) and three comparisons (discriminative stimuli: 1, 2 and 3). Pressing the correct comparison produced a coin; pressing the other comparisons, and responses other than pressing, produced no coin (see text).

lence relations do come under contextual control. And so we have the possibility that the role of experience is not to create equivalence classes, but to break such classes down (Bush, Sidman, & de Rose, 1989).

Given our failure so far to derive equivalence from something more basic, and given the qualitative change from stimulus–response to stimulus–stimulus relations in the transition from three- to four-term units of analysis, it does not seem unreasonable to suspect that equivalence relations emerge from conditional discriminations for the same reason our behaviour is reinforceable, and for the same reason our behaviour is controllable by discriminative and conditional stimuli—because contingencies of survival have made us that way.

REFERENCES

Bush, K. M., Sidman, M., & de Rose, T. (1989). Conditional control of stimulus classes. *Journal of the Experimental Analysis of Behavior*, *51*, 29–45.

Cumming, W. W. & Berryman, R. (1965). The complex discriminated operant: Studies of matching-to-sample and related problems. In D. I. Mostofsky (Ed.), *Stimulus generalization*, pp. 284–330. Stanford, Calif.: Stanford University Press.

D'Amato, M. R., Salmon, D., Loukas, E., & Tomie, A. (1985). Symmetry and transitivity of conditional relations in monkeys (*Cebus apella*) and pigeons (*Columba livia*). *Journal of the Experimental Analysis of Behavior*, *44*, 35–47.

De Rose, J. C., McIlvane, W. J., Dube, W. V., Galpin, V. C., & Stoddard, L. T. (1988). Emergent simple discrimination established by indirect relation to differential consequences. *Journal of the Experimental Analysis of Behavior*, *50*, 1–20.

Devany, J. M., Hayes, S. C., & Nelson, R. O. (1986). Equivalence class formation in language-able and language-disabled children. *Journal of the Experimental Analysis of Behavior*, *46*, 243–257.

Goldiamond, I. (1966). Perception, language, and conceptualization rules. In B. Kleinmuntz (Ed.), *Problem solving*, pp. 183–224. New York: John Wiley.

Jenkins, J. J. (1963). Mediated associations: Paradigms and situations. In C. N. Cofer & B. S. Musgrave (Eds), *Verbal behavior and learning: Problems and processes*, pp. 210–245. New York: McGraw-Hill.

Jenkins, J. J. (1965). Mediation theory and grammatical behavior. In S. Rosenberg (Ed.), *Directions in psycholinguistics*, pp. 66–96. New York: Macmillan.

Lazar, R. (1977). Extending sequence–class membership with matching to sample. *Journal of the Experimental Analysis of Behavior*, *27*, 381–392.

Lazar, R. M., Davis-Lang, D., & Sanchez, L. (1984). The formation of visual stimulus equivalences in children. *Journal of the Experimental Analysis of Behavior*, *41*, 251–266.

Lazar, R. M. & Kotlarchyk, B. J. (1986). Second-order control of sequence–class equivalences in children. *Behaviour Processes*, *13*, 205–215.

Lipkens, R., Kop, P. F. M., & Matthijs, W. (1988). A test of symmetry and transitivity in the conditional discrimination performances of pigeons. *Journal of the Experimental Analysis of Behavior*, *49*, 395–409.

Lowe, C. F. (1986). The role of verbal behavior in the emergence of equivalence relations. Paper presented at the Meeting of the Association for Behavior Analysis, Milwaukee, May.

Mackay, H. A. & Sidman, M. (1984). Teaching new behavior via equivalence relations. In P. H. Brooks, R. Sperber, & C. McCauley (Eds), *Learning and cognition in the mentally retarded*, pp. 493–513. Hillsdale, N.J.: Lawrence Erlbaum Associates Inc.

McDonagh, E. C., McIlvane, W. J., & Stoddard, L. T. (1984). Teaching coin equivalences via matching to sample. *Applied Research in Mental Retardation*, *5*, 177–197.

McIntire, K. D., Cleary, J., & Thompson, T. (1987). Conditional relations by monkeys: Reflexivity, symmetry, and transitivity. *Journal of the Experimental Analysis of Behavior*, *47*, 279–285.

Saunders, R. R., Wachter, J., & Spradlin, J. E. (1988). Establishing auditory stimulus control over an eight-member equivalence class via conditional discrimination procedures. *Journal of the Experimental Analysis of Behavior*, *49*, 95–115.

Sidman, M. (1971). Reading and auditory–visual equivalences. *Journal of Speech and Hearing Resarch*, *14*, 5–13.

Sidman, M. (1978). Remarks. *Behaviorism*, *6*, 265–268.

Sidman, M. (1986). Functional analysis of emergent verbal classes. In T. Thompson & M. D. Zeiler (Eds), *Analysis and integration of behavioral units*, pp. 213–245. Hillsdale, N.J.: Lawrence Erlbaum Associates Inc.

Sidman, M. (1987). Two choices are not enough. *Behavior Analysis*, *22*, 11–18.

Sidman, M. & Cresson, O., Jr (1973). Reading and transfer of crossmodal stimulus equivalences in severe retardation. *American Journal of Mental Deficiency*, *77*, 515–523.

Sidman, M., Cresson, O., Jr, & Willson-Morris, M. (1974). Acquisition of matching to sample via mediated transfer. *Journal of the Experimental Analysis of Behavior*, *22*, 261–273.

Sidman, M., Kirk, B., & Willson-Morris, M. (1985). Six-member stimulus classes generated by conditional-discrimination procedures. *Journal of the Experimental Analysis of Behavior*, *43*, 21–42.

Sidman, M., Rauzin, R., Lazar, R., Cunningham, S., Tailby, W., & Carrigan, P. (1982). A search for symmetry in the conditional discriminations of rhesus monkeys, baboons, and children. *Journal of the Experimental Analysis of Behavior*, *37*, 23–44.

Sidman, M. & Tailby, W. (1982). Conditional discrimination *vs.* matching to sample: An expansion of the testing paradigm. *Journal of the Experimental Analysis of Behavior*, *37*, 5–22.

Sidman, M., Willson-Morris, M., & Kirk, B. (1986). Matching-to-sample procedures and the development of equivalence relations: The role of naming. *Analysis and Intervention in Developmental Disabilities*, *6*, 1–19.

Silverman, K., Anderson, S. R., Marshall, A. M., & Baer, D. M. (1986). Establishing and generalizing audience control of new language repertoires. *Analysis and Intervention in Developmental Disabilities*, 6, 21–40.

Skinner, B. F. (1938). *The behavior of organisms: An experimental analysis*. New York: Appleton-Century-Crofts.

Skinner, B. F. (1953). *Science and human behavior*. New York: Macmillan.

Skinner, B. F. (1957). *Verbal behavior*. New York: Appleton-Century-Crofts.

Skinner, B. F. (1969). *Contingencies of reinforcement: A theoretical analysis*. New York: Appleton-Century-Crofts.

Spradlin, J. E., Cotter, V. W., & Baxley, N. (1973). Establishing a conditional discrimination without direct training: A study of transfer with retarded adolescents. *American Journal of Mental Deficiency*, *77*, 556–566.

Stromer, R. & Osborne, J. G. (1982). Control of adolescents' arbitrary matching-to-sample by positive and negative stimulus relations. *Journal of the Experimental Analysis of Behavior*, *37*, 329–348.

Vaughan, W., Jr (1988). Formation of equivalence sets in pigeons. *Journal of Experimental Psychology: Animal Behavior Processes*, *14*, 36–42.

Wetherby, B., Karlan, G. R., & Spradlin, J. E. (1983). The development of derived stimulus relations through training in arbitrary-matching sequences. *Journal of the Experimental Analysis of Behavior*, *40*, 69–78.

5 Naming and Stimulus Equivalence

N. Dugdale and C. F. Lowe
Department of Psychology, University College of North Wales, Bangor, U.K.

A major problem facing contemporary psychology is how to account for "emergent" behaviour, i.e. behaviour that is novel, has not been directly trained or reinforced, and cannot be explained by simple conditioning principles such as stimulus generalisation. Many important phenomena such as reasoning, the acquisition of language (Chomsky, 1959; 1972), the learning of arbitrary relational concepts (Williams, 1984), and indeed most of what we call symbolic activity, appear to have emergent properties. Perhaps because it provides a rigorous means of assessing emergent behaviour, the paradigm of *stimulus equivalence* has generated great interest among behaviour analysts in recent years. At last it seems that we have the basis for an experimental analysis of symbolic behaviour.

THE STIMULUS EQUIVALENCE PARADIGM

Matching-to-sample procedures are commonly employed in the study of stimulus equivalence. Figure 5.1 depicts an example of a matching-to-sample task. The subject sits in front of a stimulus-response panel and the trial begins with the presentation of a sample stimulus on the centre key (e.g. the printed word, ONE). The subject then touches the sample and several comparison stimuli appear on the outer keys (e.g. the printed digits, 1 and 2). The subject is required to select the comparison which corresponds to the sample.

When the subject has learned to match, say, each of a set of printed number word samples to the corresponding digit comparison, it is often assumed that the behaviour is symbolic and that the stimuli are acting as

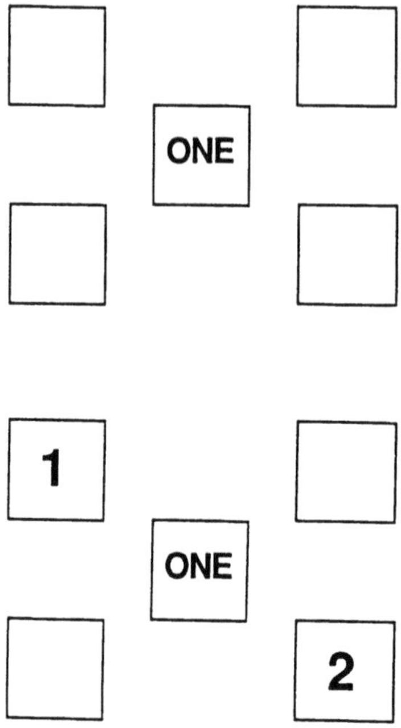

FIG. 5.1. Schematic representation of an arbitrary matching-to-sample task. At the start of the trial, a sample appears in the centre window of the five-key response panel (see upper section). Touching the sample brings on the comparisons on any two of the four outer keys (see lower section). Reinforcers are delivered for selecting the comparison that corresponds to the sample.

symbols. But this, of course, is not the only possibility; rather, it might be the case that the subject has learned a simple stimulus–response chain or conditional ("if–then") relation that has no symbolic relevance. To ascertain whether the subject is behaving symbolically or not requires a more detailed analysis.

If the stimuli were serving as symbols, then one would expect each to "stand for" the other, i.e. they should, in a sense, be equivalent or interchangeable. In the example above, the subject was taught to match set A number word samples to set B digit comparisons (AB). If the set A and corresponding set B stimuli are equivalent, then the subject should be able to do the reverse—match set B samples to corresponding set A comparisons—without any additional training or reinforcement for doing so. A new performance (BA matching) should emerge without having been explicitly taught.

This procedure of interchanging the former samples and comparisons is known as a *symmetry* test. It tests for one of the prerequisites of stimulus equivalence (tests for the other prerequisites are described by Sidman, this volume). A subject's failure on any one of these tests would suggest that the stimuli had not become equivalent and that the initial training, far from establishing a relation of symbolic status, had resulted in what was no more than a unidirectional relation of fixed sequence. The stimulus equivalence paradigm is important precisely because it enables researchers to distinguish what is truly symbolic behaviour from behaviour that may appear to be so but is not. Thus in seeking to understand symbolic behaviour, perhaps the focus of concern should be the origins of equivalence classes and the question of how stimuli become equivalent.

WHERE DOES EQUIVALENCE COME FROM?

One possibility that occurred to some psychologists quite early on is that physically different stimuli cannot become equivalent unless the subject names them (Jenkins, 1963; Miller & Dollard, 1941). One can conceive of a number of ways in which naming might mediate equivalence. Perhaps stimuli become equivalent after they are given the same name. For example, although five 10p coins and one 50p coin offer completely dissimilar perceptual cues, we can accept them as equivalent if we apply to both the common label, "fifty". Alternatively, perhaps naming can mediate equivalence even if the subject gives each stimulus a different name, provided the names can be incorporated in a verbal rule linking each sample to its corresponding comparison (e.g. "A goes with B", "A is the same as B", "A means B", and so on).

According to Sidman and colleagues, however, naming is not necessary for equivalence (Sidman, Cresson, & Willson-Morris, 1974; Sidman, Kirk, & Willson-Morris, 1985; Sidman & Tailby, 1982; Sidman, Willson-Morris, & Kirk, 1986), and others have supported this view (Hayes, Tilley, & Hayes, 1988; Lazar, Davis-Lang, & Sanchez, 1984). Having rejected verbal behaviour (i.e. naming and/or the formulation of verbal rules) as the source of equivalence, Sidman (this volume) now entertains the possibility that equivalence is a *given*, i.e. a fundamental stimulus function which cannot be derived from something more basic.

Sidman's hypothesis may appear attractive. After all, if equivalence is a given, then there is no need to trouble oneself with searching for its precursors; one simply has to accept equivalence as a basic property of some stimuli in the same way as one accepts reinforcing stimuli and discriminative stimuli as unanalysable units. But, while it is convenient, Sidman's view has notable difficulties, not least of which is that there is little evidence to support it. More specifically, the view that equivalences may be formed in the absence of naming turns out, upon close inspection, to have little empirical foundation. On the contrary, data from a number of recent studies offer compelling support for the notion that naming is indeed necessary.

THE ROLE OF NAMING IN STIMULUS EQUIVALENCE

Naming: The Evidence Against

A number of authors (Lazar et al., 1984; Sidman & Tailby, 1982; Sidman et al., 1974; 1985; 1986) have presented evidence apparently showing that some subjects pass equivalence tests without consistently naming the stimuli concerned, a finding which leads these researchers to conclude that equivalence is not dependent upon naming. However, none of these studies recorded what was actually said by the subjects "spontaneously" during equivalence testing or the preceding training sessions. Instead, subjects were prompted to name the stimuli, and this prompting typically took place after equivalence testing, in a post-experimental naming test. If the subject passed the equivalence tests but proceeded to name the stimuli inconsistently when prompted by the experimenter, then equivalence and naming were taken to be independent.

However, verbalisations elicited via prompting need not necessarily correspond with those emitted spontaneously during an experiment. This is not just a point of logic; it is supported by empirical evidence. In a series of studies, Hird and Lowe, who recorded all verbalisations made by their subjects during training and testing, found that many named the stimuli "spontaneously" and consistently during matching-to-sample trials, but then gave no evidence of having done so when they were prompted to name the stimuli in a subsequent naming test (Hird & Lowe, 1985; Lowe, 1986). During the naming test, the subjects seemed to interpret the experimenter's questions (i.e. "What is it?" and "Do you have a name for it?") in a rather complex fashion, often giving elaborate analytical descriptions of the stimuli, descriptions quite unlike the more conventional stimulus names they produced spontaneously during the experiment. It would seem, then, that the studies by Sidman and colleagues should not be accepted uncritically as satisfactory evidence against the role of naming in equivalence formation. Commenting on the recent study by Sidman et al. (1986), Stoddard and McIlvane (1986, p. 157) have also raised doubts about the validity of prompted naming responses:

> Do these data lay to rest the question of response mediation as the critical basis for stimulus equivalence? Probably not . . . . Some examples may serve to illustrate the difficulty of this research question. Suppose a given subject characterizes all the stimuli in the entire visual classes with a common descriptive *adjectival* term, like "rounded", "pointed" or "pointing that

way", perhaps derived from primary stimulus generalisation . . . . Alternatively, suppose a common descriptive term, such as "Set 1" vs. "Set 2" was applied, as we do in talking about stimuli within classes. When asked the question, "What is it?", in relation to a given stimulus, perhaps the subject's verbal conditioning history had not prepared him or her to use descriptive terms as labels, leading to "I don't know" (its name) responses on the naming tests. Would other methods of testing have evoked descriptions?

Naming: The Evidence For

If equivalence does require naming, then animals should be unable to pass equivalence tests and, indeed, it is interesting to note that to date there has been no unequivocal demonstration of stimulus equivalence with non-humans. Despite concerted efforts, studies have failed to demonstrate symmetry with, variously, pigeons (Hogan & Zentall, 1977; Holmes, 1979; Kendall, 1983; Lipkens, Kop, & Matthijs, 1988; Rodewald, 1974), cebus monkeys (D'Amato, Salmon, Loukas, & Tomie, 1985) and rhesus monkeys and baboons (Sidman et al., 1982). Thus far, there have been only two published studies claiming to find equivalence with animal subjects and, although both on close analysis fail to meet the criteria necessary to demonstrate equivalence, they merit discussion, if only to emphasise exactly what is required for satisfactory evidence. McIntire, Cleary, and Thompson (1987) taught macaques to produce a common response to a set of non-identical samples and to select the same stimuli (now appearing as comparisons) after emitting that response. The monkeys were then able to match the non-identical stimuli without differential reinforcement, thus apparently demonstrating equivalence. But this was hardly surprising. Each sample controlled a response which in turn controlled the selection of a comparison and both controlling relations had been taught via the reinforcement contingencies present throughout the training phases. Thus, although the experiment might look as if it demonstrated equivalence, a simpler and more parsimonious explanation is available in terms of behaviour directly reinforced. Equivalence, on the other hand, is not defined by formal properties of this sort, but rather by the emergence of untrained relations, and in McIntire et al.'s study nothing untrained could be said to have emerged during testing. This raises a general point which applies to any study purporting to demonstrate equivalence classes, whether with animal or human subjects (see Hall, this volume): Although performance might *look like* equivalence, in fact it may not be. One needs not only to apply rigorous testing criteria (e.g. as specified by Sidman, this volume), but also to know the prior training conditions before one can determine with any certainty whether performance demonstrates equivalence rather than the operation of simpler conditioning principles.

Vaughan (1988) has demonstrated with pigeons the formation of a functional stimulus class, using a free-operant successive discrimination procedure (see Hall, this volume). Functional classes, however, are not necessarily the same as equivalence classes (see Sidman, this volume, for a detailed account of the distinction between functional classes and equivalence classes). Although Vaughan's data might appear to provide evidence for stimulus equivalence, he himself has recognised that his testing procedure was quite different from that of standard equivalence tests; his pigeons were not, for example, presented with any test of symmetry. The fact that pigeons have been shown to be successful with his procedure but not the conventional one, suggests to him "that different behavioral processes may be operating in the two cases" (Vaughan, 1988, p. 42).

The notion that naming may be necessary for equivalence gives rise to some interesting research questions. For example, can animals pass equivalence tests after receiving some degree of language training? How might language-trained chimpanzees cope with the tests? We attempted to resolve these questions during a year spent by one of us (Dugdale) at the Language Research Center in Atlanta, U.S.A. Our subjects were three adult chimpanzees (*Pan troglodytes*), two of which were males (Sherman and Austin) and one female (Lana). All three had participated in an ape-language training programme at the Language Center. The chimps communicate by touching lexigrams (visual-graphic stimuli) arranged on a keyboard, each associated with an object, action or location. Details of their training have been described elsewhere by their principal caretakers, Professors Duane Rumbaugh and Sue Savage-Rumbaugh (see Rumbaugh, 1977; Savage-Rumbaugh, 1986). It should be noted, however, that the chimps did not have access to a lexigram keyboard at any time during our visit.

We attempted to teach the chimps the AB matching relation depicted in Fig. 5.2. The set A sample stimuli were two forms (a Y shape and a zig-zag) and the set B comparisons were two colours (one green and the other red). When the sample was a Y shape, reinforcers were contingent upon choosing the green comparison, and when the sample was a zig-zag, reinforcers were contingent upon choosing red. Sherman and Lana eventually learned this AB matching task but Austin did not, despite being exposed to a number of intervention procedures.

After learning the AB relation, Sherman and Lana were presented with BA symmetry test trials (see Fig. 5.2). Lana's performance was tested in three distinct phases. In her first test phase, correct responses on the BA symmetry test trials were not reinforced. Before the test trials were introduced, the probability of reinforcement for correct responses on AB baseline training trials was gradually lowered to 0.2, so that only 1 in 5 correct responses were reinforced. Then, during test sessions, the unrein-

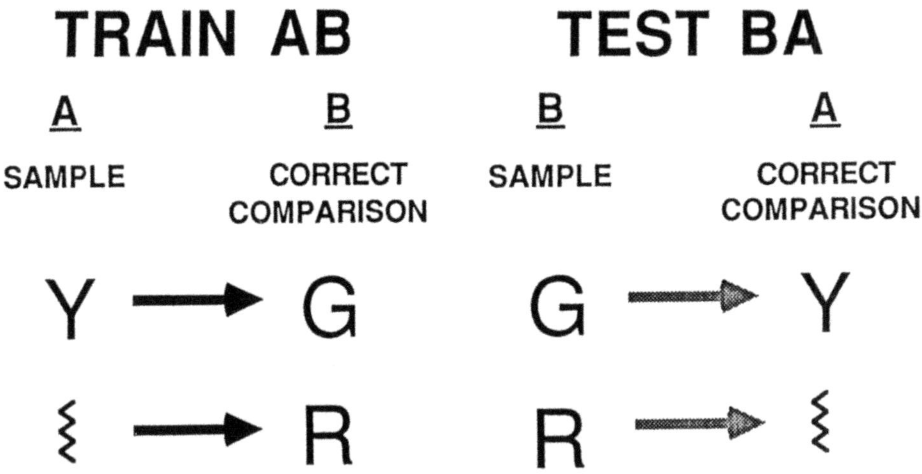

FIG. 5.2. Stimulus relations presented to the chimps during AB training trials and BA symmetry test trials. The arrows point from sample stimuli (only one presented at a time) to corresponding (correct) comparison stimuli. G, green; R, red.

forced BA test trials were interspersed among the sparsely reinforced AB baseline trials. Lana was given 12 test sessions and her scores (percentage of correct responses) for each trial-type are shown in Fig. 5.3. Lana's AB baseline performance was around 90% correct throughout the test sessions. Despite this, her performance on the critical symmetry test trials was at or around 50% correct, i.e. at chance level. Lana thus failed the symmetry test. She gave no evidence that her training had established equivalence between samples and corresponding comparisons, and therefore her behaviour on the baseline trials could not be classed as symbolic.

It could be argued, however, that Lana's failure on the symmetry test was an artefact of the test procedure. There are two possible justifications for this argument. Lana's correct responses on test trials were never reinforced, whereas those on baseline trials were reinforced, albeit only occasionally. So perhaps she had learned not to attend to the stimuli on BA test trials. Also, on symmetry test trials, Lana was presented with the colours as samples and the shapes as comparisons for the very first time. This novelty could have somehow disrupted her test performance. In order to eliminate these possibilities, two changes were made before Lana's second test phase. First, reinforcement became available for correct responses not only on baseline but also on test trials. Secondly, identity matching trials were added to the baseline; prior to the resumption of testing, Lana was required to match each set A shape and each set B colour to itself. These identity trials ensured that Lana had plenty of experience

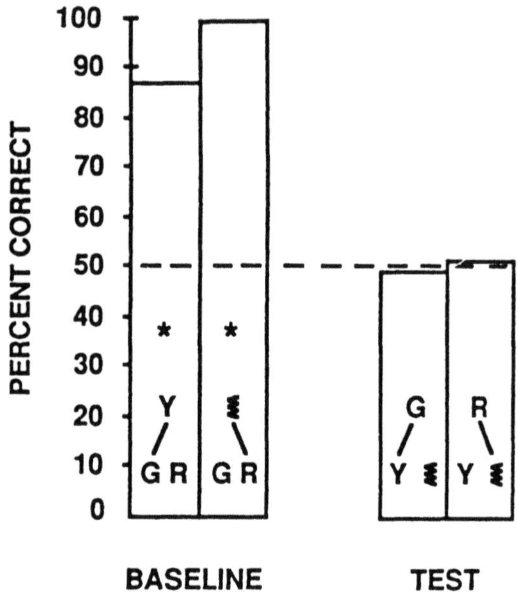

FIG. 5.3. Lana's overall performance during her first symmetry test phase (symmetry test sessions 1–12). The stimuli for each trial-type are identified at the bottom of the bars. Sample stimuli are placed above comparisons, and a line connects each sample to its corresponding (correct) comparison. The two left-hand bars depict performance (percentage of correct responses) on the AB baseline trials, and the two right-hand bars depict performance on the unreinforced BA symmetry test trials. Each baseline bar represents 192 trials and each test bar represents 96 trials.

with sample colours and comparison shapes before they were presented again on BA symmetry test trials. She was then given eight more symmetry test sessions. Once again, her performance on all the baseline trial-types was above 90% correct, but her performance on the green–Y symmetry test trial-type was still at chance level. Lana thus failed the symmetry test even with reinforced test trials and identity matching controls.

Nevertheless, as a final check, Lana received 15 more test sessions with reinforced test trials at the end of which she had still not reached criterion on the BA symmetry trial-types. To conclude, then, Lana gave no evidence of symmetry, despite receiving 35 test sessions and a grand total of 468 BA test trials.

Sherman received 12 test sessions, all of which were the same as the final series presented to Lana (i.e. all correct responses were reinforced), but he also failed the symmetry test. His performance on the symmetry test trials remained at or around chance level throughout 144 BA test trials.

To summarise, in this series of experiments, symmetry tests were applied to a single arbitrary matching problem. Within this context, and within the time available, everything possible was done to maximise the chimpanzees' chances of success. Despite this, these language-trained chimpanzees failed the symmetry tests. In fact, further manipulations were carried out which provided additional evidence that symmetry was not present (see Dugdale, 1988, for further details). Because symmetry is a necessary property of stimulus equivalence, its absence was sufficient to show that each sample and its corresponding comparison had not become equivalent.

These results extend previous findings on stimulus equivalence. Existing reports of the failure of animals on symmetry tests have been confirmed in the case of yet another animal species, namely chimpanzees. If one of our closest relatives in the animal kingdom is unable to pass these tests, then what chance is there for our other more distant relatives? What is of even greater significance is that the chimpanzees we tested are unique among all animals in that they have a history of training that is quite unprecedented in its extent and complexity. Sherman and Lana are arguably the most "test-wise" of all animals. Before this experiment they must surely have ranked among the favourites to be the first non-humans likely to pass a standard symmetry test. Despite all this, however, they did not.

Of course, some may wish to argue that failures of this kind cannot prove conclusively that animals are unable to pass equivalence tests, as a modification to the training and/or test procedure might possibly turn failure into success. But that is to miss the point. Failures may not, of themselves, prove anything, but they can support an hypothesis that the subject is unable to pass equivalence tests, and in the final analysis they are presumably the only evidence one can have that this is the case. Furthermore, although it is similarly impossible to prove a fundamental difference between animals and humans in their capacity for stimulus equivalence, there is, to date, no convincing evidence that animals (not even those as "sophisticated" as Sherman and Lana) are capable, as humans are, of equivalence formation.

While the animal data are entirely consistent with the hypothesis that equivalence requires naming, direct confirmation can, perhaps, only come from studies of humans. Apart from those referred to above, only a few studies have pursued the question of whether language and equivalence are related in humans (Beasty & Lowe, 1985; Devany, Hayes, & Nelson, 1986; Lowe, 1986; Lowe & Beasty, 1987). Devany et al. (1986) compared equivalence formation in three groups of subjects: normal 2-year-old children, 2- to 4-year-old retarded children with functional spontaneous speech and signing, and 2- to 4-year-old retarded children with no functional verbal skills. Both the normal and retarded/language groups passed the equivalence tests, whereas the retarded/no-language group failed. Devany et al. concluded that language and stimulus equivalence are closely related in some hitherto unknown way.

Our own research with children has attempted to go beyond simply correlating language and equivalence. In order to demonstrate the necessity of naming, one must show not only that equivalence is absent when naming is absent but also that equivalence emerges when naming is introduced. In one series of experiments, Lowe and Beasty demonstrated that children (younger than 4 years of age) who initially failed equivalence tests later passed these tests when they were taught to name the sample–comparison pairings while responding on baseline training trials (Beasty, 1987; Lowe, 1986; Lowe & Beasty, 1987). Their experimental paradigm is shown in Fig. 5.4. Within the context of a standard matching-to-sample procedure, the children were taught on some baseline trials to match, for example, a vertical line sample to a green comparison (AB) and a vertical line sample to a triangle comparison (AC). Equivalence tests were then presented to assess whether the subjects could match green to triangle (BC) and triangle to green (CB). The children who failed these tests were then taught to say "Up–Green" on AB baseline trials and "Up–Triangle" on AC baseline trials. This verbal intervention resulted in the immediate emergence of the BC and CB test relations.

But why should naming prove so effective in bringing about stimulus equivalence? One, but not of course the only, possibility (cf. Lowe, 1986) is that the triangle and green stimuli became equivalent because they both controlled the common word "Up" spoken by the subjects. In the case of at least some of the children, common naming may have been the active ingredient responsible for the emergence of stimulus equivalence. This possibility prompted a further series of experiments into the effects of common naming on equivalence formation (see Dugdale, 1988). The experiment reported here involved six 4- to 5-year-old children, all of whom had failed to learn the AB relations depicted in Fig. 5.2, despite, in some cases, having received many hundreds of reinforced trials. Having failed to learn the AB relation, five of the children were taught to give common labels to the stimuli which they had earlier failed to match.

The stimuli were presented one at a time, as samples, and the subjects were taught to say "Omni" to the Y shape and the green hue, and "Delta" to the zig-zag and red. These labelling relations, depicted as A'X' and B'X' in Fig. 5.5, were learned very rapidly, often within two 48-trial sessions. In the final stage before testing, reinforcement was discontinued without affecting the subjects' labelling performances. The stage was now set to determine whether each shape and its corresponding colour would become equivalent through mediation of the common set X labels. The subjects were presented with both AB and BA matching-to-sample test trials and testing was conducted in extinction; each response, whether correct or incorrect, terminated the trial and no reinforcers were delivered.

A sixth child, Jessica, who had also failed to learn the AB relation, underwent a different training procedure. She was not taught to produce common labels but rather to select set A and set B comparisons conditional upon common labels dictated by the experimenter (see Fig. 5.6). When the experimenter said "Omni", reinforcers were delivered if Jessica selected the Y shape or green comparison, and when the experimenter said "De-

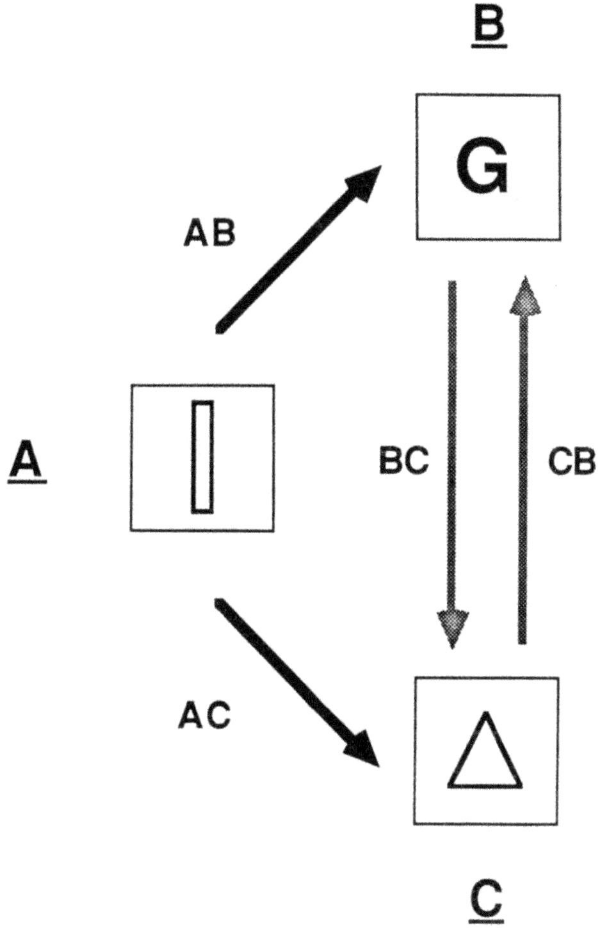

FIG. 5.4. The equivalence paradigm employed in the studies by Lowe and Beasty. The arrows point from samples to corresponding comparisons. Black arrows indicate trained relations and shaded arrows depict relations assessed during testing (see text).

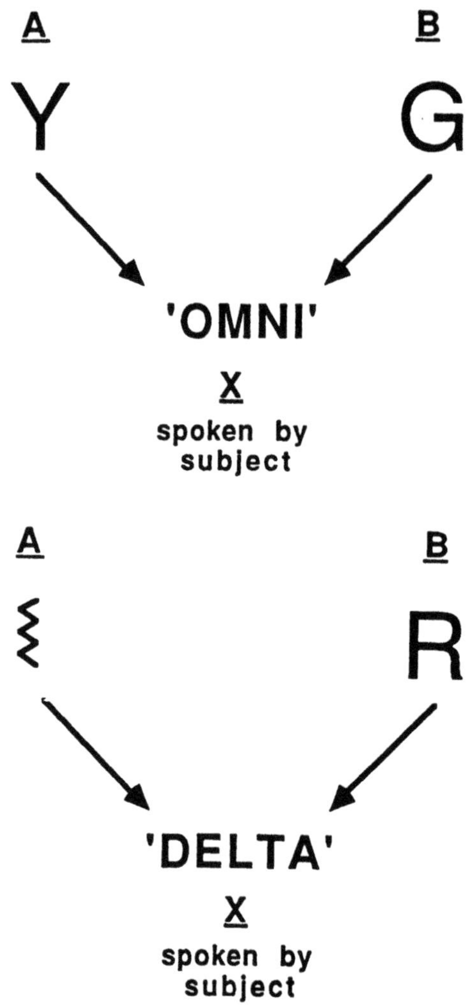

FIG. 5.5. Relations taught during A'X' and B'X' training in the experiment with 4- to 5-year-old children. The arrows point from samples to corresponding labels spoken by the subjects.

lta", reinforcers were delivered if she chose the zig-zag or red comparison. Jessica quickly learned this task.

Figure 5.7 gives the test results for all six subjects. Each bar shows the overall percentage of correct responses for a particular trial-type. The shading indicates those matching-to-sample trials on which common set X labels were correctly applied by the subjects to the set A and set B samples. Four of the subjects—Francis, Alex, Michael and Stephen—gave common

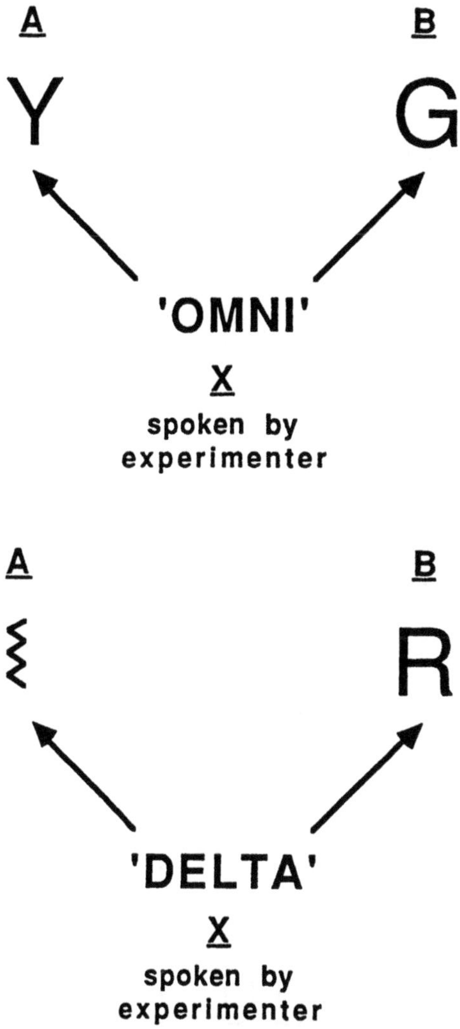

FIG. 5.6. Relations taught to one subject (Jessica) during 'X'A and 'X'B training. The arrows point from sample words, dictated by the experimenter, to corresponding comparisons.

labels to the samples right from the beginning of testing. On AB trials, they labelled the Y shape with the word "Omni" and the zig-zag with the word "Delta", and on BA trials, they labelled the green sample with "Omni" and the red sample with "Delta".

As Fig. 5.7 indicates, the scores, averaged over all the test trials, were good; indeed, by the end of testing, the subjects made no errors for at least

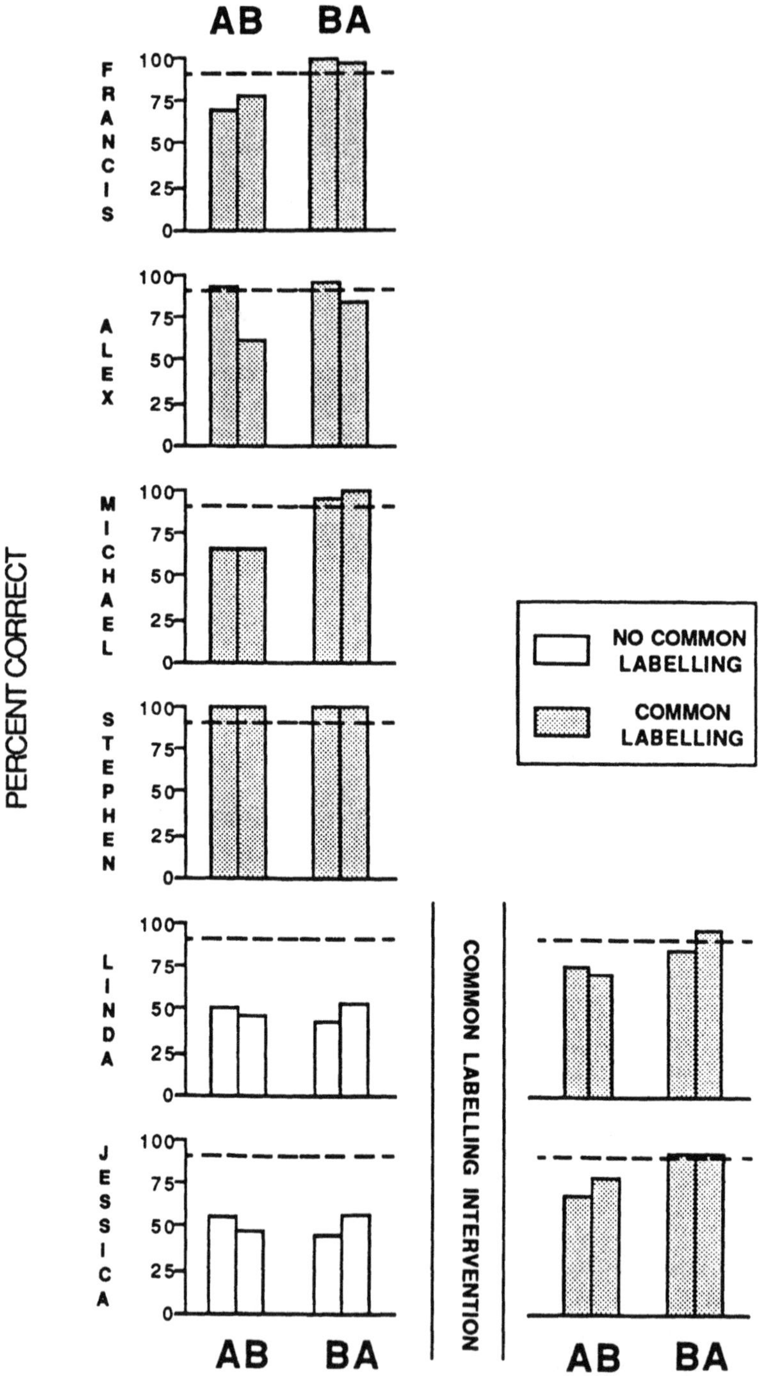

FIG. 5.7. Overall test scores (percentage of correct responses) of the six subjects on AB and BA matching-to-sample trials. In the case of two of the subjects (Linda and Jessica), the scores are shown before (unshaded) and after (shaded) the common labelling intervention (see text).

six consecutive trials per trial-type. However, Linda and Jessica did not initially apply common labels to the samples, and their performance on both AB and BA was at or around chance level or 50% correct. Therefore, both Linda and Jessica, in the absence of common labelling, failed the tests. Jessica failed even though at this stage she could select set A shapes and set B colours conditional upon common labels spoken by the experimenter. For Jessica, then, hearing common labels, as distinct from producing them herself, was apparently insufficient to mediate the emergence of the AB and BA relations. In a further manipulation (i.e. common labelling intervention: Fig. 5.7), both of these girls were prompted with the question "Is it Omni or Delta?" when the samples appeared. This resulted in both girls producing appropriate common labels to the sample stimuli as soon as they appeared, and this in turn led to an immediate improvement in their performance on the AB and BA test trials. Again, as was the case with the other four subjects, performance on both trial-types was error-free by the end of the test phase. Thus, in the case of all six subjects, each shape and its corresponding colour had become equivalent through the subjects' use of common set X labels.

However, taken overall, Fig. 5.7 shows that the BA scores were better than the AB scores for five of the six subjects. The subjects' overall scores on AB trial-types tended to fall short of the 90% criterion line, whereas their scores on BA trial-types tended to be above criterion. Figure 5.8 depicts the AB and BA matching scores from the first 48 trials in which the subjects gave common labels to the samples (in the case of Linda and Jessica, these were the first 48 trials following the common labelling intervention). The figure shows that the difference between AB and BA matching was particularly pronounced in the initial stages of the test phase.

There are thus two points to consider. First, common labels produced by the subjects resulted in the emergence of both the AB and BA relation. Secondly, although both relations emerged as a function of common labelling, BA emerged prior to AB for all subjects except Stephen who scored 100% correct on both. To find out why BA emerged prior to AB, it is necessary to examine how the subjects' labels helped them to match the stimuli. This analysis is best approached by focusing on one pair of stimuli, e.g. the Y shape and the green stimulus, though the following account applies equally well to the other stimulus pair.

On BA trials, the subjects matched the green sample to the Y shape comparison. If verbal labels are to help them to do this, then two things must happen. First, as shown in Fig. 5.9, when the Green sample appears the subjects must say "Omni" (B'X'). Secondly, when the subjects have said "Omni", they must then choose the Y comparison ('X'A). Matching Green to Y then becomes a two-stage process—B'X' and 'X'A, therefore BA. During test phases, all the subjects proved capable of B'X'; they all,

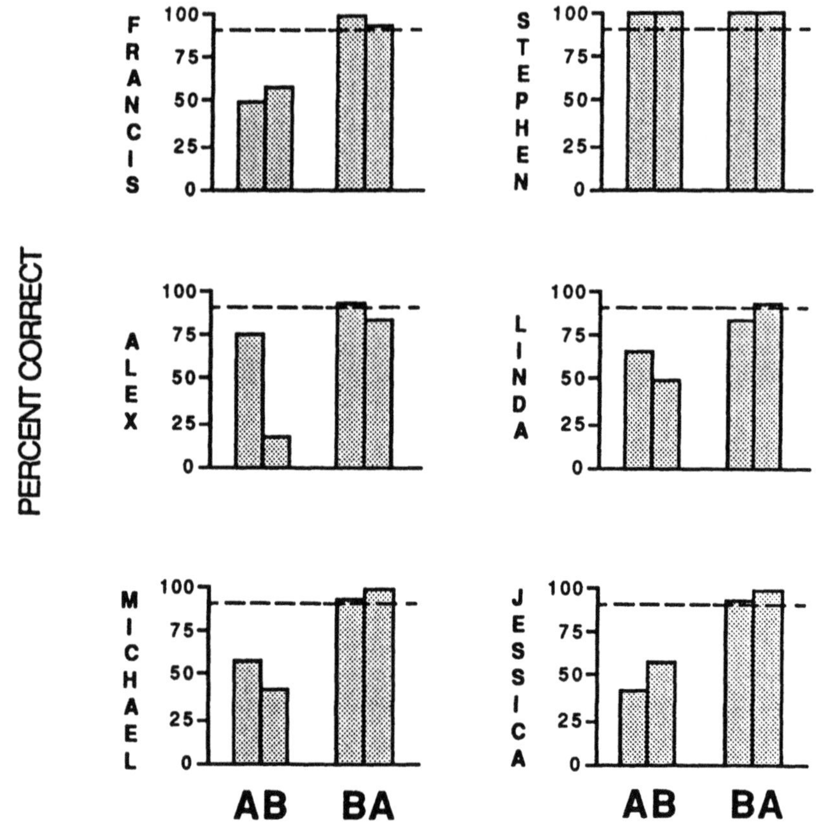

FIG. 5.8. AB and BA matching scores from the first 48 trials in which the subjects gave common labels to the samples. In the case of Linda and Jessica, these were the first 48 trials following the common labelling intervention.

for example, overtly labelled Green with the word "Omni" because their earlier training had established this skill. But none of them had been taught the second stage, 'X'A; none of them had been taught to *say* "Omni" and then choose the Y shape. We must therefore assume that this critical second component was brought about by the earlier training which established the A'X' relation. Thus, when the skill of labelling the Y shape with the word "Omni" was established, so too was the potential for its symmetrical counterpart, i.e. saying "Omni" and then choosing the Y shape. The subjects' earlier training had resulted in the formation of symmetry between the set A shapes and the subjects' spoken set X words. Had it not done, then 'X'A would have been absent during testing and the BA relation could not have emerged as a function of the subjects' set X labels.

A similar analysis may be applied to the AB relation. Although the AB relation eventually did emerge, it did not do so when the subjects first

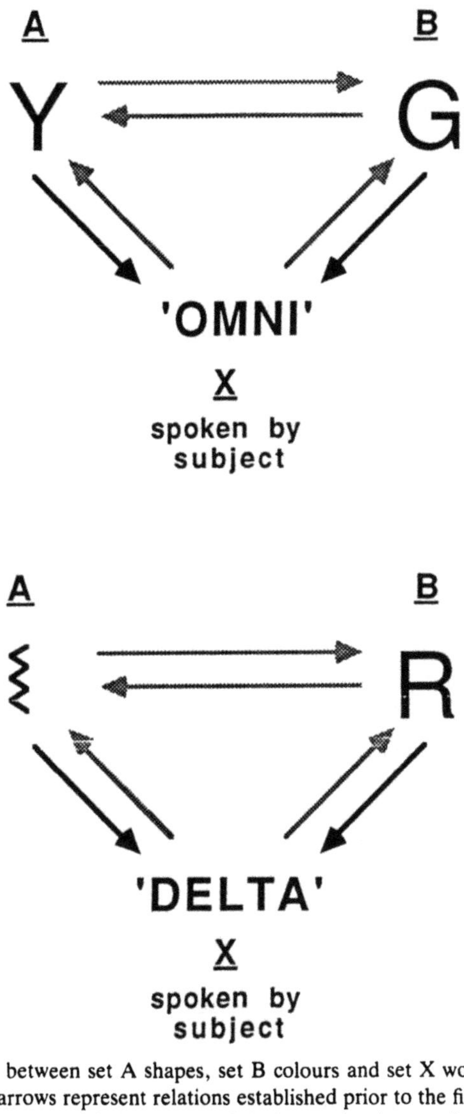

FIG. 5.9. Relations between set A shapes, set B colours and set X words (spoken by the subjects). The black arrows represent relations established prior to the final stage of testing. The shaded arrows represent relations assessed during testing (see text).

produced common labels. On AB trials, when the Y shape appeared, the subjects overtly said "Omni", but then having said "Omni" they did not at first consistently choose green. In other words, the 'X'B relation was not fully present at the outset of testing. Although the subjects had learned, from their earlier training, to label green by saying "Omni" (B'X'), they were not initially capable of doing the reverse, i.e. of saying "Omni" and then choosing green ('X'B). For some reason, the earlier establishment of

B'X' had not resulted in the immediate formation of symmetry between the set B colours and the subjects' spoken set X words.

In order to make sense of the data we need to examine the subjects' labelling skills prior to the acquisition of the A'X' and B'X' relations. There are two sources of information; first, the subjects' spontaneous naming as monitored throughout the experiment and, secondly, their responses during naming tests. All five subjects who acquired BA prior to AB also spontaneously labelled the colours with their conventional names, "Green" and "Red", prior to the establishment of A'X' and B'X'. None of the subjects, however, consistently labelled the shapes with any other than the set X words, either spontaneously or during naming tests. Therefore, it seems likely that the subjects' conventional labels, "Green" and "Red", somehow interfered with the formation of symmetry between the colours and the set X labels "Omni" and "Delta", and that this in turn interfered with the emergence of AB during testing. BA emerged straight away, perhaps because the subjects had no names for the set A shapes prior to labelling them with the set X words. The A'X' training, free of any interference from pre-existing names, could thus result in the immediate formation of symmetry between each shape and its corresponding set X word. This interference hypothesis has gained further support from our subsequent experiments with children (see Dugdale, 1988).

The set X words "Omni" and "Delta", spoken by the subjects, were symmetrically related to the set A shapes but not to the set B colours, at least not until the final trials of testing. A symmetrical relation is bidirectional, and bidirectionality, as was outlined above, appears to be one of the defining properties of symbolic behaviour (see Bates, 1976; Catania, 1986; Devany et al., 1986). Thus, because the relation between the set X words and set A shapes was bidirectional, one has grounds for claiming that the subjects were behaving symbolically when they labelled the shapes with the words "Omni" and "Delta". However, although the subjects applied the same words to the set B colours, it seemed that, in so doing, they were not at first behaving symbolically, because the B'X' relation was not initially bidirectional.

These findings raise an important conceptual issue. Given the presence of bidirectionality between words and shapes, should we say that the behaviour in this instance is best described, not merely as labelling, but as *naming*?

WHAT IS NAMING?

We are proposing that naming is itself a symbolic skill that involves bidirectionality. To put it another way, a defining characteristic of a naming response may be that it is an arbitrary (verbal) response which is symmetrically related to its controlling stimulus. It is arbitrary in the sense that the relation between stimulus and response is established, not by the contingencies of the natural environment, but by the practices and conventions of a community of users. The skill of naming would require, then, the formation of two symmetrically related components; not only should a particular stimulus control a subject's verbal response, but the subject's verbal response should also exert control over other behaviour (e.g. selection) with respect to that particular stimulus. Naming would thus involve both language production and comprehension, and it would require the subject to function both as a speaker and as a listener. But, most importantly, in a naming relation, the two skills would not be functionally independent but would be linked within a single "emergent" symmetrical relation. According to this account, the children in the experiment described above were naming the stimuli; after learning to produce a verbal response conditional upon a stimulus, they all proved able to do the reverse in the absence of any additional training or reinforcement. If, however, they had been trained on both components in question, then there would have been no compelling reason to claim that they had been naming.

Traditionally, there has appeared to be widespread agreement over what does *not* qualify as naming; suggestions as to how to positively identify the skill have been much rarer. Thus, most psychologists have recognised that terms like "paired associate", "pure performative", "conditional discrimination" and "tacting" all refer to discriminative responding which, while it bears a formal resemblance to naming, lacks the necessary symbolic relevance normally reserved for the term. A pigeon responding differentially to a stimulus is not, most of us would agree, "naming" it. However, when it comes to defining what does actually constitute naming, such accounts as do exist all too often refer to elusive conceptual properties, whereas what are needed are behaviourally specifiable characteristics. Given that naming is a symbolic skill, and that symbolic behaviour has been defined in terms of behaviourally specifiable properties such as symmetry, it is perhaps surprising that, before now, no one has explicitly defined naming in terms of a symmetrical relation between an arbitrary response and its controlling stimulus (hereafter referred to as stimulus–response symmetry).[1]

Such an account of naming would appear to have some face-validity with respect to the current data. The words "Omni" and "Delta", as spoken by the subjects, were found to be bidirectionally related to the set A shapes.

[1]We are grateful to Dr Pauline Horne for her help in formulating some of the ideas contained in this section.

Thus, the subjects were not just saying "Omni" in the presence of the Y shape and "Delta" in the presence of the zig-zag; in so doing they were also naming the shapes. The same words, however, for five of the six subjects and for the most part of testing, were not symmetrically related to the set B colours. In other words, these five subjects were not initially naming the colours with the words "Omni" and "Delta"; at first they were merely saying those words in the presence of the colours (presumably because they already had other "conventional" names for them). However, by the end of testing, the subjects were, according to our definition, naming the colours as well as the shapes with the words "Omni" and "Delta", thus enabling the stimuli to become fully equivalent.

This characterisation of naming may help to put our findings from the chimpanzee experiment into perspective. Given that Sherman and Lana have some linguistic accomplishment, it might appear puzzling that they failed a standard symmetry test and so did not satisfy the criteria for stimulus equivalence. However, the fact that they did not does not mean that they cannot. Some of the children in our studies also failed standard tests for equivalence (although it is important to note that the children were never, like the chimps, given the advantage of reinforced test trials). But these children proved capable of equivalence once they had applied a common label to each member of the stimulus set. Their success, then, confirmed that their verbal behaviour was indeed symbolic and, as argued above, that in giving common labels they were actually naming the stimuli.

The question then arises as to whether the chimps can "name" in the sense described above, and whether their lexigram responses are functionally equivalent to childrens' naming. These issues might be addressed by utilising the present paradigm's potential as a diagnostic indicator of true naming. If the chimps were to persist in failing equivalence tests after having learned to apply common labels to the stimuli on matching-to-sample trials, then we would be led to conclude that their language training had not established the skill of naming, or at least not as we have defined it here.

The data reviewed above suggest that naming is necessary not just for equivalence but also for forming a bidirectional or symmetrical relation between two visual stimuli. At the same time, it has been argued that naming is itself a kind of symmetrical relation. The apparent circularity of this argument disappears when one draws a distinction between two kinds of symmetry, *stimulus–response symmetry* (naming) and *stimulus–stimulus* symmetry, the former being primary, and necessary for the emergence of stimulus–stimulus symmetry. This, of course, in turn raises the question of where stimulus–response symmetry, or naming, comes from. One possibility is that stimulus–response symmetry emerges in the course of the training that occurs naturally within the developing child's linguistic environment (Dugdale & Lowe, 1987). During the early stages of language learning, the child is taught language production and comprehension, i.e. to function both as a speaker and as a listener. More specifically, the child is taught to say a particular word (or produce a particular sign) conditional upon a stimulus (the referent) and to do the reverse, i.e. select that stimulus conditional upon the spoken word (or sign). The child receives an extraordinarily extensive history of reinforcement for responding correctly to innumerable exemplars of such stimulus–response symmetry. Perhaps, then, the naming relation emerges in childhood as one is repeatedly exposed by the verbal community to conditions in which stimulus–response reversals are reinforced. The literature on language learning lends some support to this hypothesis. Many accounts of language development note the occurrence of some kind of transition from purely associative verbal behaviour to naming. Lock (1980, p. 120), for example, suggests that we may have evidence for naming when:

> words begin to be acquired in a different way: the laborious game of building up an association between a sound and an object recedes, and the child increases his vocabulary in some other, and as yet barely understood, way. This again implies that the basis of his ability is more than being able to associate a particular sound with a particular object, but that he has "gone beyond the information given" towards knowing some principle.

Here, Lock implies that naming has "emergent" characteristics, a view that is in accord with what has been argued in this chapter, although he clearly has difficulty in explicitly defining what naming is. His difficulty is understandable: naming cannot be identified from its surface or topographical features alone; what is required is a functional analysis of verbal behaviour.

The importance of a through-going functional analysis of verbal behaviour, particularly as it develops through childhood, and embracing all of the complexities of symbolic activity (including equivalence classes), cannot be overstressed. Skinner's (1957) book *Verbal behavior* laid the groundwork for such an analysis over 30 years ago, but much remains to be done. In the view of the present authors, whose perspective draws heavily from the theoretical writings of both Vygotsky (1962; 1978) and Skinner (see Catania & Harnad, 1988), an analysis of the role of verbal behaviour is essential to an adequate understanding of most of the important phenomena of human psychology. This has now been shown to be the case for many aspects of human operant behaviour (e.g. Bentall, Lowe, & Beasty, 1985; Lowe, 1979; 1983; Lowe, Beasty, & Bentall, 1983; Lowe & Horne, 1985; Lowe, Horne, & Higson, 1987) and, as the evidence presented here indicates, stimulus equivalence stands least of all as an exception to this general principle.

ACKNOWLEDGEMENTS

Some of this work was supported by a studentship, held by Neil Dugdale, from the Economic and Social Science Research Council. We are grateful to Professors Duane Rumbaugh and Sue Savage-Rumbaugh for their invaluable assistance and for providing us with the opportunity to work with their very special subjects.

REFERENCES

Bates, E. (1976). *The emergence of symbols*. London: Academic Press.

Beasty, A. (1987). The role of language in the emergence of equivalence relations: A developmental study. Unpublished Ph.D. thesis, University of Wales.

Beasty, A. & Lowe, C. F. (1985, April). The role of language in the emergence of equivalence classes II: Evidence from developmental studies. Paper presented to the Annual Conference of the Experimental Analysis of Behaviour Group, York.

Bentall, R. P., Lowe, C. F., & Beasty, A. (1985). The role of verbal behavior in human learning II: Developmental differences. *Journal of the Experimental Analysis of Behavior*, *43*, 165–181.

Catania, A. C. (1986). On the differences between verbal and nonverbal behavior. *Analysis of Verbal Behavior*, *4*, 2–9.

Catania, A. C. & Harnad, S. (Eds) (1988). *The selection of behavior: The operant behaviorism of B. F. Skinner*. Cambridge: Cambridge University Press.

Chomsky, N. (1959). A review of B. F. Skinner's *Verbal Behavior*. *Language*, *35*, 26–58.

Chomsky, N. (1972). *Language and mind*. San Diego: Harcourt Brace Jovanovich.

D'Amato, M. R., Salmon, D. P., Loukas, E., & Tomie, A. (1985). Symmetry and transitivity of conditional relations in monkeys (*Cebus apella*) and pigeons (*Columbia livia*). *Journal of the Experimental Analysis of Behavior*, *44*, 35–47.

Devany, J. M., Hayes, S. C., & Nelson, R. O. (1986). Equivalence class formation in language-able and language-disabled children. *Journal of the Experimental Analysis of Behavior*, *46*, 243–257.

Dugdale, N. A. (1988). The role of naming in stimulus equivalence: Differences between humans and animals. Unpublished Ph.D. thesis, University of Wales.

Dugdale, N. A. & Lowe, C. F. (1987, April). No symmetry in the conditional discriminations of language-trained chimpanzees. Paper presented to the Annual Conference of the British Psychological Society, Brighton.

Hayes, L. J., Tilley, K. J., & Hayes, S. C. (1988). Extending equivalence class membership to gustatory stimuli. *Psychological Record*, *38*, 473–482.

Hird, J. & Lowe, C. F. (1985, April). The role of language in the emergence of equivalence relations I: Evidence from studies with mentally handicapped people. Paper presented to the Annual Conference of the Experimental Analysis of Behavior Group, York.

Hogan, D. E. & Zentall, T. R. (1977). Backward associations in the pigeon. *American Journal of Psychology*, *90*, 3–15.

Holmes, P. W. (1979). Transfer of matching performance in pigeons. *Journal of the Experimental Analysis of Behavior*, *31*, 103–114.

Jenkins, J. J. (1963). Mediated associations: Paradigms and situations. In C. N. Cofer & B. S. Musgrave (Eds), *Verbal behavior and learning: Problems and processes*, pp. 210–245. New York: McGraw-Hill.

Kendall, S. B. (1983). Tests for mediated transfer in pigeons. *Psychological Record, 33*, 245–256.

Lazar, R. M., Davis-Lang, D., & Sanchez, L. (1984). The formation of visual stimulus equivalences in children. *Journal of the Experimental Analysis of Behavior, 41*, 251–266.

Lipkens, R., Kop, P. F. M., & Matthijs, W. (1988). A test of symmetry and transitivity in the conditional discrimination performances of pigeons. *Journal of the Experimental Analysis of Behavior, 49*, 395–409.

Lock, A. (1980). *The guided reinvention of language*. London: Academic Press.

Lowe, C. F. (1979). Determinants of human operant behavior. In M. D. Zeiler & P. Harzem (Eds), *Advances in analysis of behaviour, Vol. 1: Reinforcement and the organisation of behaviour*, pp. 159–192. Chichester: John Wiley.

Lowe, C. F. (1983). Radical behaviorism and human psychology. In G. C. L. Davey (Ed.), *Animal models of human behavior*, pp. 71–93. Chichester: John Wiley.

Lowe, C. F. (1986, May). The role of verbal behaviour in the emergence of equivalence relations. Paper presented to the Annual Conference of the Association for Behavior Analysis, Milwaukee.

Lowe, C. F. & Beasty, A. (1987). Language and the emergence of equivalence relations: A developmental study. *Bulletin of the British Psychological Society, 40*, A42.

Lowe, C. F. & Horne, P. J. (1985). On the generality of behavioural principles: Human choice and the matching law. In C. F. Lowe, M. Richelle, D. E. Blackman, & C. M. Bradshaw (Eds), *Behaviour analysis and contemporary psychology*, pp. 97–115. London: Lawrence Erlbaum Associates Ltd.

Lowe, C. F., Beasty, A., & Bentall, R. P. (1983). The role of verbal behavior in human learning: Infant performance on fixed-interval schedules. *Journal of the Experimental Analysis of Behavior, 39*, 157–164.

Lowe, C. F., Horne, P. J., & Higson, P. J. (1987). Operant conditioning: The hiatus between theory and practice in clinical psychology. In H. J. Eysenck & I. Martin (Eds), *Theoretical foundations of behaviour therapy*, pp. 153–165. New York: Plenum Press.

McIntire, K. D., Cleary, J., & Thompson, T. (1987). Conditional relations by monkeys: Reflexivity, symmetry and transitivity. *Journal of the Experimental Analysis of Behavior, 47*, 279–285.

Miller, N. E. & Dollard, J. (1941). *Social learning and imitation*. New Haven, Conn.: Yale University Press.

Rodewald, H. K. (1974). Symbolic matching-to-sample by pigeons. *Psychological Reports, 34*, 987–990.

Rumbaugh, D. M. (1977). *Language learning by a chimpanzee: The Lana Project*. New York: John Wiley.

Savage-Rumbaugh, E. S. (1986). *Ape language: From conditioned response to symbol*. New York: Columbia University Press.

Sidman, M., Cresson, O., Jr, & Willson-Morris, M. (1974). Acquisition of matching-to-sample via mediated transfer. *Journal of the Experimental Analysis of Behavior, 22*, 261–273.

Sidman, M., Kirk, B., & Willson-Morris, M. (1985). Six-member stimulus classes generated by conditional-discrimination procedures. *Journal of the Experimental Analysis of Behavior, 43*, 21–42.

Sidman, M., Rauzin, R., Lazar, R., Cunningham, S., Tailby, W., & Carrigan, P. (1982). A search for symmetry in the conditional discriminations of rhesus monkeys, baboons, and children. *Journal of the Experimental Analysis of Behavior, 37*, 23–44.

Sidman, M. & Tailby, W. (1982). Conditional discrimination vs. matching to sample: An expansion of the testing paradigm. *Journal of the Experimental Analysis of Behavior, 37*, 5–22.

Sidman, M., Willson-Morris, M., & Kirk, B. (1986). Matching-to-sample procedures and the development of equivalence relations: The role of naming. *Analysis and Intervention in Developmental Disabilities*, *6*, 1–19.

Skinner, B. F. (1957). *Verbal behavior*. New York: Appleton-Century-Crofts.

Stoddard, L. T. & McIlvane, W. J. (1986). Stimulus control research and developmentally disabled individuals. *Analysis and Intervention in Developmental Disabilities*, *6*, 155–178.

Vaughan, W., Jr (1988). Formation of equivalence sets in pigeons. *Journal of Experimental Psychology: Animal Behavior Processes*, *14*, 36–42.

Vygotsky, L. S. (1962). *Thought and language*. New York: John Wiley.

Vygotsky, L. S. (1978). *Mind in society: The development of higher psychological processes*. Cambridge, Mass.: Harvard University Press.

Williams, B. A. (1984). Stimulus control and associative learning. *Journal of the Experimental Analysis of Behavior*, *42*, 469–483.

6 The Development of Thinking in Mentally Retarded Children: Has Behaviourism Something to Offer?

Jean-Luc Lambert
Institut de Padagogie Curative, Université de Fribourg, Fribourg, Switzerland

> Human thought is human behavior
> B. F. Skinner

TWO DIFFERENT PSYCHOLOGIES

When Itard finished writing his report on Victor, he characterised his own experiment as a failure. Since the end of the eighteenth century, a great deal of systematic research has been directed towards the understanding of the thought processes of retarded persons. Psychological research concerned with thinking in retarded children followed and paralleled developments in general psychology. If the psychometric focus dominated the field 30 years ago, the importance of learning studies became more and more obvious (Clarke & Clarke, 1987), because notions such as I.Q. and mental age were demonstrated to be insufficient bases for understanding the nature of the differences between retarded and non-retarded people. The history of psychological research in mental retardation would encompass the scope of this paper. It would be the history of the emergence of theories, controversies, contradictory results, but also of progress and educational applications. Today, it is recognised that a gap exists between two groups of researchers. On the one hand, we have the behaviourists who consider that the study of thinking in retarded people is the study of retarded behaviour. On the other hand, the cognitivists argue that thought in retarded people can best be understood in terms of a wide range of component cognitive processes. This state of affairs has led to the development of what Baumeister (1984) calls "two different experimental psycho-

TABLE 6.1
Two Experimental Psychologies in Mental Retardation: General Trends

Dominant paradigm	Behaviourist	Cognitivist
Basic research design	Single-subject	Group contrast
Level of retardation	Profound–severe Moderate	Mild–borderline "Normal"
Age of subjects	All ages	Adolescents
Vocabulary	Experimental analysis of behaviour	Information processing; higher processes
Procedures	The simplest task	Complex tasks

logies in mental retardation with little commerce and a lot of antagonism between them" (Table 6.1).

Before reviewing some of the characteristics of the cognitive trend, it is necessary to underline two aspects of this situation. First, the two groups of researchers deal with the same basic phenomena: the analysis of the changes in behaviour as a result of experimental intervention. Secondly, when they try to explain mental retardation, both psychologies are limited. In a recent review on cognitive psychology and mental handicap, O'Connor (1987) illustrated a dilemma: Evidence against a unitary concept of intelligence has accumulated as a result of experiments with the mentally retarded. The experimental cognitive psychology approach has failed to identify one distinctive function whose weakness would explain general cognitive deficit. On the other hand, behaviourist psychology has also failed to produce a model which could explain retarded behaviour.

The Cognitive Trend

At the end of the 1970s, a growing number of researchers in mental retardation suggested the demise of the behaviourist paradigm, claiming that cognitive psychology has provided a new framework for research on strategy acquisition, maintenance and generalisation in the mentally retarded (cf. Borkowski & Cavanaugh, 1979; Campione & Brown, 1977). A new terminology entered into the field. Metacognition, control processes, metamemory, higher-order executive mechanisms and executive functioning became the key words in the study of thinking.

Metacognition refers to introspective knowledge about one's cognitive states and processes. The function of metacognition is to inform and regulate cognitive routines and strategies. According to this view, problem solvers integrate metacognitive knowledge with strategic behaviours (control processes) in order to solve problems. Learners are supposed to select, modify and invent strategies to meet problems and to alter metacognition, through feedback mechanisms that follow successful problem solving. For those who support this trend, production deficiencies, so common in the retarded, can be interpreted in terms of failures of metacognition. At this point of the discussion, I think that we need some clarifications. "Failures of metacognition" means that retarded children may have a strategy in their cognitive repertoires applicable to the task at hand, but simply lack the knowledge regarding when, how and why that strategy might be applied (Borkowski, Reid, & Kurtz, 1984).

The development of these concepts raises at least three questions: What is their empirical base in the retarded? Do they bring something new to the field of special education? What can a behaviourist do when confronted with the claim that his favourite paradigm is disappearing?

Cognitive researchers admit themselves that "whereas metacognition has interesting theoretical and applied implications, its empirical base is limited" (Borkowski et al., 1984). Cavanaugh and Borkowski (1980) found that metacognition has not been closely linked to problem-solving behaviours in the retarded or to strategy use across a variety of learning tasks. The same statement can be made about the nature of metamemory–memory connections (Cavanaugh & Borkowski, 1980), and the concepts of executive functioning and superordinate processes (Butterfield, 1985).

The education of the retarded is, in my opinion, the final proof of the validity of any theory. Here, the results published by cognitive psychologists go rarely beyond the statement that "There seems little doubt about the potential utility of the concept of executive functioning for improving the problem-solving behavior of the retarded" (Borkowski et al., 1984). Recommendations are given, but without explanations. What can special teachers do with statements like these:

1. Train subordinate processes.
2. Train superordinate processes and instruct on the co-ordination of lower- and higher-level processes.
3. Teach, through examples and feedback, the reasons and goals of both subordinate and superordinate processes (Borkowski, Reid & Kurtz, 1984).

The problem is the same with strategy generalisation: Only a handful of successful studies have been reported in the retardation literature (Belmont, Butterfield, & Borkowski, 1978; Campione & Brown, 1977; Sternberg, 1981). Some programmes have been developed to train cognitive processes and metacognitive components. Feuerstein's (1980) model and instructional work is actually sold all over the world. Feuerstein reports that his programme can modify successfully the cognitive structure of retarded adolescents. On the basis of a thorough scientific analysis, Bradley (1983) concluded that claims that research lends "substantial support" to the effectiveness of Feuerstein's programme must be rejected.

What can the behaviourist do when confronted with the development of cognitive psychology in mental retardation? I see two directions. First of all, he should ask himself whether a large number of the concepts of cognitive psychology cannot be analysed in light of the theoretical and methodological backgrounds of beahviourism. Secondly, he should try to contribute to the elimination of theoretical confusion which often seems to be the only higher-order process developed by a great deal of cognitive research.

Behind the Concepts

The conceptual escalation accompanying the emergence of the cognitive trend deals with what are fashionably called higher-order processes. Two types of considerations must be developed if we wish to characterise the research in this framework.

First, from a theoretical viewpoint, it is necessary to consider this question: Is it really progress to interpret a behaviour as the outcome of a higher-order process if this behaviour can be understood in terms of simpler behaviour? This question does not seem to interest many cognitivists. They are centred on the identification and the manipulation of metathings, mostly influenced by the information processing models (Baumeister, 1984). Even old controversies have subsided somewhat in favour of interactionist positions. The best example is the structure *vs* process issue which is less salient today (Sternberg, 1981). Traditionally, researchers in the field of mental retardation tried to arrange the environment and to observe behaviour. The simplest tasks were used in order to isolate simple processes. Today, cognitivists are well obliged to recognise that what they can do is to arrange the environment and to observe behaviour. But they have designed very complex experimental tasks, thinking that the existence of higher-order processes could be inferred from task complexity. With Baumeister (1984), I do not deny the fact that human thought processes are very complex. I am simply saying that in mental retardation the greatest part of the cognitive trend brought mentalism back into the field and that it is not an advance in terms of explaining mental retardation. Circularity is the core of most explanations. Fifty years ago, mental retardation was considered to be caused by a lack of intelligence. Today, this phenomenon is caused by the non-functioning of metacomponents. Nothing is explained.

One example can be found in the use of some concepts and especially the notion of generalisation. The current literature on the problem of generalisation in mental retardation is highly confusing because the term is used in so many different ways (Baumeister, 1984). It is amusing to examine the controversy developed by Zeaman and House (1984), cognitive psychologists who strongly advocated the existence of structural deficiencies in the retarded, against other cognitivists like Borkowski, Cavanaugh, Brown and Butterfield. For Zeaman and House (1984), strategy generalisation as it is often used in research is in fact discriminative learning. There is a tendency among cognitivists to avoid contact with the systematic literature on a problem. In fact, at least two different meanings of generalisation are used. On the one hand, the concept is used in terms of results from experimental manipulations that require the test stimulus to be different in some ways from the conditioned stimulus. On the other hand, generalisation is used to mean generalised strategies, as referring to a strategy that will work in many situations, a mechanism driven by the "executive functioning".

The second group of considerations are methodological ones. It is surprising to observe that a great number of concepts used in the literature are not clearly defined. Let us take a few examples. In the problem of achieving the acquisition of problem-solving strategies, it is recognised that the most important factor conducive to maintenance is the amount of strategy training. Extended training can mean anything from "overlearning" trials on the same material to spending 2 years on a particular programme (Borkowski & Cavanaugh, 1979). "Near" and "far" transfer are other problematic concepts used in many experiments. It seems that every researcher has his own definition, making the interpretation of results highly confusing. It is extremely easy to criticise the experimental value of hypothetical constructs like metacognition or executive functioning. In fact, when authors claim that "all tests for strategy transfer represent an assessment of executive functioning" (Belmont & Butterfield, 1977), I believe that we have made little progress since the beginning of this century when Binet defined intelligence as the things measured by his test.

Another methodological problem present in much cognitive research is the use of the conventional group design. It is beyond the scope of this chapter to analyse the interpretive problems inherent in comparative studies: A number of commentators have already contributed some rigorous papers to this issue (Chapman & Chapman, 1974; Winters, 1977). Baumeister (1984) exhausted the methodological difficulties that characterise much of the research and made a plea for a greater use of single-subject designs in experiments. The fundamental question in research has to do with the degree of experimental control that can be demonstrated over responding. Designs comparing groups of retarded and non-retarded people are not sensitive to individual response rates, and experimental control is often not apparent in the examination of group means.

I do not believe that I will have convinced the cognitivists with my observations. I do not know what the future of cognitive psychology in mental retardation will be. But, I do know that it is far too early to claim that the demise of the behaviourist paradigm is now accomplished. As a matter of fact, the cognitive psychology of mental retardation based on the information processing approach forgets two important things. First, there is an almost complete disregard for the motivational characteristics of the individuals, Zigler's (1966) work being the exception. Little is said about the consequences of the activity. Secondly, many cognitivists seem to ignore that behaviour occurs within a context from which behaviour derives its meaning. As Baumeister and Brooks (1981) noted, if we do not understand the context, we cannot understand the behaviour.

ADVANCES IN THE ANALYSIS OF RETARDED BEHAVIOUR

First, I would like to illustrate the fact that some concepts introduced by cognitivists to explain thinking processes in mentally retarded children can be studied in the frame of the behaviourist paradigm.

The Zone of Proximal Development

A number of clinicians have attempted to design testing procedures, termed dynamic assessment, in order to provide information on a child's ability to learn. These forms of testing extend the focus of the evaluation to potential developmental levels. Vygotsky (1978) referred to the discrepancy between a child's current and potential levels of development as the zone of proximal development. He defined this zone as the distance between the level of performance that a child can reach unaided and the level of participation that the child can accomplish when he is guided by another, more knowledgeable individual. Vygotsky's notion of the zone of proximal development has stimulated a large body of recent research (Brown & Ferrara, 1985; Day, 1983; Ferrara, Brown, & Campione, 1986; Rogoff & Wertsch, 1984). These studies are centred on specific populations: normal or mildly mentally retarded children. One reason for this selection of subjects is that the measures are based upon the performance of tasks, like letter series completion and Raven's Matrices Test, that need rather good developmental prerequisites. To my knowledge, there is no report of measures of zones of proximal development in children falling in the range of moderate and severe retardation.

Vygotsky's notion of the zone of proximal development has been concerned primarily with the amount of improvement that takes place following guided instruction. We have chosen another measure proposed by Ferrara et al. (1986): The amount of instruction needed to bring children to some specified level of competence. The zone of proximal development is thus defined in our study as an inverse function of the number of prompts that children need both in achieving successful independent performance within a problem domain and, subsequently, in transferring their acquired knowledge to a similar problem.

In this example, three severely retarded children (T, J and M) participated in the study. Their ages ranged from 9 to 14 years. Their developmental levels ranged from 19 to 24 months.

The experiment was conducted in a special classroom during an activity designed by the teacher—the construction of a "musical instrument" as part of a programme of sensory stimulation. The task consisted of filling a large plastic can with objects and shaking it in order to make noise. The experiment involved three sessions: initial prompted learning (the acquisition phase), maintenance and transfer. The transfer phase consisted of the construction of the same toy with objects differing from those used in the previous phases.

The data recorded were the responses of the children and the instructions given by the teacher in order to help the children. The teacher's behaviours were recorded according to the frequency and the nature of the instructions given: demonstration (imitation), guidance, indications and arrangement of the material.

Figure 6.1 shows that there is a constant decrease in the number of prompts given by the teacher across the sessions. The slope of the decrease in the number of prompts is considered to be a measure of the zone of proximal development. The more assistance a child requires, the lower her potential developmental level. There is a correlation between the decrease in the number of prompts needed across acquisition and transfer phases and learning efficiency. Figure 6.2 shows the number of steps performed by the children without assistance.

These results present nothing new for behaviourist researchers in mental retardation. I can say that they are the basis of experiments conducted by many graduate students. What we did not know until recently is that this kind of simple research is in fact a study in the zone of proximal development. According to Vygotsky, the proposed measure assesses the child's ability to internalise what he or she is taught. Every time behaviourists have demonstrated that severely retarded children were able to learn a task which was beyond the scope of their actual level of development, they have measured zones of proximal development. In this example, the use of simple operant conditioning principles and the analysis of the results are

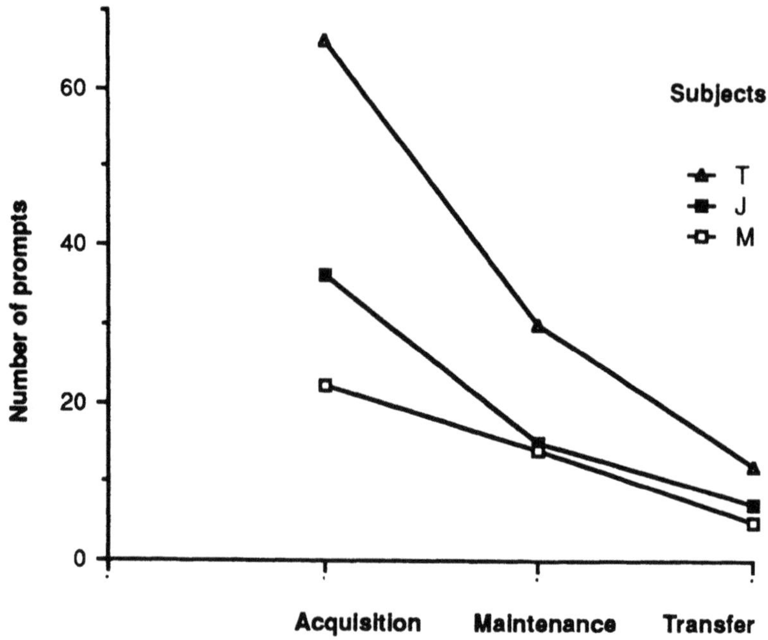

FIG. 6.1. Number of prompts required on each session.

sufficient in themselves to study the behaviour. But, in my opinion, such an analysis is not complete. As a matter of fact, it tells us nothing about the way children integrate what is learned. In other terms, the problem of the structures is forgotten. The notion of the zone of proximal development is a very challenging concept in Vygotsky's theory that brings something new in order to study the relationships between development and learning. What the behaviourist can avoid is the use of the concept of zone as a hypothetical construct. In fact, it does not help to say that retarded children have different zones of proximal development or that they are retarded because of the narrowness of their zone, a reasoning held by theorists and researchers (Day, 1983; Ferrara et al., 1986).

In many cases, the experimental analysis of behaviour forces us to reconsider the meaning of concepts widely used in the cognitive literature on mental retardation. The study of children's classification of simple sets of objects is another instance of concepts that can be studied in the frame of the behaviourist paradigm. Classification means the organisation of objects according to their similarities and differences. "Thinking" in this context refers to the judgements children make as they select objects and manouevre them into one arrangement or another. Piaget postulated little organisational change in early representational thought, the period be-

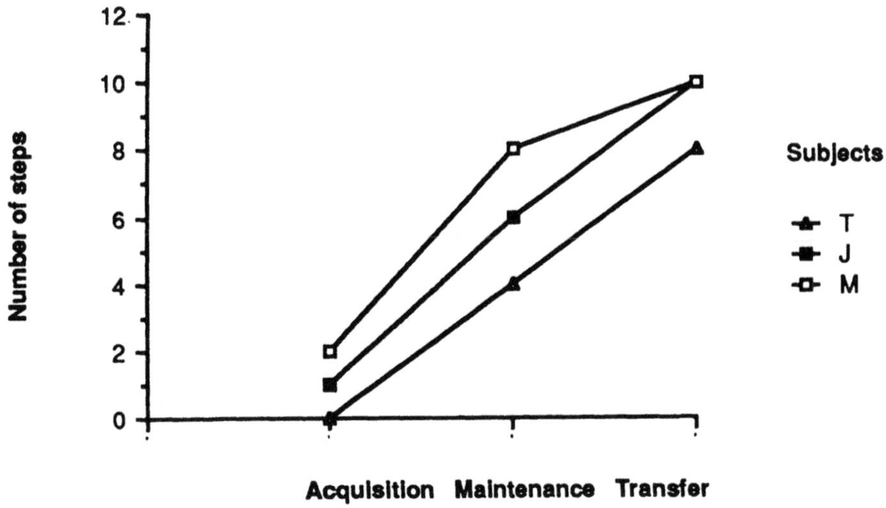

FIG. 6.2. Number of steps performed without assistance on each session.

tween 2 and 4 years of age. Classification is one of the activities produced by children that can be studied in Piaget's framework as well as in behaviourist principles. Classification is said to exist when two or more discrete events are treated as equivalent. As such, classification may be found in the lowest organisms as well as in our most creative intellectuals. Finally, the criterion of equivalent treatment is fortunate, as it identifies a phenomenon that exists in children throughout our target population range. Recent research led by cognitivists has provided a new insight into the levels of organisation in the classification abilities of young children. Despite very interesting results, this research—especially Sugarman's (1983) work—concluded that these questions do not translate in any simple way into behavioural observations. Tattarletti (1988) studied the organisation of classification in severely non-speaking retarded children, with a chronological age ranging from 7 to 9 years and developmental levels between 24 and 30 months. The results showed that these children were able to arrange ("class") the objects according to various criteria and that their behaviours were under the control of specific features of the objects (shapes, colours, figurative *vs* non-figurative). All the cognitivist concepts used in the classification literature could be applied to arrangements produced by the children which depend on the stimuli presented.

It would be an over-simplification to identify thinking with stimulus control. But it helps us to consider that many questions raised by cognitivists in order to study thought processes are in fact instances of stimulus control. For example, given an environment in which we know that retarded children can discriminate one kind of thing from another, how do they organise what they see? To what extent do they interrelate individual elements? To what extent do they see further relations among these relations?

Stimulus Control

Terrace (1966) suggested that the term stimulus control refers to the extent to which an antecedent stimulus determines the probability of a conditioned response occurring. Terrace's work has given impetus to the study of stimulus control in both developmentally normal and retarded children. It is important to analyse the methods used to establish stimulus control, not only for theoretical purposes, but also for educational reasons, as it is demonstrated by Spradlin and Spradlin's (1976) first synthesis on the application of stimulus control in special education for the moderately and severely retarded. Since Hogg's (1976) review of stimulus control studies on retarded children, the experimental work has followed three main directions: the analysis of constructs, the effectiveness of error-free learning and the training of new behaviours via equivalence relations.

The notion of inhibition is an example of the need for experimental analysis. The inhibitory process and its use in explaining learning and the lack of it as exhibited in retarded learning is popular in the literature and has been used to account for individual differences in learning in both normal and retarded children (Heal & Johnson, 1970).

A demonstration of the validity of the concept of inhibition in learning rests on the behavioural demonstration that stimuli which have become associated with non-reinforcement have active negative properties, as opposed to neutral properties. Evans (1982) conducted a series of experiments designed to analyse the notion of the inhibition deficit as an explanatory concept using a go/no-go discrimination learning design in which S+ and S− are presented in separate trials. The regular incremental inhibitory gradients replicated across children and stimuli conditions gives reasonable evidence of inhibitory dimensional control. For the groups observed, S− functions as an active inhibitory stimulus in interdimensional go/no-go discrimination learning.

The conclusions of Evans' (1982) experiments are two-fold. There is little formal evidence to support the inhibition deficit hypothesis, a view widely held in the literature over the last 20 years. On the other hand, there is evidence to suggest that there are individual differences along an excitation–inhibition dimension within at least the severely retarded population. These differences may reflect fairly stable behavioural characteristics. According to Evans (1982, p. 117): "A notion of inhibition deficit is probably not a worthwhile project unless these individual variations can be taken into account." The notion of individual differences in terms of the child's susceptibilities to reinforcing and non-reinforcing events would take the place of the notion of inhibition deficit from the point of view of understanding learning processes in the retarded.

Terrace's (1966) work on error-free discrimination learning has had a wide resonance. The possibility of devising strategies capable of establishing discrimination without relying on errors appeared of great value for many retarded children who, in fact, may fail to acquire even simple discriminations by means of trial-and-error training. Errors seem to contribute to a deterioration in their performance, rather than helping them to acquire a discrimination. Five different procedures of error-free discrimination training are now available (Fig. 6.3).

Stimulus fading involves the manipulation of one or more dimensions of one of the stimuli to be discriminated. In the example, the final discrimination is to be between a circle and a triangle and stimulus fading is made along the dimension of intensity. The discrimination starts with the circle (S+, the correct choice) at full intensity, while the S− is invisible. The triangle will appear progressively on the white card. Stimulus shaping involves manipulations along the configuration of the stimuli to be discriminated. In the example, the final discrimination is to be between a circle and a triangle. Stimulus shaping starts with the drawings of an apple and of a tree. The configuration of the apple is changed into the circle and the configuration of the tree is altered into the triangle. Superimposition and fading involves the use of known stimuli as prompts for the discrimination of new stimuli. In the example, superimposition and fading start by pairing the stimuli with colours already discriminated by the subject (e.g. red for the circle; yellow for the triangle). The colours are gradually faded out. Superimposition and shaping is similar to superimposition and fading. For the discrimination of two letters, in the example, the discrimination starts by superimposing the drawings of the objects on the letters. The configuration and the size of the drawings are then modified until they completely overlap with the letters. In the delayed cue procedure, one of the stimuli to be discriminated (in the example, S+, a circle) is paired with a prompt (e.g. finger pointing). In the example, the discrimination starts with the experimenter pointing to the S+ at each presentation. When the subject responds correctly, the pointing is gradually delayed. The prompt is discontinued once the subject can respond before its occurrence.

Lancioni and Smeets (1986) recently proposed a very clear and complete synthesis of error-free training in retarded children. The results obtained with these procedures compare favourably with those obtained with trial-and-error training. General guidelines can be stated as follows (Fig. 6.4). Within-stimulus manipulations are directly concerned with the stimuli to be discriminated. These manipulations are involved to a large extent in

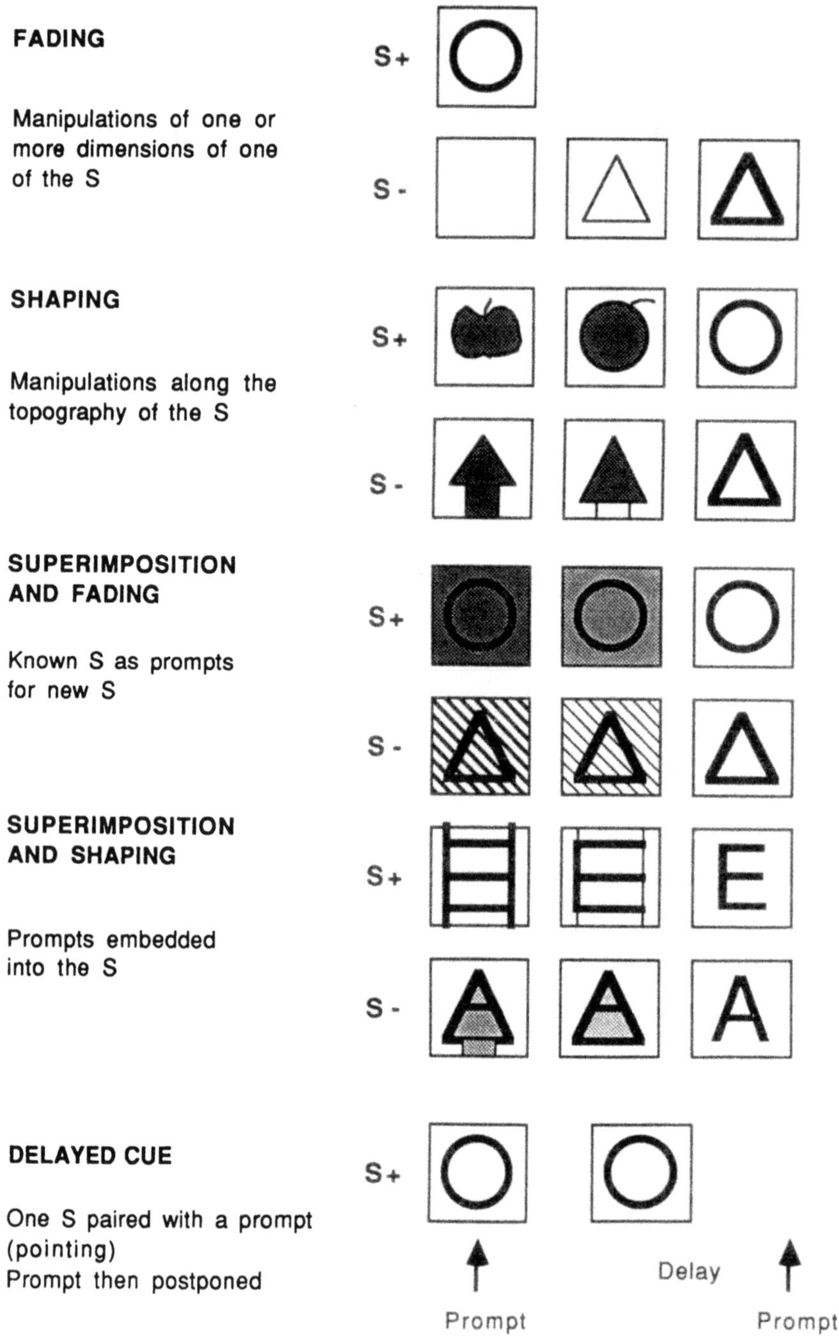

FIG. 6.3. Parameters of error-free discrimination learning.

WITHIN-STIMULUS

(Shaping - Fading)

Criterion related	**Non criterion related**
Change: one dimension of the S present at the final discrimination (ex: size)	Change: one dimension of the S (ex: size) not present at the final discrimination (ex: shape)

EXTRA-STIMULUS

(Superimposition and fading - and shaping - Delayed cue)

Connected with a feature	**Nonconnected with a feature**
Change: a prompt that emphasizes a relevant portion of the S	Change: a prompt not related to a relevant portion of the S

FIG. 6.4. Types of stimulus manipulations in error-free learning.

stimulus shaping and stimulus fading. In a criterion-related procedure, the change is made along a dimension of the stimulus present at the final discrimination (e.g. Fig. 6.3: the shapes of the circle and the triangle in the shaping procedure). In a non-criterion-related procedure, the change is made along a dimension of the stimuli that is not present at the final discrimination (e.g. Fig. 6.3: the intensity of the triangle is changed, while the final discrimination is based on shape).

Extra-stimulus manipulations are concerned with modifications of stimuli other than those to be discriminated. They are found in superimposition and fading, superimposition and shaping, and delayed cue procedures. Two different manipulations can be considered: those connected and those non-connected with a distinctive feature of the stimuli. In the connected manipulation, the changes are made along a dimension that emphasises a differentiating portion of the stimuli to be discriminated. In Fig. 6.4, the example is the fading out of a pretrained cue (black mark) superimposed on the leg of the E in a E-F discrimination. Non-connected manipulation involves changes of a prompt that is not related to any relevant portion of the stimuli to be discriminated. In Fig. 6.4, the example is the fading out of a green background used to prompt responding to F in a E-F discrimination.

According to Lancioni and Smeets (1986), procedures involving within-stimulus, criterion-related manipulations could be indicated as being effective across a range of subjects and situations. Procedures using extra-stimulus, distinctive-feature manipulations are also highly successful. Procedures involving within-stimulus, non-criterion-related manipulations may provide better results if combined with criterion-related (self-cueing) motor responses. The use of a large number of training steps is unlikely to be detrimental to learning. There is no doubt that progress has been made in the last two decades in the quest for better methods for establishing stimulus control in retarded children.

Sidman has developed a series of tests designed to study the equivalence relation that defines matching-to-sample performances (Sidman et al., 1982; Sidman & Tailby, 1982). The examination of the effects of the matching-to-sample procedure upon the subject's performance leads Sidman to the discovery of complexities that are related to fundamental issues in cognition. Equivalence relation must possess three necessary properties: reflexivity, symmetry and transitivity. Mackay and Sidman (1984) have designed a basic equivalence paradigm for testing symmetry and transitivity. Figure 6.5 illustrates this paradigm, which is used in our laboratory in order to teach matching printed words to pictures in severely retarded adults.

In Fig. 6.5, D, P and W represent stimuli. The arrows point from the sample to the comparison stimuli. The test requires the subject to do new tasks: matching picture samples to a printed-word comparison (PW) and printed-word samples to a picture comparison (WP). The thin arrows represent relations that emerge after the others have been taught. If the subject succeeded in these new tasks, the two original relations had to be both symmetric and transitive. Symmetry in the DP and DW relations establishes PD and WD. Given transitivity, PD and DW, for example, yield PW.

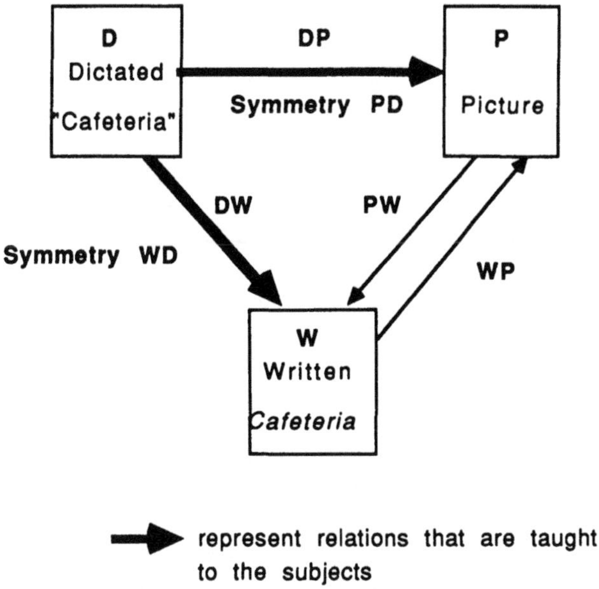

FIG. 6.5. A basic equivalence paradigm used with retarded adults (adapted from Mackay & Sidman, 1984).

Using this paradigm, the results recorded in severely retarded children proved to be unexpected, and they showed that the procedure accomplishes its teaching function with considerable economy. Moreover, the teaching technique can deal with procedures involved in cognition, such as oral and written naming, class creation of equivalent stimuli (a basis for the establishment of semantic relations), and receptive and expressive aspects of elementary linguistic repertories. In fact, the matching-to-sample techniques can serve a dual function, that of both generating and testing for equivalence relations. A complete analysis of Sidman's work would encompass the scope of this chapter (but see Sidman, this volume). By creating new things with old words, Sidman's contribution to the study of thinking processes in retarded children is highly valuable.

THE FUTURE

It is quite surprising to realise that no more than a decade ago, behaviourists working in the field of mental retardation made a clear distinction between the importance of teaching specific behaviours—the role of applied behaviour analysis, their own role—and the study of the organisation of behaviour, which they considered as the role of cognitive theory (Spradlin & Spradlin, 1976). If this position is no longer tenable, such statements were too often the credo of many behaviourists and contributed progressively to isolate the tenets of a rigorous analysis of learning conditions in retarded people. Today, the study of the rules organising and integrating behavioural units in complex entities is considered as one of the tasks of the experimental analysis of behaviour (Thompson & Zeiler, 1986). The evolution of the behaviourist paradigm in mental retardation deserves other conceptual and methodological observations.

The introduction into the field of constructs developed in developmental and cognitive psychology, education or sociobiology is a reality that we cannot avoid. Concepts such as attention, rehearsal and retrieval mechanisms, storage, disability, readiness, metacognition, etc., are present. The task is to recognise that each of these constructs often represents some behavioural reality not yet analysed as such (Baer, Wolf, & Risley, 1987). As I have demonstrated with a few examples, I am not sure that these realities are likely to be analysed as such by their parent disciplines, but might well be studied and clarified within the behaviourist paradigm. In fact, theorists could develop collaboration on the basis of what is happening in special education where there are emerging signs of cooperation between functional cognitivists and behaviour modifiers (Turnure, 1985).

Behaviourists, themselves, would benefit from the rediscovery of some basic concepts of their science in the analysis of retarded behaviour. The individual's own response rate is almost absent from the studies. The fundamental question has to do with the degree of experimental control which can be achieved over responding. Response rate was one of the major discoveries of the experimental analysis of behaviour. Its disappearance gives an impetus to the development of complex experimental designs where sophisticated statistics often seem to replace careful observation of the behaviour. In fact, intra-individual response variability, one of the hypothesised striking characteristics of retarded people (Baumeister, 1968), has never received a close interest from behaviourist researchers. Actually, it is almost impossible to draw firm conclusions about the molar response variability of the retarded. The research is non-systematic and has yielded ambiguous and sometimes unreliable data. This is another field in which the usual caveat "More rigorous basic research is needed" is in order (Smith & Siegel, 1986).

Developmental considerations continue to be absent from behavioural studies in mental retardation. This focus, which is difficult to explain, contributes to the exclusion of the experimental analysis of behaviour from many recent important contributions, because most of the cognitive literature is developmental in nature.

Nearly all the reviews or articles dealing with learning in retarded people end with a sentence such as: "Experimental studies pay very little attention to the issue of generalisation across stimuli or settings." This is another mystery of the application of operant principles in mental retardation: The behaviourist paradigm offers tracks for the study of generalisation, but never follows them. The problem is the same in applied behaviour analysis where the analysis of the generality of any intervention effort is one of the most urgent tasks.

Finally, the identification of the major methodological problems which characterise our research indicates that two designs should be reintroduced in order to provide more valuable data upon the behaviour of retarded children. These designs are longitudinal studies which use single-subject models.

In *About behaviorism*, Skinner (1974, p. 231) wrote: "It is simpler to say that 'mental retardates show reactive inhibition' than to examine the defective relation between their behavior and the environments to which they are exposed." I think that this latter focus is the best way to describe what should constitute the analysis of thinking in retarded children.

REFERENCES

Baer, D. M., Wolf, M. M., & Risley, T. R. (1987). Some still-current dimensions of applied behavior analysis. *Journal of Applied Behavior Analysis*, *20*, 313–327.

Baumeister, A. A. (1968). Behavioral inadequacy and variability of performance. *American Journal of Mental Deficiency*, *73*, 477–483.

Baumeister, A. A. (1984). Some methodological and conceptual issues in the study of cognitive processes with retarded people. In P. H. Brooks, R. Sperber, & C. McCauley (Eds), *Learning and cognition in the mentally retarded*. Hillsdale, N.J.: Lawrence Erlbaum Associates Inc.

Baumeister, A. A. & Brooks, P. H. (1981). Cognitive deficits in mental retardation. In J. M. Kauffman & D. P. Hallahan (Eds), *Handbook of special education*. Englewood Cliffs, N.J.: Prentice-Hall.

Belmont, J. M. & Butterfield, E. C. (1977). The instructional approach to developmental cognitive research. In R. V. Kail & J. W. Hagen (Eds), *Perspectives on the development of memory and cognition*. Hillsdale, N.J.: Lawrence Erlbaum Associates Inc.

Belmont, J. M., Butterfield, E. C., & Borkowski, J. G. (1978). Training retarded people to generalize memorization methods across memory tasks. In M. M. Gruneberg, P. E. Morris, & R. N. Snykes (Eds), *Practical aspects of memory*. London: Academic Press.

Borkowski, J. G. & Cavanaugh, J. C. (1979). Maintenance and generalization of skills and strategies by the retarded. In N. R. Ellis (Ed.), *Handbook of mental deficiency, psychological theory and research*. Hillsdale, N.J.: Lawrence Erlbaum Associates Inc.

Borkowski, J. G., Reid, M. K., & Kurtz, B. E. (1984). Metacognition and retardation: Paradigmatic, theoretical, and applied perspectives. In P. H. Brooks, R. Sperber, & C. McCauley (Eds), *Learning and cognition in the mentally retarded*. Hillsdale, N.J.: Lawrence Erlbaum Associates Inc.

Bradley, T. B. (1983). Remediation of cognitive deficits: A critical appraisal of the Feuerstein model. *Journal of Mental Deficiency Research*, *27*, 79–92.

Brown, A. L. & Ferrara, R. A. (1985). Diagnosing zones of proximal development. In J. V. Wertsch (Ed.), *Culture, communication, and cognition: Vygotskian perspectives*. Cambridge: Cambridge University Press.

Butterfield, E. C. (1985). Testing process theories of intelligence. In M. Friedman, J. P. Das, & N . O'Connor (Eds), *Intelligence and learning*. New York: Plenum Press.

Campione, J. C. & Brown, A. L. (1977). Memory and metamemory development in educable retarded children. In R. V. Kail & J. W. Hagen (Eds), *Perspectives on the development of memory and cognition*. Hillsdale, N.J.: Lawrence Erlbaum Associates Inc.

Cavanaugh, J. C. & Borkowski, J. G. (1980). Searching for the metamemory–memory connections. *Developmental Psychology*, *16*, 447–453.

Chapman, L. J. & Chapman, J. P. (1974). Alternatives to the design of manipulating a variable to compare retarded and normal subjects. *American Journal of Mental Deficiency*, *79*, 404–411.

Clarke, A. D. B. & Clarke, A. M. (1987). Research on mental handicap, 1957–1987: A selective review. *Journal of Mental Deficiency Research*, *31*, 317–328.

Day, J. D. (1983). The zone of proximal development. In M. Pressley & J. R. Levin (Eds), *Cognitive strategy research: Psychological foundations*. New York: Springer-Verlag.

Evans, P. L. (1982). Inhibition and individual differences in inhibitory processes in retarded children. In N. R. Ellis (Ed.), *International review of research in mental retardation*, Vol. 11. London: Academic Press.

Ferrara, R. A., Brown, A. L., & Campione, J. C. (1986). Children's learning and transfer of inductive reasoning rules: Studies of proximal development. *Child Development*, *57*, 1087–1099.

Feuerstein, R. (1980). *Instrumental enrichment: An intervention program for cognitive modifiability*. Baltimore: University Park Press.

Heal, L. W. & Johnson, J. T. (1970). Inhibition deficits in retardate learning and attention. In N. R. Ellis (Ed.), *International review of research in mental retardation*, Vol. 4. London: Academic Press.

Hogg, J. (1976). The experimental analysis of retarded behaviour and its relation to normal development. In M. P. Feldman & A. Broadhurst (Eds), *Theoretical and experimental bases of the behaviour therapies*. Chichester: John Wiley.

Lancioni, G. E. & Smeets, P. M. (1986). Procedures and parameters of errorless discrimination training with developmentally impaired individuals. In N. R. Ellis & N. W. Bray (Eds), *International review of research in mental retardation*, Vol. 14. London: Academic Press.

Mackay, H. A. & Sidman, M. (1984). Teaching new behavior via equivalence relations. In P. H. Brooks, R. Sperber, & C. McCauley (Eds), *Learning and cognition in the mentally retarded*. Hillsdale, N.J.: Lawrence Erlbaum Associates Inc.

O'Connor, N. (1987). Cognitive psychology and mental handicap. *Journal of Mental Deficiency Research*, *31*, 329–336.

Rogoff, B. & Wertsch, J. V. (Eds) (1984). *Children's learning in the "zone of proximal development"*. San Francisco: Jossey Bass.

Sidman, M., Rauzin, R., Lazar, R., Cunningham, S., Tailby, W., & Carrigan, P. (1982). A search for symmetry in the conditional discriminations of rhesus monkeys, baboons, and children. *Journal of the Experimental Analysis of Behavior*, *37*, 23–44.

Sidman, M. & Tailby, W. (1982). Conditional discrimination vs. matching-to-sample. An expansion of the testing paradigm. *Journal of the Experimental Analysis of Behavior*, *37*, 5–22.

Skinner, B. F. (1974). *About behaviorism*. New York: Knopf.

Smith, S. A. & Siegel, P. S. (1986). Molar variability and the mentally retarded. In N. R. Ellis & N. W. Bray (Eds), *International review of research in mental retardation*, Vol. 14. London: Academic Press.

Spradlin, J. E. & Spradlin, R. R. (1976). Developing necessary skills for entry into classroom teaching arrangements. In N. G. Haring & R. L. Schiefelbusch (Eds), *Teaching special children*. New York: McGraw-Hill.

Sternberg, R. J. (1981). Cognitive-behavioral approaches to the training of intelligence in the retarded. *Journal of Special Education*, *15*, 165–183.

Sugarman, S. (1983). *Children's early thought: Developments in classification*. Cambridge: Cambridge University Press.

Tattarletti, C. (1988). Observation de conduites pré-opératoires de classification chez des enfants handicapés mentaux. In J. L. Lambert (Ed.), *Enfants et adultes handicapés mentaux: Recherches et applications*. Delval: Cousset.

Terrace, H. S. (1966). Stimulus control. In W. K. Honig (Ed.), *Operant behavior: Areas of research and application*. New York: Appleton-Century-Crofts.

Thompson, T. & Zeiler, M. D. (Eds) (1986). *Analysis and integration of behavioral units*. Hillsdale, N.J.: Lawrence Erlbaum Associates Inc.

Turnure, J. E. (1985). Communication and cues in the functional cognition of the mentally retarded. In N. R. Ellis (Ed.), *International review of research in mental retardation*, Vol. 13. London: Academic Press.

Vygotsky, L. S. (1978). *Mind in society: The development of higher psychological processes*. Cambridge, Mass.: Harvard University Press.

Winters, J. J. (1977). Methodological issues in psychological research with retarded persons. In I. Bialer & M. Sternlicht (Eds), *The psychology of mental retardation*. New York: Psychological Dimensions.

Zeaman, D. & House, B. (1984). Intelligence and the process of generalization. In P. H. Brooks, R. Sperber, & C. McCauley (Eds), *Learning and cognition in the mentally retarded*. Hillsdale, N.J.: Lawrence Erlbaum Associates Inc.

Zigler, E. (1966). Research on personality structure in the retardate. In N. R. Ellis (Ed.), *International review of research in mental retardation*, Vol. 1. London: Academic Press.

7 Reasoning and Associative Learning

Geoffrey Hall
Department of Psychology, University of York, York, U.K.

The various associative accounts of learning and behaviour share a single core notion—the suggestion that central representations of specified elements can become linked so that activation of one can excite its associate. Although intended to have widespread (even universal) applicability, this notion is most easily exemplified (and has been most rigorously explored) in studies of conditioning in non-human animals. When a pigeon receives a series of trials in which the illumination of a keylight is reliably followed by the presentation of food, the change in its behaviour (the development of a tendency to approach and peck the lit key) has been taken to reflect the formation of an association between (the central representations of) keylight and food. Operant conditioning has received a similar analysis, it being assumed that a pattern of behaviour can be treated as an element that can enter into association.

Although (perhaps, indeed, because of the fact that) the concept of association has been central to philosophical and psychological discussions of the acquisition of knowledge over the last 300 years, it has been the target for constant criticism. We need mention only two classes of critic here who may be caricatured as those who argue that the associative interpretation is too "cognitive" and those who believe that it is not cognitive enough. The former class comprises radical behaviourists who object to any sort of theorising that tries to explain behaviour by postulating mechanisms that are supposed to underlie it. They are, however, perfectly prepared to use conclusions drawn from experimental studies of conditioning in non-human animals in their analysis of seemingly more complex behaviour. And even those who hold that human language might radically influence the way in which our species is able to interact with its environment, are keen to apply operant conditioning principles to the analysis of verbal behaviour.

The other class of critic perhaps includes the majority of psychologists (and philosophers and laymen who have considered the matter). They might accept that the associative account of conditioning is adequate for describing the way in which animals learn but would argue that humans, perhaps by virtue of their language, can acquire knowledge and interact with the world by means of a quite different cognitive mechanism, that responsible for rational thinking. Some would follow Aristotle and set rationality aside as a uniquely human attribute; others might accept Hume's view that the difference between man and non-human animals in their powers of reasoning is merely quantitative. But even the latter would want to distinguish the mechanisms required for reasoning from those involved in conditioning. Munn's (1947) once-influential textbook makes the point clearly. After describing early studies (e.g. by Maier, 1929) designed to demonstrate reasoning in the rat, Munn (1947, p. 177) comments:

> It is quite possible that the rats used in our experiments on reasoning reasoned then for the first time in their lives. . . . In order to induce these organisms to reason, it was necessary to confront them with problems which could not be solved by mere reproduction of former solutions, by conditioning, or by overt trial-and-error.

Apparently, reasoning starts where conditioning ends.

I want to argue that to impose such a limitation on conditioning theory is premature. It may well turn out that the principles derived from studies of conditioning are inadequate to explain rational thought, but we can determine this only by giving those principles a fair try. This general approach will be congenial to the behaviour analyst; the specific associative principles I intend to apply may be less so. But, to anticipate, I hope that the associative perspective will be able to shed some new light on the notion of "equivalence" that has been much discussed of late in the behaviour analytic context (see Sidman, this volume) and that it will be possible to discern some convergence between the two approaches.

INDUCTIVE REASONING

If we take reasoning to be a process that allows the acquisition of knowledge (and hence the solution of some problem) in the absence of any training that could directly impart that knowledge, then the grounds for wanting to make a firm distinction between this process and those involved in conditioning seem quite clear, at least at first sight. A closer look, however, makes the distinction less clear. A rat given a single conditioning trial in which the presentation of a tone has been followed by a moderately severe electric shock will behave appropriately (e.g. by freezing) when the tone is presented again, even though the animal has no direct knowledge as to what the consequences of this second presentation might be. This tendency to generalise from a particular experience, to assume that the future will resemble the past, is what we refer to in humans as inductive reasoning.

Some might want to debate the extent to which simple induction involves rational thought, perhaps accepting Hume's dismissive assertion, in the *Enquiry* of 1748, that "all inferences from experience . . . are effects of custom not reasoning" (Hume, 1902, p. 43). But elsewhere Hume was willing to consider induction as a form of reasoning, particularly in the case where the pattern of conjunction between two events rendered plausible the inference that there might be a causal relation between them. It is of some interest, therefore, to pursue the possibility (Dickinson, 1980; see also Catania & Keller, 1981) that experimental studies of conditioning reveal that animals tend to behave as though they make plausible inferences about the causal relationships that might hold between the events they experience.

Causation and Conditioning

We shall proceed by assuming that when, in classical conditioning, an animal comes to emit a conditioned response (CR) to a conditioned stimulus (CS) that has been presented along with an unconditioned stimulus (US), it does so because it has made the inference that the US is an effect of which the CS is the likely cause. If this assumption is correct, then the readiness with which the CS comes to evoke the CR should depend upon the extent to which the scheduling of the CS and US mimics the features that typify a true causal relationship. For examples of such features we can do no better than to return to Hume and consider some of those that he lists in his *Treatise* of 1739 (Hume, 1888, pp. 173–176).

First, the cause must be prior to the effect. We should expect, therefore, that conditioning would be successful only when the CS precedes the US, and, by and large, this is so. Figure 7.1. presents a summary of the results reported by Smith, Coleman, and Gormezano (1969) from a study of eyelid conditioning in the rabbit. Different groups of subjects experienced different intervals between the onset of the CS (a tone) and the occurrence of the US. CRs tended to occur when the inter-stimulus interval was positive, but no conditioning was evident when the two stimuli occurred together (0 msec in Fig. 7.1), or when the US preceded the CS (−50 msec).

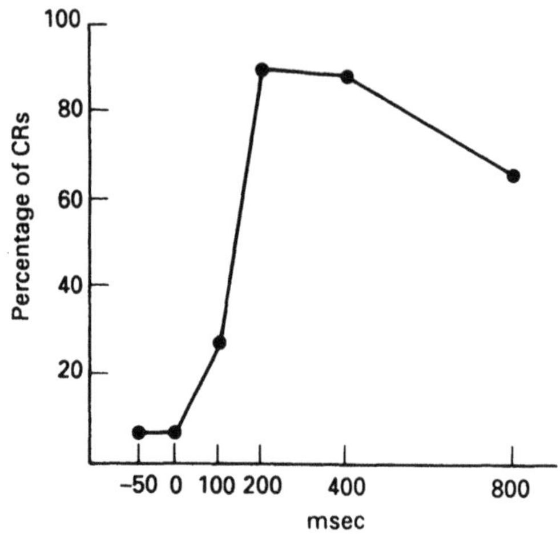

FIG. 7.1. Conditioning of the rabbit's nictitating membrane response as a function of the interval between onset of the CS and onset of the US (from data reported by Smith et al., 1969).

Similar results have been reported for a range of other conditioning preparations. It should be acknowledged, however, that there has been a persistent trickle of experimental reports claiming to demonstrate that "backward conditioning" can occur. We will not discuss the issue here except to say that most would agree that the backward procedure is at best a rather ineffective means of producing excitatory conditioning (see, e.g. Heth & Rescorla, 1973) and that the most common outcome of this procedure (see Wagner & Larew, 1985) is for the CS to come to function as an inhibitor. An inhibitory CS can be construed as a cause, the effect of which is to reduce for a time the likelihood of a certain event, the occurrence of the US. The possibility that some form of conditioning might occur when CS and US are presented simultaneously will be taken up below.

Next, Hume states, cause and effect must be contiguous in space and time. Spatial contiguity has received little experimental attention (but see Rescorla & Cunningham, 1979), but the importance of temporal contiguity is well established and is again illustrated in Fig. 7.1, which shows that as the interval between CS and US is increased beyond 200 msec, the percentage of trials on which the CS evokes a CR declines.

The other rules listed by Hume all concern, in one way or another, the proper interpretation of cases in which there is not a constant conjunction between the events being considered. Such procedures are common in the study of conditioning. Thus Wagner, Logan, Haberlandt, and Price (1968) report a series of experiments in which subjects received a schedule of

TABLE 7.1
Design of Experiment by Wagner et al. (1968)

	Trial types
Uncorrelated group	$T_1L \rightarrow$ US $T_1L \rightarrow$ no US $T_2L \rightarrow$ US $T_2L \rightarrow$ no US
Correlated group	$T_1L \rightarrow$ US $T_2L \rightarrow$ no US

Note: L represents a light; T_1 and T_2 are tones differing in frequency. The auditory cue and the light were presented as a simultaneous compound.

partial reinforcement in which the US followed the CS on only 50% of occasions. The details of two of the conditions they studied are presented in Table 7.1. Both groups experienced training in which a compound CS consisting of a tone and a light sometimes preceded the US. Two different tones were employed and, in the uncorrelated condition, these were presented equally often reinforced and non-reinforced. As Fig. 7.2 shows, the light acquired the ability to evoke the CR but neither of the tones did so. In the correlated condition, the US occurred only on trials on which the light was accompanied by T_1. For this group, T_1 came to govern a CR and T_2 and the light did not (Fig. 7.2). The uncorrelated group, in apparently attributing the US to the light, appear to be following Hume's rule "that where several different objects produce the same effect, it must be by means of some quality, which we discover to be common amongst them" (Hume, 1888, p. 174). The correlated group follows the converse rule that "the difference in the effects of two resembling objects must proceed from that particular in which they differ" (p. 174), in this case in the difference between the two tones.

Event Correlations

This last experimental example constitutes a special case of what is perhaps the most important feature of any system that is required to detect causal relations—the ability to appreciate that "an object may be contiguous and prior to another, without being consider'd as its cause" (Hume, 1888, p. 77). The system must be able to discriminate between chance conjunctions of two events and conjunctions depending upon a causal relation.

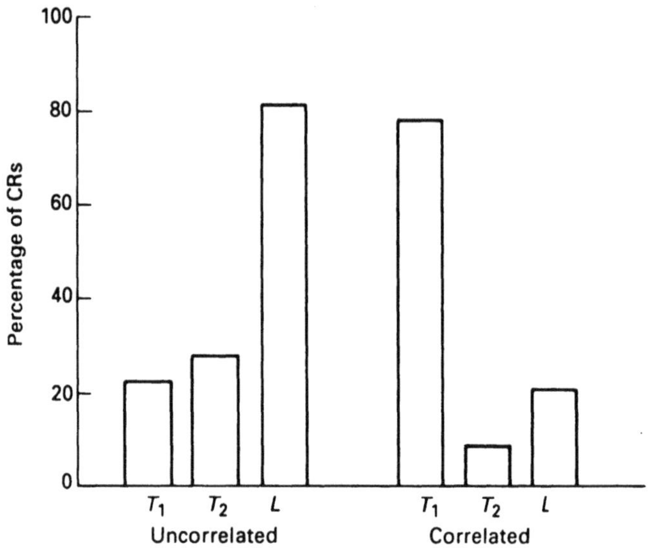

FIG. 7.2. Conditioned responding in rabbits trained according to the procedures outlined in Table 7.1 and tested with the tones and light presented separately (from data reported by Wagner et al., 1968).

Consider the two schedules illustrated in Fig. 7.3. Subjects exposed to the partial reinforcement schedule might infer that the event labelled CS is a cause (albeit not a sufficient cause because the schedule is partial) of that labelled US. But subjects given the "truly random" schedule in which CS and US are uncorrelated, should make no such inference despite their having had equivalent experience of CS and US occurring together—the occurrence of the US in the absence of the CS implies that their conjunction on two of the trials was a matter of chance. A much-cited experiment by Rescorla (1968) shows that rats are sensitive to the correlations established by various schedules of reinforcement. Four groups of subjects received presentations of a tone during which the probability of receiving a shock was 0.4. One group received no other shocks. For the other groups, the probability of a shock occurring in the absence of the tone was 0.1, 0.2, or 0.4. The suppression governed by the tone on the various groups is shown in Fig. 7.4. The group that received shocks only in the presence of a tone developed a strong CR, as shown by a suppression ratio near zero. An increase in the probability of the shock in the inter-trial interval led to a decrease in the magnitude of the CR. The group receiving the uncorrelated treatment (having a probability of shock of 0.4 both in the presence and absence of the tone) showed no conditioning, its suppression score (0.5.) being identical to that recorded for a control group that experienced the tone with no shocks at all.

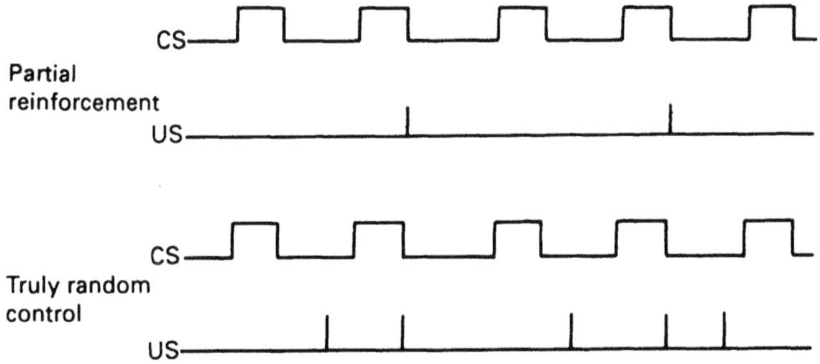

FIG. 7.3. The probability of a US in the presence of a CS is the same in both these schedules of reinforcement. In the truly random control procedure (the uncorrelated schedule), the US is just as probable in the absence of the CS as in its presence.

The finding that excitatory conditioning depends upon there being a "contingency" (a positive correlation) between the events associated and not upon simple contiguity has been cited as strong evidence in favour of the hypothesis that conditioning should be construed as the detection of causality. It has been objected, however, that an ability to detect regularities involving causally related events is not the same as having a "concept

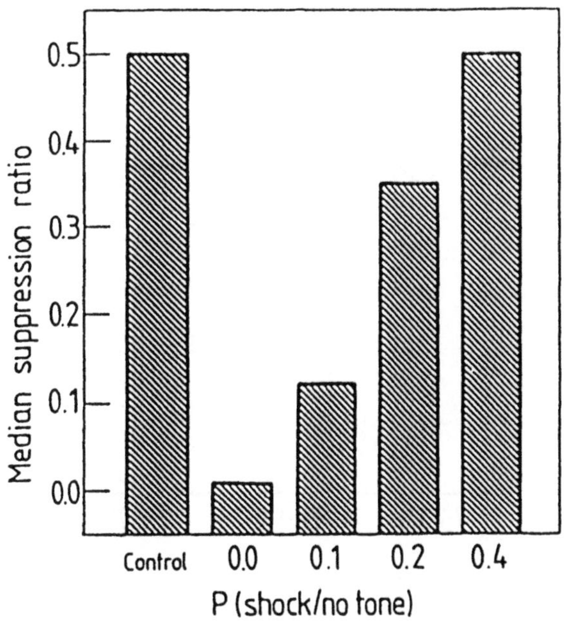

FIG. 7.4. Conditioned suppression to a tone in rats. The control subjects received no shocks. The other four groups all experienced shocks with a 0.4 probability in the presence of the tone but differed in their experience of shocks in the absence of the tone (from data reported by Rescorla, 1968).

of causality" (see Macphail, 1982). Unfortunately, it is difficult to see what else might be required of an animal subject (in addition to the features of conditioning noted above) in order to convince the doubter that the animal's behaviour depended upon its having a concept of causality. Perhaps an approach to a solution can be made by looking at the effects produced in human subjects by training procedures that are conceptually equivalent to those used in experiments on conditioning in non-human animals.

Dickinson, Shanks, and Evenden (1984; see also Dickinson & Shanks, 1985) have performed a study with human subjects that is formally equivalent to that by Recorla (1968) and discussed above. Their task took the form of a "video game" in which a representation of a tank moved across the screen, on some occasions successfully but on others "blowing up" at some point on its traverse (the tank was supposedly crossing a minefield). The subjects could press a button on the computer keyboard which represented their firing a shell at the tank. This, too, might (not all shells were able to penetrate the tank's armour) bring about the destruction of the tank. In the first experiment reported by Dickinson et al. (1984), the subjects received several blocks of trials in which the probability of the

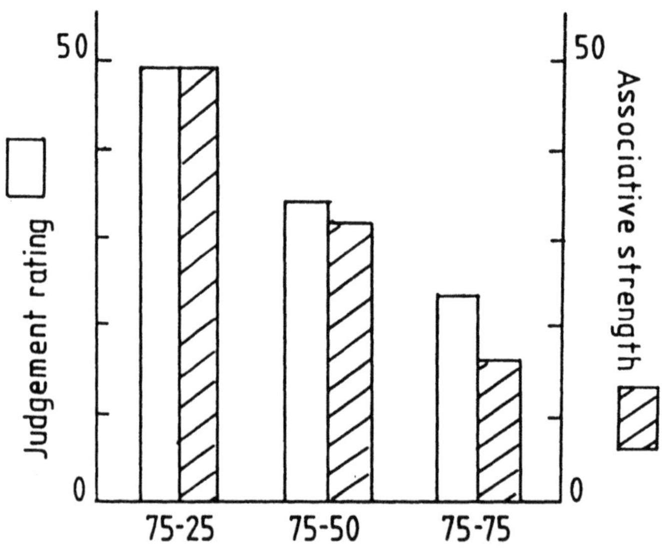

FIG. 7.5. Judgements (on a scale from 0 to 100) of the effectiveness of an action in producing a given outcome after three types of training. In all, the probability of the outcome given the action was 0.75, but the probability of the outcome in the absence of the action was 0.25, 0.50, or 0.75. Also shown is the "associative strength" of an action–outcome association computed using the Rescorla–Wagner equations (adapted from Dickinson et al., 1984).

tank's exploding given that a shell had been fired was fixed at 0.75, but in which the probability of this outcome occurring without a shell being fired was varied from one block to another. The subjects were asked to rate the effectiveness of the shells in bringing about the destruction of the tank.

The results of some of the conditions included in this study are presented in Fig. 7.5. They show that human subjects, like Rescorla's rats, are sensitive to contingency in that the likelihood of their attributing an outcome to a particular event that often accompanies it (an explosion often follows firing a shell) will decline when the probability of that outcome's occurring in the absence of the event is increased. A behavioural test given at the end of each block of trials in which the subjects were allowed to fire shells under a specified pay-off structure generated responding that paralleled the judgement ratings.

The significance of these findings is that in this experiment the subjects were specifically being asked about causality, and the inferences reflected in their judgement ratings exactly matched both their non-verbal behaviour and that shown by rats in conceptually equivalent conditioning experiments. If, as I suspect may be the case, some would only believe that an individual has a concept of causality when he explicitly tells us that he has, then the results of conditioning experiments in animals could never supply the necessary evidence. But the parallel between the behaviour shown by rats and the explicit statements made by human subjects given equivalent training may go some way towards convincing the sceptic.

Associative Interpretations

It remains to assess the extent to which an interpretation of conditioning as a process, whereby animals detect causal relationships, can be accommodated by our associative theories. As we have already implied, the essence of any associative account of classical conditioning is that an established CS, by virtue of a newly formed link, becomes capable of evoking activity in some representation of the US. It has been common to describe this process as the CS evoking an expectation (or an "image", Konorski, 1967; or a "memory", Pearce & Hall, 1980) of the US; but we can just as readily adopt the formulation that the link embodies knowledge that the CS is a cause of the US. But a full associative interpretation requires rather more than this—it requires that our formal theories of the conditions in which an association is formed should be able to predict that "associative strength" will be acquired particularly readily when the conjunctions of CS and US are such as to justify the inference that there is a causal link between them.

Current theories (derived largely from that proposed by Rescorla & Wagner, 1972) have been partially successful in this. They are designed to predict a gradual increase in strength as a result of repeated pairings of the

CS and US and in this they follow common psychology (if not logic) which tends to attribute causality more readily as a result of repeated exposure to the paired events. They emphasise the role of temporal contiguity, assuming that CS and US representations must be active at the same time for a link to be formed. And they introduce various supplementary mechanisms (see, e.g. Wagner & Larew, 1985; Wagner & Rescorla, 1972) which ensure that backward conditioning procedures do not result in excitatory conditioning.

What these theories excel at, however, is explaining the role of event correlations: Indeed, the results presented in Fig. 7.2 and 7.4 constituted the foundations upon which the Rescorla–Wagner model was built. This model asserts that the co-occurrence of a CS and a US will result in a strengthening of the link between them only when there is a discrepancy between the outcome of the conditioning trial (i.e. the activity evoked by the US itself) and that expected on the basis of such CSs as are present (i.e. the activity evoked by CSs as a consequence of their associative links). Thus if one CS becomes strongly associated with the US, this will limit the ability of another CS to gain strength. In the correlated condition depicted in Fig. 7.2, T_1 gains substantial strength because it is always presented prior to the US and, accordingly, the light (which in the uncorrelated condition is able to gain strength by virtue of its 50% partial reinforcement schedule) is not able to do so. The results presented in Fig. 7.4 may be explained by assuming that the conditioning context itself can come to act as a CS. The presentations of shocks in the interval between tones allows the context to gain strength and thus limits the acquisition of strength by the tone.

This simple theoretical notion is also effective when applied to the results of experiments on human causality attribution. Dickinson et al. (1984) chose a plausible set of parameters and, treating the explosion of the tank as the US and the minefield and firing the shell as CSs, used the formal version of the Rescorla–Wagner model to derive the expected associative strength of firing a shell. The results of their simulations are presented in Fig. 7.5, and it is apparent that the match between the data and theory is close. Subsequent research has revealed a need to modify the Rescorla–Wagner model when applied to these data, but Shanks and Dickinson (1987) remain confident that associative mechanisms play an important part in the process by which human subjects make judgements about causality. We might expect that current associative theories would not be fully adequate (after all, no current theory can successfully accommodate all the data from studies of conditioning in animals); but perhaps enough has been demonstrated to justify our taking seriously the notion that conditioning reflects a process whereby causal relationships can be detected and that an associative mechanism might underlie this process.

This conclusion would come as no surprise to Hume (1888, p. 177), who wrote that:

> a dog, that avoids fire and precipices, that shuns strangers, and caresses his master, affords us an instance [of actions that] proceed from a reasoning, that is not in itself different, nor founded on different principles, from that which appears in human nature.

DEDUCTIVE REASONING AND RELATED MATTERS

We may query the extent to which inductive inference involves rationality, but there is no doubting the status of deduction—the deductive syllogism (all As are Bs, all Bs are Cs, and therefore all As are Cs) constitutes a paradigm case of rational thought and it is on this form of reasoning that we shall concentrate initially. The questions that we need to consider are, as before, whether or not non-human animals show the phenomenon of interest and the extent to which their behaviour can be explained in terms of associative principles.

Integration Across Associations

Human subjects required to solve a syllogism are supplied with two items of information and must derive a conclusion. To find a possible parallel in animals, therefore, we need to consider cases in which the subjects are trained on two separate conditioning tasks and tested on some further task that requires integration of the information they have previously acquired. An experiment reported by Holland and Straub (1979) provides a good example of such a case.

In the first phase of their study, Holland and Straub (1979) gave training in which the presentation of a noise was followed by food and, as Fig. 7.6 shows, the rats acquired the CR of approaching the site of food-delivery. Experimental subjects then received a second phase of training in which consumption of the food pellets was followed by an injection of nausea-inducing lithium chloride. A final test stage revealed that for subjects given this treatment the noise was no longer effective in evoking the CR.

If we accept the characterisation of conditioning advanced in the previous section, as the detection of causal relationships, then a deductive interpretation of these findings follows readily. The animals are given training which allows them to establish two propositions: in Holland and Straub's study, these might be that "noise causes food" and that "food causes illness". The test phase of the experiment shows that the rats are capable of putting the two things together, of deducing a relationship between noise and illness. The notion of excitatory associative links

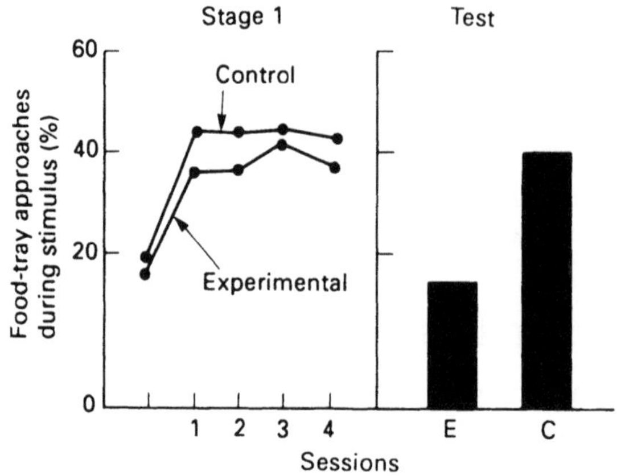

FIG. 7.6. In stage 1, the control and experimental groups of rats learned to approach the food tray in the presence of a CS. Pairings cf food and illness for experimental subjects in a second phase reduced the frequency of this behaviour in the test phase (from data reported by Holland & Straub, 1979).

provides a possible underlying mechanism—presentation of the noise would be able to activate a representation of food which in turn activates a representation of illness.[1]

Sensory Preconditioning and Equivalence

This same associative analysis applies readily to the related phenomenon of sensory preconditioning in which subjects are given a first phase of training with two motivationally neutral stimuli (CSA → CSB), followed by orthodox conditioning (CSB → US) with the second of these. The ability of CSA to elicit the CR on a subsequent test trial implies integration of the information acquired in the two separate phases of training, with CSB providing the linking term between CSA and the US and allowing CSA to control the same behaviour as CSB.

An interesting consequence of this interpretation is that it provides a possible explanation for the transitivity effects revealed in experiments on the "equivalence relation" of the sort pioneered by Sidman and his collaborators (e.g. Sidman & Tailby, 1982). In these experiments, subjects

[1]Having noted this success for associative theory, a word of qualification is needed concerning its general applicability. It has been persuasively argued (see, e.g. Mackintosh & Dickinson, 1979) that operant conditioning too depends upon a process of inference from propositions. It has proved difficult, however, to supply an excitatory-link account of the mechanism involved in this case, and Dickinson (1989) has argued that an interpretation in terms of semantic and computational processes is required.

are taught a conditional discrimination in which the choice of B rather than C is rewarded when stimulus A has been presented previously. They also learn a further discrimination in which B is used to indicate that D rather than E must be chosen. (On other, intermixed trials, other conditional cues dictate the choice of B rather than A and of E rather than D.) For some subjects and with some training procedures (see, e.g. D'Amato, Salmon, Loukas, & Tomie, 1985; McIntire, Cleary, & Thompson, 1987), transitivity is evidenced in that A is able to take the place of B in the second task; that is, on test trials with A as the conditional cue, subjects given a choice between D and E will choose the former. If it is allowed that training on the initial task is likely to establish an A–B association, then this outcome follows from our analysis of sensory preconditioning. A will be able to activate a representation of B and then behaviour appropriate to the presence of B itself (in this case a particular choice response) will be evoked.

To this extent at least, sensory preconditioning can be regarded as a procedure that renders stimuli A and B equivalent. But they will not be logically equivalent, because our associative analysis of the phenomenon implies an asymmetry between them—the first phase of training will establish A as a cause of B but, given what was said above about backward conditioning, it does not allow the inference that B is a cause of A. Things may be different, however, when A and B are presented simultaneously in the first phase of a sensory preconditioning experiment.

Although it has often been assumed that A and B should be presented serially in the first phase of training, recent work has amply confirmed Brogden's (1939) original demonstration that the sensory preconditioning effect can be found when they are presented simultaneously (e.g. Rescorla & Cunningham, 1978). Indeed, Rescorla (1980) has presented some evidence to suggest that the simultaneous method of presentation may actually be superior.

We have interpreted the orthodox sensory preconditioning procedure (in which A precedes B in the first phase of training) as generating a proposition (A causes B) which could be integrated with other information to allow a conclusion. This interpretation seems inappropriate when A and B are presented simultaneously (cause must precede effect); rather, the information acquired in the first phase of training is likely to be that A and B go together.[2] An associative mechanism for such learning is provided by

---

[2]It is interesting to note that Hume (1888) considers the effects of exposure to a simultaneous compound when discussing the relation between the taste of a fruit or its colour. The role of causality here is not clear ("whichever of them be the cause or effect . . .", p. 237) but for him the important consequence of their "coexistence" is that either "must have such an effect on the mind, that upon the appearance of one it will immediately turn its thought to the conception of the other" (p. 237).

the suggestion (e.g. Rescorla, 1981) that simultaneous presentation of stimuli allows the formation of symmetrical links, so that A becomes capable of exciting a representation of B, and vice versa. This associative structure allows a new process by which sensory preconditioning could occur. In the second phase of training, when stimulus B is presented along with the US, a representation of stimulus A will also be activated by virtue of the A–B link formed in the first phase of training. There is good evidence that such an associatively activated representation can enter into further associations. Holland (1981) gave rats orthodox conditioning with a tone as the CS and distinctively flavoured food as the US, and then a second phase of training in which presentation of the tone preceded an injection of lithium chloride. In a final test, the rats, although hungry, proved unwilling to consume the food. Holland's interpretation was that the second phase of training allowed the formation of an association between the illness produced by the injection and the CS-evoked representation of the food that preceded it.

It is tempting to conclude, therefore, that exposure to two events as a simultaneous compound renders them effectively equivalent by establishing a symmetrical pair of excitatory links between them. But before accepting this conclusion we should acknowledge the existence of an alternative possible interpretation for the findings discussed above. As Rescorla (1981) has pointed out (see also Hall & Honey, 1989), we have no need to accept the associationist position with its assumption that the organism starts off with a set of distinguishable elements and learns the relations among them. Rather than analysing a simultaneous compound into its component parts and then reassociating them, the animal might form an undifferentiated representation of the total compound. Each of the elements of the compound would be perceptually similar to such a compound and any training given to one in isolation would thus generalise back to the compound and to the other element. Sensory preconditioining produced by this mechanism would not imply that some equivalence had been established between A and B; it would mean only that A and B are both mistaken for AB by the organism.

This "perceptual" account of sensory preconditioning has most plausibility when applied, as it has chiefly been, to experiments in which the simultaneous compound consists of a mixture of two novel flavours—indeed, in these experiments, it is often difficult to see how the organism could analyse the compound into the two components identified by the experimenters. But there is no doubt that it could apply in other preparations too (see Hall & Honey, 1989, for a discussion of this issue) and, accordingly, it seems sensible to look elsewhere for evidence on the learning of an equivalence relation.

Acquired Equivalence of Cues

The notion that physically quite different stimuli might acquire equivalence as a consequence of some types of training was given an important role in early (i.e. S–R) associative accounts of the "higher mental processes". In a chapter with this title, Miller and Dollard (1941) use the notion of acquired equivalence in their account of simple reasoning. The instance they cite is that of an individual who has learned to attach the verbal label "enemy" to several quite different people. This verbal response produces a cue that is common to all of them and so behaviour that is reinforced in the presence of one of them becomes attached to that cue and is likely to be evoked in the presence of other enemies. Although the example they cite involves verbal behaviour (and Miller and Dollard emphasise that the possession of a language is important in reasoning because it equips the individual with an "enormous arsenal of cue-producing responses"—these authors seem fond of militaristic analogies!), it is not supposed that the processes responsible for acquired equivalence are unique to man. Any response attached to two different stimuli will, it is supposed, allow response-mediated generalisation.

In fact, experimental evidence to confirm the existence of acquired-equivalence effects is sparse for both human and non-human animals. Experiments with humans have usually taken the form of exposing the subjects to presentations of a range of different visual stimuli (e.g. fingerprints in a study by Robinson, 1955; random geometrical figures in a study by Ellis & Muller, 1964) and requiring them to apply the same verbal label to a randomly chosen set of stimuli. Performance is then assessed on a subsequent task that requires discrimination among these stimuli, the comparison being made with a control condition that has not received equivalence training or with a condition in which the subjects have had to learn different verbal labels for the different stimuli. (In this last condition, the converse of acquired equivalence, the acquired distinctiveness of cues, might be expected.) Acquired distinctiveness should yield enhanced performance on the final task; acquired equivalence should retard performance. Unfortunately, however, the various experiments that have employed this general design have not yielded a very consistent pattern of results (see Epstein, 1967, for a review). Quite often the various pretraining treatments do not differ in their effects on the test task, perhaps implying no more than that human subjects always tend to apply a different verbal label to each stimulus, no matter what the experimenter tells them to do.

The best-known experiment on this topic using animal subjects (Lawrence, 1949) was concerned with the acquired distinctiveness case. Here the results are not in doubt—rats that had learned different responses to two stimuli (e.g. to approach one for food and to avoid the other) were better able to learn another discrimination between these two stimuli than rats for whom these stimuli had not been associated with differing consequences. But there is some doubt as to whether this result should be interpreted in terms of the mechanism hypothesised by Miller and Dollard (1941). One possibility is that the initial phase of discrimination training has its effect by boosting the animal's tendency to attend to the dimension on which the stimuli differ (Sutherland & Mackintosh, 1971); another is that the specific patterns of response acquired in the first phase of training transfer to and influence performance on the (supposedly independent) task used in the second stage (Siegel, 1967). Similar problems of interpretation trouble experiments concerned with acquired equivalence. There is no doubt that animals pre-exposed to a pair of stimuli sharing a common consequence and requiring the same response (e.g. both may be reliably followed by food) learn a subsequent discrimination between these stimuli rather slowly (e.g. Hall, 1976; Hall & Channell, 1980). But an attentional explanation is readily available—pre-exposed stimuli tend to lose "associability", whereas for novel stimuli associability is high and conditioning will proceed readily (Pearce & Hall, 1980).

In an attempt to avoid some of these problems, R. C. Honey and I have recently conducted a series of experiments that tried to demonstrate acquired equivalence (and distinctiveness) using a rather different procedure. In one of these experiments, the subjects were two groups of rats that received 12 sessions of phase-one training in each of which two presentations of each of three auditory stimuli occurred. For both groups, stimuli A and B (a tone and a clicker, counterbalanced so that for half the subjects in each group A was the tone and for half it was the clicker) had different consequences. Stimulus B was always followed by food and stimulus A was not. The groups differed in the treatment given to the third stimulus, a noise (N). For group 1, the noise was non-reinforced, but for group 2 its presentation was followed by food. We hoped that this training would induce the subjects to treat as equivalent the pair of stimuli that had the same consequence: A and N in group 1; B and N in group 2. Similarly, group 1 might be better able to discriminate between B and N and group 2 between A and N.

In order to reveal any such effects, we gave a second phase of training designed to endow the noise with new properties. We then assessed the extent to which the effects of this training generalised back to A and B. In the second phase, all subjects received six trials on which the noise was followed by a shock. The results shown in Fig. 7.7 come from a final test session in which the (generalised) tendency of A and B to evoke suppression of lever-pressing was assessed. Suppression on this test was not profound, but for both groups there was significantly ($P < 0.05$) more suppression to the stimulus (A for group 1, B for group 2) that had received phase-one training equivalent to that given for the noise.

This effect is not likely to be an attentional one. Our current theories for attentional effects (e.g. Pearce & Hall, 1980) suggest that both A and B are likely to lose associability during phase-one training and that this loss is likely to be less profound for the reinforced stimulus (B) than for A. But

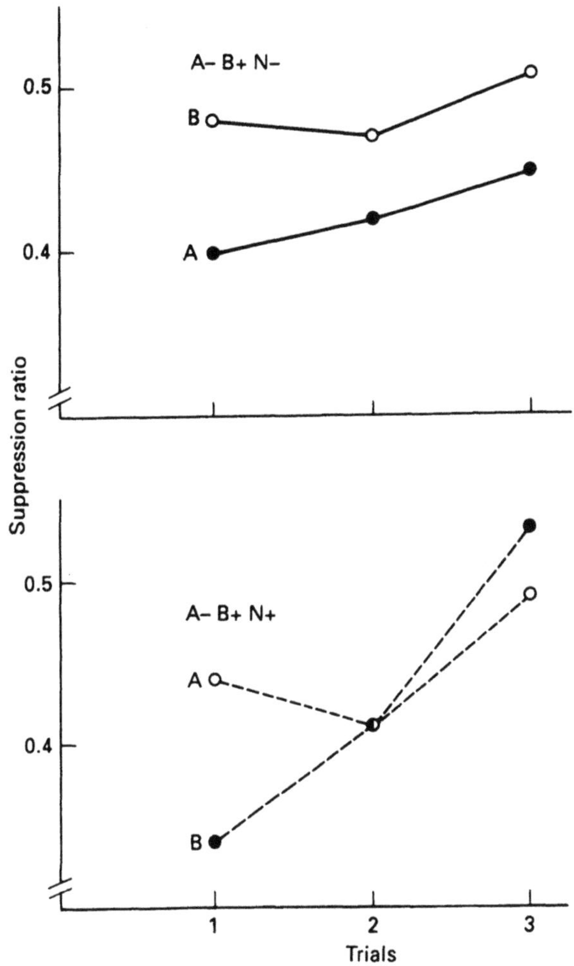

FIG. 7.7. The results of the test phase of an unpublished experiment by Honey and Hall. All subjects received initial training with three stimuli: for group 1 (top panel) only B was followed by food; for group 2 (lower panel) B and N were followed by food. All subjects then received pairings of N and shock. The test assesses the generalisation of conditioned suppression to A and B over three non-reinforced test trials with each stimulus.

this difference between the stimuli cannot account for the test results, because in one group it is A that evokes more suppression and in the other group it is B. Nor is the pattern of results to be explained in terms of the transfer of specific responses acquired in the first phase. One could postulate that the food-reinforced training given to B might allow the stimulus to evoke responses that compete with the suppressive tendencies acquired by generalisation from N, but such an effect would apply only to the results for group 1 in which B evoked less suppression than A. For group 2, by contrast, it was stimulus B that evoked more suppression.

Our general conclusion, therefore, is that stimuli that have been accompanied by identical consequences will tend to be treated as equivalent. The mechanism responsible could well be that proposed by Miller and Dollard (1941). Two stimuli that have both been followed by food (e.g. B and N for group 2 of the experiment just described) will tend to elicit the same response. Any cues elicited by this response will become associated with shock when the noise is presented along with shock in the second phase of training. Stimulus B, by virtue of the fact that it tends to elicit these same cues, will thus be likely to evoke the response that was conditioned to them during training with the noise.

This analysis can be applied with success to other experimental procedures that have been used to demonstrate acquired equivalence. Vaughan (1988) trained pigeons with 40 different pictorial stimuli, 20 of which were arbitrarily designated as positive (response to these yielded food) and 20 of which were designated as negative. When this discrimination had been learned, the reinforcement contingencies were reversed. After a series of such reversals, the birds demonstrated acquired equivalence in that, on the first session of a reversal, experience of the changed contingencies for just some of the stimuli engendered an appropriate change in the pattern of behaviour shown to the remainder. Thus, for example, by the end of the session, the birds were tending to respond only slowly to instances of the "positive" class as a consequence of the fact that other instances of this class had been associated with non-reward earlier in the session. We can interpret this finding by noting that all instances of the positive class will, at the start of the test session, tend to evoke the same response (e.g. an approach to the response-key). This response will, however, not be followed by reinforcement. It would, therefore, become a cue signalling non-reward that will be effective in suppressing key-pecking when it is elicited by other members of the class of (previously) positive stimuli.

Vaughan's (1988) experiment adopts a quite different procedure from that more usually employed in studies of the equivalence relation. More typical is the procedure used by McIntire et al. (1987), in which their subjects (monkeys) were trained initially on a conditional discrimination (if A has just been seen, choose B rather than C) and were then tested with B as the conditional cue. In this experiment (in contrast to several others of similar design that have used non-human animals as the subjects), it was found that A and B were equivalent in that using B as the conditional cue was effective in promoting the choice of A. A unique feature of the experiment by McIntire et al. (1987), which may be responsible for the effect they obtained, was that the subjects were required to make topographically quite different responses to stimuli that were designated by the experimenter as belonging to different classes. For stimuli belonging to the same class (e.g. A and B in the example cited above), the same response pattern was required. Thus the response evoked by A could have become a cue signalling that choice of a stimulus (B) associated with a similar pattern of response would be reinforced. If so, appropriate choice would be maintained when the roles of A and B were interchanged. This interpretation of their results (which is essentially that adopted by McIntire et al. themselves) can be seen as a further example of the general principle, outlined above, that stimuli having common consequences (i.e. common associates) tend to be treated as equivalent.

THE EMERGENCE OF RATIONAL THOUGHT

Recent computational, connectionist theories of cognition have made great play with the notion of "emergence", being concerned to demonstrate that the ability to perform "higher mental functions" might emerge from interactions within a system composed of really rather simple "units". But this suggestion has long been current among those working in associative learning theory, and this chapter can be seen as an exercise in that tradition. It has taken the excitatory link between event-representations as its basic unit and has tried to demonstrate (with what success the reader must judge) that phenomena taken by many to characterise rational thought can emerge from a consideration of the ways in which these units interact and of the conditions that determine the formation of associative links.

The associative mechanisms postulated here are usually supposed to be common to all vertebrate species (Macphail, 1982), and this brings us to another sense in which rational thought might be described as "emerging". Given the widespread interpretation of rational thought as being essentially an ability to manipulate the world using symbols, and given that human language is a very extensive system of symbolic representation, it is no surprise to come across the view that rationality will emerge only with the (phylogenetic and ontogenetic) emergence of language. But if reasoning depends only on associative processes, why should language make such a difference—why do not non-human species (and humans lacking linguistic capacity) reason as adult, intelligent humans do?

In answer to this question, I will restrict myself to making three (somewhat contentious) points. The first (and least contentious) is simply to state a standard criticism of much comparative (and developmental) psychology, i.e. that much of it consists of demonstrating that a given species (or age group) cannot perform a given task and that such demonstrations cannot prove the null hypothesis. Given appropriate conditions of training, many animals may be better at reasoning than we have supposed. Secondly, it may be inappropriate to make any rigid distinction between the processes involved in associative learning and those involved in reasoning by the manipulation of symbols. A monkey may treat two stimuli as equivalent because each has come to control the same motor response; but is this in principle different from what human beings do when they learn to attach the same word to physically different events? The final point follows from this: Monkeys may need special training to learn to apply "names" to stimuli and the range of such names available to them will be rather limited. Adult humans have, by way of their language, a much more elaborate system for symbolic representations which they seem to apply automatically. But however great the gulf between monkey and man in their reasoning ability, the difference appears to be quantitative rather than qualitative.

Lacking empirical evidence to support these assertions, I can only offer argument from authority and turn again to the works of Hume with which we began this chapter. Hume (1888, p. 610) acknowledges that "men are superior to beasts principally by the superiority of their reasoning", but he also states the following:

> No truth appears to me more evident, than that beasts are endowed with thought and reason as well as men . . . when any hypothesis is advanced to explain a mental operation, which is common to both men and beasts, we must apply the same hypothesis to both . . .. The common defect of those systems, which philosophers have employed to account for the actions of the mind, is, that they suppose such a subtility and refinement of thought, as not only exceeds the capacity of mere animals, but even of children and the common people of our own species (Hume, 1888, pp. 176–177).

ACKNOWLEDGEMENTS

Some of the experimental work described in this chapter was supported by a grant from the UK Science and Engineering Research Council. I thank C. Bonardi, R. Honey, E. Macphail and, particularly, P. Reed for their comments on an earlier version of this chapter.

REFERENCES

Brogden, W. J. (1939). Sensory pre-conditioning. *Journal of Experimental Psychology*, *25*, 323–332.

Catania, A. C. & Keller, K. J. (1981). Contingency, contiguity, correlation, and the concept of causation. In P. Harzem & M. D. Zeiler (Eds), *Predictability, correlation, and contiguity*, pp. 125–167. Chichester: John Wiley.

D'Amato, M. R., Salmon, D. P., Loukas, E., & Tomie, A. (1985). Symmetry and transitivity of conditional relations in monkeys (*Cebus apella*) and pigeons (*Columba livia*). *Journal of the Experimental Analysis of Behavior*, *4*, 35–47.

Dickinson, A. (1980). *Contemporary animal learning theory*. Cambridge: Cambridge University Press.

Dickinson, A. (1989). The expectancy theory of animal conditioning. In S. B. Klein & R. Mowrer (Eds), *Contemporary learning theories: Pavlovian conditioning and the status of traditional learning theory*, pp. 279–308. Hillsdale, N.J.: Lawrence Erlbaum Associates Inc.

Dickinson, A. & Shanks, D. (1985). Animal conditioning and human causality judgement. In L.-G. Nilsson & T. Archer (Eds), *Perspectives on learning and memory*, pp. 167–191. Hillsdale, N.J.: Lawrence Erlbaum Associates Inc.

Dickinson, A., Shanks, D., & Evenden, J. (1984). Judgement of act-outcome contingency: The role of selective attribution. *Quarterly Journal of Experimental Psychology*, *36A*, 29–50.

Ellis, H. C. & Muller, D. G. (1964). Transfer in perceptual learning following stimulus predifferentiation. *Journal of Experimental Psychology*, *68*, 388–395.

Epstein, W. (1967). *Varieties of perceptual learning*. New York: McGraw-Hill.

Hall, G. (1976). Learning to ignore irrelevant stimuli: Variations within and between displays. *Quarterly Journal of Experimental Psychology*, *28*, 247–253.

Hall, G. & Channell, S. (1980). A search for perceptual differentiation produced by non-differential reinforcement. *Quarterly Journal of Experimental Psychology*, *32*, 185–195.

Hall, G. & Honey, R. C. (1989). Perceptual and associative learning. In S. B. Klein & R. Mowrer (Eds), *Contemporary learning theories: Pavlovian conditioning and the status of traditional learning theory*, pp. 117–147. Hillsdale, N.J.: Lawrence Erlbaum Associates Inc.

Heth, C. D. & Rescorla, R. A. (1973). Simultaneous and backward fear conditioning in the rat. *Journal of Comparative and Physiological Psychology*, *82*, 434–443.

Holland, P. C. (1981). Acquisition of representation-mediated conditioned food aversions. *Learning and Motivation*, *12*, 1–18.

Holland, P. C. & Straub, J. J. (1979). Differential effects of two ways of devaluing the unconditioned stimulus after Pavlovian appetitive conditioning. *Journal of Experimental Psychology: Animal Behavior Processes*, *5*, 65–78.

Hume, D. (1888). *A treatise of human nature* (edited by L. A. Selby-Bigge). Oxford: Clarendon Press. (Originally published 1739)

Hume, D. (1902). *Enquiries concerning the human understanding and concerning the principles of morals* (edited by L. A. Selby-Bigge). Oxford: Clarendon Press. (Originally published 1748)

Konorski, J. (1967). *Integrative activity of the brain*. Chicago: University of Chicago Press.

Lawrence, D. H. (1949). Acquired distinctiveness of cues: I. Transfer between discriminations on the basis of familiarity with the stimulus. *Journal of Experimental Psychology*, *39*, 770–784.

McIntire, K. D., Cleary, J., & Thompson, T. (1987). Conditional relations by monkeys: Reflexivity, symmetry, and transitivity. *Journal of the Experimental Analysis of Behavior*, *47*, 279–285.

Maier, N. R. F. (1929). Reasoning in white rats. *Comparative Psychology Monograph*, No. 6.

Mackintosh, N. J. & Dickinson, A. (1979). Instrumental (type II) conditioning. In A. Dickinson & R. A. Boakes (Eds), *Mechanisms of learning and motivation*, pp. 143–167. Hillsdale, N.J.: Lawrence Erlbaum Associates Inc.

Macphail, E. M. (1982). *Brain and intelligence in vertebrates*. Oxford: Clarendon Press.
Miller, N. E. & Dollard, J. (1941). *Social learning and imitation*. New Haven, Conn.: Yale University Press.
Munn, N. L. (1947). *Psychology*. London: Harrap.
Pearce, J. M. & Hall, G. (1980). A model for Pavlovian learning: Variations in the effectiveness of conditioned but not of unconditioned stimuli. *Psychological Review*, *87*, 532–552.
Rescorla, R. A. (1968). Probability of shock in the presence and absence of CS in fear conditioning. *Journal of Comparative and Physiological Psychology*, *6*, 1–5.
Rescorla, R. A. (1980). Simultaneous and successive associations in sensory preconditioning. *Journal of Experimental Psychology: Animal Behavior Processes*, *6*, 207–216.
Rescorla, R. A. (1981). Simultaneous associations. In P. Harzem & M. D. Zeiler (Eds), *Predictability, correlation, and contiguity*, pp. 47–80. Chichester: John Wiley.
Rescorla, R. A. & Cunningham, C. L. (1978). Within-compound flavour associations. *Journal of Experimental Psychology: Animal Behavior Processes*, *4*, 267–275.
Rescorla, R. A. & Cunningham, C. L. (1979). Spatial contiguity facilitates Pavlovian second-order conditioning. *Journal of Experimental Psychology: Animal Behavior Processes*, *5*, 152–161.
Rescorla, R. A. & Wagner, A. R. (1972). A theory of Pavlovian conditioning: Variations in the effectivenes of reinforcement and nonreinforcement. In A. H. Black & W. F. Prokasy (Eds), *Classical conditioning II: Current research and theory*, pp. 64–99. New York: Appleton-Century-Crofts.
Robinson, J. S. (1955). The effects of learning verbal labels for stimuli on their later discrimination. *Journal of Experimental Psychology*, *49*, 112–114.
Shanks, D. & Dickinson, A. (1987). Associative accounts of causality judgement. In G. H. Bower (Ed.), *The psychology of learning and motivation*, Vol. 21, pp. 229–261. London: Academic Press.
Sidman, M. & Tailby, W. (1982). Conditional discrimination *vs* matching to sample: An expansion of the testing paradigm. *Journal of the Experimental Analysis of Behavior*, *37*, 5–22.
Siegel, S. (1967). Overtraining and transfer processes. *Journal of Comparative and Physiological Psychology*, *64*, 471–477.
Smith, M. C., Coleman, S. R., & Gormezano, I. (1969). Classical conditioning of the rabbit's nictitating membrane response at backward, simultaneous, and forward CS–US intervals. *Journal of Comparative and Physiological Psychology*, *69*, 226–231.
Sutherland, N. S. & Mackintosh, N. J. (1971). *Mechanisms of animal discrimination learning*. London: Academic Press.
Vaughan, W. (1988). Formation of equivalence sets in pigeons. *Journal of Experimental Psychology: Animal Behavior Processes*, *14*, 36–42.
Wagner, A. R. & Larew, M. B. (1985). Opponent processes and Pavlovian inhibition. In R. R. Miller & N. E. Spear (Eds), *Information processing in animals: Conditioned inhibition*, pp. 233–265. Hillsdale, N.J.: Lawrence Erlbaum Associates Inc.
Wagner, A. R., Logan, F. A., Haberlandt, K., & Price, T. (1968). Stimulus selection in animal discrimination learning. *Journal of Experimental Psychology*, *76*, 171–180.
Wagner, A. R. & Rescorla, R. A. (1972). Inhibition in Pavlovian conditioning: Application of a theory. In R. A. Boakes & M. S. Halliday (Eds), *Inhibition and learning*, pp. 301–336. London: Academic Press.

III BEHAVIOUR ANALYSIS AND LANGUAGE

8 Some Determinants of the Production of Temporal Markers

J. P. Bronckart
Faculté de Psychologie et des Sciences de l'Education, Université de Genève, Genève, Switzerland

The primary objective of this chapter is to present several aspects of a research project which is currently underway and the goal of which is to identify the parameters which govern temporal markers in texts produced by children.

The study has three main features. First, it is developmental in that we are working with children of three different ages: 10, 12 and 14 years. Secondly, it is comparative in that five languages are being studied simultaneously: German, Basque, Catalan, French and Italian. Thirdly, for theoretical reasons we will discuss later, it deals with four different types of texts: narratives, reports, conversational stories and explanatory texts.

For each of the five languages and each of the three age levels, we asked four groups of 30 pupils to produce the four types of text. Our study thus involves 1800 texts produced by 1800 different subjects.

The object of our investigation (the dependent variables of the experimental design) is temporal markers; that is, the following linguistic units:

1. The verbs themselves (or the verbal lexemes);
2. The verbal endings (or "tenses");
3. The different kinds of auxiliaries;
4. The temporal adverbs distributed within the verbphrase;
5. The various types of temporal connectives distributed within the sentence unit (conjunctions, temporal adverbs, temporal prepositional phrases).

In what follows, we will present successively:

1. A short recapitulation of research already done in this area.
2. The theoretical framework we have adopted and the hypotheses which are derived from it.
3. The general characteristics of our methodology and some results with regard to French.

THE EVOLUTION OF THE RESEARCH PROBLEM

An analysis of the vast amount of research carried out in this area shows a clear evolution which can be summarised as the transition from a sentence-oriented outlook to a textual or discursive outlook.

The Sentence-oriented Outlook

Research based on this approach has been conducted by Antinucci and Miller (1976), Bloom, Lifter, and Hafitz (1980), and Bronckart (1976), among others. Our experiment had the following characteristics:

Materials. A collection of toys was used: dolls (two boys and two girls), cars, trucks, one dog, one cat, one sheep, one fish, a basin of water, a farm with several animals, several fences, a ball, a bottle, a garage, etc.

Experimental Design. The experimenter first showed the toys to the child and explained what they were if the child did not seem to recognise them. Secondly, he gave the following instructions: "I'm going to do something with the toys and you are going to look carefully at what happens and, after that, you are going to tell me everything. Try not to forget anything." The experimenter then proceeded to perform some actions with the toys (e.g. the dog knocks over the bottle; the horse jumps over the fences; a fish swims in the basin). He induced the child to give an adequate description of the event, and he made it quite clear that the child had to wait until the action was finished before starting his description.

Two categories of parameters were monitored and made up the independent variables:

1. The "internal" characteristics of the event mimed: duration (1–15 sec); distance travelled (from 0 to 100 cm); attainment or non-attainment of a result.

2. The time between the end of the action and the start of the production of the sentence (from 2 to 25 sec).

Dependent Variables. The temporal markers analysed were verbs, verb tenses, and temporal adverbs. The main observed tenses were as follows:

Présent	"le cheval *saute*"
Passé composé	"le cheval *a sauté*"
Passé simple	"le cheval *sauta*"
Imparfait	"le cheval *sautait*"
Plus-que-parfait	"le cheval *avait sauté*"

In this type of experimental situation, the results showed a very clear developmental pattern.

1. In children under 6 years of age, the use of verb tenses is clearly dependent on internal characteristics of the action. In French, for example, the shorter an event and the more evident the result, the more likely the verb used to describe it will be conjugated in the *passé composé*; if the event does not have a result or if it is of long duration, the verb will generally be conjugated in the *présent*; if the event lasts a long time and involves displacement over a long distance, it will be conjugated in the *imparfait*. Although the results are clear at the statistical level, a large proportion of the subjects did not produce the anticipated tense. In these cases, it can be shown that it is the choice of the verb which determines the choice of the tense; certain verbs (e.g. "*être*" are always conjugated in the *présent*; others, such as "*venir*", are always conjugated in the *passe compose*. It should also be noted that at this age, the variable "time lapse" between the end of the action and the beginning of the production has no bearing on the use of tenses.
2. At 6 years of age, the situation begins to evolve and, at 8 years, there is a reversal of the tendency. At age 8, it is the "time lapse" factor which influences the use of tenses. When the lapse is short (2 sec), all the verbs are conjugated in the *présent*; when it is long, all the verbs are conjugated in the past, regardless of the internal characteristics of the action. The dependence on the type of verb chosen also vanishes at this stage, and the appearance of syntagmatic adverbs which specify certain internal characteristics of the event ("*vite*", "*lentement*", etc.) is to be observed.

These results were subjected to a two-fold interpretation—linguistic and cognitive. At the linguistic level, the evolution observed was summarised by the formula *aspect before time*. At an initial stage, the use of temporal markers is dependent on the characteristics of the action (either directly or through the lexical choices), and subjects therefore attribute an aspectual function to these markers. At a second stage, the use of the same markers becomes dependent on the temporal distance and the subjects therefore attribute to the markers the temporal function they appear to have for adults. At the cognitive level, the same data were interpreted in terms of progressive decentring (the "Strong Decentring Hypothesis" modelled after Piaget): Children under 6 years of age, because of the egocentrism of their reasoning, are only able to take into consideration the internal characteristics of the action; with access to concrete operations and the resultant development of decentring abilities, they become capable of situating the moment of the action in relation to the moment of production and, thus, to construct genuine temporal relations.

The Discursive Outlook

These initial data have been criticised on three accounts. First, a series of replication studies using similar experimental paradigms were carried out (Di Paolo & Smith, 1978; Harner, 1980; 1981; Smith, 1980). These studies did not refute the general trends observed (they confirmed, in particular, the clear dependence of the choice of tenses with regard to the verbal item in the case of young children), but they also showed that children of less than 6 years of age are capable, in certain situations, of using verb endings to code temporal relationships. The "Strong Decentring Hyopthesis" must therefore be abandoned.

Secondly, many authors have stressed the distinctly artificial character of the experimental situations used, on two points:

1. The technique of the mime (and the use of toys) considerably reduces the types of actions which can be carried out and, hence, the types of sentences which can be proposed to the subjects.
2. The sentences are context-free, which makes it possible only to deal with one aspect of language, namely its *representative* function, which is not its most interesting aspect when one is attempting to investigate a category as clearly deictic (and, hence, *communicative*) as time.

The third type of criticism concerns the very conceptualisation of the categories "time" and "aspect". Rejecting the sentence-oriented outlook which is implicit in the works we have just mentioned and adopting a resolutely textual approach, many authors revealed the existence of other factors (or determinants) likely to govern the use of temporal markers in a text. The following factors, in particular, were mentioned:

1. *The type of text produced*. Researchers such as Benveniste (1959) and Weinrich (1964) have distinguished between "discursive" texts and "narrative" texts and have shown that these two forms use clearly distinct paradigms of temporal markers. Further investigations were carried out by Vet (1980) and Simonin-Grumbach (1975), the latter showing that in French, there existed at least four subsystems of temporal markers: two systems on the "discourse" side (discourse in situation and theoretical

discourse) and two on the "narrative" side (conversational story and the narrative proper).

2. The *text plan*. With respect to stories and narratives—in particular, since Propp (1928)—there is evidence of the existence of superstructures (i.e. relatively precise text plans) organised in successive phases. Building on the work of Labov and Waletzky (1967), most researchers define these phases in terms of *origin*, *exposition*, *complication*, *evalutation*, *resolution* and *coda*. Various authors (e.g. Schiffrin, 1981, for English; Fayol, 1981; 1985, for French) have shown that the distribution of various temporal markers is dependent on the phase of the plan.

3. The *mechanisms of cohesion*. Weinrich (1964) was the first to hypothesise that temporal markers also served to distinguish the foreground from the background of a text, and this theory was confirmed by Hopper and Thompson (1980), who stressed the more generalised role of temporal markers in maintaining textual cohesion (this concerns a new analysis of the phenomenon described classically as the "sequence of tenses").

4. The *modalisation mechanisms*. Various temporal markers apparently help express the enunciator's stand in relation to certain aspects of the content he is evoking (expression of probability, certainty, etc.).

These studies have two important implications for us. First, any analysis of the determinants of the production of temporal markers in a text implies that not only should the two traditional factors of the characteristics of the action and the temporal relationship be taken into account, but also the four factors listed above. Secondly, the setting up of an experimental research to ascertain the respective weight of these factors implies the formulation of a general model of discourse production which arranges these various potential determinants in hierarchical order. We will now discuss the general characteristics of this model, on which we have been working for around 10 years and which was first described exhaustively in our collective work *Le fonctionnement des discours* (Bronckart et al., 1985).

FRAME OF REFERENCE

Two aspects of our frame of reference are presented here. First, the general principles modelled on the theory of *social interactionism*, specifically on Vygotsky and Leontiev's theory of activity (see Wertsch, 1979). These principles will enable us to formulate hypotheses on the status of verbal behaviour and its determinants. Next, some proposals are put forward concerning the *linguistic operations* which underlie the production of these same behaviours, in particular, the production of temporal markers. The term "linguistic operation" is related to that of "cognitive operation", as used by Piaget.

General Principles of Social Interactionism

First, human beings form groups and function within these groups; their behaviour develops within the framework of various interactions or activities which find their expression in actions of diverse kinds. These actions can be defined as sets of behaviours oriented by a goal and determined by four social parameters:

1. The social setting, or the institution in which the action takes place.
2. The social role (or social situation) of the enunciator.
3. The social role of the addressee.
4. The purpose of the interaction or the goal which we define as the "projection of the effect of the action on the addressee".

The value which each of these parameters of *social interaction* take on (What institution is concerned? What social roles are being played? What goal is pursued?) define a given linguistic action. For example, in the social context "university", a linguistic action is initiated by an individual playing the role of teacher, for the benefit of other individuals having the status of students, in order to convince the latter to read Skinner's book *Verbal behavior* in its entirety.

Secondly, although linguistic actions are primarily social, they are also concretely anchored in a physical situation which we call the *enunciation situation* and which is defined by four other parameters: the time of the action, the place of the action, the producer and the co-producers (the interlocutors).

The parameters of social interaction, as well as those of the enunciation situation, define the *context* of a linguistic action.

Thirdly, linguistic actions are executed in the form of verbal signs which convey a certain number of representations of the world. We suggest that these representations are organised in the memory of the interlocutors, prior to being translated into verbal behaviour. They constitute the *referent* of a linguistic action.

Fourthly, the two aspects of the context (the parameters of social interaction on the one hand, and the physical act of enunciation on the other), together with the referent, make up the entire set of *potential determinants of a linguistic action*. They provide a possible explanation for the characteristics of verbal behaviour.

Fifthly, the observables of the linguistic action (or of verbal behaviour) are textual corpora, which can be broken down into linguistic units (morphemes). These minimal units of textual corpora could be the object of a first, descriptive analysis; they can be identified, labelled and categorised using the strict distributional approach proposed by Bloomfield (1933).

Finally, these same observables can also be the object of a second analysis, this time explanatory. Indeed, if every linguistic unit is under the control of extralinguistic determinants (referent and context), from a psychological point of view, we can consider that the production of each unit is the result of operations performed on the context and on the referent within the constraints imposed by the system of the natural language being used. The notion of "linguistic operation" accounts for the psychological processing to which extralinguistic parameters need to be subjected if effective verbal behaviour is to result.

The Linguistic Operations

In *Le fonctionnement des discours*, we constructed a first operations model. I will now present certain aspects of this model, limiting myself to the elements pertinent to temporal markers. It is a simplified sampling, which deliberately bypasses a number of thorny problems, such as lexicalisation in the case of natural languages and those related to the heterogeneity of texts. Let us recall that the object of these operations is the different types of processes that subjects have to perform on the parameters of the content and the context, within the constraints of a given natural language, to culminate in a text *per se*. These operations are extemporaneous in character and in no way compromise processes which subjects initiate, in real time, in the actual production of statements. I will present four categories of operations.

Category 1. The first category of operations involves the structuring of the referent and its lexicalisation. Let us look at its two main aspects:

1. As we have already said, the referent of a text (its content) is preorganised in the mind of the speaker. We postulate that this organisation is based on a distinction between two forms of representation: "notions" (representations of objects) and "relations" (representations of relationships between notions). We likewise postulate that these representations have properties, the result of the empirical experiences of the subject in the world. With regard to relations, which alone concern us here, the two main properties are the degree of transitivity and the degree of perfectivity. A relation can be transitive to various degrees (it can link one or more notions) and it can be perfective to various degrees (it can change more or less profoundly the notions to which it applies). To simplify, the combina-

tion of these two classes of properties makes it possible to distinguish relations of state (generally expressed by a sentence like "John is tired"), imperfective processes ("John sees a three"), and perfective processes ("John broke a chair"). The properties of these relations, which pre-exist in the memory of the speaker, correspond in part to what is customarily called "aspect" in linguistics and constitute the first potential determinant of the use of temporal markers.

2. When a text is produced, the various representations of the world are the object of lexicalisation within the framework of the natural language used: They are concretised by means of one of the signifiers available in the language and familiar to the speaker. In the case of relations, this concretisation will generally consist in the choice of a verb, and this choice (as shown in experiments mentioned in the first part of this chapter) constitutes the second potential determinant of the use of temporal markers.

Category 2. The second category of operations concerns the choice of the type of text. In every language, there exist different kinds of textual organisation, which are sometimes referred to as "forms of text": story, narrative, theoretical discourse, report, explanation, argumentation, etc. One must be clearly aware that several types of text can be chosen for a given linguistic action, defined by the parameters of social interaction which we have already discussed. Let us use our previous example. A university professor initiates a linguistic action consisting in persuading a student to read *Verbal behavior*. He then has the choice between several discourse possibilities:

1. He can elaborate a discourse emphasising the intrinsic qualities of this book. The result will be a theoretical and/or argumentative text.
2. He can also tell how he discovered the book, the difficulties he experienced at the outset in reading it and, finally, the interest he took in the book. In this case he would produce a story.
3. He can question his students about the reservations they might have and discuss these reservations with them, in which case he will construct a discourse in situation.
4. He could perhaps think up a parable or a symbolic story and thus enter into the narrative form of discourse.

To our view, the operation consisting in the choice of the type of text is the result of a double calculation, involving the parameters of the social interaction—a calculation of the relationship existing between the content (or referent) and the parameters of the interaction—and a second calculation of the relationship between the material parameters of the enunciation and the same parameters of social interaction.

The first calculation consists in establishing a relationship of *disjunction* or *conjunction* between the referent and the interaction. The referent may either be placed "outside" of the interaction, in which case it is disjoint and this disjunction is marked by an "origin" (*yesterday*, *one day*, *once upon a time*)—this is the case with stories and narratives; or, the referent is not placed outside, in which case it is conjoint, whether the conjunction be real or symbolic—consequently, there is no origin as is the case in theoretical texts and discourse in situation.

The second calculation consists in establishing a relationship of either *involvement* or *autonomy* between parameters of the social interaction and the enunciation situation. Either the goal and the mode of interaction "involve" and "solicit" the time-space of the enunciation or the interlocutors (this is indicated by the presence of deictic pronouns and deictic adverbs, and this is typical of the discourse in situation and of the story); or, the goal and the mode of interaction do not interact, and this is indicated by the absence of these very markers, which is characteristic of narratives and of theoretical texts.

The product of these two calculations enables us to define the four textual archetypes of French (see Table 8.1): the DS ("discourse in situation"), the CS ("conversational story"), the TD ("theoretical discourse"), and the N ("narratives").

With regard to the observables of verbal behaviour, the choice of the type of text has two main consequences:

1. The selection of a *subset of linguistic units*, more or less specific in type, especially a subset of temporal markers.
2. The construction of a *form of plan*, which is also specific; narrative superstructure: story, theoretical argumentation or discourse in situation plans.

The choice of the type of text, therefore, makes up the third potential determinant of the use of temporal markers, and, as many authors have shown, the text plan phases constitute a fourth.

TABLE 8.1
The Four Textual Archetypes of French

	Conjunction	*Disjunction*
Involvement	DS	CS
Autonomy	TD	N

DS, Discourse in situation; CS, conversational story; TD, theoretical discourse; N, narrative (after Bronckart et al., 1985).

Category 3. The third set of operations corresponds to what is traditionally referred to as *temporal relations*. On this point, we draw on Reichenbach's (1947) trichotomous conceptualisation. According to the solutions proposed by Reichenbach, establishing a temporal relation means setting up a relationship between three elements: the moment of the event referred to, the moment of speech, and a moment of reference which Reichenbach calls "psychological". Let us take as an example the following statement:

> *Cette année, je donne un cours de linguistique générale à l'Université de Genève.*

One immediately observes that the use of the present tense does not express a relation of simultaneity between the moment of speech and the moment of the event (I am not teaching a course at this very moment!); rather, it expresses that the moment of the event and the moment of speech are both within a moment of reference expressed by *cette année*. Transposing this concept to the textual plane, we can consider that each type of text contains an axis of reference which has a precise relationship to the moment of speech, and that the different events or states mentioned in the text are pinpointed or situated in relation to this axis of reference. Let us take a classic example of a narrative text.

> *Le 12 décembre 1602*, les savoyards établirent leur camp sur la colline de Cologny; *le lendemain*, il pleuvait et ils firent une brève reconnaissance de la ville de Genève; *trois jours après*, leur capitaine, qui avait beaucoup réfléchi, décida d'attaquer à la nuit tombée . . .

In this excerpt, the origin (*le 12 décembre 1602*) expresses the relation between the moment of speech and the text's temporal axis of reference. This axis consists of the same origin together with its temporal relays, which are in the text (*le lendemain, trois jours après*) and each event expressed by a verb is situated in relation to this axis. Direct temporal pinpointing gives the two basic tenses of the narrative in the French text, the *passé simple* and the *imparfait*; more complex pinpointing, which we will not describe here, produces tenses such as the *plus-que-parfait* (*avait réfléchi*) the *passé antérieur*, and so on.

Category 4. The fourth type of operation which we will mention concerns one of the mechanisms of textualisation; in this case, the preservation of the *cohesion* of the text and, more precisely, the distinction between the foreground and the background. In our example, this distinction is expressed by the opposition between *imparfait* and *passé simple*. It makes up the sixth potential determinant of the use of temporal markers in a text.

There exist still other potential determinants (e.g. with regard to modalisations), but the six we have described are amply sufficient for our purposes.

RESEARCH METHODOLOGY

Our research approach relies on the *experimental analysis of behaviour* and we consider that the object of our study is the role played by *extralinguistic factors* (the parameters of the context and content) in the development and functioning of verbal behaviour; given, of course, the fact that these extralinguistic factors are the object of a set of psychological treatments or operations in the sense in which we have just defined them. Consequently, at the methodological level, we have adopted the following approach. We try to control the extralinguistic parameters, that is to say, we define precise, limiting conditions of text production, in which the independent variables are the referent (the content) and the parameters of the context, as defined by us. We collect the texts produced under these conditions, and our dependent variables are the linguisitc units observable in the textual corpora. The dependent variables are subjected to a first, distributional and statistical analysis, which enables us to categorise linguistically the corpus of texts produced. Finally, a second analysis aims at measuring the effect of the controlled independent variables on the use of the various linguistic units, which allows us to formulate hypotheses on the operations which their use implies, i.e. the respective weights of their different potential determinants.

This methodological approach will now be illustrated by the presentation of the research project dealing with temporal markers.

Background Information Concerning the Population

The experiment involved five different languages and was carried out in five cities: Modena for Italian, Barcelona for Catalan, San Sebastian for Basque, Bern for German, and Geneva for French. For each language, we worked with children of three ages (10, 12 and 14), and for each age group, we set up four groups of 30 subjects, who were subjected to four text production conditions. The four production conditions were the same for each language and each age group.

The Text Production Conditions

For three of the four production conditions, we showed the subjects a silent film for 3–4 min, illustrating the content of the text to be produced. In this way we controlled the referential content of the text. For each production condition we also elaborated a complex set of directions, designed to control contextual parameters: for whom the text was intended, for what purpose it was written, what social role the writer was to play, etc.

In condition A, the videotape showed an excerpt from the story of *Snow White* and the directions can be summarised as follows:

> Tell the story of Snow White as you would to a pupil who is younger than you and who is not familiar with it.

In condition B, the videotape showed a news item (the arrest of a driver by the police) and the directions can be summarised as follows:

> Imagine you are a journalist. Write a newspaper article reporting the events which occurred in the City of X this afternoon.

In condition C, the videotape showed the operation of a lock and the directions can be summarised as follows:

> Explain what a lock is for and how it functions to a pupil younger than you and who has never seen one.

In condition D, there was no videotape. The directions can be summarised as follows:

> Write a letter in which you tell a story which is funny, sad or exciting, an adventure you had recently. Write it to X (a pupil in a parallel class), who is your age and who is also going to write you a letter.'

These production conditions were designed to limit the choice of text as much as possible—in condition A, we expected a "narrative" type of text; in B, a "report" type of text; in C, a "theoretical explanation", and in D, a "conversational story".

Analysis of the Data

The analysis of the data comprised three distinct phases. In the first phase, we applied to each text the global text analysis grid presented in *Le fonctionnement des discours* (Bronckart et al., 1985). This grid (which, fortunately, is partly automated) makes it possible to detect the frequency of occurrence of 27 linguistic marks (the different pronouns, verb tenses, auxiliaries, connectives, adverbs, etc.). An index of relative frequency is computed for each mark according to the number of words and the number of verbs in the text. Obviously, the grids are different for each of the five languages.

These data are the object of extensive statistical treatment (analysis of variance and correspondency), the purpose of which is to identify the type of text effectively produced by each subject. To do this we relied on a previous study involving several thousands of texts already identified as being narratives, reports, theoretical explanations and conversational stories. Analysis of variance and discriminant analysis procedures enabled us to define the profiles of linguistic units characteristic of these texts. A comparison of the earlier data and the data from the present investigation allow us to ensure that the texts produced indeed correspond to the type expected, i.e. that the texts produced in condition A are narratives, in B, reports, etc. The texts which did not correspond to the type expected were excluded from the subsequent analysis.

The second phase focused more specifically on temporal markers, i.e. on the paradigm of units defined at the beginning of this article (tenses, auxiliaries, adverbs, etc.). It consists in the characterisation of each text from this point of view and comprises the following analyses:

1. An examination of the statisical parameters of the distribution of each unit.

2. An examination of the typical text profiles with regard to tense usage. Using an analysis of correspondences, we grouped the texts along an axis according to the tense profiles used. The example which follows (see Fig. 8.1) concerns report texts (or news items) in French produced by 12-year-olds. The texts in this group are represented by a cross. Two factors, represented by the two axes, explain 45 and 39% of the total inertia, respectively, and therefore account for 84% of the variance. The horizontal axis is essentially made up of the opposition of the *passé simple* to the positive pole and of the *présent* to the negative pole. The vertical axis contrasts essentially the *passé composé* and the *passé simple*. Fig. 8.1 indicates to us in fact that we can consider these texts to be distributed in three subsets: those which are saturated in the *présent* (11 cases), those which are saturated in the *passé simple* (11 cases), and those saturated in the *passé composé* (4 cases). The crosses which stand outside these three dense areas represent the few texts which mix the three basic tenses. One can also note that the other tenses are close to the intersection of the two axes. This mean that their distribution in the three groups is equivalent, with the *imparfait* and *plus-que-parfait* more in accord with the group of texts saturated in the *passé simple*.

3. A study, using an analysis of correspondences, of the phenomena of interaction between different types of markers.

4. Finally, using the same technique, an analysis was carried out of the groupings among the groups of texts and markers, making it possible to identify the typical or discriminant units in each type of text, for a given age group.

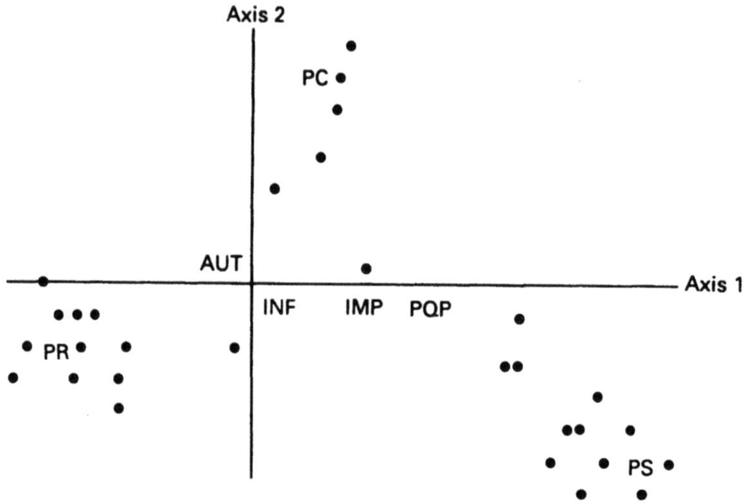

FIG. 8.1. An analysis of correspondences representing the distribution of tenses and reports texts in an axial plan (French 12-year-olds). PR, *présent*; PC, *passé composé*; PS, *passé simple*; IMP, *imparfait*; PQP, *plus-que-parfait*; INF, *infinitif*; AUT, other tenses.

Once these various analyses were completed, we obtained a set of measures of the effect of one of the potential determinants of the use of temporal markers, i.e. the choice of the type of text.

The third phase consists in calculating the degree of dependence of each of these classes of temporal markers in comparison to four other potential determinants:

Determinant 1: The degree of perfectivity of the event. Based on an analysis of the content of the videotapes, we will classify *a priori* the expressible relations as state, perfective process and imperfective process, and calculate the incidence of this variable on the distribution of temporal markers, limiting ourselves to the verbphrase which acts as the vehicle of the relation.

Determinant 2: The type of verb. On a sampling of relations (those expressed most often in the texts), we will proceed to classify the verbal items chosen, and we will calculate the incidence of this choice on the temporal marks of the verbphrase.

Determinant 3: The text plan. On the basis of our analysis of the content of the videotapes, we will define *a priori* the phases of the plan and calculate the incidence of this variable on the distribution of all the temporal markers in each sentence.

Determinant 4: The distinction between foreground and background. Again, on the basis of our analysis of the content of the videotapes, we will distinguish two levels in the text, and calculate the incidence of this opposition on the distribution of temporal markers as a whole.

This, then, is our programme of research. At the present time, all of the corpora have been collected and have been transcribed on the computer (with a system of codification of all markers); the first two phases of the analysis have been carried out on the five languages, and phase three is underway. The results available to date show a very significant effect of the text production conditions on the distribution of the temporal markers in the five languages. Three groups of texts are to be distinguished:

1. The theoretical explanation, with a tense profile always in the present.
2. The narrative and the report, with different systems of past tenses in the five languages (one basis tense in German, two tenses in Catalan, French and Italian, and three past tenses in Basque).
3. The conversational story, which always combines two subsystems of tenses, clearly dependent of the phases of the plan: one in the present, the other in the past.

Much remains to be done with respect to each language and with respect to the comparison of the results between the five languages, before general conclusions can be drawn.

ACKNOWLEDGEMENTS

This research was supported by Grant 1.406-0.86 from the Fonds National Suisse de la Recherce Scientifique.

REFERENCES

Antinucci, F. & Miller, R. (1976). How children talk about what happened. *Journal of Child Language*, *3*, 167–189.

Benveniste, E. (1959). Les relations de temps dans le verbe français. *Bulletin de la société de Linguistique*, *54*, 69–82.

Bloom, L., Lifter, K ., & Hafitz, J. (1980). Semantics of verbs and the development of verb inflection in child language. *Language*, *56*, 386–412.

Bloomfield, L. (1933). *Language*. New York: Holt, Rinehart and Winston.

Bronckart, J. P. (1976). *Genèse et organisation des formes verbales chez l'enfant*. Bruxelles: Dessart et Mardaga.

Bronckart, J. P., Bain, D., Davaud, C., Pasquier, A., & Schneuwly, B. (1985). *Le fonctionnement des discours*. Paris: Delachaux et Niestlé.

Di Paolo, M. & Smith, C. S. (1978). Cognitive and linguistic factors in the acquisition of temporal and aspectual expressions. In P. French (Ed.), *The development of meaning*. Tokyo: Bukka Hyoron.

Fayol, M. (1981). *L'organisation du récit écrit chez l'enfant*. Unpublished doctoral thesis, Université de Bordeaux.

Fayol, M. (1985). *Le récit et sa construction*. Paris: Delachaux et Niestlé.

Harner, L. (1980). Comprehension of past and future revisted. *Journal of Experimental Child Psychology*. *29*, 170–182.

Harner, L. (1981). Children talk about time and aspect of actions. *Child Development*, *52*, 498–506.

Hopper, P. J. & Thompson, S. A. (1980). Transitivity in grammar and discourse. *Language*, *56*, 251–299.

Labov, W. & Waletzki, J. (1967). Narrative analysis: Oral versions of personal experience. In J. Helm (Ed.), *Essays in the verbal and visual arts*. Seattle, Wash.: University of Washington Press.

Propp, W. (1928). *Morfologija skazki*. Leningrad: Akademia.

Reichenbach, H. (1947). *Elements of symbolic logic*. Berkeley, Calif.: University of California Press.

Schiffrin, D. (1981). Tense variation in narrative. *Language*, *57*, 45–62.

Simonin-Grumbach, J. (1975). Pour une typologie des discours. In J. Kristeva, J. C. Milner, & N. Ruwet (Eds), *Langue, discours, société: Pour Emile Benveniste*. Paris: Editions du Seuil.

Smith, C. S. (1980). The acquisition of time talk: Relations between child and adult grammar. *Journal of Child Language*, *7*, 263–278.

Vet. C. (1980). *Temps, aspects et adverbes de temps en français contemporain: Essai de sémantique formelle*. Genève: Droz.

Weinrich, H. (1964). *Tempus*. Stuttgart: Kohlammer.

Wertsch, J. V. (1979). *The concept of activity in Soviet psychology*. New York: Sharpe.

9 Language and Theory of Mind: Vygotsky, Skinner and Beyond

Angel Rivière
Universidad Autonoma de Madrid, Madrid, Spain

The reflections that will be presented here originated from clinical work carried out over the past few years with autistic children. In a certain sense, childhood autism provides us with a natural experiment, the correct interpretation of which could be of great importance for understanding the nature and acquisition of language and symbolic behaviour in general. The present interpretation is one that will take us on a path beginning with Skinner, continuing with Vygotsky, and leading us finally beyond them.

Skinner has probably done more for autistic children than even he himself realises. At a time when the perspectives on the treatment of infantile autism were scarce and poor, the rigorous procedures for intervention developed from the experimental analysis of behaviour offered a relatively effective path for alleviating their problems. In the field of language, *Verbal behavior* (Skinner, 1957) exerted its influence above all through the work of Lovaas (1977), and this influence may still be clearly traced in the most recently developed and most sophisticated procedures directed at developing communication in autistics. I suspect that this influence may be explained, in part, by the fact that *Verbal behavior* was a pragmatic work in a double sense; first, it opened up roads to practical intervention and did so independently of particular hypotheses regarding the possible causes of autism and its supposed "underlying mechanisms"; and, secondly, *Verbal behavior* was fundamentally a work of pragmatic psychology which conceived of language as an activity which is a function of a context. Thus it anticipated, in many respects, ideas about language which have been developed and elaborated upon, with the predominance of the pragmatic focus in psycholinguistics in the 1980s.

Now that we are able to understand better the profound influence of *Verbal behavior* on the treatment of autism, it happens that, in a not-so-metaphorical sense, autism is a species of "pragmatic illness". It displays a disturbance of the usual pattern of social interaction in general and of language interaction in particular. In work on autistic language carried out by our own team (Rivière, Belinchon, Pfeiffer, & Sarria, 1988) and by others (Curcio, 1978), we find subtle alterations related to the pragmatic functions of language: for example, the lack of declaratives (Skinner's *tacts*) and a relative preservation of imperatives (*mands*), the scarcity of "psychological verbs" or intentional statements in the speech of autistics, and an enormous difficulty in conversing and maintaining the balance between reciprocity and sensitivity to the signals emitted by listeners that characterises normal human speakers. The latter includes difficulties adapting the volume of the voice to the listener's physical distance and connecting the content of the emissions with its prosodic aspects.

Although the guides for intervention derived from the experimental analysis of behaviour are effective for developing certain aspects of language behaviour in autistics, the cited disturbances are not very sensitive to intervention and, above all, are very difficult to explain from the positions sustained in *Verbal behavior*.

This difficulty of explication does not seem, moreover, to be of secondary or minor importance, but is directly related to the premises held by Skinner. Allow me to elaborate on this point, which I think is important: One of the obstacles to proposing a "non-mentalistic" or, perhaps, "non-intensional" view of the nature of language—if such an explanation is possible—is the fact that persons *de facto* employ mentalistic and intensional statements in their habitual symbolic transactions. We speak of our beliefs, thoughts and memories. We mutually attribute intentions and mental states to each other. We construct, in the first-person singular, statements with "intentional" verbs that transmit, for better or worse, information about what we believe are our internal states. In other words, we do precisely and with facility, exactly what autistics do not do. They do not speak of their beliefs, nor attribute intentions, nor appear to employ intentional declaratives in the first-person singular.

Without doubt, these statements of intention in the first-person singular have always been epistemological obstacles to the construction of a scientific psychology. They refer to a private world, whose *prima facie* acceptance would lead us to a totally implicit and non-scientific psychology with ideographic, teleologic and mentalistic presuppositions difficult to accommodate within scientific method. If we want to conduct a scientific psychology, we must avoid the explanatory tangles and difficulties of ordinary intentional language. These comments can be related to Place (1981), who demonstrated lucidly that the essential aspect of Skinner's exercise in

Verbal behavior consisted of developing a theory of verbal behaviour established entirely in non-intensional—that is extensional—terms. The problem, according to this analysis, is that any explication of language established entirely in intensional terms is condemned to circularity, from the moment that one has to explain the acquisition of linguistic skills based on the supposition that the speaker possesses, *a priori*, these types of skills.

I think that, arriving at this point, we must carefully differentiate two questions: The first, which requires extensive debate, is whether it is possible to develop a scientific theory which is completely explicative of linguistic behavior in exclusively extensional terms. The second refers to the fact that, although intensional terms are not adequate for a scientific explanation of language, people use such terms in their everyday talk. This second point is the one which is the most pertinent for the analysis of linguistic deviations in autistics, and for that reason I shall discuss it briefly.

Our ordinary language is full of statements and terms which pose puzzles that are as difficult to solve for logicians as for psychologists. Terms such as "believe", "know that", "think that", etc., and expressions such as "I think that the congress is interesting", or "John thinks that Laura does not love him". It turns out that the propositions within these statements possess peculiar logical properties:

1. The references of these propositions are "opaque" (Quine, 1961), i.e. it is not the case that if one proposition is true a different proposition with the same meaning and the same referent may be substituted for it and also be true. Thus, if Laura is the only professor of learning psychology at the Universidad Autónoma de Madrid, and if it is true that "Laura is blonde", then it is also true that "The professor of learning psychology at the Universidad Autónoma de Madrid is blonde". However, if it is true that "John thinks that Laura does not love him", it does not follow from this that "John thinks that the professor of learning psychology at the Universidad Autónoma de Madrid does not love him". In this case, the substitutability principle of extensional logic is not applicable.

2. Moreover, the truth or falsity of an intensional proposition does not imply the truth or falsity of propositions embedded in the intensional context created by this proposition. For example, in the previous case, although it is true that "John thinks that Laura does not love him", it could turn out that she is madly in love with him.

3. Finally, the truth or falsity of statements that contain intensional terms is not logically relevant to the existence or non-existence of the objects mentioned and embedded in the intensional contexts. From the statement "John believes that God is infinitely good", it does not follow that God exists, even though certain mediaeval theologians thought the contrary.

We can call these properties, analysed by Place in his analysis of *Verbal behavior*, "referential opacity", "non-entailment of truth" and "non-entailment of existence".

From a psychological point of view, these propositions pose the difficult question of how it is possible for humans to learn to interchange statements that lack external referents. How do we learn the meaning of verbs such as "think", "believe" or "pretend", whose referents are mental states enclosed "within the skin"? From Wittgenstein to Skinner there has been a wealth of speculation on the problem. However, what interests us here is to look at the problem from a somewhat special perspective: There are in fact certain subjects, i.e. autistics, who do not have the ability to learn easily to employ nor understand these expressions and terms. Moreover, these same subjects have shown other disturbances that appear to be subtly related to this incapacity: global alterations in the symbolic mechanisms of imitation and play, marked deficiencies in decoding the emotional expressions of others, and severe problems interacting.

It was necessary to find a theoretical framework which would permit us to explain why these disturbances appear together and how they are related to one another. The task was thus to find an explanatory perspective that could be added to the pragmatic vision provided by the experimental analysis of behaviour and which would permit us to optimise its methods. In this way, we began to move slowly towards the "inside of the skin", and there we found ourselves with Vygotsky and with his attempt to explain objectively the genesis of the higher mental functions in general, and the symbolic mechanisms in particular.

Our problem was to try to explain psychologically the "pathological affiliation" that exists (Wing & Gould, 1979) between the disturbances in communication and language, the problems of social interaction, and the enormous difficulties autistics have with the symbolic world. Our clinical and research experience with autistics had made us more sensitive to certain subtle and important aspects of what could be called the "developmental design" of normal children. More than once, upon going back home, we had the curious experience of being strangely surprised by normal children. How is it possible that they so quickly and effectively develop systems of relation, symbolic functions and mechanisms of identity that we only barely manage to achieve in autistics after years of continuous work? This strangeness provided the drive to investigate the normal development of children. It made us sensitive to normal functions that are so obvious that we often allow them to pass unnoticed.

Permit me to refer to some of these obvious functions so that they do not pass unnoticed here. To do this, an obvious example will serve well, i.e. what is happening when a speaker communicates about certain topics with his listeners. In order that the communication be adequate, it is necessary that the speaker subtly adapt to the conditions of the listeners, especially if he wants to fulfil the implicit contract between the "given and the new" that, according to Clark and Clark (1977), guides the communicative processes. The communication of the speaker will fail if it only refers to information already known by (in other words, "given to") the listener. But it will also fail if it only refers to new topics without providing the listeners with the "pegs" that couple the new to the given. The effective speaker makes use of a complex set of cues for reconstructing states of knowledge, interests, beliefs, etc., in the listeners: thematic cues (the speaker's knowledge in relation to the listener's knowledge with regard to the specific topics of the interlocution), interpersonal cues (the speaker's knowledge about the listener himself), contextual cues (dependent on sharing or not sharing a common situation at the moment of communication), paralinguistic cues (gestures and expressions of the listener), linguistic cues (as already discussed), etc. To say it in a few (and dangerous) words: It is as if the speaker had constantly to construct "theories" or "hypotheses" about the mental state of the listener. I am not speaking of conscious or explicit theories, but perhaps of non-conscious inferences that guide the communicative process.

One autistic subject, diagnosed by Kanner and later examined by Bemporad (1979), who was sufficiently intelligent to describe his "experience", stated: "It seemed as if others were capable of reading each other's thoughts, but I wasn't capable of reading the thoughts of others." What is this about "reading the thoughts" or of having theories about the mental states of others? What does this have to do with intensional language? How does this relate to the gross alterations of language, symbolic capacities and communication we find in autistics?

Vygotsky's (1930) theory offers us a promising initial path for uniting the pieces of this puzzle. It allows us to understand the aspects of autism which have not been explained by either "affective" theories—more or less psychodynamic, and which predominated from the 1940s through to the 1960s—or by the "cognitive" theories, which predominated from the 1960s to the 1980s. The affective theories considered the obvious cognitive disturbances as secondary, or even "false" effects, of affective and personality anomalies which were of a psychogenetic origin. The cognitive theories viewed the affective perturbations as secondary disorders to the cognitive, generally considered to have an organic origin. However, from the interactionist point of view suggested by the work of Vygotsky, this type of discussion lacks sense.

From this point of view we can consider that what is fundamentally altered is the social interaction which forms the basis for both the cognitive and affective functions. Since the end of the 1970s, investigations into the psychological development of children have emphasised more and more clearly that not only does the child interact as a function of a solid base of cognitive and affective structures, but also that the genesis of such functions resides in the interaction itself. And, as Vygotsky (1930) suggested, they are not the result of an endogenous preformation or of pure experience of an empty organism, but of the development of the child as a social being.

Vygotsky's interactionist solution originated in his attempt to explain the origins of the sign complexes that constitute human culture and that, from the culture, form the reflexive consciousness. He considered as equally insufficient and solipsistic the reductionistic thesis of classical objectivism, which analysed consciousness as a set of reflex elements, and the descriptive (and non-explanatory) project of the idealist psychology of the 1920s. His solution had something in common with that of Skinner's: In order to explain the origin of the higher mental functions, he considered it necessary to go outside the subject. These functions were considered to be products which originated in the culture and were made subjective through processes of social interaction. Higher mental functions—language and signs, even consciousness itself, with its semiotic structure—are nothing but refined forms of interaction.

A second characteristic which draws Vygotsky somewhat close to the position of Skinner is what we might call his "instrumentalism". His unit of analysis was instrumental behaviour. He thought that the possibility of transforming the material world by means of tools established the conditions for the modification of reflexive behaviour and its qualitative transformation in consciousness. This process is further mediated by a special class of tools: those which permit the realisation of transformations in others. We call these tools "signs" and they are essentially provided by the culture—by the persons that surround, and in a certain sense "construct", the child during development. At this point one can understand the claim that the fundamental path of development is that which is defined by the internalisation of those instruments and signs, by the conversion of the external systems of regulation into means of self-regulation. It is this notion which creates a decisive separation between the instrumentalism of Vygotsky and that of Skinner, because Vygotsky thought the systems of self-regulation, when internalised, dialectically modify the structure of external behaviour, which can no longer be understood as an expression of reflexes. In other words, consciousness, which was for him "social contact with oneself", exerts a causal influence over behaviour.

Vygotsky formulated these interactionist ideas in a manner that appears particularly useful for bringing us closer to a better comprehension of the strange experiment that is autism. He called this formulation the "law of double formation", which in 1930 he expressed in the following way:

> In the cultural development of the child all functions appear twice: first, at a social level, and then, at an individual level; first between persons (interpsychological) and later in the interior of the child itself (intrapsychological) . . . all of the higher mental functions appear as relations between human beings (Vygotsky, 1930, p. 94).

This has been termed Vygotsky's general genetic law of cultural development (Wertsch, 1985).

To show the importance this way of thinking had on our way of understanding autistic children (which was becoming more and more an attempt to understand normal children), it will be useful to summarise, very concisely, the fundamental propositions of Vygotsky's interactionist solution:

1. Instrumental activity is the unit of analysis for a psychology of higher mental functions.
2. The higher mental functions involve the combination of elements and signs in psychological activity.
3. The conversion of the instrumental activity into meaningful sign activity is mediated and made possible by relations with others.
4. The conversion of an activity into a sign involves its condensation.
5. The signs originate as mediators for regulating the behaviour of others. With them, others regulate the behaviour of the child, and the child the behaviour of others.
6. The main path of development of higher mental functions is the internalisation of social processes.
7. As such, the origin of these functions is not to be found in the unfolding of the spirit or in cerebral connections, but in social history.
8. The culture provides the necessary symbolic tools for the construction of consciousness and the higher mental functions. These tools are, fundamentally, linguistic symbols.
9. Development does not essentially consist of the progressive socialisation of an individual who is initially "autistic", but of the individualisation of an individual who was basically social from the beginning.

These positions, which I have been obliged to present very schematically, permit us to begin to better unite the pieces of our conceptual puzzle: If higher symbolic functions are internalised forms of interaction, it is logical that one would see them altered when the early structures of interaction are altered. And, if signs are, as we say, types of instruments, it is also logical that these alterations will be accompanied by deviations in instrumental behaviour and in causality and means–ends notions that serve as the basis for this behaviour. And if development does not consist of the progressive socialisation of an individual who is initially autistic, but rather in the individualisation of a social being, then autistics do not suffer the arresting of development proposed by certain psychodynamic theorists, but a serious deviation of development that *ab initio* impedes the construction of higher mental functions such as language and ultimately consciousness. And if, as seems evident, consciousness is the only thing on which we can predicate intentionality, then autistics would show a perturbation of intentionality in general and of communicative intentions in particular.

All of these reflections are very general, but they accommodate much of the research data on autistic children as well as normal children. Data on perceptual preferences in neonates, for example, show that the idea of the child existing as a social being from the beginning has a clear empirical sense. Epidemiological studies on children with abnormal patterns of social behaviour demonstrate that, in addition to the case of autism, there is a consistent association between alterations of social relations, of symbolic abilities, and of instrumental and intentional behaviours (Wing & Gould, 1979). In more specific research, I have demonstrated that it is possible to predict, to a high degree, the likely success of a programme to teach sign-language to mute autistics based on their level of development in notions of causality and means–end relations; In other words, in those notions that are most closely related to instrumental behaviour. On the basis of Vygotsky's theory and also on the basis of an ample corpus of developmental data, we constructed theoretical models of the early development of normal children, which turned out to be applicable and effective for understanding and treating autistics (Rivière, 1983; Rivière & Coll, 1987).

These models start out from an "outside-in" perspective that is also common to the positions of Vygotsky and Skinner. Contrary to many of the dominant positions in developmental psychology which postulate a strong innate component of interpersonal behaviours, we were working to elaborate a constructivist position. In particular, we were opposed to Trevarthen's (1982) idea that infants possess a "primary intersubjectivity" which is manifested, from the first 2–3 months, in the complex exchange of expressions between babies and their mothers, in the fascinating ability that babies possess to mirror emotional expressions of their partners in interaction. If subjectivity itself is a product of social relations, as Vygotsky would hold, it is difficult to accept the idea that there is a primary intersubjectivity that is a basic and non-notional ability to enter into the emotional internal world of others by means of the exchange of emotional expressions.

We accepted, however, the idea of Trevarthen and Hubley (1978) that towards the end of the first year infants develop what they call a "secondary intersubjectivity", a group of social skills based on the implicit notion that others possess a mental world whose structure is essentially identical to their own. With the development of this ability comes a fundamental motivation to share experience, which is above all expressed in the pragmatic mechanisms that Bates (1976) labels "proto-declaratives", and which correspond to Skinner's *tacts*. These prelinguistic "tacts" find their expression in the behaviour of pointing, which does not have the goal of obtaining objects, accomplishing situations or pursuing activities, but rather that of sharing experience or commenting on it.

The study of these "tacts" (or proto-tacts, perhaps) has been of great importance for us. In the first place, these social behaviours of pointing have a close developmental relation to the child's first symbolic forms. Moreover, they are very specific to our species and (as opposed to "proto-imperatives" or "proto-mands"), they do not seem to appear in the natural behaviour of gorillas or chimpanzees. Finally, the research of Curcio (1978) and Rivière et al. (1988) demonstrates that the lack of proto-declaratives or "proto-tacts" is the clearest characteristic of autistic children without language, and the scarcity of declarative linguistic forms is a frequent peculiarity of autistics with language.

It turns out, however, that an explication of the *tact* mechanism poses serious difficulties for any non-intensional explication of the nature of language and, indeed, for any "outside-in" explication of its origin. This is another aspect discussed by Place (1981) in his analysis of *Verbal behavior*. There he noted that *tacts*, in a pragmatic sense, are reinforced by generalised verbal or social reinforcers on the part of the listener, in contrast to mands which are reinforced by verbal or non-verbal behaviours specific to the statement itself. We would give a more mentalistic interpretation of the reinforcement capacity of "tacts". We believe they are reinforcing because, for human beings, it is gratifying to know that we are sharing an experience with others. The hypothesis that prelinguistic proto-declaratives demand higher intersubjective prerequisites than proto-imperatives was indirectly put to the test in a study about communicative patterns in babies between 8 and 12 months. The complex and somewhat mystical concept of intersubjectivity was operationalised by means of the concept of "imitation". We based this on the supposition that imitation is not merely a "copying of behaviour", but that it is an intersubjective expression of the child. As we hypothesised, significant correlations appeared between proto-declaratives and imitation, but not between imitation and proto-imperatives (Sarria, Rivière, & Brioso, 1988).

Our puzzle was slowly being unravelled: For autistics (as well as for the higher anthropoids), imitation is much less frequent and less elaborated than in normal children. Actually, the objective of establishing imitation by means of reinforcement is frequently one of the first steps in intervention programmes based on the experimental analysis of behaviour. But in this case, we also have doubts about the possibilities inherent in an exclusively external analysis of the mechanism: What is it that reinforces spontaneous imitation in normal children? We remind ourselves that there are early forms of imitation in neonates, as has been demonstrated by Meltzoff and Moore (1977) and others.

Moreover, in normal infants, social reinforcers appear to exert, from very early on, a very different effect from that of non-social reinforcers. This was demonstrated in an experiment employing the "perception of contingencies" paradigm with 3-month-old babies. We established a situation in which, every time the baby moved her head to the right, a contingent sound was presented, which could be either a speaking voice or a brief fragment of music. The behaviour of the babies was very different between the two conditions. The operant response was established and extinguished much more rapidly and abruptly in the case of the voice, and the baby showed more marked emotional expressions (Gonzales del Hierro & Rivière, in press).

These investigations, together with an ample base of experimental data by other investigators, have provided consistent empirical support for Vygotsky's idea that the child is a social being from the very beginning. At the same time, we are getting closer to Trevarthen's hypothesis that there is a primary intersubjectivity, which is demonstrated in the elaborate exchange of expressions between infants that are a few months old and their mothers. In contrast to this notable ability for coding the emotional expressions of others at a very early age, autistic children are unable to accomplish tasks that demand emotional discrimination, as has been conclusively demonstrated by Hobson (1986a; 1986b).

The conceptual framework taking shape was, in very general terms, the following: The first intentional communicative behaviours, which appear in babies around 8–9 months of age, are certainly elaborated forms of instrumental activity. They are related, first and foremost, to the notions of causality and means–end relations which form the basis for patterns of activity. But it is not only the development of instrumental mechanisms that explains the appearance of these behaviours. For the declarative type, above all, the "input" of a rudimentary form of intersubjectivity is necessary, which consists of the baby's capacity to experience emotion when others do. This primary intersubjectivity is followed by a secondary intersubjectivity that implies the cognitive notion that others possess a world of mental structures identical to his own. This second level of intersubjectivity, whose development coincides with the first proto-declaratives towards the end of the first year of life, is a product of the child's cognitive development, but also of the elaboration that occurs of the primary intersubjectivity itself. The concept of primary intersubjectivity, which we rejected in principle for its innatist and, at the same time mentalistic, character, permits us to give a provisional answer to some old philosophical themes to which I have referred during this discussion. Children are able to acquire a language of private referents because, before language, they have shared private internal states with others: first, states of emotion, by means of early emotional exchanges; shared cognitive states of interests, knowledge and attention are achieved afterwards by means of communicative forms (in other words, by means of sophisticated forms of instrumental behaviours of exchange).

These behaviours are converted into symbolic forms when they refer to objects that are not present and, as a consequence, require specific signifying gestures for "representing" these absent objects, in a way that is more specific than the relatively unspecific behaviour of pointing or extending the arms towards a desired and immediately present object. As Vygotsky said, symbols are always elaborated communicative patterns, including when they are converted into forms of communication with oneself, whereupon they are called "consciousness".

However, these elaborated forms of pointing to "the absent" give rise to much more complicated philosophical and psychological problems than those posed for previous forms of communication. I have referred to some of these problems already. First is the problem of the high genetic correlation in the appearance and development of the first symbolic behaviours in the child, and the high correlation which marks their alteration or disturbance. In autistic children, as well as in those that present syndromes of receptive developmental dysphasia, the alterations and deficiencies of language are accompanied by global deficiencies in symbolic mechanisms, expressed in the alteration or lack of play, delayed imitation, and in difficulties acquiring non-linguistic mechanisms of symbolic communication.

What do these symbolic behaviours have in common that would allow us to account for the closeness with which they develop and are disturbed? Wolf and Gardner (1981) have proposed a hypothesis that is very suggestive for investigators working with autistics, and which has a definitive Vygotskian flavour. They suggest that the organisation of the first symbols conserve, in a way, the traces of their roots in the schemata of action and interaction. This organisation is defined by Wolf and Gardner as "structuration of roles"; that is to say, the ability to understand, represent and signify the functions of persons and objects in action sequences.

Probably, the behaviours that express the symbolic mechanisms in the most genuine manner, from the second year, are those of pretending. Leslie (1987, p. 412) has noted:

> pretending ought to strike the cognitive psychologist as a very odd sort of ability. After all, from an evolutionary point of view, there ought to be a high

> premium on the veridicality of cognitive processes. The perceiving, thinking organism ought, as far as possible, to get things right. Yet pretense flies in the face of this fundamental principle. In pretense, we deliberately distort reality. How much more odd, then, that this ability is not the sober culmination of intellectual development but instead makes its appearance playfully and precociously at the very beginning of childhood.

As Leslie notes, "pretending" present properties that are parallel to those presented by intensional language. We recall that these properties were the "referential opacity", "non-entailment of truth" and "non-entailment of existence". In the "pretense-play" and "acting-if behaviours" of children, we see the substitution of some objects for others (e.g. a block scooted along the floor represents a car) without confusing them. This corresponds to "referential opacity"—the attribution of imaginary properties which parallels "non-entailment of truth"—and the creation of imaginary objects, which is related to "non-entailment of existence". Leslie supposes that for the development of behaviours with these properties, the organism has to be able to construct "representations over representations", suspending for them the relations of reference, truth and existence that hold for the primary representations.

The foregoing observations are closely related with a concept which is becoming increasingly important in developmental psychology and seems very useful for explaining some of the cognitive peculiarities of intelligent autistic subjects. I refer to the concept of the "theory of mind", which arose out of research by Premack and Woodruff (1978) on chimpanzees, in which they demonstrated that, in certain conditions, chimpanzees appear to be able to comprehend the purposes and intentions of humans in problematic situations. Premack and Woodruff say that, in order to explain these skills, it is necessary to acknowledge that they are able to employ a "theory of mind":

> In saying that an individual has a theory of mind, we mean that the individual imputes mental states to himself and to others (either to conspecifics or to other species as well). A system of inferences of this kind is properly viewed as a theory, first because such states are not directly observable, and second, because the system can be used to make predictions specifically about the behavior of other organisms (Premack & Woodruff, 1978, p. 515).

The skills of attributing intentions and mental states to others that are distinct from one's own develop from the second year in normal children, and their development is closely related to the skill of using and understanding "psychological verbs" and intensional statements. It is necessary to observe that this skill supposes a further step with respect to the concept of "secondary intersubjectivity", which only involves the notion that others have a mental world whose essential structure is identical to one's own. After arriving at this notion, children acquire the skill of recognising that, while the essential structure of mental worlds may be identical, their transitory states of knowledge, intention, interest, etc., can be different from the child's own. It is easy to imagine the relation between this skill and "pretending".

Baron-Cohen, Leslie, and Frith (1985) have recently demonstrated that intelligent autistic children are particularly unable to solve "theory of mind" tasks. They presented the same task to autistic children, retarded children of equal mental age, and to normal 4-year-olds. In the task, two dolls (A and B) were in a room and each had a bag. One of the dolls, A, had a marble in her bag. Taking advantage of a moment when A was out of the room, B hid the marble in her own bag. Later, when A came back into the room, the child was asked where A would look for the marble. Naturally, the correct answer was that A would look for the marble in her own bag (where she thought it was) despite the fact that the child knew that the marble was in B's bag. The solution to this task involves a clear differentiation between the other's state of knowledge and one's own. Normal and retarded children were able to solve this task, whereas autistic children were not.

In an experiment using this same paradigm, Rivière and Castellanos (in press) demonstrated that, while normal 4-year-olds who are unable to solve Piagetian-type operational tasks are able to give the correct response in the doll task, autistic children could solve the doll task only when they were able to solve formally equivalent operational tasks. This result suggests that normal children employ special cognitive procedures for solving formally complex "theory of mind" tasks, whereas autistics have, we might say, "only one mental world".

Normal children are very skilled in "warm" cognitive tasks which involve attributing intentions to others, deliberately lying, taking advantage of creating incorrect knowledge states in others, and in inferring emotions, thoughts and beliefs. Humphrey (1984) has speculated that these types of skills have been more important than instrumental and technical skills in the phylogenetic origins of our species, which has more frequently obtained advantages from the cultural transmission of techniques in complex social groups than from technological invention as such. For Humphrey, what characterises us as a species is being good "natural psychologists", with a great capacity for interpersonal calculating and predicting the behaviour of others.

In other words, the adaptive context of the phylogenetic evolution of man has favoured, perhaps, the development of complex skills directed towards constructing theories of others' minds. These skills do not develop in the same way in autistic children. They have to solve interpersonal tasks as if they were non-personal tasks, as if they were purely formal problems without reference to persons with whom they might identify or in whose shoes they might walk. This incapacity seems to be closely related to that of the "pretending" skills and using psychological language. For some reason unkown to us, autistics are not good natural psychologists; indeed, they find the mental world of others particularly opaque.

Our hypothesis is that the concept of "theory of mind" could be fundamental for any pragmatic explication of language. When we communicate linguistically with others, we bring into play our skill for calculating their knowledge and interests. We modify our language as a function of the presuppositions we think we share with them. We make our language more predicative and elliptical according to our understanding of the distance between their world and ours. We do it still more when we communicate with ourselves because, all said and done, we share all presuppositions with ourselves.

REFERENCES

Baron-Cohen, S., Leslie, A. M., & Frith, U. (1985). Does the autistic child have a "theory of mind". *Cognition*, *21*, 37–46.

Bates, E. (1976). *Language and context: The acquisition of pragmatics*. London: Academic Press.

Bemporad, J. (1979). Adult recollections of a formerly autistic child. *Journal of Autism and Developmental Disorders*, *9*, 179–197.

Clark, H. N. & Clark, B. V. (1977). *Psychology and language*. San Diego, Calif.: Harcourt Brace Jovanovich.

Curcio, F. (1978). Sensorimotor functioning and communication in mute autistic children. *Journal of Autism and Childhood Schizophrenia*, *8*, 282–292.

Gonzales del Hierro, A. & Rivière, A. (in press). La influencia de los estimulos en los procesos de percepcion de contingencias en bebés.

Hobson, R. P. (1986a). The autistic child's appraisal of expressions of emotion. *Journal of Child Psychology and Psychiatry*, *27*, 321–342.

Hobson, R. P. (1986b). The autistic child's appraisal of expressions of emotion: A further study. *Journal of Child Psychology and Psychiatry*, *27*, 671–680.

Humphrey, N. (1984). *Consciousness regained: Chapters in the development of mind*. Oxford: Oxford University Press.

Leslie, A. M. (1987). Pretense and representation: The origin of "theory of mind". *Psychological Review*, *94*, 412–426.

Meltzoff, A. & Moore, M. (1977). Imitation of facial and manual gestures. *Science*, *198*, 75–80.

Place, U. T. (1981). Skinner's *Verbal Behavior I*—Why we need it. *Behaviorism*, *9*, 1–24.

Premack, D. & Woodruff, G. (1978). Does the chimpanzee have a theory of mind? *Behaviour and Brain Sciences*, *4*, 515–526.

Quine, W. V. (1961). *From a logical point of view*. Cambridge, Mass.: Harvard University Press.

Rivière, A. (1983). Interaccion y simbolo en autistas. *Infancia y Aprendizale*, *22*, 8–25.

Rivière, A. & Castellanos, J. L. (in press). Teoria de la mente y desarrollo operatorio en autismo.

Rivière, A. & Coll, C. (1987). Individuation et intraction avec le sensoriomoteur: notes sur la construction génétique du sujet et de l'objet social. In M. Siguan (Ed.), *Comportement, cognition, conscience. La psychologie à la recherche de son objet*. Paris: Presses Universitaires de France.

Rivière, A., Belinchon, M., Pfeiffer, A., & Sarria, E. (1988). *Evaluacion y alteraciones de las funciones psicologicas en autismo infantil*. Madrid: Cide.

Sarria, E., Rivière, A., & Brioso, A. (1988). Observation of communicative intentions in infants. Paper presented to the Third European Conference on Developmental Psychology, Budapest.

Skinner, B. F. (1957). *Verbal behavior*. New York: Appleton-Century-Croft.

Trevarthen, C. (1982). The primary motives for cooperative understanding. In G. Butterworth & P. Light (Eds), *Social cognition: studies on the development of understanding*, pp. 77–109. Brighton: Harvester Press.

Trevarthen, C. & Hubley, P. (1978). Secondary intersubjectivity: Confidence, confiding and acts of meaning in the first years. In A. Lock (Ed.), *Action, gesture and symbol: The emergence of language*. London: Academic Press.

Vygotsky, L. S. (1930). Internalizacion de las funciones psicologicas superlores. In L. S. Vygotsky, *El desarrollo de los procesos psicologicos superiores*. Barcelona: Critica, 1979. (English translation: *Mind in society: The development of higher psychological processes*. Cambridge, Mass.: Harvard University Press, 1978).

Wing, L. & Gould, I. (1979). Severe impairments of social interaction and associated abnormalities in children: Epidemiology and classification. *Journal of Autism and Developmental Disorders*, *9*, 11–30.

Wolf, D. & Gardner, H. (1981). On the structure of early symbolization. In R. L. Schiefbusch & D. D. Bricker (Eds), *Early language. Acquisition and intervention*. Baltimore: University Park Press.

10 Properties of Rule-governed Behaviour and their Implications

A. Charles Catania, Byron A. Matthews and Eliot H. Shimoff
*University of Maryland Baltimore County, Catonsville, Maryland, U.S.A.**

A fundamental property of behaviour is its sensitivity to its consequences. Much research on learning in non-human organisms has concentrated on how behaviour changes when its consequences change. When behaviour is determined by its consequences, it is called contingency-shaped. For example, the rate and temporal patterning of a pigeon's pecks at a key are determined by the schedule according to which its pecks produce food. The rate is higher when food deliveries depend on response number than when they depend on elapsed time (interval *vs* ratio schedules), and different temporal patterns emerge when number and time requirements are constant than when they vary from one food delivery to the next (fixed *vs* variable schedules). These performances are determined by contingencies between responses and their consequences. The behaviour of non-human organisms is sensitive to such contingencies, in the sense that it changes consistently when contingencies change.

Human behaviour, however, is often rule-governed rather than contingency-shaped: It is often determined by verbal behaviour and therefore only indirectly by its consequences (Skinner, 1969). Such behaviour is necessarily less sensitive to its consequences than behaviour that is contingency-governed; it does not easily change when contingencies change. For example, human schedule performances are typically accompanied by verbal behaviour related to those performances, and humans

*A. Charles Catania and Eliot H. Shimoff are in the Department of Psychology, Byron A. Matthews is in the Department of Sociology.

typically produce high and relatively constant rates under schedules that produce varied rates and temporal patterning in other organisms. When verbal behaviour is involved, initiated either by the experimenter through instructions or by the human responder through private talk, the performance becomes rule-governed rather than contingency-shaped (Catania, Shimoff, & Matthews, 1989).

It is paradoxical that verbal behaviour can make human behaviour less rather than more sensitive to its consequences. Rule-governed behaviour is sensitive to contingencies only to the extent that verbal rules are consistent with them. When this is not so, the contingencies that maintain rule-following, even though often remote, may override other consequences of the behaviour. We usually assume that verbal behaviour is beneficial, but in these cases it gets in the way. This is the sense in which verbal behaviour can be said to insulate behaviour from its consequences. Concerns about what happens when people thoughtlessly do what they are told or blindly obey orders are concerns about the properties of rule-governed behaviour.

Some of these properties have been demonstrated experimentally (Catania, Matthews, & Shimoff, 1982; Matthews, Catania, & Shimoff, 1985; Shimoff, Matthews, & Catania, 1986). In one study, students' presses on left and right buttons occasionally produced points later exchangeable for money. Lights above the buttons lit alternately, indicating which button was operative. A number-based schedule operated for the left button (random ratio or RR: points were arranged for the first press after a random number of presses) and a time-based schedule operated for the right (random interval or RI: points were arranged for the first press after a random time had passed since the last point delivery). Between periods of responding, the student filled in "guess sheets" with sentences to be completed, such as "The way to earn points with the left button is to:". Guess sheets were returned to the student with points awarded for guesses; the points were used to shape the student's verbal behaviour, i.e. they were awarded for successively closer approximations to particular statements about contingencies or performances. (cf. Greenspoon, 1955).

The non-verbal performance, button pressing, was determined not by the contingencies arranged for pressing, but rather by the student's verbal behaviour. Statements that points depended on slow left pressing and fast right pressing, when shaped, reliably produced corresponding pressing rates, slow left and fast right, even though these actual schedules respectively produce high and low rates in typical non-human contingency-shaped performances. Pressing rates typically conformed to the shaped verbal behaviour even when such responding reduced the student's net earnings (as with low rates given a number-based schedule).

But verbal responses may describe contingencies as well as performances. People often tell others about the contingencies operating in some environment, assuming that a description of the contingencies will somehow produce behaviour appropriate to them. A description of contingencies having implications for performance, however, is not equivalent to an explicit description of that performance. In the button-pressing experiments, shaping performance descriptions was more consistently effective than shaping contingency descriptions (e.g. "The left button produces points after a random number of presses"), depending mainly on whether verbal behaviour was available to the student relating performance to contingencies. Furthermore, shaping verbal behaviour was more consistently effective than establishing verbal behaviour by instructions (telling the student what to say about the performance).

In other words, shaping what people say about their own behaviour appears to be a more effective way to change their behaviour than either shaping their behaviour directly or telling them what to do. Once nonverbal behaviour has come to be determined by verbal behaviour, it appears sensitive to contingencies only indirectly, to the extent that changing contingencies may lead to changes in the corresponding verbal behaviour.

THE INSENSITIVITY OF RULE-GOVERNED BEHAVIOUR TO ITS CONSEQUENCES

In a different experimental design for studying the sensitivity of behaviour to its consequences, Catania, Shimoff, and Matthews (1987) used a computer joystick as a response device for students whose responding earned points exchangeable for money. Directions and latencies of joystick movement were recorded over trials. The dimension on which verbal feedback was given was a more important determinant of performance than the dimension upon which consequences depended. For example, if the student was consistently given the latency but not the angle of the last joystick response, latencies rather than angles were likely to be repeated on trials following those earning points, even if points depended systematically on angle rather than latency.

In this experiment, undergraduates were seated at a video monitor with a joystick assembly consisting of a box with a single button on one side and a protruding rod. A metal plate concentric to the rod limited its movement from the vertical resting position. The response of interest was moving the rod from the centre until it touched the metal plate, when the angle was calculated; the spring-loaded rod returned to its vertical position when released.

The following instructions were presented at the top of the screen:

> Your task is to earn as many points as possible. You can earn points by using the joystick. When the READY signal appears on the screen, start the trial by pressing the button on the joystick box; this will make the READY signal go off. Next, move the joystick until it touches the metal cover of the joystick

> box. The screen will then show either a white bar or the flashing message CORRECT along with your total point earnings. You will be paid 1 cent for every point you earn.

Trials began with the word "READY" at the bottom centre of the screen; the word disappeared when the subject pressed the joystick button. Trials ended when the rod touched the metal plate or after 10 sec. Whether responses earned a point depended on either angle (position to which the rod was moved) or latency (time between the button-press and the end of the trial). Correct responses produced the word "CORRECT" and the total points earned on the bottom right of the screen; for incorrect responses, that portion of the screen remained blank. In addition, one of two forms of feedback was presented on the bottom left of the screen. For latency feedback, the screen showed "TIME" with latency to the nearest 0.05 sec. For position feedback, it showed "ANGLE" with the angle in degrees.

Shaping was carried out by the computer. Angle shaping began with any angle from 0 to 60 degrees producing a point. The 60-degree range was constant, but minimum angle increased as a function of performance; with two constraints, it was set at the mean of the last 10 correct angles. First, if the current angle equalled the minimum, the minimum increased 3 degrees regardless of the last mean. Second, three consecutive identical correct responses raised the minimum to that angle. The minimum never decreased. Sessions ended when the minimum exceeded 300 degrees or after 400 trials, whichever came first. Thus, angle shaping gradually moved the position criterion clockwise from 0 to 300 degrees.

Latency shaping was similar, with a range of 1 sec and a starting minimum of 0 sec; the minimum was raised in 0.05-sec increments (latencies of 5–10 sec were treated as 5 sec). Thus, a session started with latencies from 0 to 1 sec eligible to produce points. The minimum was set to the mean of the last 10 correct latencies, with two constraints: latencies equal to the mimimum increased it by 0.05 sec, and three consecutive identical correct latencies raised it to that latency, regardless of the previous mean. Shaping continued until the minimum latency was 4 sec or after 400 trials, whichever came first.

When latency was shaped with latency feedback for three subjects, latencies gradually increased, whereas angles were not systematically affected by point deliveries. Similarly, when angle was shaped with angle feedback for another three subjects, angles gradually increased, whereas latencies were not systematically affected by point deliveries. Shaping was successful for all six subjects for whom feedback was consistent with the dimension along which responding was shaped and took a mean of 152 trials.

But when feedback was inconsistent with the dimension along which responding was shaped (i.e. shaping of angle with latency feedback or of latency with angle feedback), shaping was not consistently successful. In shaping of angle with latency feedback for four subjects, shaping progressed slowly; when a response produced a point, the next response was similar in latency and often varied in angle, even though the point depended on angle. The inverse occurred during shaping of latency with angle feedback for another four subjects: Again shaping progressed slowly, and when a response produced a point, the next response was often similar in angle and substantially shorter in latency, even though the point depended on latency. Shaping was successful within the 400-trial maximum in only three of these eight cases, and in those three cases took a mean of 249 trials (a mean of 344 trials if the other five cases are counted as 401 trials each). Similar results were obtained in subsequent conditions for these subjects, during which different combinations of shaping and feedback dimensions were arranged.

In other words, responding was insulated from the effects of contingences by a verbal intervention, the verbal feedback that specified one or the other response dimension. Note that a defining property of a reinforcer is that the response that produces it is repeated. To the extent that the feedback was a more important determinant of which feature of the response was repeated on the next trial than was the contingent relation between response properties and points, the feedback insulated the response from its consequences.

In at least a general sense, the present phenomena can be regarded as examples of blocking (e.g. Kamin, 1969), but the various manipulations of verbal behaviour and its relations to the subject's performance involve different temporal relations among the possible stimulus and response terms than those in classical blocking procedures. Furthermore, any account in such terms must deal with the verbal history that could allow words to produce such effects.

It is reasonable to assume that the feedback contributed to these results by way of its effect on each subject's verbal behaviour with respect to the experimental contingencies. Feedback with respect to a response dimension presumably generates talk about that dimension, even if only at a covert level. Other ways of manipulating verbal behaviour experimentally (e.g. by instructions or by shaping of verbal behaviour) have functionally equivalent effects, though all such procedures have an intrinsic source of variability in the different sorts of verbal behaviour subjects enter such experiments with or produce in the course of them.

THE INSTRUCTIONAL FUNCTION OF LANGUAGE

The primary function of verbal behaviour is that it allows one to do things via the mediation of another organism. It follows that this behaviour is quintessentially social and can emerge only in organisms whose behaviour is already sensitive to social contingencies. Discriminating the behaviour of other organisms, whether of one's own or of other species, has clear selective advantages.

Discriminations of the behaviour of others are at the heart of our human concept of intentionality (cf. Dennett, 1987): We say we understand someone's intentions when our discriminations of the various properties of that individual's past and current behaviour enable us to act appropriately with respect to what that individual is likely to do in the future. In fact, if discriminating one's own behaviour is a special case of discriminating the behaviour of others (e.g. Bem, 1967), this topic encompasses all of the phenomena considered under the rubric of intentionality. Judgements of the intentions of others are, above all, social judgements, and it takes no special assumptions about the selective contingencies that must have operated on both intraspecific and interspecific social behaviour to see that such contingencies could phylogenically shape well-prepared capacities for social discriminations.

This social function of verbal behaviour is therefore the primary candidate for providing the basis of language origins and evolution (Catania, 1985; in press). Once intraspecific social discriminative stimuli have become important to the members of a species, the stage is set for verbal behaviour because the organism so discriminating has become a potential listener. (It is of interest that many of the problems in teaching symbol use to our highly social primate relatives arise because the primates are more likely to attend to the behaviour of their human handlers than to the inanimate apparatuses in the context of which symbolic materials are presented: cf. Savage-Rumbaugh, 1986).

The distinction between contingency-shaped and rule-governed behaviour captures this instructional function of verbal behaviour. In this usage, rules are defined functionally, in terms of their roles as antecedent verbal stimuli, rather than structurally, by topographic or syntactic criteria. Thus, definitions or statements of fact may function as rules as effectively as commands or instructions, to the extent that they generate relevant verbal or non-verbal behaviour. A speaker can instruct what another says as well as what another does. Giving definitions and stating facts are instructions with respect to the listener's future verbal behaviour. Speaking need not have the grammatical character of the imperative to influence the behaviour of the listener.

By definition, contingency-shaped behaviour is never insensitive to contingencies. Rule-governed behaviour, however, is often so, and it may be established by verbal communities precisely because of its insensitivity to contingencies. We often attempt to establish responding by instruction when natural consequences are weak (as when we tell children to study), or when they are remote (as when we tell drivers to wear seatbelts), or when they are likely to maintain undesirable competing behaviour (as when we warn against drug abuse). It is not necessary to tell people to do what they would do even if not told.

Rules may or may not be consistent with contingencies. When they are consistent with contingencies, the rule-governed performances they occasion may change with contingencies accordingly. But rule-governed behaviour, though sometimes sensitive to contingencies in this sense, cannot be sensitive to contingencies in the same way as behaviour that is contingency-shaped. In fact, we can only be certain that behaviour is controlled by rules when rules and contingencies are pitted against each other. If we studied rules and contingencies that produced comparable performances, we would have no basis for deciding whether the rules or the contingencies were in control. The terminology of rule-governed and contingency-shaped behaviour identifies rules or contingencies as controlling variables; placing particular instances of behaviour in one or the other class is a matter of experimental analysis.

Consider again the student whose button-presses produced points. If a rule specified high-rate button-pressing while contingencies operated that would otherwise generate low-rate pressing, we could distinguish between rule-governed and contingency-shaped performance on the basis of whether the response rate was high or low. We must allow for the possibilities that either type of control may operate alone or that both may enter into intermediate cases in which performance is jointly controlled by contingencies and by rules. In any case, the distinction between the two classes of responding is in terms of the sources of their control and not in terms of their topographies.

RULE-GOVERNED BEHAVIOUR AS A HIGHER-ORDER CLASS

The contingencies that establish rule-governed behaviour are presumably effective because they make consequences depend on the relation between verbal antecedents and the behaviour that follows. Thus, they may establish and maintain rule-following as a response class. Once such a class is established, the consequences involved in maintaining it are likely to differ from those involved in specific instances of behaviour. For example, when a child is told to put on boots before going out to play in the snow, the social consequences of obeying or disobeying the parents must be distinguished from the natural consequences of shod or unshod feet. In other words, it is important to distinguish between the direct consequences that operate for specific responses and the indirect consequences that establish and maintain rule-governed behaviour.

The insensitivity to contingencies of subclasses within a higher-order class is not an incidental empirical byproduct. Insensitivity to the contingencies arranged for a particular response class is a necessary condition for the establishment of higher-order behavioural units (cf. Estes, 1971, p. 23).

Consider, for example, the higher-order class of behaviour referred to as generalised imitation (e.g. Baer, Peterson, & Sherman, 1967; Gewirtz & Stingle, 1968). A puppet models several instances of behaviour, such as pressing a lever, stamping its foot or shaking its head. If we reinforce a child's imitation of all of these but the head-shaking, the child will ordinarily continue to imitate the head-shaking along with the others even though the head-shaking is never reinforced. Imitation of head-shaking does not extinguish, and we therefore say it is a member of the generalised class.

But this failure to extinguish is precisely the condition that leads us also to say that this response is insensitive to contingencies. The practical corollary is that when we fail to change behaviour with contingencies in application, as in trying to deal with self-injurious behaviour, it is worth asking whether the behaviour is insensitive to contingencies because it is a member of a higher-order class (for example, in some cases, a self-injurious child's head-banging might be part of a larger class, all the members of which have some other function such as attracting attention).

The characteristics of higher-order classes must depend at least to some extent on the contingencies that create and maintain them. Presumably, rule-governed behaviour is initially shaped by social contingencies, but complex instructional control demands that verbal behaviour must also be correlated reasonably well with environmental contingencies. Thus, rules may come to conform to those contingencies, and performances may then be jointly determined both by the specific contingencies for particular instances of behaviour and the social contingencies that maintain the higher-order class of rule-following. In other words, verbal behaviour that constitutes a rule may be shaped by contingencies that would otherwise operate on the non-verbal behaviour itself: Rules that work remain effective as rules, whereas those that do not lose their power to govern behaviour (but such contingencies are undermined when rules specify very remote contingencies, as in promises of reward or punishment after death).

THE ELUSIVENESS OF HUMAN CONTINGENCY-SHAPED BEHAVIOUR

Much human behaviour is rule-governed and therefore insensitive to its consequences. In fact, apart from the area of motor skills, it is difficult to find instances of adult human behaviour that are unequivocally contingency-shaped, though characteristic performances can be obtained from preverbal children (Lowe, Beasty, & Bentall, 1983).

Rule-governed behaviour is well-established in humans by an early age. For example, Bentall, Lowe, and Beasty (1985) studied the performances of children from about 2 to 5 years of age on simple tasks in which responses such as button-presses produced simple consequences, such as snacks or opportunities to hear music, according to various schedules. For children under 2, performances were not substantially different from those of non-verbal organisms such as pigeons. Between the ages of about 2 and 4 or 5, the performances of most children were transitional, with variable properties apparently related both to contingency-governed and to rule-governed behaviour. By the age of 5, the performances of most children had become almost exclusively rule-governed, with the relatively stereotyped and inflexible properties that characterise adult performance. As with adults, such insensitivities to schedule contingencies can be overridden by the shaping of verbal behaviour (Bentall & Lowe, 1987; Catania, in press).

In a variety of contexts, human performance is likely to be determined by verbal behaviour rather than by current contingencies (cf. Lowe, 1979; Luria, 1961; Zivin, 1979), but clearly there must be points at which human behaviour makes direct contact with contingencies. Many skilled motor performances probably do not allow verbal mediation (e.g. in athletics, or in tying shoelaces). In some performances that begin with large instructional components (e.g. as in learning to drive a manual or stick-shift car), verbal behaviour seems eventually to drop out, at which point the performance is sometimes called automatic; in such cases, abrupt changes in contingencies sometimes trigger the reappearance of relevant verbal behaviour. But such behaviour may not be sensitive to contingencies in the same way as contingency-shaped behaviour that has never been under rule-governed control (cf. Dreyfus & Dreyfus, 1986).

Bringing human contingency-shaped behaviour into the laboratory has been a concern of experiments on learning without awareness (e.g. Dulany, Carlson, & Dewey, 1985). The problem with such experiments is that the failure to identify or record relevant verbal behaviour does not rule out its possible involvement in the subject's performance. It cannot even be assumed that subjects can accurately report whether or not they have been engaging in private talk.

Consider the invisible thumb twitch studied by Hefferline and Keenan (1961). Their subjects were not able to report that this small-scale muscle movement served as their avoidance response, though this response varied with an avoidance contingency (turning off noise that masked music). But might verbal mediation unrelated to the specific thumb movement have affected general activity levels (e.g. "the music sounds better when I relax")? When this experiment was conducted, it was not technically feasible to record simultaneously from several fingers and to arrange consequences based on an independent small-scale movement from only one of them (verbal mediation has also been implicated in biofeedback procedures involving autonomic responses: Hopkinson, 1988).

In modifying human non-verbal behaviour, one is more likely to be successful indirectly, by shaping relevant verbal behaviour, than directly, by shaping the non-verbal behaviour itself. The search for human contingency-shaped behaviour might well begin here, with verbal behaviour itself as a prime candidate. If nowhere else, this must be the point at which contingencies enter directly. The very fact of shaping implies that this verbal behaviour must be sensitive to contingencies even if the behaviour it controls is rule-governed.

One reason for the susceptibility of verbal behaviour to the direct effects of contingencies might be that our everyday language does not include an effective vocabulary dealing with the variables that control our verbal behaviour. We may distinguish between what we have been told and what we have arrived at on our own, and our discrimination of these different sources may make instructed verbal behaviour less sensitive to contingencies than verbal behaviour that has been shaped by contact with contingencies. But contingencies may also generate verbal behaviour that in turn produces non-verbal behaviour consistent with natural consequences. One's behaviour then may become sensitive to its consequences because one has developed a good verbal formulation of contingencies and related performances; in such cases, the sensitivity, mediated by verbal behaviour, is indirect.

The distinction between shaped and instructed verbal behaviour has practical implications. For example, formal procedures based on explicit instructions are often described as cookbook, but the mark of a great chef is being able to deviate from the recipe when appropriate (e.g. as when some ingredients are unavailable). The same point can be made with respect to a scientist's deviation from recipes for experimental design. The training of laboratory researchers can emphasise formal statistical designs or the interaction of the experimenter's behaviour with the natural contingencies of the laboratory. Both forms of instruction may lead to rule-governed experimenting, but the experimental behaviour generated by the latter is more likely to be consistent with the contingencies of the research environment. To the extent that they shape correspondences between verbal behaviour and environmental contingencies, the practices of science help to counteract the ways in which language can insulate behaviour from its consequences.

EQUIVALENCE CLASSES AND CORRESPONDENCES BETWEEN SAYING AND DOING

Following instructions implies a correspondence between verbal behaviour and the rule-governed behaviour that it occasions. Correspondences between saying and doing enter into a variety of relations between human verbal and non-verbal behaviour. These correspondences are typically symmetrical. For example, a child's doing may precede the saying, as in describing past behaviour, or the saying may precede the doing, as in keeping a promise. The symmetry implicit in these verbal functions is a property of equivalence classes (cf. Sidman, Rauzin, Lazar, Cunningham, Tailby, & Carrigan, 1982).

Discriminative control is unidirectional—a stimulus sets the occasion on which responding has consequences. For example, the relation between a red traffic light and stepping on the brakes is not reversible. That between the red light and the word "stop," however, is: One can produce the word on seeing the light or attend to the light on hearing the word. Such symmetries exist in the relations among verbal responses and non-verbal events. We can produce a pencil upon hearing the word "pencil" and we can produce the word "pencil" upon seeing the writing implement. These kinds of equivalences are what make verbal behaviour symbolic. Unlike non-verbal events, verbal events function both as stimuli and as responses (lever presses and key pecks are not analogously interchangeable with lights and tones). Such equivalences characterise verbal behavior.

Many features of the social interactions that may have been central to the evolution of language involve symmetries. Even the simplest verbal episodes include reciprocities in the roles of the speaker and the listener. To the extent that the speaker sometimes functions as listener and vice versa, such reciprocities may be the precursors of equivalence classes, which may be linked to instructional control in turn by way of the correspondences that must develop between the speaker's instructions and the listener's rule-governed behaviour occasioned by those instructions.

It is not possible to say whether equivalence classes are a prerequisite for language or language is a prerequisite for equivalence classes. Perhaps these alternatives are not even appropriate; both language and equivalences may be two different aspects of a single behavioural competence. In any case, equivalences allow verbal units and environmental events to enter into classes (objects and their names); verbal behaviour that describes one's own behaviour may then strengthen the correspondences between saying and doing that make verbal contingencies override non-verbal ones. Once saying and doing are members of an equivalence class, changes in one will be accompanied by changes in the other. Thus, changes in non-verbal behaviour are likely to be accompanied by corresponding verbal reports, and changes in verbal reports are likely to be accompanied by corresponding non-verbal behaviour.

SELF-INSTRUCTIONS AND DISCRIMINATIONS OF ONE'S OWN BEHAVIOUR

Rule-governed behaviour would be limited in scope if a listener followed the speaker's instructions only when the speaker was present. The temporal extension of rule-governed behaviour presumably comes about because the listener can repeat what the speaker has said. At this point, we can only speculate about the ways in which speakers can become their own listeners and vice versa, but discriminations of one's own behaviour must play an important role in such elaborations of the effects of rule-governed behaviour.

Verbal behaviour cannot exist in the absence of discriminations of one's own behaviour (the autoclitic processes of Skinner, 1957; cf. Catania, 1980). For example, appropriately saying "I am pleased to report that this is so" rather than "I am sorry to report that this is so" requires that one discriminate between the respective conditions under which one may be speaking. Words like "is" and "not" and "if" are similarly built on the speaker's discriminations among other aspects of the speaker's own verbal behaviour. Autoclitic verbal behaviour is verbal behaviour built upon other verbal behaviour; its function is to modify the effects on the listener of the other verbal behaviour (e.g. as effects of the instruction "go" are modified by the word "not"; particles, words, phrases and grammatical structures can have autoclitic functions). The propositional character of language is based on such functional relations rather than on logical ones.

If discriminations of one's own behaviour are an intrinsic property of language, such discriminations may enter into the effectiveness of verbal control. For example, once instructions have been repeated by a listener, the listener may begin to discriminate among the sources of this verbal behaviour. It is one thing to respond to what someone else has said; it is another to respond to one's own repetition of the other's utterance. Discrimination of the sources of instructional control may have marked the beginnings of those processes we speak of as consciousness or self-awareness. In the evolution of rule-governed behaviour, repetitions of the speaker's instructions presumably began in an overt vocal form, but the argument can also be made in terms of covert behaviour (cf. Jaynes, 1977).

Both remembered voices and hallucinated voices begin as repetitions of heard voices. The main difference is in the listener's discrimination between their sources: Remembered voices are discriminated from heard voices, whereas hallucinated voices are not.

An implication is that one might talk to oneself without knowing that one is doing it. To the extent that much human behaviour is rule-governed, it also follows that instructions will be especially effective when a single organism produces both the instructions and the instructed behaviour. We humans often talk to ourselves and thereby generate our own rules (cf. Hayes, 1986; Lowe, 1979). It may be that rule-governed behaviour that depends on our own talk is even more likely to be insulated from its consequences than rule-governed behaviour that depends on the talk of others.

A problem in studying such phenomena is that self-generated rules are not easily accessible. The ease with which we can identify a rule as a part of a particular verbal environment depends on who generated it, on whether it is overt or covert, and on which properties of behaviour it specifies. In an experimental setting, for example, a rule overtly provided by the experimenter in a set of instructions will probably be easier to identify than one covertly generated by the subject. The difference, however, is one of accessibility and not one of the behavioural dimensions of the relevant verbal behaviour.

CLINICAL AND EXPERIMENTAL IMPLICATIONS

Natural contingencies may favour correspondences between verbal and non-verbal behaviour over the long run, but the joint effect of social and non-social contingencies in the shaping of an individual's verbal behaviour may produce anomalies. For example, some pathologies of human behaviour (e.g. compulsions) may be interpreted as rule-governed behaviour gone awry.

We have observed that one is more likely to be successful in modifying human non-verbal behaviour indirectly by shaping relevant verbal behaviour than directly by shaping the non-verbal behaviour itself. This observation may be clinically relevant, because verbal manipulations are common in therapeutic treatments. Consider the implicit shaping of the client's talk in Rogerian therapy (Truax, 1966; other therapies combine shaping with instructional manipulations, as in rational-emotive therapy or cognitive behaviour modification). If human behaviour is dominated by rule-governed rather than by contingency-shaped behaviour, it makes sense to work on a client's verbal behaviour rather than directly on the client's non-verbal behaviour. This is one practical way in which behaviour change established within the therapeutic setting may transfer to environments outside that setting: Shaping what the client says about behaviour in other settings may produce changes in the client's behaviour in those settings.

But one other hope of clinical interventions is that the behaviour established in therapy will be maintained outside the therapeutic setting when it is taken over by the natural contingencies that operate there. For example, if a therapist establishes appropriate social behaviour in a shy individual through verbal means, the therapist would like to assume that natural social contingencies will eventually support the newly established appropriate social behaviour. The problem, however, is that establishing appropriate social behaviour through verbal means will necessarily make that behaviour rule-governed and therefore insensitive to its natural consequences, thereby slowing or even blocking transfer of control from its verbal origins to those natural consequences.

These clinical problems are closely related to experimental problems that have been studied in such contexts as probability judgement (Estes, 1976; Tversky & Kahneman, 1983), hypothesis theory (Levine, 1971) and implicit learning (Reber, 1976). In these cases, human judgements involve verbal formulations that produce behaviour that is inconsistent with nonverbal (usually quantitative) contingencies. The present approach is distinguished from these others primarily in its focus on the origins of the verbal formulations and the ways in which these formulations can determine other behaviour. These might be appropriate settings in which to explore further the properties of rule-governed behaviour. For example, if subjects are to be asked to choose alternatives in a probability matching study, it might be of more interest first to teach them relevant verbal behaviour by shaping accurate probability estimations than later to try to interpret performances that will necessarily be based on the unknown self-instructions with which they entered the experimental setting.

Given the central role played by verbal behaviour in contemporary social, political, economic and environmental settings, this subject matter could hardly have a higher priority. We need to learn as much as we can about rule-governed behaviour.

REFERENCES

Baer, D. M., Peterson, R. F., & Sherman, J. A. (1967). The development of imitation by reinforcing behavioral similarity to a model. *Journal of the Experimental Analysis of Behavior*, *10*, 405–416.

Bem, D. J. (1967). Self-perception: An alternative interpretation of cognitive phenomena. *Psychological Review*, *74*, 183–200.

Bentall, R. P. & Lowe, C. F. (1987). The role of verbal behavior in human learning: III. Instructional effects in children. *Journal of the Experimental Analysis of Behavior*, *47*, 177–190.

Bentall, R. P., Lowe, C. F., & Beasty, A. (1985). The role of verbal behavior in human learning: II. Developmental differences. *Journal of the Experimental Analysis of Behavior*, *43*, 165–181.

Catania, A. C. (1980). Autoclitic processes and the structure of behavior. *Behaviorism*, *8*, 175–186.

Catania, A. C. (1985). Rule-governed behavior and the origins of language. In C. F. Lowe, M. Richelle, D. E. Blackman, & C. Bradshaw (Eds), *Behavior analysis and contemporary psychology*, pp. 135–156. Hillsdale, N.J.: Lawrence Erlbaum Associates Inc.

Catania, A. C. (in press). The phylogeny and ontogeny of language function. In N. A. Krasnegor (Ed.), *Biobehavioural foundations of language acquisition*. Hillsdale, N.J.: Lawrence Erlbaum Associates Inc.

Catania, A. C., Matthews, B. A., & Shimoff, E. (1982). Instructed versus shaped human verbal behavior: Interactions with nonverbal responding. *Journal of the Experimental Analysis of Behavior*, *38*, 233–248.

Catania, A. C., Shimoff, E., & Matthews, B. A. (1987). How language insulates behavior from its consequences. *Proceedings of the Annual Meeting of the British Psychological Society*, *4*.

Catania, A. C., Shimoff, E., & Matthews, B. A. (1989). An experimental analysis of rule-governed behavior. In S. C. Hayes (Ed.), *Rule-governed behavior: Cognition, contingencies and instructional control*, pp. 119–150. New York: Plenum Press.

Dennett, D. C. (1987). *The intentional stance*. Cambridge, Mass.: MIT Press.

Dreyfus, H. L. & Dreyfus, S. E. (1986). *Mind over machine*. New York: Free Press.

Dulany, D. E., Carlson, R. A., & Dewey, G. I. (1985). On consciousness in syntactic learning and judgment: A reply to Reber, Allen, and Regan. *Journal of Experimental Psychology: General*, *114*, 25–32.

Estes, W. K. (1971). Reward in human learning: Theoretical issues and strategic choice points. In R. Glaser (Ed.), *The nature of reinforcement*, pp. 16–36. London: Academic Press.

Estes, W. K. (1976). The cognitive side of probability learning. *Psychological Review*, *83*, 37–64.

Gerwirtz, J. L. & Stingle, K. G. (1968). Learning of generalized imitation as the basis for identification. *Psychological Review*, *75*, 374–397.

Greenspoon, J. (1955). The reinforcing effect of two spoken sounds on the frequency of two responses. *American Journal of Psychology*, *68*, 409–416.

Hayes, S. C. (1986). The case of the silent dog—Verbal reports and the analysis of rules: A review of Ericsson and Simon's *Protocol Analysis: Verbal Reports as Data. Journal of the Experimental Analysis of Behavior*, *45*, 351–363.

Hefferline, R. F. & Keenan, B. (1961). Amplitude-induction gradient of a small human operant in an escape–avoidance situation. *Journal of the Experimental Analysis of Behavior*, *6*, 41–43.

Hopkinson, P. (1988). Operant modification of electrodermal responses: An analysis of individual behaviour. Doctoral dissertation, University of Southampton.

Jaynes, J. (1977). *The origin of consciousness in the breakdown of the bicameral mind*. Boston: Houghton Mifflin.

Kamin, L. J. (1969). Predictability, surprise, attention and conditioning. In B. A. Campbell and R. M. Church (Eds), *Punishment and aversive behavior*, pp. 279–296. New York: Appleton-Century-Crofts.

Levine, M. (1971). Hypothesis theory and nonlearning despite ideal S-R-reinforcement contingencies. *Psychological Review*, *78*, 130–140.

Lowe, C. F. (1979). Determinants of human operant behaviour. In M. D. Zeiler & P. Harzem (Eds), *Reinforcement and the organization of behaviour*, pp. 159–192. Chichester: John Wiley.

Lowe, C. F., Beasty, A., & Bentall, R. P. (1983). The role of verbal behavior in human learning: Infant performance on fixed-interval schedules. *Journal of the Experimental Analysis of Behavior*, *39*, 157–164.

Luria, A. R. (1961). *The role of speech in the production of normal and abnormal behavior*. New York: Liveright.

Matthews, B. A., Catania, A. C., & Shimoff, E. (1985). Effects of uninstructed verbal behavior on nonverbal responding: Contingency descriptions versus performance descriptions. *Journal of the Experimental Analysis of Behavior*, *43*, 155–164.

Reber, A. S. (1976). Implicit learning of synthetic languages: The role of instructional set. *Journal of Experimental Psychology: Human Learning and Memory*, *2*, 88–94.

Savage-Rumbaugh, E. S. (1986). *Ape language*. New York: Columbia University Press.

Shimoff, E., Matthews, B. A., & Catania, A. C. (1986). Human operant performance: Sensitivity and pseudosensitivity to contingencies. *Journal of the Experimental Analysis of Behavior*, *46*, 149–157.

Sidman, M., Rauzin, R., Lazar, R., Cunningham, S., Tailby, W., & Carrigan, P. (1982). A search for symmetry in the conditional discrimination of Rhesus monkeys, baboons, and children. *Journal of the Experimental Analysis of Behavior*, *37*, 23–44.

Skinner, B. F. (1957). *Verbal behavior*. New York: Appleton-Century-Crofts.

Skinner, B. F. (1969). An operant analysis of problem solving. In B. F. Skinner, *Contingencies of reinforcement*, pp. 133–157. New York: Appleton-Century-Crofts.

Truax, C. B. (1966). Reinforcement and nonreinforcement in Rogerian therapy. *Journal of Abnormal Psychology*, *71*, 1–9.

Tversky, A. & Kahneman, D. (1983). Extensional versus intuitive reasoning: The conjunction fallacy in probability judgment. *Psychological Review*, *90*, 293–315.

Zivin, G. (Ed.) (1979). *The development of self-regulation through private speech*. New York: John Wiley.

IV BEHAVIOURAL MEDICINE

11 Behaviour and Visceral Functions

György Ádám, Eszter Láng, György Bárdos, László Balázs and Julia Weisz
Department of Comparative Physiology and Psychophysiology, Hungarian Academy of Science, University of Budapest, Budapest, Hungary

Today, it seems commonplace to emphasise that behavioural modifications affect the functions of our internal organs and, vice versa, that visceral changes can modify behaviour. This statement—which may now appear to most of us as banal—has a long and controversial history which cannot be regarded as having been clarified. On the contrary, it hides a series of unresolved, open problems. In this paper, we try to approach some of them.

Before delivering our own results, we would like to make it clear that the Setchenovian-Pavlovian mentality with which the research started has regarded the process of reinforcement as the cornerstone of the interrelations between the visceral functions and behaviour (Adam, 1967). Programmes and algorithms of reinforcement ensure the two-way interaction between covert or overt visceral activity and behavioural phenomena. This well-documented finding enabled us a smooth and easy transition to Thorndikeian and Skinnerian principles of behavioural analysis.

Based upon our early data of visceral learning, we have undertaken, in recent years, experiments in two different directions concerning the reciprocity of behavioural and visceral functions. Our first approach concerns centrifugal relations, i.e. how higher brain functions and behavioural changes modify the activity of internal organs. Our second approach refers to centripetal influence, namely, how visceral sensory events may alter behaviour.

CENTRIFUGAL INFLUENCE OF BEHAVIOUR ON VISCERAL FUNCTIONS

In the framework of our first approach, we selected heart rate and heart period conditioning as a model of instrumental visceral learning, as this model has a wide literature—although some basic issues are far from being resolved. Two different human experimental series will be outlined, both using visual feedback of heart rate changes as reinforcement.

In the first series, heart rate feedback *vs* pre-experimental instructions were investigated. Each of the 24 subjects took part in 14 sessions over a period of five consecutive weeks. The sessions were divided into four blocks. After the first adaptation block, the second block consisted of three sessions where subjects were instructed to try to slow down their heart rate. In the third block, the same instructions were given but, in addition, heart-period visual feedback was presented for heart rate decrease. The visual feedback was displayed in the form of a beating heart scheme on a TV monitor. In the last block, the feedback was again taken away. Each session consisted of ten 30-sec pre-trials and 90-sec trials.

The results indicate that the ability to decrease heart rate depends on personality traits, rather than on the presence or absence of a visual feedback. Instruction—in given typologies—might be as powerful as feedback! Six different slowing strategies could be observed. Of the six behaviours, two displayed a higher level of decreased heart rate when feedback was absent (Fig. 11.1).

In the second series of our heart rate feedback programme, we raised the question of whether feedback training for decreases in heart rate improves a subject's ability to detect heart beat, because (as will be outlined later) detection of visceral signals is one of the main issues of our research endeavours. We presumed that heart rate decreasing behaviour is partly or totally dependent on the heart beat detection ability of the subject, and vice versa.

Two groups were used, each consisting of 16 males ranging in age from 18 to 25 years. For all subjects, the experiment consisted of one session as follows: At the beginning and at the end of the session, each group performed a heart beat discrimination task according to Whitehead et al. (1977). Using this technique, the subjects were asked to discriminate between two sets of stimuli, both of which are contingent on the R-wave, but presented at different time delays. The subjects were asked to indicate whether the stimuli were presented "immediately" after the heart beat or whether they were "delayed". The discrimination test involved presenting 10-sec trials: on half, a light flashed 128 msec after each R-wave of the ECG; on the other half, a light flashed 384 msec after each R-wave. A delay of 128 msec was chosen to represent immediate feedback because

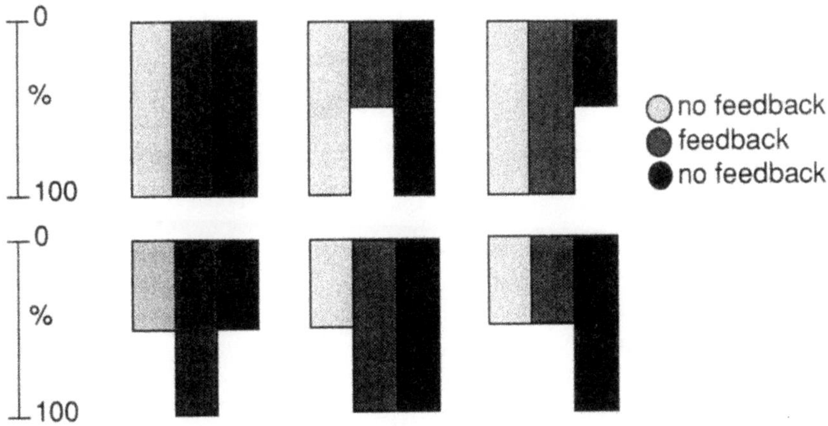

FIG. 11.1. Six types of heart rate decrease strategies performed by subjects in a no feedback–feedback–no feedback situation. 100% on the y-axis indicates the maximal performance of a given subject. Note that only in one group of subjects was the feedback more effective than the instructions.

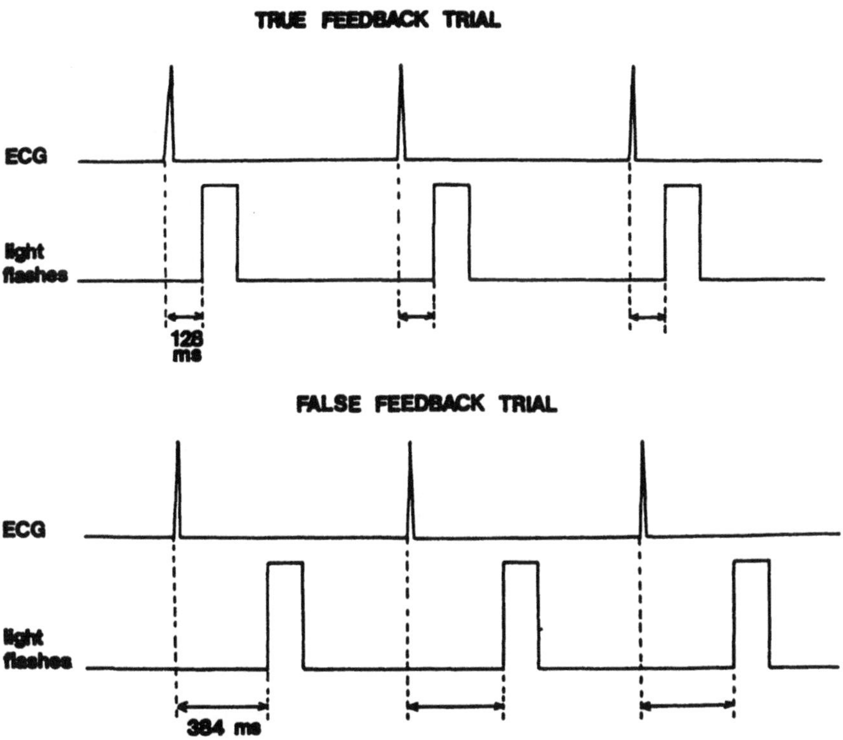

FIG. 11.2. The heart beat detection technique according to Whitehead et al. (1977) (see text for further explanation.)

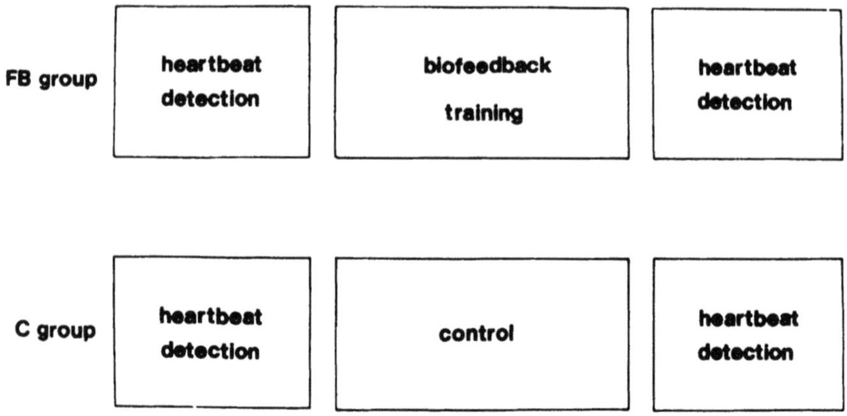

FIG. 11.3. Experimental design of heart beat detection experiments combined with feedback-training (FB) *vs* control (C) (see text for a detailed explanation.)

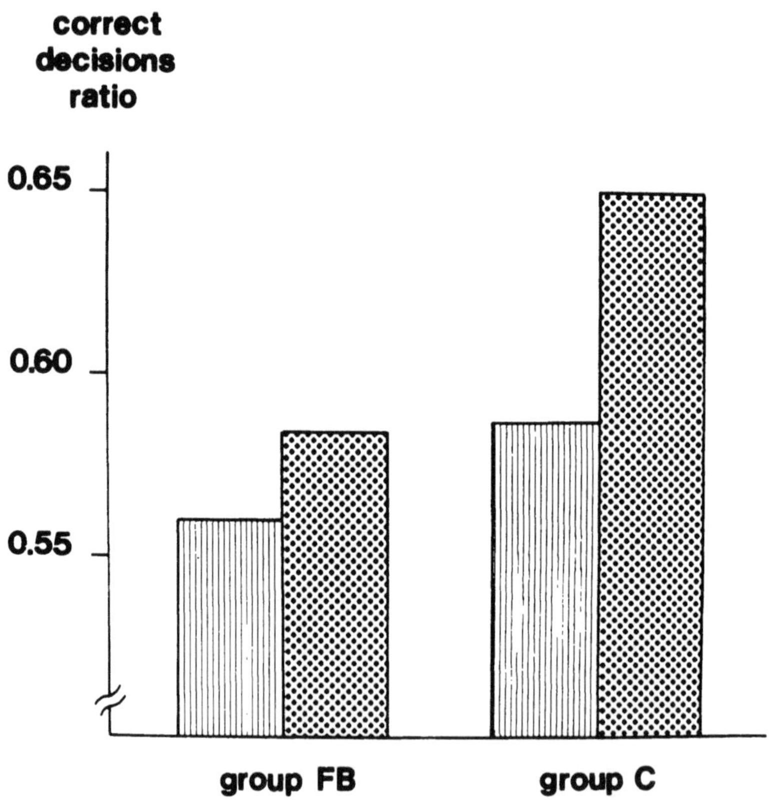

FIG. 11.4. Heart beat detection with and without feedback training. The group without feedback (C) performed as well as the feedback (FB) group if the correct detection ratios of the first (striped columns) and the second (dotted columns) detection series are compared.

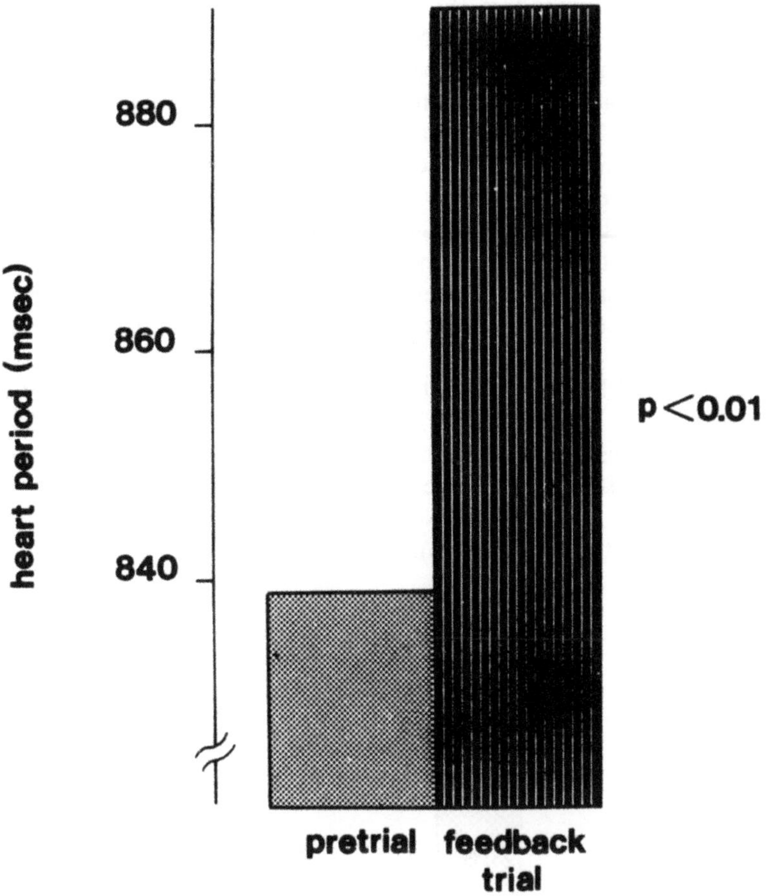

FIG. 11.5. Increase in heart-period following heart beat decrease training before (dotted columns) and following (striped columns) feedback.

100–150 msec is required for a blood pulse wave to reach the neck (Fig. 11.2). The percentage of correct decisions was computed for each heart beat detection task. Following the first heart beat discrimination task, the only difference between the groups was that whereas in the feedback group 22 essentially similar training trials were given as in the previous study (i.e. visual display of a pulsating heart scheme), the subjects in the control group were reading a text (Fig. 11.3). Each part of the experiment was preceded by a 3-min baseline period during which the subjects were sitting quietly. Their ECG and respiration were recorded throughout the session.

The ratios of correct decisions during the first and second heart beat detection tasks were calculated for both groups. Analyses of variance were performed using procedure (FB,C) as between- and order (of detection task) as within-group factor. No reliable effects for procedure were obtained, showing that the feedback training used to control heart rate did not improve heart beat discrimination (Fig. 11.4). A reliable main effect obtained for order indicated that the subjects in both groups improved their accuracy in heart beat discrimination equally from the first to the second task. These data do not support the hypothesis that control over heart rate and discrimination of heart beat are very closely related. Our data suggest that this control can be acquired without an improvement in heart beat detection. Our data even illustrate how the subjects decreased their heart rate during feedback training from the pre-trials to the trials (Fig. 11.5).

We recorded heart-period data during the first and second heart beat detection tasks. Analyses of variance were performed with procedure as between- and task order (heartbeat detection) as within-group factor. A reliable order effect was obtained reflecting a heart period increase from the first to the second task. Neither a main effect for procedure nor interaction was found (Fig. 11.6).

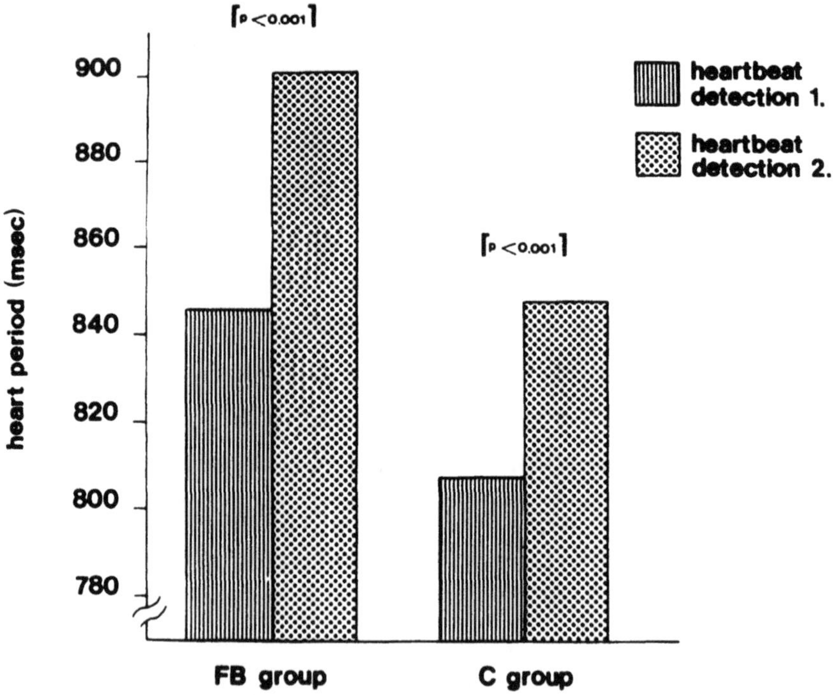

FIG. 11.6. The changes in heart-period between heart beat detection tasks 1 and 2 in the feedback (FB) and control (C) groups.

In conclusion, it seems that decreases in heart beat via feedback cannot be regarded as a reinforcement for the ability to detect heart beat. It seems that these two processes are somehow independent from each other.

CENTRIPETAL INFLUENCE OF VISCERAL SENSATIONS ON BEHAVIOUR

The experiment described above leads us to our second line of investigation, in which we analysed the detection and discrimination capacities of animals and humans for visceral sensory input via reinforcement, i.e. through instrumental conditioning strategies.

For more than 25 years we have been engaged in the analysis of behavioural changes following the non-painful stimulation of several internal organs. As an example, I will briefly describe some of our operant conditioning experiments in animals and humans by using intestinal stimulation in a discrimination task (S-d *vs* S-delta).

Our pilot studies with rhesus monkeys have proved that the mild distension of the wall of an isolated intestinal loop can be used as a

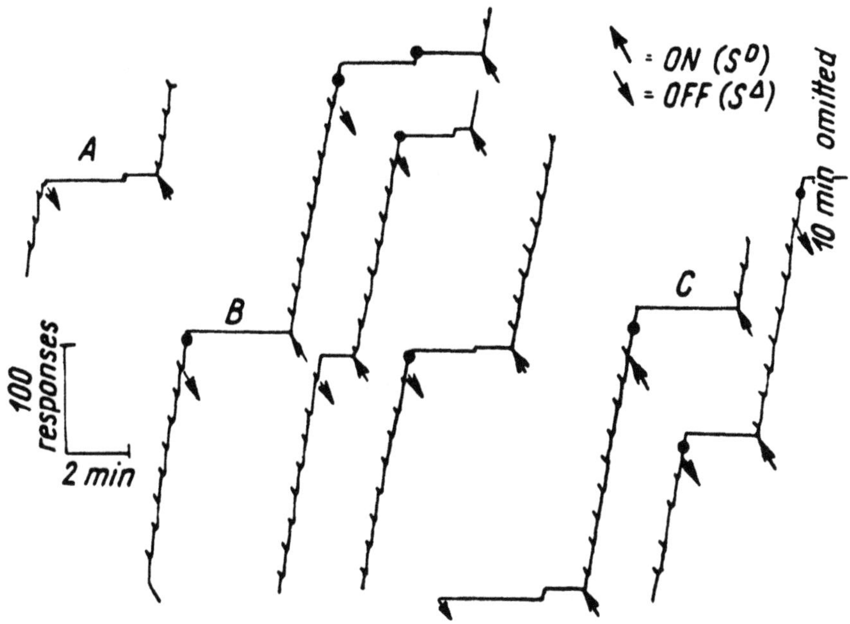

FIG. 11.7. Detection of intestinal distension by a rhesus monkey in an operant conditioning situation. The pips indicate reinforcement, the dots the reset of the stepper. Sample cumulative lever-press curves. The arrows indicate the onset and offset of the intestinal stimulus (Ádám, 1967).

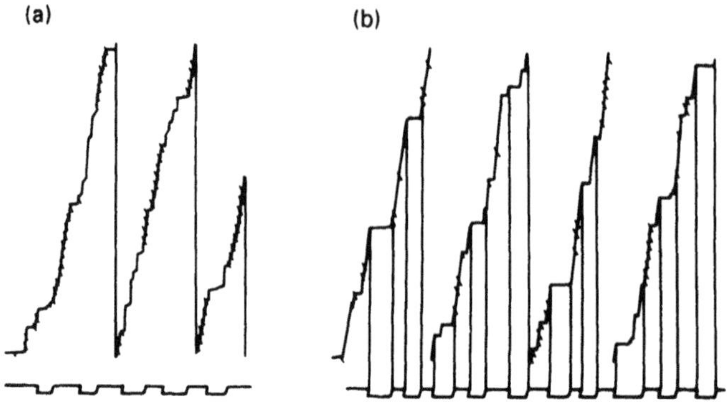

FIG. 11.8. Unsuccessful (a) and successful (b) detection of intestinal distension in a rat in an operant conditioning situation. The intestinal stimuli are marked by indentations of the horizontal lines below the cumulative lever-press curves.

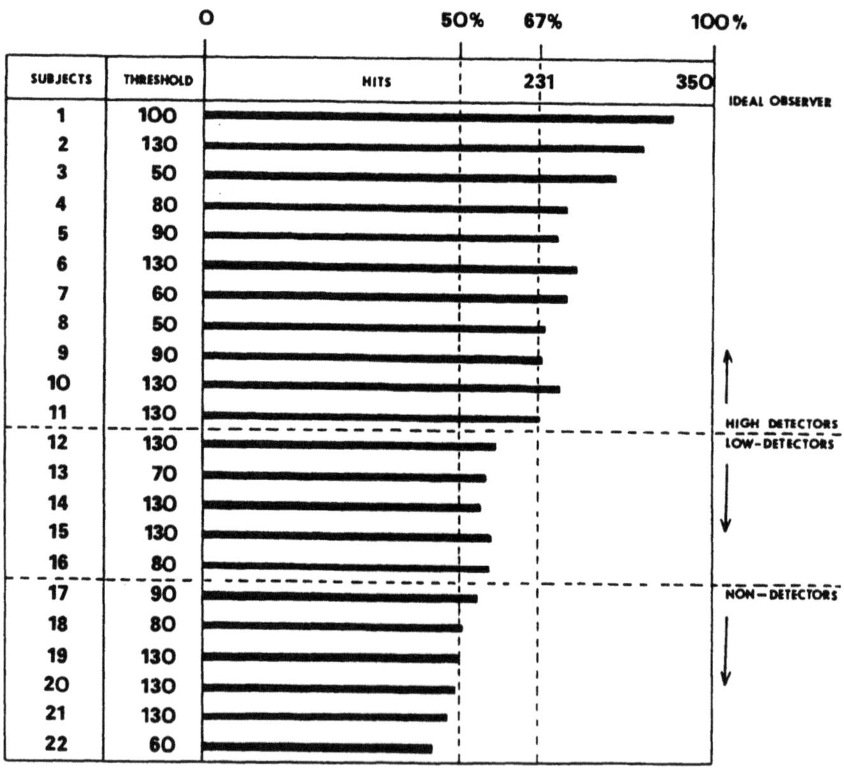

FIG. 11.9. The performance of 22 colonostomy patients on colon-distension detection. Each of the 22 horizontal columns indicates the total number of correct decisions of the given subject in the three experimental sessions. Note that 16 subjects displayed performance above the 50% chance level (175 hits out of 350), and 11 subjects above the 67% level (231 or more hits out of 350).

discriminative stimulus. In these first experiments, we did not pay attention to the exact threshold of our mechanical stimuli (Fig. 11.7). In more recent investigations, however, it turned out that the ability to detect and discriminate was highly dependent on the intensiveness of the stretch stimuli applied. Less intensive intestinal stimuli resulted neither in learning nor in reconditioning. More intensive gut stimuli were as effective in operant conditioning situations as visual or auditory ones (Fig. 11.8). Indeed, gut stimuli proved to be more effective in aversive situations than in the case of alimentary reinforcement. All these findings are based upon experiments with rats.

But, what is the situation in humans? Based on the early data of the ability to detect duodenal stimuli in a group of subjects, a new series has recently been undertaken in colonostomy patients. We examined the ability to detect mild, non-painful distension of the sygmoid colon in 22 patients who underwent colonostomy 1 year or more before the investigation.

The colon was distended by a balloon inserted 10 cm below the orifice of the artificial anus. Each subject participated in three sessions on three consecutive weeks with several experimental tasks in each session. During the tasks, the patients received the colon stimulus (the "signal") 25 times in

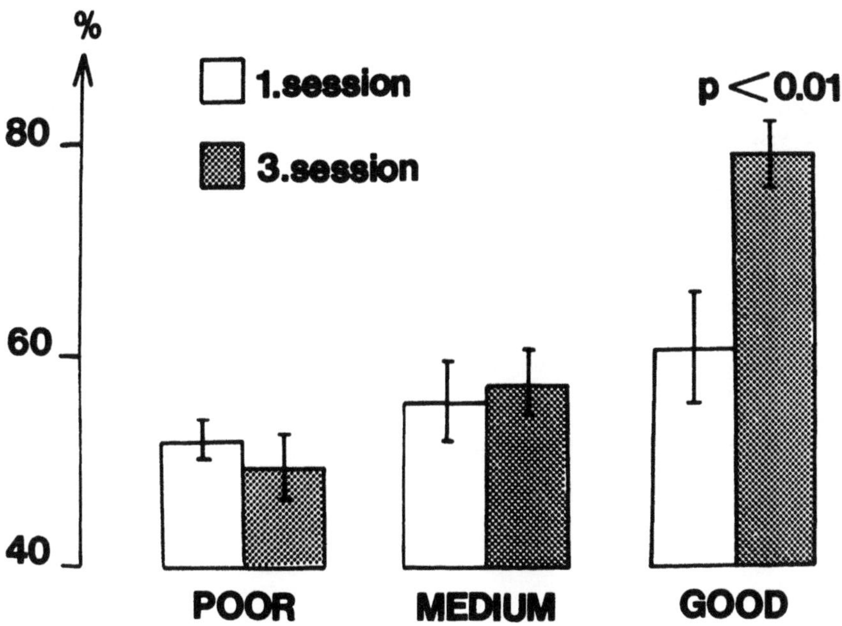

FIG. 11.10. Colon-distension detection by poor, low and high detector groups before (white columns) and after (dotted columns) training via auditory feedback.

random order, masked by simultaneously delivered—either auditory or annular—skin stimuli, administered in series of 50, representing "noise" according to signal detection paradigms. Each subject had to make a yes/no choice after each time the warning "noise" stimulus was administered. In all three sessions, learning tasks were included using operant conditioning paradigms. Of the 22 subjects, 9 were considered "good perceivers", 6 "medium perceivers", and the remaining 6 "poor perceivers" (Fig. 11.9). According to the data, it can be hypothesised that most patients have some inherent sensitivity to colon distension and that learning improves this initial ability (Fig. 11.10).

CONCLUSION

Two main issues have been addressed in this paper:

1. How instrumental conditioning mechanisms act on the centrifugal processes which commence in the brain and influence modifications in heart activity.
2. How visceral (more precisely, intestinal) signals act on the centripetal processes which commence in the internal organs and influence detection, i.e. the modification of cognitive behaviour.

With both of these, it turned out that reinforcement, regarded both as a brain mechanism and a procedure, is essential in initiating and modifying cerebro-visceral interrelations both "downwards" (i.e. commencing in the brain and influencing visceral activity), and "upwards" (i.e. commencing in the visceral receptors and influencing the perceptive mechanisms of the brain).

It is our strong belief that an experimental analysis of behaviour cannot omit visceral functions.

REFERENCES

Ádám, G. (1967). *Interoception and behavior: An experimental study*. Budapest: Akadémiai Kiadó.

Whitehead, E. W., Drescher, V. M., & Heiman, P. (1977). Relation of heart rate control to heartbeat perception. *Biofeedback and Self-regulation*, *2*, 371–392.

12 The Contribution of Behavioural Medicine to the Research and Prevention of AIDS

Ramon Bayés
Universidad Autonoma de Barcelona, Barcelona, Spain

AIDS: A PUBLIC HEALTH PROBLEM

The World Conference on AIDS Prevention Programmes organised by the World Health Organisation (WHO) in London from 26 to 28 January 1988, brought together health ministers and experts from 152 countries (Criado, 1988). The fact that this conference took place shows how concerned WHO and governments around the world are with the spread of AIDS, and the importance attached to preventive measures. The Fourth International Conference on AIDS, held in Stockholm in June 1988 in the presence of 7000 health experts, confirmed these concerns.

By June 1988, the number of declared cases of AIDS worldwide had reached 96,433 in 136 countries, though the actual number is considered to be considerably higher. The greatest number of cases has been reported in the Americas—71,343 (61,850 in the U.S.A. alone)—followed by Europe with 12,414 cases (Salgado, 1988). In Europe, the number of official cases tripled between September 1986 and June 1988. Although AIDS is to be found throughout Europe, its incidence varies from country to country, with Switzerland, France, Denmark and Belgium being the most badly affected (see Table 12.1). The distribution of AIDS also varies within each country (see Table 12.2 for the situation in Spain).

Almost half of the people who have been affected have died. Although once someone has been diagnosed as having AIDS the average life expectancy is only 2 years, some recent studies have shown that 15% of patients can survive for 5 years (Rothenberg et al., 1987).

Bloom and Carliner (1988) have estimated the average cost of caring for an AIDS patient to be $80,000. This would mean in Zaire, for example,

TABLE 12.1
Estimated Number of AIDS Cases in Europe (per million people) Officially Reported to WHO, 30 September 1987

1. Switzerland	46
2. France	46
3. Denmark	40
4. Belgium	28
5. The Netherlands	26
6. West Germany	23
7. Iceland	20
8. Luxembourg	20
9. Italy	19
10. United Kingdom	19
11. Malta	18
12. Sweden	17
13. Spain	16

Source: INED (Paris). Reproduced by Comunidad de Madrid (1988).

TABLE 12.2
Estimated Number of AIDS Cases in Spain (per million people), 1988

1. Baleares	55
2. Madrid	52
3. Catalunya	46
4. País Vasco	42
5. Navarra	26
6. País Valenciano	19
7. Asturias	19
8. Rioja	19
9. Aragón	18
10. Andalucía	15
11. Cantabria	14
12. Canarias	13
13. Galicia	13
14. Castilla-León	12
15. Murcia	10
16. Castilla-La Mancha	9
17. Extremadura	2

Source: Adapted from Tijeras et al. (1988).

that the budget of its biggest hospital would allow for the treatment of only 10 patients from a developed nation (Panos Institute, 1987). In some countries, the indirect economic losses related to AIDS outweigh medical expenses, because 80% of those diagnosed as being infected are aged between 20 and 40, the very age group which makes up the core of the workforce. In West Germany, for example, it is estimated that the indirect economic loss to the nation is DM100 million for every 300 AIDS cases (Velimirovic, 1986).

At the time of writing, there is no vaccine or therapeutic agent which can fight the human immunodeficiency virus (HIV) effectively. Although zidovudine (AZT) has brought some hope, it is not the long-term answer:

1. It will not eradicate the illness, although it may help to stop the virus replicating.
2. It has important side-effects in the short term, and its long-term effects are unknown.
3. Its application requires a high level of therapeutic compliance.
4. It is very expensive to administer (in Spain at the present time, it costs $41 a day).

Therefore, we are faced with an epidemic that is caused by a retrovirus with the following features:

1. It is spreading worldwide.
2. It affects young people especially.
3. It is fatal for the great majority of those infected.
4. It creates, and will continue to create, an enormous burden on health care services and losses in production.
5. There is no effective therapeutic agent which is free from side-effects (both in the short and long term), easy to administer and inexpensive.

For these reasons, our best weapon in the fight against AIDS is *prevention*, especially as we know a great deal about how the virus is transmitted. However, before looking at preventive behaviours, it is important to consider some other aspects of the disease.

Unlike other viruses, the HIV virus can remain in a latent state for a period that ranges from several months to 10 years or more. Then, one day, without apparent reason, it becomes active and the AIDS symptoms appear. It is important to point out, however, that although during the latent period the affected person, or *carrier*, may show no symptons at all, he or she is able to transmit the virus to other people. In fact, it has been calculated that every carrier infects on average one person per year (Brouard, 1987). Therefore, we have a kind of virus that:

1. May remain latent for many years, or even throughout the whole lifetime of the carrier.
2. May be ignored or even hidden by an indeterminate number of infected persons.
3. May be transmitted by these apparently healthy carriers or by others who already show some signs of the disease.

The body defends itself against viruses by manufacturing antibodies. At present, there are normalised tests for detecting HIV antibodies in the blood. However, apart from the small margin of error with these tests, it is important to take into account what has been termed the "window-period". For 6 weeks to 6 months or more after being infected, carriers do not show the presence of HIV antibodies, the very thing that the standardised tests are used to register.

However, at a social level, the most serious aspect is not the number of AIDS patients, or even that the disease is fatal, but the probably very high number of people who are infected but do not show any symptoms and who continue to spread the virus. It has been calculated that for each person diagnosed as having AIDS, there are 50–100 asymptomatic carriers (Delgado, 1988; de la Loma, 1987).

Although the following estimates are debatable (Segura, 1987a; 1987b), they give us an idea of the magnitude of the problem that we will face in the near future. WHO (OMS, 1987a), for example, has stated that the number of worldwide virus carriers could be between 5 and 10 million at the present time, and that by 1991 could reach between 50 and 100 million (OMS, 1987b). It was estimated that if 10–30% of carriers developed AIDS between 1987 and 1991, there could be between 0.5 and 3 million AIDS sufferers in total (OMS, 1987a). However, some think this estimate to be conservative. The National Academy of Sciences in the U.S.A., for example, indicates that possibly between 25 and 50% of carriers will develop full-blown AIDS in the same period. Moreover, a group of scientists from the University of Frankfurt believe this figure should be up to 50% for this 5-year-period and up to 75% over 7 years (cf. Panos Institute, 1987). In 1988, Moss et al. stated that:

> at three years an estimated two thirds of the seropositive subjects [included in the San Francisco Hospital cohort] showed clinical AIDS, an AIDS related condition, or laboratory results that were highly predictive of AIDS . . . [and that] . . . we should regard progression to clinical AIDS after infection with HIV as the norm rather than the exception.

Therefore, the AIDS epidemic can be considered as a time bomb which we do not know how to defuse.

It is not surprising, therefore, to find that WHO and many national health departments see prevention and health education as the most likely means of helping to solve the problem, especially as their own health care services are unable to cope and therapeutic solutions risk creating an economic collapse.

RISK BEHAVIOURS

Having outlined some of the relevant data regarding AIDS, we will now focus upon prevention. To do so, we must analyse the ways in which infection can take place and those factors that may facilitate or interfere with the infection process. The routes of infection are:

1. Sexual penetration: anal, vaginal and oral.
2. The sharing of needles or syringes by intravenous drug users.
3. Mother-to-child: before, during or after birth.
4. Blood transfusions or blood byproducts, e.g. the coagulation factor given to haemophiliacs.
5. Organ transplantation and artificial insemination.
6. Accidental contacts: wounds, sores, etc.; the fluids of infected or ill people; infected instruments such as shavers, knives, tattooing equipment, unsterilised medical equipment, etc.

At present in the West, the chances of becoming infected as a result of blood transfusion, blood byproducts, organ transplantation or artificial insemination are, although possible, highly unlikely, due to the existing safety measures. In many Third World countries, on the other hand, these safety measures are not so stringent, and the possibility of infection is high (OMS, 1987b).

The patterns of the spread of HIV vary according to the geographical location. In Europe, for example, the most prevalent behaviours leading to infection are:

1. Anal coitus, both in homosexual and heterosexual couples—the recipient is especially at risk.
2. The sharing of needles or syringes by intravenous drug users.

Apart from Italy and Spain, the highest incidence of AIDS in Europe has, until now, been found among the homosexual population. In Italy and Spain, however, intravenous drug users, especially heroin addicts, have been the group presenting most frequently with the HIV virus (see Table 12.3).

TABLE 12.3
Mode of Transmission of AIDS in Europe, 30 September 1987

Mode of transmission	*Total Europe*		*Europe without Italy and Spain*		*Italy and Spain*	
	N	%	*N*	%	*N*	%
Homo/Bisexual	4987	60	4595	69	392	24
Intravenous drug users	1498	18	514	8	984	59
Others	1817	22	1530	23	287	17
Totals	8302	100	6639	100	1663	100

Source: Adapted from Comunidad de Madrid (1988).

The high incidence of infection among homosexual men is due to:

1. A high level of promiscuity and, consequently, an increased likelihood of finding a partner who is infected. In 1986, Velimirovic found that the average homosexual male with AIDS in the U.S.A. had had 60 different sexual partners in a year.
2. The high level of anal intercourse, which is more dangerous than vaginal coitus (Bosch, 1986).
3. The infrequent use of condoms. From June 1986 to December 1987, of 593 assisted homosexuals at a primary care centre in Madrid, only 30% used condoms (Ortiz, 1988). It should be noted, however, that there is a high rate of accidents (including holes and rips) with condoms during anal intercourse (Fumento, 1987).

There is also a heated debate as to whether or not in the near future we will experience a large increase in the number of heterosexuals presenting with HIV. Many experts believe that too many people are not taking enough preventive measures when taking sexual risks (e.g. prostitutes and their clients, the partners of intravenous drug users, and promiscuous teenagers), and that they may well become infected. Bennett (1987), for example, considers that in many parts of the world, 60–70% of prostitutes are already carriers of the virus. In Spain, the incidence is not as high as this yet. In Barcelona in 1987, for example, of 121 prostitutes examined, 7% were found to be carriers (Capdevila et al., 1988). In a study carried out in Madrid between 1985 and 1988, of 218 non-intravenous drug-using prostitutes, there were no carriers, but in a group of 55 intravenous drug-using prostitutes, 70% were found to be carriers (Ortiz, 1988).

The three most important objectives for future preventive programmes in Europe should be to:

1. Discourage anal (homo- or heterosexual) intercourse, unless there are full guarantees that neither partner is infected.
2. Ensure that every person who undertakes sexually risky contacts (vaginal, anal or oral), whether infected or not, always uses condoms and a spermicide with antiviral properties.
3. Ensure that every person who injects intravenous drugs or medicines, or who is contemplating having a tattoo, always uses new or sterilised needles.

It is important to remember that most of the data collected on AIDS comes from self-reports and, as Huang, Watters, and Case (1988) have found, they are not always reliable. At a family planning clinic in Madrid, for example, 20% of the seropositive women who said their sexual partner used a condom came to the centre because of an unwanted pregnancy (Sojo et al., 1988). Similarly, in a hospital in Barcelona, of the 10% of intravenous drug users who said that they did not share needles, half were infected (Tor et al., 1988).

There is no doubt about the need to improve the validity and reliability of the ways in which the data are collected, especially as it will otherwise be difficult to assess the efficacy of any programme.

INFORMATION AND PREVENTION

Behavioural psychologists have known for a long time that in most cases *information is necessary but insufficient* to change behaviour. A clear example of this, in Spain at least, is that those who are best informed of the risks of smoking (physicians, nurses, teachers and, probably, psychologists) are those who smoke the most (Bayés, 1985). However, other health professionals and politicians do not seem to realise this fact. Therefore, it is important to state at the outset that pamphlets, advertisements and didactic television campaigns, although necessary, will not solve the AIDS problem by themselves. Information is not enough to change people's behaviour—it is only a first step.

During the last 3 months of 1987, for example, 107 intravenous drug users attended a primary care centre in Madrid. Despite the fact that 94% of them possessed adequate information about AIDS and its sources of infection, only 13% systematically used condoms and only 17% said they did not share syringes (de la Loma, 1988).

Even if by providing adequate information we change people's attitudes (which would be an important step in the right direction) but not their risk behaviours, we will have failed, because information and attitudes do not transmit the virus—*behaviours do*. And to change people's risk behaviours will not be easy, as shown by the failure to control syphilis, gonorrhoea, smoking, alcoholism and the use of heroin.

On the other hand, it is important to remember that even if we are able to change people's risk behaviours or get them to adopt effective preventive measures, there is no guarantee that such behaviours will be maintained. For example, Pardell, Salleras, and Salvador (1982) reported that only 15–25% of those who stopped smoking after an anti-smoking programme continued to do so after 1 year. Therefore, how many homosexuals who have changed their sexual behaviour because of AIDS will continue to do so? In fact, the facilitating factors of change are not necessarily those that allow for consolidation and maintenance of the new behaviour (Bayés, 1987). I think that there are important questions which need to be answered:

1. For a given person, what factors account for the practice, or non-practice, of a risk behaviour?
2. For a given person, what factors account for the practice, or non-practice, of effective preventive behaviours?
3. For a given person, what factors account for the maintenance of risk behaviours and/or the compliance with effective preventive behaviours?

FUNCTIONAL ANALYSIS OF BEHAVIOUR AND AIDS

The functional analysis of behaviour suggests some reasons why, in the case of AIDS, individuals continue practising dangerous behaviours despite being well-informed of the risks involved, or why individuals do not adopt or maintain effective preventive behaviours.

1. The most frequent risk behaviours (i.e. sexual penetration and intravenous drug use) almost *always*, *immediately*, and often *intensively*, imply *pleasure or stress release as a consequence*. When intravenous drug users are undergoing withdrawal, for example, it is very difficult for them to adopt or maintain preventive behaviours (des Jarlais, Friedman, & Strug, 1986).

2. The *harmful consequences* (infection by the HIV virus followed, perhaps, by AIDS) that may result from the practice of risk behaviours *always appear after a long period of time*, i.e. a person may be infected yet not show any symptoms for a number of years. The fact that the coping strategies of intravenous drug users usually consist of denial or an unreal sense of invulnerability (Solomon & DeJong, 1986), may further sever the link between risk behaviours and their consequences. Therefore, the

presence of a previous verbal stimulus which links the behaviour with a harmful consequence is broken down by this kind of strategy.

It is interesting to note that these coping strategies are also used by others at risk, including non-intravenous drug users. For example, it has recently been shown in the U.S.A., that only one-third of the sexual partners of haemophiliacs had asked for an HIV antibody test, despite the high prevalence of AIDS among the haemophiliac population (Centers for Disease Control, 1987).

The fact that there is probably a large number of carriers who practise risk behaviours, and who behave as if the virus did not exist, constitutes an added important risk, both for their sexual partners as well as for their future children.

3. In short, *there is not a perceived link* (e.g. a progressive deterioration or a growing symptomatology) *that can bind the moment of infection with the beginning of the disease*. Moreover, some of the early signs of AIDS in intravenous drug users, such as weight loss, fatigue, fever without apparent reason, night sweating, etc., may often be masked by the fact that they are also the frequent symptoms of drug use (Friedman, des Jarlais, & Sotheran, 1986).

4. The very practice of a dangerous behaviour does not always produce the same harmful consequences—infection by the virus or a transition from asymptomaticity to seropositivity. The *harmful consequences of a risk behaviour come about by chance*. The specific factors that may increase or reduce the probability of infection from a concrete episode (e.g. a single episode of vaginal coitus with an infected person) are unknown (Redfield & Burke, 1987).

Fischl et al. (1987) carried out a longitudinal study of a number of established heterosexual couples, in which the males were infected with the HIV virus but the females were not. Of the 14 women who continued their sexual relationship with their partner, but without using condoms, 12 became infected. Of the eight women who abstained from intercourse, none became infected. Finally, of the 10 women who continued to have intercourse and their partner used a condom, only one became infected. Therefore, it can be seen that not only does using condoms as a preventive measure not guarantee protection (though the chance of infection is low), but ignoring preventive measures does not guarantee that one will become infected (though the risk is very great).

In summary, the knowledge we possess about AIDS allows us to claim that:

1. There are risk behaviours that lead to:
   - pleasant sensations (sometimes of great intensity) or the release of anxiety or tension, almost immediately and universally;

- probable highly harmful consequences in the long term, that imply intense suffering and even death.

2. There are effective preventive behaviours that lead to:
   - immediate and overall self-deprivation, attenuation or delay of pleasant consequences, or a decrease in anxiety or tension;
   - a reduced probability of suffering highly harmful consequences in the long term, implying intense suffering and even death.

Under these conditions, the functional analysis of behaviour indicates that individuals often choose the effective and immediate pleasant stimulation, despite the terrible consequences that this action may have in the future (Perry & Markowitz, 1988), unless they are able to:

1. Delay or deprive themselves of satisfaction—completely against the Western philosophy of consumer satisfaction.
2. Find other equally effective and immediate pleasant satisfaction through the practice of non-risk behaviours, which can be accomplished by:
   - practising alternative behaviours that do not have any harmful consequences, neither in the short or long term;
   - dropping from the risk behaviours the harmful elements without substantially changing the nature of the satisfaction they provide.

It is my point of view that programmes developed to accomplish the preventive objectives outlined in this chapter must bear in mind these functional aspects. Nevertheless, there are other factors that need to be considered if we are to succeed: patterns of personal behaviour, affective social support, etc. The problem is a very complex one, and may be even more difficult to solve than finding a vaccine.

Taking into account the restricted funding by governments for psychosocial research, it would seem that politicians and officials have yet to realise the fact that, for example, a $10 million programme of research which resulted in the protection of only 100 people from AIDS during their lifetimes, would be a profitable investment from a strict economic viewpoint.

VULNERABILITY AND AIDS

Besides the practice of risk behaviours and effective preventive measures, there are other important aspects about AIDS which behavioural psychologists need to examine, such as the concept of vulnerability (Bayés & Arranz, 1988) and the possibility of conditioning the immune system

(Ader, 1981; Ader & Cohen, 1985; Ader, Cohen, & Felten, 1987; Bayés, 1988; Glaser & Kiecolt-Glaser, 1987).

In contrast with the epidemiological data on AIDS which shows the disease to be spreading, the HIV virus is difficult to transmit. Whereas genital contact alone is enough to contact syphilis, gonorrhoea or herpes, the HIV virus (like the hepatitis B virus) needs direct contact with blood. Furthermore, if we compare the probability of infection with the HIV and hepatitis B viruses, we find that 27% of health workers who prick themselves with a contaminated needle become infected with hepatitis B, whereas only 1% become infected with AIDS (Fumento, 1987). In Madrid, for example, of 82 health workers who accidentally suffered a virus inoculation, none presented antibodies after 1 year (Communidad de Madrid, 1988). In other words, the probability of infection with an HIV virus due to an isolated risk episode is very low. However, why does it occur on some occasions but not on others? What are the factors which account for the infection?

On the other hand, if we observe those who are already infected but who show no symptoms, we get a rather similar picture: in some, AIDS appears a few months after infection with the virus; in others, the virus may remain latent for years; and in still others, AIDS may never appear. What, therefore, are the factors which account for the development of AIDS at a specific moment in time in a person in which the virus had been latent? What are the conditions which favour or interfere with the activation of the virus and the development of full-blown AIDS?

Whether a person remains healthy, is asymptomatic yet infected, or is ill, depends in general on two factors:

1. The degree of harmfulness of the condition and/or the stimuli to which the organism is exposed.
2. The degree of the organism's vulnerability to these conditions or stimuli.

Even under the most suspicious conditions and with the usual agents of infection, some people become ill whereas others do not. If one thinks of an organism's vulnerability as a variable along a continuum, and that at any given moment in time it is placed somewhere along that continuum, allows us to establish our main priority, i.e. *to ensure that every person remains the least vulnerable possible, whether they are healthy, asymptomatic yet infected, or ill.*

With HIV infection, given the continuous interaction between the nervous, immune and endocrine systems, any disturbance initiated through any of these systems by stimuli that have this natural or acquired capacity, may be able to alter this fine balance, increase the organism's vulnerability, and facilitate the infection or the progression from carrier to AIDS patient. There are four kinds of stimuli capable of disturbing the immune system (Bayés & Arranz, 1988):

1. Stimuli that are intrinsically capable of producing this effect, e.g. a new infection produced by the same or another virus, or a vaccine, drug or medicine which has immunosuppressive effects, etc.
2. Stimuli intrinsically capable of altering the endocrine system and, therefore, capable of affecting indirectly the immune system, e.g. pregnancy.
3. Stimuli capable of producing psychological stress and, through it, changes in the endocrine and immune systems, depending on the cultural and biographical history of an individual.
4. Previously neutral stimuli which have been accidentally associated with the preceding conditions and have, for this reason, acquired the ability to disturb directly the endocrine, immune or nervous sytems.

It is also necessary to remember that sexually transmitted diseases (syphilis, gonorrhoea, herpes, etc.), additional to any disturbance to a patient's immune system, also constitute an important risk factor, because a sore, though it may be small, offers the virus a suitable pathway for penetrating the organism.

As psychologists, we are especially interested in the following:

1. Establishing any relationship between psychological stress and vulnerability, when acquiring the AIDS virus.
2. Establishing any relationship between psychological stress and replication of the virus on:
   - those who are seropositive;
   - those who have an AIDS-related complex; and
   - those who have been diagnosed as having AIDS.

One of the main problems with those people who are found to be asymptomatic seropositive, or who, after practising a risk behaviour think they have perhaps been infected, comes from the emotional upheaval they experience, without the knowledge of how to cope with it (García-Huete, 1988). Besides such suffering, are emotions also a modulating factor which increases the probability of activating the virus and, consequently, of developing AIDS?

CONCLUSIONS

To end this chapter, I would like to call attention to the need for the following:

1. To establish, for each of the risk behaviours and for different cultural groups, those factors which account for the practice or non-practice of these behaviours.
2. To develop programmes to train people in the practice and maintenance, over time, of effective preventive behaviours.
3. To establish the possible relationship between stress and people's vulnerability to the acquisition and/or activation of the AIDS virus.
4. To develop programmes which are devoted to achieving and maintaining, at the very least, the level of vulnerability of:
   - those who are seronegative and who practise risk behaviours;
   - those who are asymptomatic seropositive;
   - those who suffer from an AIDS-related complex;
   - those diagnosed as having AIDS; and
   - anyone who is connected in any way with the aforementioned, in particular sexual partners, family members and health workers.

In order to accomplish these goals, it is necessary to develop reliable and valid assessment tools that allow us, at any time, to know:

1. The level, type and frequencies of the relevant behaviours involved with risk and prevention.
2. The expansion, decline or stabilisation of the virus and/or its destructive action; and/or the expansion, decline or stabilisation of the disease.
3. The level of vulnerability.

By accomplishing these goals, we may be able to begin to solve the AIDS problem.

Although medical laboratories will continue to work towards a vaccine and an effective antiviral drug for combating AIDS, it is necessary for governments to promote AIDS research, especially as regards preventive behaviours, without cutting funding. Otherwise, the disease will continue to spread. The problem of prevention will not be solved by television campaigns. It can only be solved through scientific research.

In the short term, even if a vaccine and an effective and reasonably inexpensive drug are developed, prevention will still be important. For example:

1. It has been shown that 5 million children die each year due to diseases for which a vaccine exists and for which treatment is inexpensive.
2. Although effective treatments for sexually transmitted diseases (and AIDS can, to a certain extent, be considered as one of them) have existed for many years, they have not been eradicated in the West. Indeed, their incidence is increasing. For example, in the U.S.A., the number of cases of syphilis increased by 35% in 1987 over the previous year (Gascón, 1988).
3. It is possible that we may be faced with a new retrovirus—or a new mutation of the present AIDS virus—which could be more lethal, contagious and difficult to detect.

ACKNOWLEDGEMENTS

This work was supported by Direccion de Investigacion Cientifica y Tecnica del Ministerio de Educacion y Ciencia's Grant PB 86/0124.

REFERENCES

Ader, R. (Ed.) (1981). *Psychoneuroimmunology*. London: Academic Press.

Ader, R. & Cohen, N. (1985). CNS-immune system interactions: Conditioning phenomena. *Behavioral and Brain Sciences*, *8*, 379–394.

Ader, R., Cohen, N., & Felten, D. L. (1987). Editorial: Brain, behavior and immunity. *Brain, Behavior, and Immunity*, *1*, 1–6.

Bayés, R. (1985). *Psicología oncológica*. Barcelona: Martínez Roca.

Bayés, R. (1987). El "efecto placebo" en los procesos de cambio terapéutico. *Estudios de Psicología*. *31*, 71–81.

Bayés, R. (1988). Modulación psicológica de la respuesta inmmunológica. *Revista Cubana de Hematología, Inmunología y Hemoterapia*, *4*, 7–29.

Bayés, R. & Arranz, P. (1988). Las variables psicológicas como cofactores del síndrome de inmunodeficiencia adquirida. *Jano, Medicina y Humanidades*, *34*, 1313–1322.

Bennett, F. J. (1987). AIDS as a social phenomenon. *Social Science and Medicine*, *25*, 529–539.

Bloom, D. E. & Carliner, G. (1988). The economic impact of AIDS in the United States. *Science*, *239*, 604–610.

Bosch, F. X. (1986). La transmissió sexual de virus carcinògens: Nous conceptes en l'origen de tumors humans. *Ciència*, *5*, 419–424.

Brouard, N. (1987). SIDA: Durée d'incubation, taux de croissance, taux de reproduction nette. *Population*, *6*, 797–818.

Capdevila, J. M., Armengol, P., Bou, D., Calmet, M., Solé, J. M., & Soriano, R. (1988). Seguiment d'anticossos HIV en diferents collectius socials de Barcelona. *Annals de Medicina*, *74*, 34.

Centers for Disease Control (1987). HIV infection and pregnancies of sexual partners of HIV-seropositive hemophilic men—United States. *Morbidity and Mortality Weekly Reports*, *36*, 593–595.

Comunidad de Madrid (1988). *Vigilancia epidemiológica del SIDA*. Informe No. 1. Madrid: Ayuntamiento de Madrid.

Criado, A. (1988). Los trabajos de la Conferencia Internacional sobre el SIDA se centran en las medidas de prevención. *El País*, 27 January, p. 24.

de la Loma, A. (1987). Aspectos epidemiológicos del SIDA. In R. Usieto (Ed.), *SIDA: Un problema de salud pública*, pp. 49–139. Madrid: Diaz de Santos.

de la Loma, A. (1988). Aportaciones a la epidemiología del SIDA desde un centro de atención primaria. In *Resumen de Ponencias de la II Conferencia de Información Sanitaria sobre el SIDA*. Madrid: Ayuntamiento de Madrid.

Delgado, A. (1988). *Manual S.I.D.A.: Aspectos médicos y sociales*. Madrid: IDEPSA.

des Jarlais, D. C., Friedman, S. R., & Strug, D. (1986). AIDS among intravenous drug users: A sociocultural perspective. In D. Feldman & T. Johnson (Eds), *The social dimensions of AIDS: Methods and theory*, pp. 111–126. New York: Praeger.

Fischl, M. A., Dickinson, G. M., Scott, G. M., Kilmas, N., Flechter, M. A. & Parks, W. (1987). Evaluation of heterosexual partners, children, and household contacts of adults with AIDS. *Journal of the American Medical Association*, *257*, 640–644.

Friedman, S. R., des Jarlais, D. C., & Sotheran, J. L. (1986). AIDS health education for intravenous drug users. *Health Education Quarterly*, *13*, 383–393.

Fumento, M. A. (1987). AIDS: Are heterosexuals at risk? *Commentary*, *84*, 21–27.

García-Huete, E. (1988). SIDA: Aspectos psicológicos. In *Resumen de Ponencias de la II Conferencia de Información Sanitaria sobre el SIDA*. Madrid: Ayuntamiento de Madrid.

Gascón, P. (1988). Preocupante aumento de la sífilis en Estados Unidos. *Jano. Medicine y Humanidades*, *34*, 186–187.

Glaser, R. & Kiecolt-Glaser, J. (1987). Stress-associated depression in cellular immunity: Implications for acquired immune deficiency syndrome (AIDS). *Brain, Behavior, and Immunity*, *1*, 107–112.

Huang, K. H. C., Watters, J. K., & Case, P. (1988). Psychological sequelae of HIV testing among intravenous drug users.

Moss, A. R., Bacchetti, P., Osmond, D., Krampf, W., Chaisson, R. E., Stites, D., Wilber, J., Allain, J. P., & Carlson, J. (1988). Seropositivity for HIV and the development of AIDS or AIDS related condition: Three year follow up of the San Francisco General Hospital cohort. *British Medical Journal*, *296*, 745–750.

OMS (1987a). *Programme special de lutte contre le SIDA. Rapport de la Troisieme Reunion des Partes Participantes*. Geneva, 27–28 April.

OMS (1987b). *Programa especial sobre el SIDA. Estrategias y estructura. Necesidades previstas*. Geneva: Mars.

Ortiz, C. (1988). Actuación de un centro de salud municipal en la prevención del SIDA en Madrid. In *Resumen de Ponencias de la II Conferencia de Información Sanitaria sobre el SIDA*. Madrid: Ayuntamiento de Madrid.

Panos Institute (1987). *AIDS and the Third World*, 2nd revised edn. London: Panos Institute.

Pardell, H., Salleras, L., & Salvador, T. (1982). *Manual de prevenció i control del tabaiquisme*. Barcelona: Generalitat de Catalunya.

Perry, S. W. & Markowitz, J. C. (1988). Counseling for HIV testing. *Hospital and Community Psychiatry*, *39*, 731–739.

Redfield, R. R. & Burke, D. S. (1987). Shadow on the land: The epidemiology of HIV infection. *Viral Immunology*, *1*, 69–81.

Rothenberg, R., Woelfel, M., Stoneburner, R., Milberg, J., Parker, R., Truman, B. (1987). Survival with the acquired immunodeficiency syndrome. *New England Journal of Medicine*, *317*, 1297–1302.

Salgado, A. (1988). La cumbre de Suecia abre nuevas vías contra el SIDA. *La Vanguardia*, p. 15, 13 June.

Segura, A. (1987a). El SIDA como problema de salud pública. Paper presented at *Reunión de la Sociedad Española de Epidemiología*, June.

Segura, A. (1987b). SIDA: Soluciones viejas para un problema nuevo. *Gaceta Sanitaria, 1* (2), 47–48.

Sojo, D., Freneda, A., Babin, F., Lázaro, A., Abad, S., & San Román, R. (1988). S.I.D.A. y planificación familiar. In *Resumen de Ponencias de la II Conferencia de Información Sanitaria sobre el SIDA*. Madrid: Ayuntamiento de Madrid.

Solomon, M. Z. & DeJong, W. (1986). Recent sexually transmitted disease prevention efforts and their implications for AIDS health education. *Health Education Quarterly, 13*, 301–316.

Tijeras, R., Canales, L., & Esteban, T. (1988). Sanidad prepara una campaña contra el Sida en las playas. *Tribuna de Actualidad, 1*, 10–14.

Tor, J., Muga, R., Ribera, A., Llibre, J. M., Clotet, B., Melús, R., Ginestà, C., Rey-Joly, C., & Foz, M. (1988). Infecció per VIH en addictes a drogues per via parenteral a Barcelona, 1984–1987. *Annals de Medicina, 74*, 43.

Velimirovic, B. (1986). Social, ethical, psychological and financial dilemmas of AIDS: Implications for health policy. *AIDS-Forchung (AIFO)*, 307–317.

13 MammaCare: A Case History in Behavioural Medicine

H. S. Pennypacker
Department of Psychology, University of Florida, and Mammatech Corporation, Gainesville, Florida, U.S.A.

Margaret M. Iwata
Mammatech Corporation, Gainesville, Florida, U.S.A.

Breast cancer is a leading killer of women. It is estimated that during 1988 in the U.S.A. alone, approximately 135,000 new cases will have been diagnosed and nearly 42,00 women will have lost their lives due to it. Breast cancer incidence increases with age, making it the leading cause of death in U.S. women aged 40–44 and the leading cause of cancer death in women aged 25–74. One woman in ten will contract the disease at some time during her life.

Worldwide, the annual death rate is approximately 20.6 per 100,000, with higher values observed in the northern industrialised countries, such as England (34.5), Netherlands (32.7) and Belgium (32.2). These rates have remained fairly stable over the past four decades with increases in the absolute mortality figures maintaining a fairly constant relationship to increases in population (Silverberg & Lubera, 1988).

In addition to mortality, the morbidity associated with breast cancer is extensive. Surgery is nearly always required and often results in disfigurement and even partial disability. Adjuvant chemotherapy and radiation treatments, with associated hair loss, nausea and tissue destruction, serve to compound the debilitation. Moreover, the possibility of recurrence is a lifelong concern, thereby diminishing further the quality of the victim's life.

There is no means presently known for preventing breast cancer. It is possible, however, to reduce substantially both the morbidity and mortality through early detection (Cole & Austin, 1981). Such indicators as extent of lymph node involvement, probability of recurrence, and 5-, 10-

and 15-year survival rates all vary significantly as a function of the size of the primary tumour at the time of detection and treatment (see Henderson & Canellos, 1980, for a thorough review of the relevant literature). Fisher, Slack, and Bross (1969) have estimated that we could halve the death rate if we could halve the tumour size at the time of detection. Additionally, new methods of treatment involving less extensive surgery have been shown to be effective in cases where the tumour is small and isolated (Fisher, Bauer, & Margolese, 1985; Veronisi, Saccozzi, & del Vecchio, 1981).

BREAST CANCER DETECTION

Imaging

There are two basic procedures for detecting breast cancer: imaging and manual palpation. The most widely advocated imaging procedure is mammography, a low-dose X-ray that permits the visualisation of structures whose density or composition vary substantially from those characteristics of the surrounding tissue. The utility of mammography was first documented by the well-known Health Insurance Plan of New York (HIP) study (Shapiro, 1977) in which 62,000 female subscribers participated in a randomised clinical trial comparing voluntary mammography to standard medical screening by physical examination. Although only 65% of the experimental group actually elected for mammography, there were significantly fewer deaths (91 *vs* 128) in that group over the 10- to 14-year follow-up. The likelihood of lymph node involvement was twice as great in the control group, lending credence to the assertion that mammography enhanced detection at an earlier stage.

Since the HIP study, there have been many demonstrations of the value of mammography. The most ambitious was the Breast Cancer Detection Demonstration Project (BCDDP) conducted jointly by the National Cancer Institute and the American Cancer Society during the late 1970s and early 1980s. A total of nearly 275,000 women were screened with mammography, examined clinically, and offered instruction in breast self-examination (BSE). The massive data resulting from this programme are still being evaluated, but preliminary summaries (e.g. Baker, 1982) again confirm the benefits of mammography in screening for breast cancer. There is now widespread advocacy of mammography in the media and frequent campaigns conducted by the American Cancer Society to provide low-cost mammography throughout communities during "Breast Cancer Awareness Weeks".

As effective as mammography is for breast cancer screening, it has certain limitations. Often mentioned is the expense and inconvenience, although both have been reduced by the willingness of insurance companies to underwrite the expense and the growing availability of mobile facilities. Nevertheless, in a recent survey, only 41% of the respondents reported *ever* having had mammography, although 22% had had it done in the past year (Silberner, 1988).

Concern over radiation is another impediment to widespread use of mammography (Bailar, 1977). Technological advances have reduced the level of exposure required to approximately that of a dental X-ray, yet both the American Cancer Society and the American College of Radiology have issued guidelines recommending limited use for women under 40.

These recommendations coincide with other data on the utility of mammography as a function of patient age. The breast tissue of younger (<40 years) women tends to be both firmer and denser than that of older women, making it more opaque to X-rays. Thus, even if routine mammography were recommended, cancers in the early stages of development would more likely be missed in this age group. Other imaging technologies, including ultrasound, transillumination and thermography have been developed but have not attracted the widespread medical support accorded mammography.

Manual Palpation

The vast majority of breast cancers are discovered by manual palpation, either by a clinician during a routine physical examination or by the patient herself. In fact, it has been variously estimated (e.g. Strax, 1984) that between 80 and 95% of all breast cancers are first discovered by the patient, then confirmed by a clinician as a result of manual palpation and/or mammography. Unfortunately, the sensitivity of physicians' physical examinations is quite modest compared to mammography (Hicks, Davis, & Layton, 1979; Moskowitz, 1983), partly, at least, because they spend so little time conducting the examination (Fletcher, O'Malley, & Bunce, 1985).

Breast self-examination (BSE) has been shown in a number of prospective studies to favourably affect prognosis, measured in terms of the tumour size at the time of detection and the degree of lymph node involvement. Foster, Lang, and Costanza's (1978) classic study looked at 246 breast cancer patients and found that those who reported practising BSE monthly presented significantly smaller primary tumours (m = 2.1 cm) than did those who practised less frequently (m = 2.5 cm) or not at all (m = 3.6 cm). They also had significantly less axillary node mestastases than did the other groups.

Huguley and Brown (1981) presented similar findings with a group of 2092 breast cancer patients. Of this group, 67% reported practising BSE and the average tumour presented by this subset was nearly 0.75 cm smaller than that of the non-practising patients. Of special interest in Huguley and Brown's study was the fact that the BSE technique of individuals in the practising group was evaluated by an oncology nurse who concluded that only 51% performed BSE in a competent manner.

BSE appears to confer some benefit in terms of earlier detection, even if practised infrequently and improperly. What would be its contribution if it were:

1. Practised at levels of proficiency approaching the limits allowed by:
   - the sensory physiology of the pressure receptors in the fingertips, and
   - a state-of-the-art behavioural training technology.
2. Practised on a mass scale?

The remainder of this paper will attempt to summarise a 14-year, and still ongoing, effort to answer these questions.

THE CHALLENGE OF BREAST CANCER DETECTION FOR BEHAVIOURAL MEDICINE

Mammography and the various other imaging technologies have been shown to impart considerable prognostic benefit to those women who are both old enough and otherwise able to avail themselves of its sensitivity. Because of its cost and relative unavailability throughout much of the world, we can expect only slight reductions in breast cancer mortality resulting from the current emphasis on mammography. Other means of early detection that are both affordable and readily available must be found, developed and disseminated. Fortunately, such a means exists and is resident in the fingertips of virtually every member of the species. The potential sensitivity of the fingertips to the subtle pressure sensations that would result from palpation of a small lump are dramatically documented by the skill of the blind at reading Braille.

Being an external organ, the breast is ideal for manual palpation. Self-examination has been recommended since 1946 (Haagensen, 1971) and has been strenuously advocated by lay and professional groups alike. Given the sensitivity of the receptors, why then has BSE been practised so infrequently and with so little proficiency? The answer would appear to lie with the methods of instruction.

BSE has traditionally been taught by two methods—individually by a clinician or by conventional audio-visual means, often in a group situation. In neither case does the patient have an opportunity to learn the "feel" of the enemy. Moreover, the technique advocated has been derived from that customarily used by physicians in the course of clinical practice. Fletcher et al. (1985) have documented the wide variability in both manual palpation techniques and sensitivity of practising physicians. They also comment on the lack of uniform training in physical examination of the breast that characterises contemporary medical education. In short, manual examination of the breast, whether by a physician or the patient herself, is essentially an art form that has hitherto escaped the scrutiny of experimental analysis.

The opportunity afforded by this state of affairs seemed extremely attractive in 1974 when we began our research. Although the lack of proficiency on the part of physicians had not yet been documented, it was suspected and generally acknowledged. The disparity between the known tactile sensitivity of the fingertips (Boring, 1942) and the tumour sizes reported as a result of manual palpation (Phillips, 1974), suggested that a proper experimental analysis of the skill of lump detection could support the creation of an effective instructional technology that would eventually save lives. Hall, Goldstein, and Stein (1977) presented in detail our early assessment of the problem and the strategies required for its solution. We will briefly review them here.

Overall Strategies

A programme of behavioural research into the problem of breast lump detection via manual palpation could take one of two general forms. The first is relatively traditional and would involve survey research into the attitudes of women, their beliefs about health and disease prevention, and the assumption that BSE behaviour is determined by such factors. The intervention strategy is then clear: conduct educational campaigns aimed at altering attitudes and beliefs, provide conventional instruction on a mass scale, and then observe any changes in the frequency and quality of BSE performance. A minor variation on this strategy would include the use of "behavior modification", say, by offering Green Stamps to women who complete the course of instruction and demonstrate BSE at some level of proficiency.

This strategy has prompted massive amounts of research (see O'Malley & Fletcher, 1987, for a brief review) and has succeeded principally in sustaining the scepticism of medical authorities concerning the benefits of BSE (Cole & Austin, 1981; Moore, 1978). We chose a different strategy based on the natural science approach to the experimental analysis of behaviour (Bernard, 1957; Johnston & Pennypacker, 1980; Sidman, 1960; Skinner, 1956).

Basically, our strategy involved three elements:

1. Analysing the lump detection skill into its psychophysical and topographical components.
2. Synthesising the topographical elements into a complex behaviour chain.
3. Developing and validating an instructional technology capable of placing the chain in the repertoire of virtually any woman, regardless of her educational history.

In order to achieve our ultimate objective of reducing morbidity and mortality due to breast cancer, a fourth objective—universal dissemination—must also be achieved.

Let us now turn to a brief review of the research carried out in pursuit of this strategy (Saunders et al., 1982). Because space does not permit a detailed recapitulation of all of the studies performed, we will examine only the milestone experiments. (The interested reader may pursue the references or contact the senior author for more details of the procedure, etc.)

Psychophysical Studies

Model Development. A critical decision was taken at the outset. We recognised that it would be virtually impossible to conduct meaningful psychophysical analysis *in vivo*, so we began our work by developing a life-like model of the human female breast. The basic requirement was to fashion a simulation of the breast that would duplicate the natural firmness and indigenous granularity of breast tissue, thus providing a realistic context for the presentation of simulated tumours. Unfortunately, although a number of breast prostheses and training aids were commercially available, none exhibited physical characteristics (such as firmness) that closely matched real tissue.

With the help of our colleagues in the Department of Materials Science in the College of Engineering, we became acquainted with the vast array of biomedical polymers then being used in the construction of heart valves, internal mammary prostheses, catheters and dental appliances. We also made physical measurements on volunteers and developed a small databank describing the size, volume and shape of the adult human female breast. Curiously, no such quantitative data existed in the anthropological, anatomical or biophysical literature at the time (Yamada & Williams, 1970).

After extensive trial and error, we fabricated hemispherical breast models using a thin silicone rubber (General Electric RTV 7100) membrane as a skin and silicone gel (General Electric RTV 619) to simulate the interior breast tissue. This gel cures to a semi-solid consistency and the resulting firmness varies with the amount of catalysing agent used in the curing process.

Models of differing sizes (125, 250 and 500 ml) were constructed and subjected to load deflection tests. Four female volunteers allowed the firmness of their breasts to be evaluated by load deflection measurement. The resulting families of load deflection curves (Fig. 13.1) demonstrate that we had succeeded in matching the firmness of living breast tissue (Madden, et al., 1978).

The next step was to estimate the size threshold for detecting a lump through the medium of the silicone model. Eight volunteers palpated 250 ml

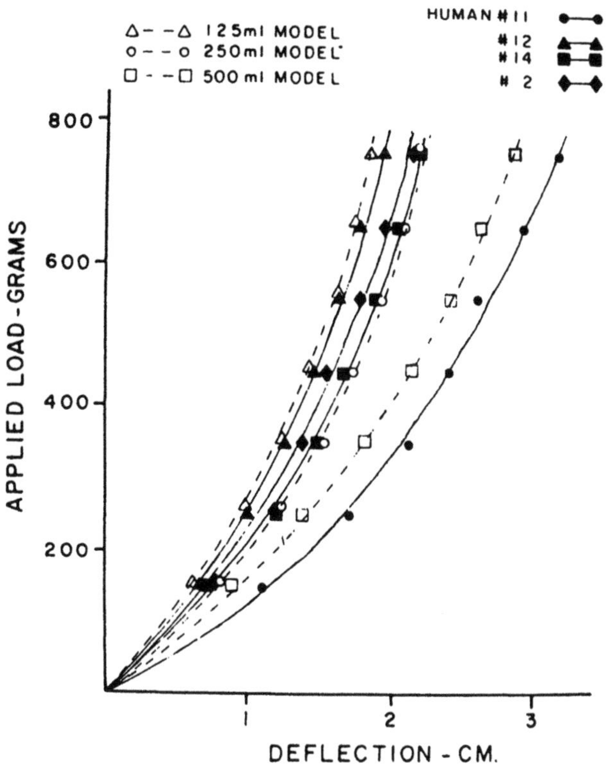

FIG. 13.1. A comparison of the load deflection properties of the breast models and real breast tissue (from Madden et al., 1978). Reprinted with the permission of Pergamon Press.

breast models, on the backs of which were placed ball-bearings varying in diameter from 1.6 to 12.7 mm. A lump-free model was also used on certain trials in an effort to assess false detection rates. The model rested on a firm foam pad and was visually isolated from the subject by a black cloth stretched across an upright frame. Armhole slits in the cloth permitted the subject to insert her preferred hand and palpate the model. A modification of the method of constant stimuli was used over repeated sessions in order to evaluate the effects of practice as well as to arrive at stable threshold determinations. The principal results of this experiment are shown in Fig. 13.2. Not surprisingly, orderly psychophysical functions were obtained, suggesting that lump detection through a medium of simulated breast tissue is similar to the process of signal detection involving other sensory modalities. The fact that stable thresholds of less than 2 mm

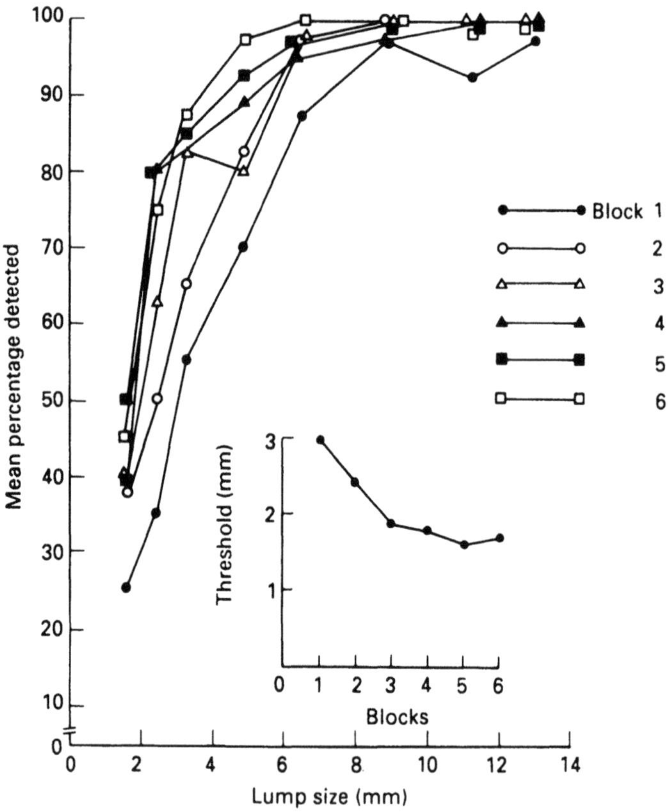

FIG. 13.2. Lump detectability as a function of size with trial blocks as the parameter (from Adams et al., 1976). Reprinted with the permission of The Psychonomic Society.

were observed, confirmed our earlier conviction that the problems with manual palpation of the breast as a means of early detection of breast cancer were not traceable to deficiencies of the sensory apparatus. Further, the observation that size thresholds decrease with practice encouraged us to believe that behavioural phenomena associated with the detection task would be amenable to analysis and eventual modification. The outcome of such an enquiry could lead to previously unsuspected levels of proficiency in manual examination.

The results of an early clinical investigation (see Hall et al., 1980) convinced us of the need to modify the physical attributes of the breast models to achieve simulation of naturally occurring structures such as glands, connective tissue and fatty deposits and to make the tumour simulations resemble real tumours with respect to size and firmness. Accordingly, Hester Bloom (*née* Stephenson) arranged to make *in vitro* measurements of the firmness of tumour samples and surrounding breast structures during surgical procedures at the local teaching hospital. Using a hand-held device called a Type 00 Durometer (Rex Guage Co., Glenview, Ill.), she collected sufficient data to enable us to alter our silicone curing procedures and fashion small structures that could be inserted into the interior gel so as to yield the sensation of palpating the differentiated structures listed above.

Resolution of the problem of simulating tumours was achieved by Mr Ken Miner (Patter Products, Beaverton, Minn.) who was formerly an engineer with the corporation that developed the first silicone breast implant. Using the data collected by Ms. Bloom as a standard for the firmness parameter, he formulated a special extruded polymer that would retain its original shape after prolonged palpation and not interact chemically with the silicone gel surrounding it in the interior of the model. The firmness of this polymer could also be controlled precisely, allowing it to be produced at a given durometer value. This development permitted us for the first time to vary the depth of placement of the tumour simulations, their firmness and the amount of surrounding nodularity, in addition to the size of the "tumour" and the firmness of the model. In the next study, we examined the effect of these variables on lump detection proficiency.

Bloom et al. (1982) recruited five adults who served as paid participants in an extended three-phase study. In all three phases, the breast models used differed from the simple hemispheres previously described in that they were "pancake"-shaped (14.5 cm in diameter, 1.7 cm thick) and were presented in a stack. Lumps were glued to thin silicone membranes which were inserted between the pancakes.

Two search patterns were used. Under the *restricted search* (RS) procedure, the subject's fingers were placed over a spot on the model stack and the subject was told to palpate that spot and report any lump detections.

Under the *unrestricted search* (US) procedure, the subject was told to search the model stack thoroughly, palpating it entirely, and report all lump detections. A visual barrier was used as in the previous study.

In phase 1, steel ball-bearings were again used as lump simulations, the variables of interest being depth of lump and search pattern. As expected, threshold values increased with depth of lump and were greater under the unrestricted search procedure. In all cases, however, they were less than 1.5 mm, probably a result of the fact that, unlike the previous study, threshold determinations were made after extended training and practice by paid participants.

Lumps of varying hardness were introduced in phase 2. The durometer readings ranged from 6.0 to 44.0 and all lumps were cut to approximate a cube measuring 3 mm each side. All other procedures were identical to phase 1.

The results of phase 2 were unexpected in that lump hardness did not contribute to variations in detection accuracy, nor did depth of placement. As before, unrestricted search was associated with lower detection accuracy. The characteristics of the lumps missed were not systematic, however, suggesting that gaps in the search pattern produced the decrement. Phase 3 was undertaken in an effort to push the complexity of the task as close to the limits of the *in vivo* lump detection task as possible.

In phase 3, only two model sections were used, but the lumps were embedded in the sections rather than being affixed to a rubber membrane between sections. This allowed substantial moveability of the lumps in the horizontal dimension, simulating a property of any breast mass not attached to the chest wall. The durometer readings of the lump materials used were 6.0, 14.0, 24.0, 38.0 and 51.0. The lump diameters were 3, 5, 7 and 10 mm and all combinations of firmness and size were presented.

As in the earlier phases, the sessions were conducted using both unrestricted and restricted search procedures. Additionally, two of the subjects (P3 and P4) were recalled 6 months after the conclusion of data collection and their skills were again assessed. The performance of P3 during the last four sessions of unrestricted search and at the 6-month follow-up is presented in Fig. 13.3. In general, it may be said that the larger, firmer and nearer the surface a breast lump is, the greater is the likelihood it will be detected. Lumps of 1 cm are nearly always detected, regardless of depth or firmness, whereas 3-mm lumps must be relatively firm and near the surface if they are to be felt. Firmness exerts its greatest influence with the 5-mm lumps; at durometer values near that of the surrounding nodularity (10 d), they are likely to be confused with normal tissue, because size is not a reliable cue and both are moveable. This mimics exactly the clinical situation with soft, fluid-filled cysts which are often only discernible with either mammography or ultrasonography.

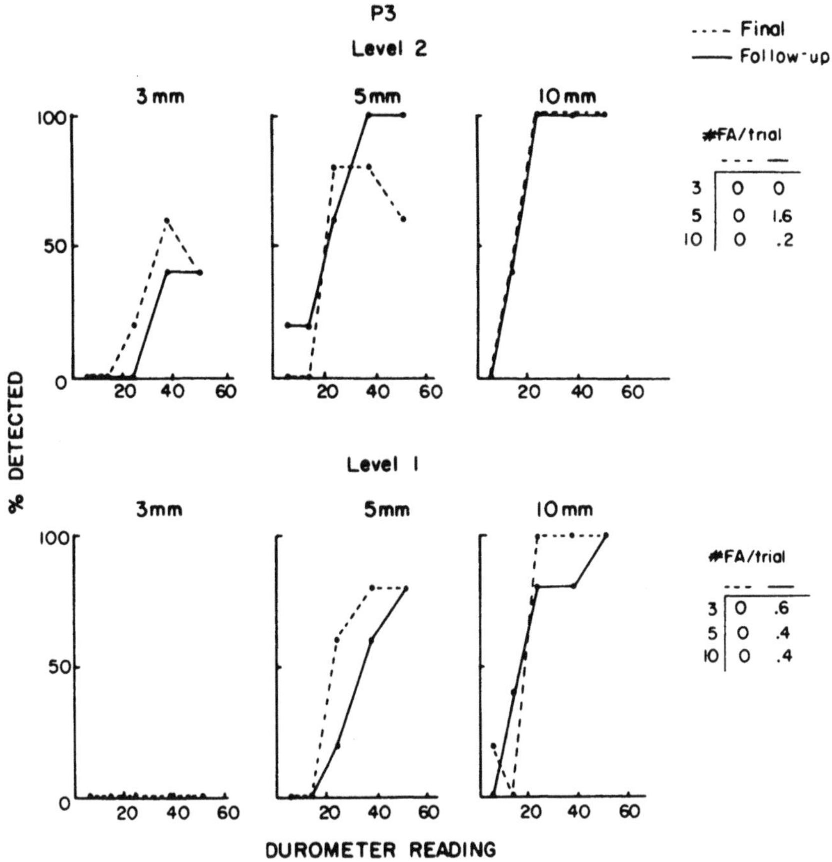

FIG. 13.3. The percentage of lumps detected in both levels of the model as a function of lump hardness with time of testing as the parameter. Inset data are the mean numbers of false alarms associated with each lump size (from Adams et al., 1976). Reprinted with the permission of The Psychonomic Society.

The 6-month follow-up data show no serious skill loss on the part of either subject. This finding has important implications for an eventual training technology: If levels of proficiency such as those exhibited by P3 and P4 can be routinely established, they can probably be maintained with only occasional practice.

The importance of search pattern is clearly demonstrated in Fig. 13.4. The combined performance of P2 and P4 during the last three restricted search sessions and the last unrestricted search session are collapsed across the depth variable and shown as a function of lump hardness with size as a parameter. The unrestricted search (US) panel to the right of Fig. 13.4

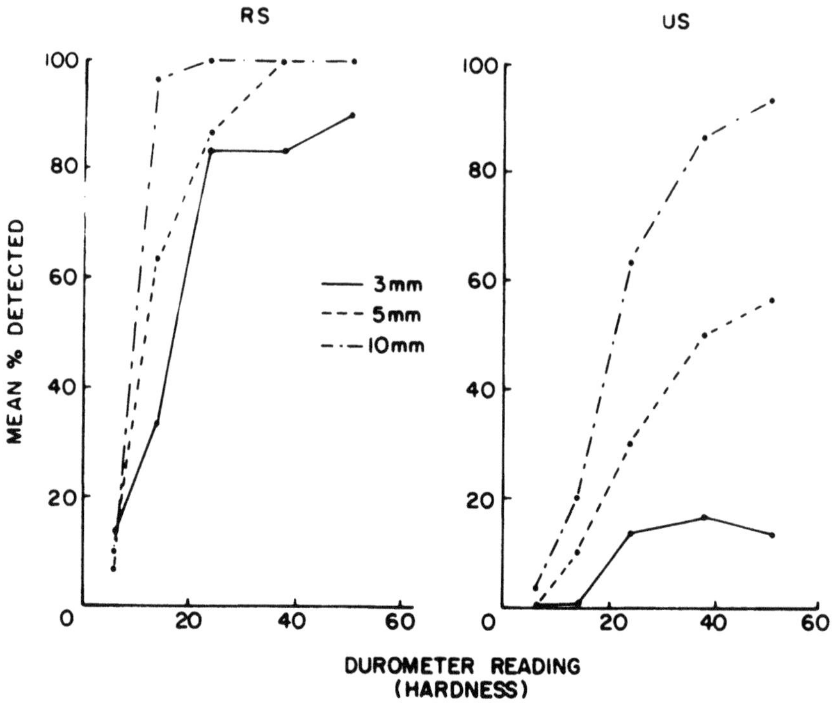

FIG. 13.4. Lump detectability under two search conditions as a function of lump hardness with lump size as the parameter.

describes almost exactly what one observes clinically (Fletcher et al., 1985), whereas the restricted search (RS) panel to the left of Fig. 13.4 shows the limits of palpability given that the fingers are brought into contact with the tumour simulations.

Clearly, the discrepancy between the two panels in Fig. 13.4 is a result of a behavioural, rather than psychophysical, limitation. It is widely believed that tumours smaller than 0.75–1.0 cm are "non-palpable" (Spence, 1988) and are therefore subject to discovery only by mammography. To the extent that the models prepared for the present study accurately simulate breast tissue with embedded tumours, we would argue that the potential sensitivity of the fingertips approaches or may even exceed that of mammography. Before the lower limits of clinical palpability can be determined, a breast examination *technique* must be developed that will ensure that fingers trained to the limits of their sensitivity come into contact with each and every fragment of breast tissue that could harbour a tumour. It is to this aspect of the research programme that we now turn our attention.

Behavioural Studies

The need for the complex breast models developed for the previous study was established in an earlier clinical investigation. Shortly after the data for the original threshold determination study (Adams et al., 1976) were collected and analysed, Robert Q. Marston, then President of the University of Florida and formerly Head of the National Institutes of Health, urged that we document the relevance of practice in palpating simulated lumps placed under a silicone hemisphere to the skill of detecting breast masses *in vivo*. We complied (Hall et al., 1980) and remain profoundly grateful for Dr. Marston's wisdom and encouragement.

Six women with a total of 13 benign breast lesions were recruited through an advertisement in the local newspaper. Their breast masses were located, measured and mapped independently by two physicians and the senior investigator. The masses ranged from 0.30 to 2.50 cm in diameter and were irregular in shape and consistency. One woman had one mass, three had two, and two had three. The role of these women was to serve as "stimuli", allowing their breasts to be palpated by trainees. Each was paid $100 for her participation in the experiment.

Twenty female volunteers, ranging in age from 19 to 38 years (mean = 24.3), served as subjects. None had professional experience in breast examination and six admitted never having examined their own breasts. These volunteers were divided into two groups of 10, differing only with respect to the order of training conditions.

All 20 trainees received a pre-test (P_0) and two post-tests (P_1 and P_2). The first post-test followed a period in which the trainees in group A received 30 min of individualised instruction that involved palpating hemispherical breast models under which had been placed ball-bearings ranging in diameter from 0.8 to 3.6 mm. The trainees in group B passed this time in a supervised, unrelated activity; both groups then palpated the stimulus women a second time (P_1). Thereafter, the trainees in group B received the palpation instruction while group A engaged in unrelated activity. Then, both groups conducted a final examination (P_2) of the stimulus women.

The accuracy of detection by both groups for each of the three examinations is shown in Fig. 13.5. A statistically significant ($P < 0.01$) effect of training was obtained, despite substantial variability. Both groups nearly doubled their detection accuracy after training and neither showed any remarkable effect of mere practice. Unfortunately, the effect of the training was insufficient to elevate accuracy above approximately 50%, suggesting that the stimuli used in training failed to simulate adequately the stimuli encountered *in vivo*.

An important clue concerning the critical disparity between the training stimuli and the benign masses embedded in real breasts is found in Fig. 13.6;

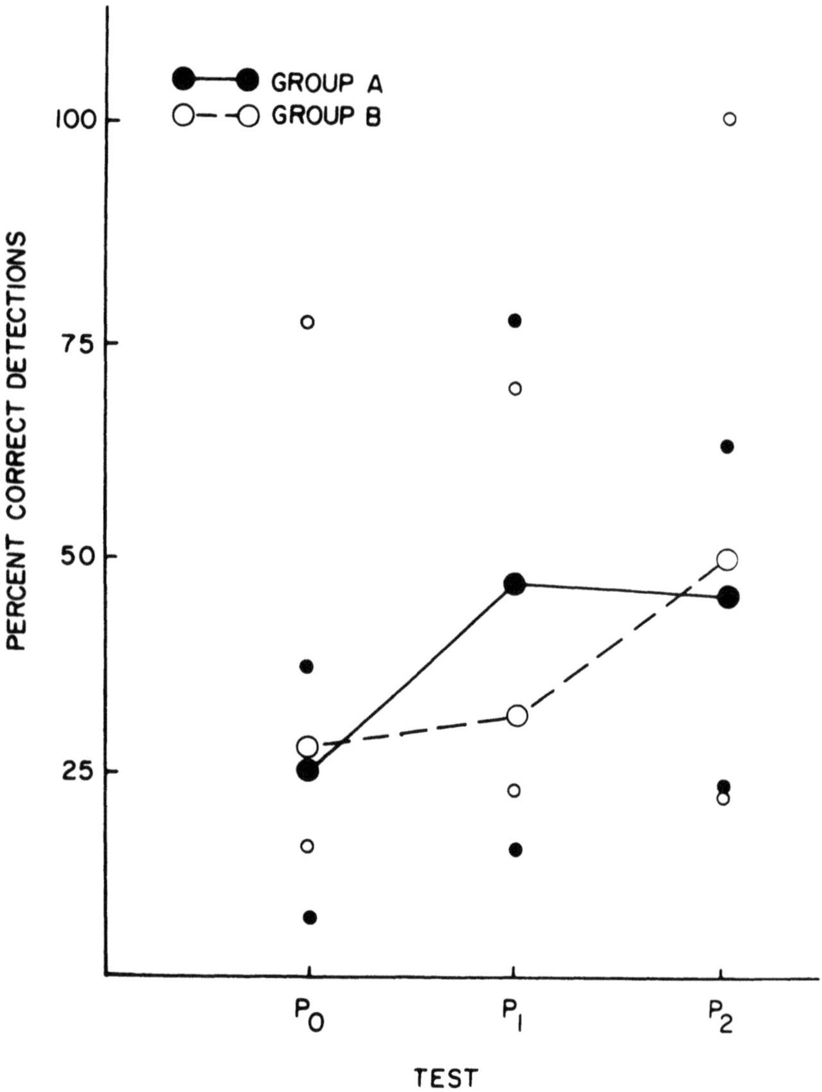

FIG. 13.5. Mean percentage of correct detections for groups A and B. Smaller symbols denote the ranges around each mean (from Hall et al., 1980). Reprinted with the permission of the American Cancer Society.

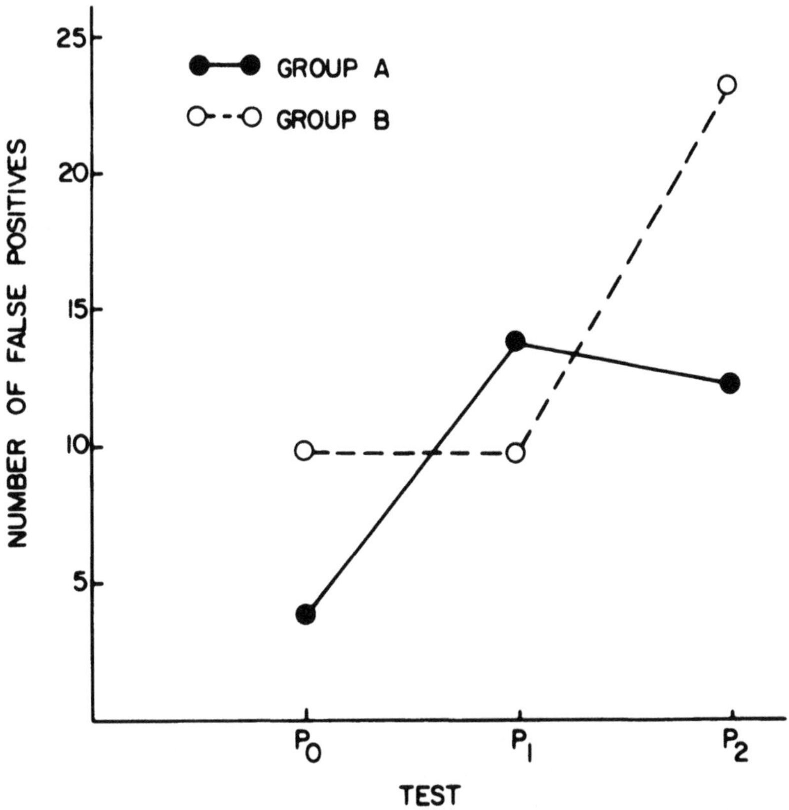

FIG. 13.6. Mean number of false positive responses for groups A and B (from Hall et al., 1980). Reprinted with the permission of the American Cancer Society.

which shows the effects of the training procedure on false positive responding (identifying a normal structure as a lesion). Here, again, a statistically significant ($P < 0.01$) increase occurs as both groups more than doubled their false positive rates.

One must remember that the models used in training were clear silicone hemispheres, resembling real breasts only in size and firmness. The lump simulations were steel spheres and were placed beneath, rather than within, the models. It is evident that palpating these media taught a discrimination between "something" and "nothing", which, when applied to real tissue, permitted a variety of normal structures (glands, fatty deposits, etc.) to evoke a detection response. Any technology designed to teach breast examination with the aid of simulation, then, would have to achieve a higher level of fidelity in the simulator or be forever plagued with unacceptable levels of false positive responding. For this reason, the more complex models used in Bloom et al.'s (1982) study were developed.

Functional Analysis of Topographical Components

The results of the Bloom et al. (1982) study (see Fig. 13.4) augured strongly for an improvement in examination techniques as a prerequisite to devising a technology for teaching breast examination that would approach the limits of sensitivity afforded by the sensory systems involved. In a previously unpublished study, Saunders et al. (1982) looked at the effects on lump detection accuracy of three specific topographical components: using a systematic search pattern, moving the flats of the fingers in three small circles at each spot palpated, and using three levels of pressure at each spot palpated.

Six adult females between the ages of 26 and 50 served as paid participants in 36–160 daily sessions. Three measures of performance were continually monitored: model area covered, duration of search, and number of lumps detected. The measurement of the area searched was accomplished with the aid of an infrared light-emitting diode (L.E.D.) taped to the middle finger of the participant's preferred hand. Light from the L.E.D. was detected by a Periphicon 511 camera mounted 96 cm above the examining surface. The movements of the L.E.D. activated picture elements (pixels) in a 32 × 32 grid located behind the camera's lens. The grid was scanned three times per second by an Apple II microcomputer which stored the data magnetically. An on-line visual display was provided on a Sony Cum 131 video monitor, allowing the experimenter to follow the progress of pixels lighting as the area on the model's surface was searched.

The participant was seated in a small room with her arm extended through a small hole in the wall. She recorded lump detections by depressing the game key of the Apple II. Timing circuitry in the Apple II recorded the durations of all searches and the temporal location of any lump detections.

The models were of the complex variety described by Bloom et al. (1982). The lumps ranged in size from 0.3 to 1.0 cm and in hardness from 20 to 60 d. The model was appropriately positioned on a "torso" fashioned of gauze and foam, permitting definition of a search area that extended beyond the boundaries of the model.

Data were collected from each participant in each phase until a criterion of performance stability ($k < 1.05$; Johnston & Pennypacker, 1980) was reached. Successive phases were defined by the addition of specific training in finger motion, palpating with three different pressures, lump *vs* normal nodular tissue discrimination, and search pattern. The order in which these training elements were introduced varied across participants.

The results of this investigation may be summarised briefly as follows: Each of the training conditions produced an increment in the performance (compared to baseline) of at least four of the six participants. The order of presentation emerged as an important consideration, e.g. the search pattern should not be taught until the palpation technique is mastered. Providing explicit training in lump *vs* nodular tissue discrimination improved the detection accuracy of all but one participant; for her, it was the last component introduced and she was already near the upper limit of proficiency.

The mean detection accuracy at stability (last five sessions within a phase) across all participants and conditions was 68.9%, well above the 44% reported later by Fletcher et al. (1985), who used almost identical models in their study of physicians' examination skills. The reader should remember, however, that the lumps used in both studies were at or below the size range considered clinically palpable (Spence, 1988) and that participants in the present study had the benefit of prolonged training.

The foregoing study taught us how to use the complex model developed by Bloom et al. (1982) to improve performance in lump detection. Specifically, it demonstrated the importance of teaching (1) a discrete palpation technique, (2) application of varying pressures during palpation, (3) an explicit discrimination between simulated nodular tissue and simulated lumps, and (4) a systematic search pattern. It also suggested an order—molecular to molar—in which these components should be presented for optimal effectiveness. We were now ready to compare this technology with the other methods of teaching breast examination that were available.

Training Comparison Studies

Two closely related studies, also previously unpublished (Neelakantan et al., 1981; Pennypacker et al., 1981), allowed us to isolate the necessary and sufficient procedures for teaching breast self-examination to a level of proficiency exceeding that of most physicians and approaching the sensitivity of mammography. In the first study (Pennypacker et al., 1981), performance on the model was the criterion of interest, whereas in the second (Neelakantan et al., 1981), quantitative and qualitative measures of the participants' performance on their own tissue were obtained.

Five groups of 15 women each were recruited through advertisements in the local paper. Each was paid $5.00 for participating in a single 1-hour session. The median age was 26 years (range 19–84 years).

The measurement and recording apparatus was identical to that used in the previous study, as were the breast models. The foam and gauze torso was abandoned, however, because no search pattern training was to be conducted in the testing environment.

Each participant began the experiment by providing a baseline measurement of her model examination skill. She entered the booth, had the L.E.D. taped to her middle finger, and was told to examine the model in any manner and for as long as she wished, pressing the game key if she encountered a lump, and to signal completion by placing her hand to the side. At the conclusion of her baseline performance, she was assigned to one of five training conditions:

A. Pass 30 min quietly reading material unrelated to breast examination.
B. Receive instruction on her own breast tissue, including palpation technique and search pattern.
C. Read a widely circulated pamphlet describing BSE.
D. Receive model-based instruction as developed in the previous study.
E. Receive a combination of B and D.

Participants in groups B and E were conducted to an isolated training room which contained a privacy screen and an examining table. The participant disrobed from the waist up and lay supine on the examining table, draped with a sheet at all times except when actual breast palpation was in progress. The model training for participants in group E was done with the model placed on the participant's chest, following a suggestion made by Lindsley (personal communication) to the effect that this would minimise transfer decrement due to changing arm position, etc.

The participants in groups A, C and D received their training, if any, in another unoccupied room in the laboratory suite. All training, regardless of condition, was conducted by a female experimenter.

Following training, each participant again examined the model under the same instructions she had received prior to baseline measurement. At the conclusion of this step, she was debriefed, paid, and cautioned not to discuss her experience with others in the community as we needed inexperienced participants to ensure the validity of the training research.

The obvious measure of benefit imparted by the various training conditions involves a comparison between performances during baseline and following training. To achieve comparability across measures, a post-pre-ratio was calculated (Johnston & Pennypacker, 1980) and the resulting group means are presented in Fig. 13.7. Interpretation of such ordinal values is straightforward: Values less than 1.0 indicate a decrease, whereas values greater than 1.0 can be viewed as coefficients or converted to percentages. Thus, a value of 2.0 denotes a doubling or a 100% increase.

The principal result portrayed in Fig. 13.7 may be simply stated: The acquisition of the skills required for breast self-examination requires "hands-on" instruction. Reading a pamphlet about BSE is comparable to

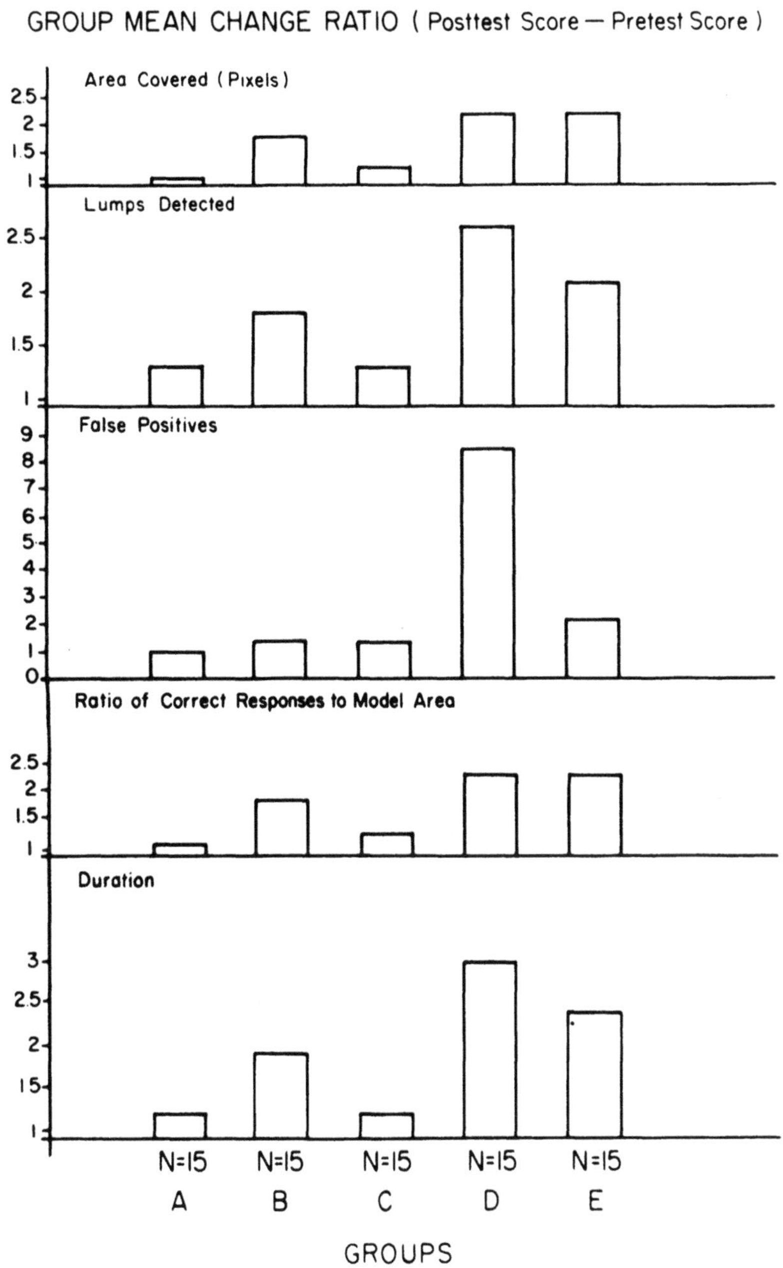

FIG. 13.7. Mean post-test/pre-test change ratios in five measures for each of the five groups. A, No training; B, trainee's breast tissue; C, pamphlet; D, model alone; E, model and breast tissue.

reading unrelated materials in its effect on subsequent performance of the model search and lump detection task.

Of special interest is the effect on false positive responding observed in group D who received model-alone training. The more than eight-fold increase that resulted from detailed instruction on the complex model suggests that extreme caution should be observed when using models alone (as many physicians and clinics do for reasons of economy) to attempt to teach BSE. The patient who thereafter attempts to perform BSE on herself is likely to react with confusion and fear, suspecting every normal structure of being a tumour.

Modulating the impact of training with the model by simultaneous comparison and practice on the trainee's own breast (group E) attenuates the tendency for false positive responding to acceptable levels. There is an attendant decline in lump detection proficiency, perhaps because the smaller lumps in the testing models are identified as normal nodularity similar to examples encountered during palpation of the trainees' own tissue. It must be remembered, however, that training and testing on similar models gives a natural advantage to group D; this advantage will disappear when testing is done on the actual breast (see below).

The fourth panel in Fig. 13.7 displays the results in terms of a derived measure that takes into account true negatives as well as true positives in defining a "correct" response. Dividing this value by the area actually searched gives a measure of palpation quality that corrects for deficiencies in search pattern. Again, the superiority of the "hands-on" procedure is apparent.

The changes in examination duration pictured in the fifth panel are almost identical to the lump detection data shown in the second panel. This fits with the clinical observation that more lumps are found when more time is taken to search (Fletcher et al., 1985). The fact that the greatest increase in duration occurred in the model-alone condition (group D) is probably a result of the demand characteristics of the situation. Model training gave the subjects an opportunity to discover that a large number of lumps were likely to be in the test model and they may have devoted more effort to trying to find them all. Subjects in group E, on the other hand, spent a good deal of their training time learning about their own breast tissue.

In the second training comparison study, participants were again solicited through the local paper and paid $5.00 for their participation. Forty-five women were recruited, ranging in age from 18 to 69 years (median = 26 years). They were assigned to one of three groups according to whether their training would consist of reading the pamphlet, using the model alone, or using the model in combination with their own tissue. Thus, the training conditions were a replication of those provided to groups C, D and E in the first study.

Each participant initially disrobed to the waist, assumed the supine position on an examining table, and provided a baseline demonstration of her self-examination technique. This performance was evaluated by one of the female experimenters with the aid of an overhead projector that projected a numbered grid on the participant's torso. Each square of the projected grid measured 1.0 cm each side. The observer outlined the area of breast tissue subtended for each trainee on a grid-ruled scoring sheet with numbers corresponding to those in the projected image. The observer could then tally the squares palpated, count the palpations in each, and note other aspects of the trainee's technique.

Observers were calibrated (Johnston & Pennypacker, 1980) to a criterion of five consecutive errorless scorings of examinations conducted by another of the female experimenters. Pre- and post-test observation and measurement were done by the same observer for each trainee. The observer was not involved in (and was blinded with respect to) the training procedure.

The training procedures were identical to those of the previous experiment. Following baseline measurement, the trainee was conducted to another room to receive instruction in accordance with her group assignment. The trainee then returned to the measurement room for post-testing.

Quantitative results, again expressed in terms of post-/pre-ratios, are presented for the three groups in Fig. 13.8. The superiority of the combination training procedure is evident with respect to all of the measures taken except frequency (palpations per second) where it does not differ from the model-alone procedure. The pamphlet produced slightly greater gains in this study as compared to the previous one, perhaps because of the publicity the research was receiving and some resulting demand characteristics. None the less, the conclusion is firm that the method of choice (among those investigated) for teaching BSE involves using the complex model to teach palpation, lump/normal tissue discrimination, and pressure, and then transferring these elements immediately to the woman's own tissue and teaching an appropriately individualised search technique.

This conclusion is supported by the results of several qualitative observations. Figure 13.9 shows the proportion of each group that exhibited each of the characteristics of proficient BSE before and after training. The black bars in Fig. 13.9 represent the effect of the training and make clear that with the exception of instructing a systematic search pattern, the pamphlet does not adequately teach the skill components of BSE. This, we contend, is not the fault of this pamphlet *per se*, but rather is the inevitable result of the assumption that a passive cognitive activity (reading) is sufficient to shape a complex sensori-motor skill. When this method of instruction fails, as it demonstrably has with respect to BSE and early detection of breast cancer, the usual recourse is to assign an explanatory role to motivational, intellectual or attitudinal deficiencies on the part of the learners (Skinner, 1985).

Figure 13.9 shows that the pamphlet actually did a fairly good job of teaching a systematic search pattern. Unfortunately, because neither clinical nor self-examination of the breast had previously been subjected to experimental analysis, the search pattern taught by the pamphlet proved to be less than maximally effective. In the last study we shall review, evidence for that conclusion will be presented.

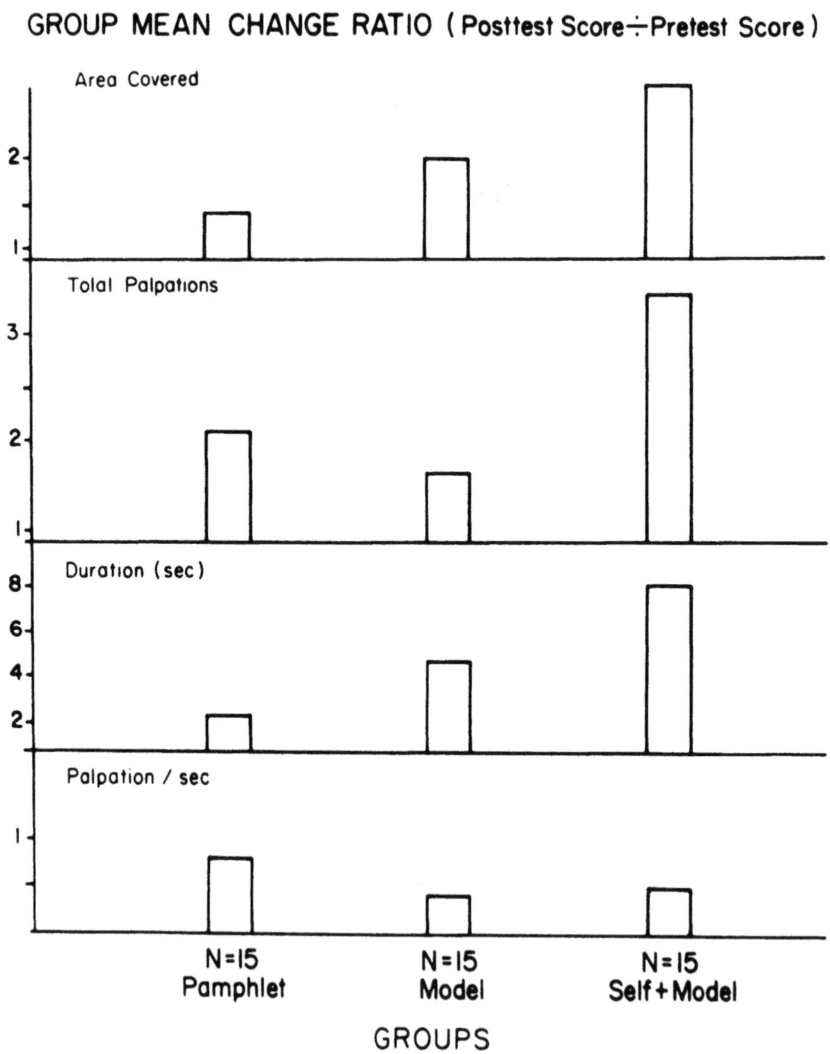

FIG. 13.8. Mean post-test/pre-test change ratios in four measures as a function of training conditions.

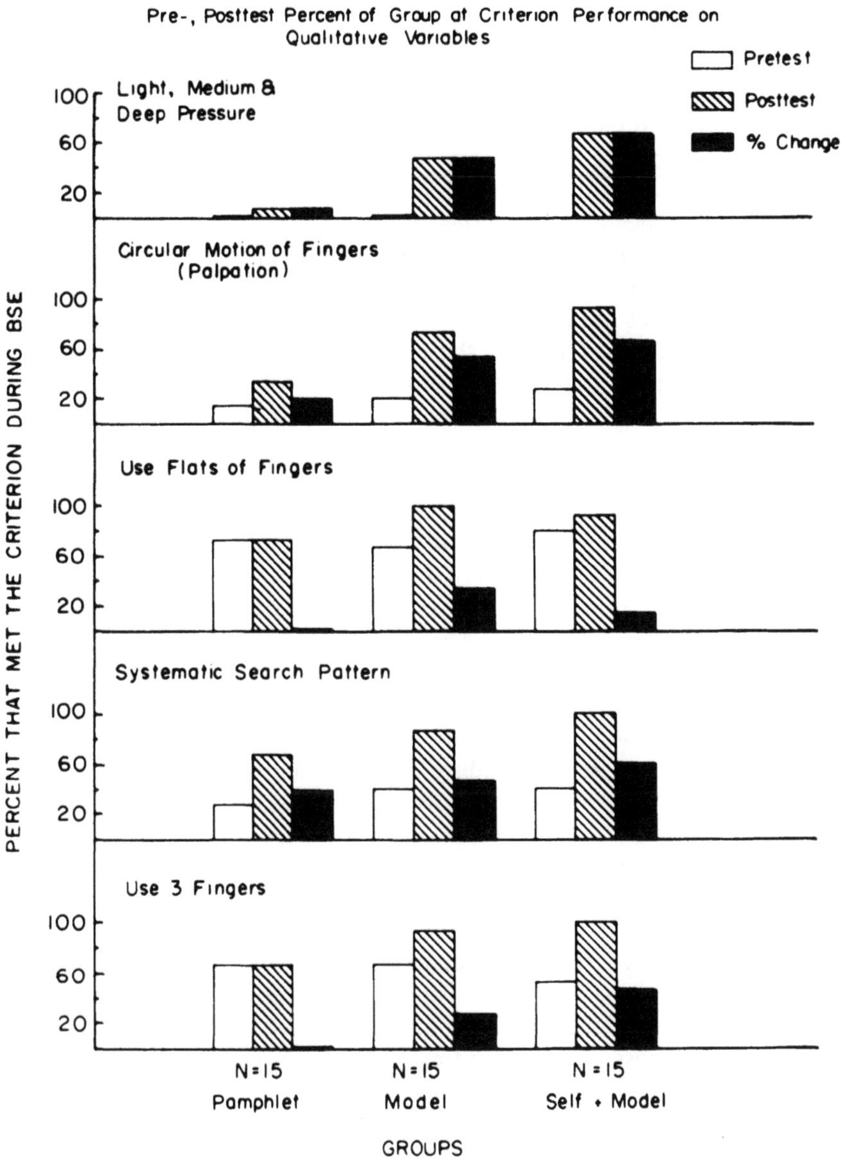

FIG. 13.9. Percentages of each group reaching criterion on five qualitative measures before and after training as a function of training conditions.

Search Pattern Analysis

The most finely honed palpation skills, no matter how sensitive the fingers may be to small breast lesions, are of no value if the fingers fail to come into contact with the portions of the breast tissue where the lesion(s) exist(s). A critical component of breast examination, then, is the use of a systematic search pattern that guarantees such contact.

During the course of the previous behavioural investigations, it gradually dawned on us that the traditional practice of searching the breast in a pattern of concentric circles leaves large areas unexamined. Tumours have been found in an area bounded by the clavicle, the midline, the fifth rib (braline) and a plumb line from the armpit to the fifth rib. The boundaries of this area are ignored by a search procedure which concentrates on the fullness (cone) of the breast. Moreover, searching in circles, no doubt originally the result of stimulus control exerted by the conical shape of the breast, often leaves a path best described as an Archimedes spiral. This causes the upper, outer quadrant to be examined relatively cursorily, despite the fact that this region accounts for over 50% of cancer finds (Case, 1984).

An alternative pattern has been advocated and is widely practised in Europe and Canada. It consists of a spoke pattern—a series of radii from the nipple. It is sometimes described as the "hands of the clock" method: Women are instructed to visualise a clock face on their breast and to initiate a line of search at the location of each hour. This method, too, guarantees decrease in coverage with increasing distance from the nipple.

We verified these phenomena on the breast models with the aid of the automated measurement procedure described above. We also established informally that the hemispheric model, despite its conical shape, could be searched thoroughly in a pattern of linear strips. We suggested to the subjects that they visualise the pattern they might use in mowing a lawn, even a lawn that contained an ancient Indian burial mound!

It remained for us to demonstrate the relative benefits of this pattern when examining real breasts. In an experiment conducted in 1982 but not reported until 1986, Saunders, Pilgrim, and Pennypacker recruited 28 female college students to serve in each of two experiments. College students were chosen for the first time in the entire programme because we considered it likely that they would have had little or no experience in breast self-examination and would therefore not show a learned preference for any of the patterns under investigation.

In Experiment 1, we compared the vertical linear strip (VS) pattern with the concentric circle (CC) pattern, whereas in Experiment 2, the VS pattern was compared to the radial spoke (RS) pattern. The subjects in both experiments initially provided a baseline demonstration of a breast examination. This was followed by basic instruction in the palpation technique, emphasising the use of the middle three fingers, small circular motions, and varying pressures. Uniform instruction in palpation provided a standard topography which facilitated later scoring of examination proficiency.

The subjects in Experiment 1 were then divided into two groups which received written instruction in either the VS pattern or the CC pattern. Instruction in either pattern consisted of a written and graphic presentation designed to acquaint the subject with the importance and nature of a systematic search pattern for breast examination. The CC instructions were taken from a widely distributed pamphlet which included diagrams of the pattern. The VS instructions were prepared in the same format by the experimenters so that the only difference was in the actual pattern described.

Following instruction, a second breast examination was performed, using the pattern just learned. The subject then immediately learned the alternative pattern and a third breast examination was conducted. Each subject therefore learned and demonstrated both search patterns, the two groups differing only with respect to order of presentation.

The procedure for Experiment 2 was identical to that of Experiment 1, except that the radial spoke (RS) pattern was substituted for the CC pattern and different subjects were used. Experiment 2 is therefore a partial replication of Experiment 1 and provides information on the stability of the effect of VS training across groups.

The measurements in both experiments were similar to those used in the second training comparison study. Calibrated observers tallied the squares of a projected grid that the subject palpated in each of her three examinations. Because thoroughness of coverage was the only performance dimension of interest, qualitative measures of palpation skill were not obtained.

The results of Experiments 1 and 2 are shown, respectively, in Fig. 13.10 and 13.11. In the top panel of each figure, we show the proportion of the entire area of clinically involved breast tissue examined under each condition. Because the CC and RS patterns do not instruct specifically for examination of the peripheral areas, we thought it prudent to evaluate the thoroughness of their coverage in the conical area alone. These comparisons are presented in the bottom panel of each figure.

There can be little doubt that the vertical strip (VS) pattern provides more thorough coverage than either of the other two, regardless of which area is considered. Of a total of 112 intrasubject comparisons involving the VS pattern, it was superior in all but 9, 4 of which were ties. It is of some interest that the RS pattern was statistically superior by *t*-test ($P < 0.05$) to the CC pattern in both areas; the tendency for the search to deteriorate into a widening spiral is peculiar to the CC pattern. All statistical compari-

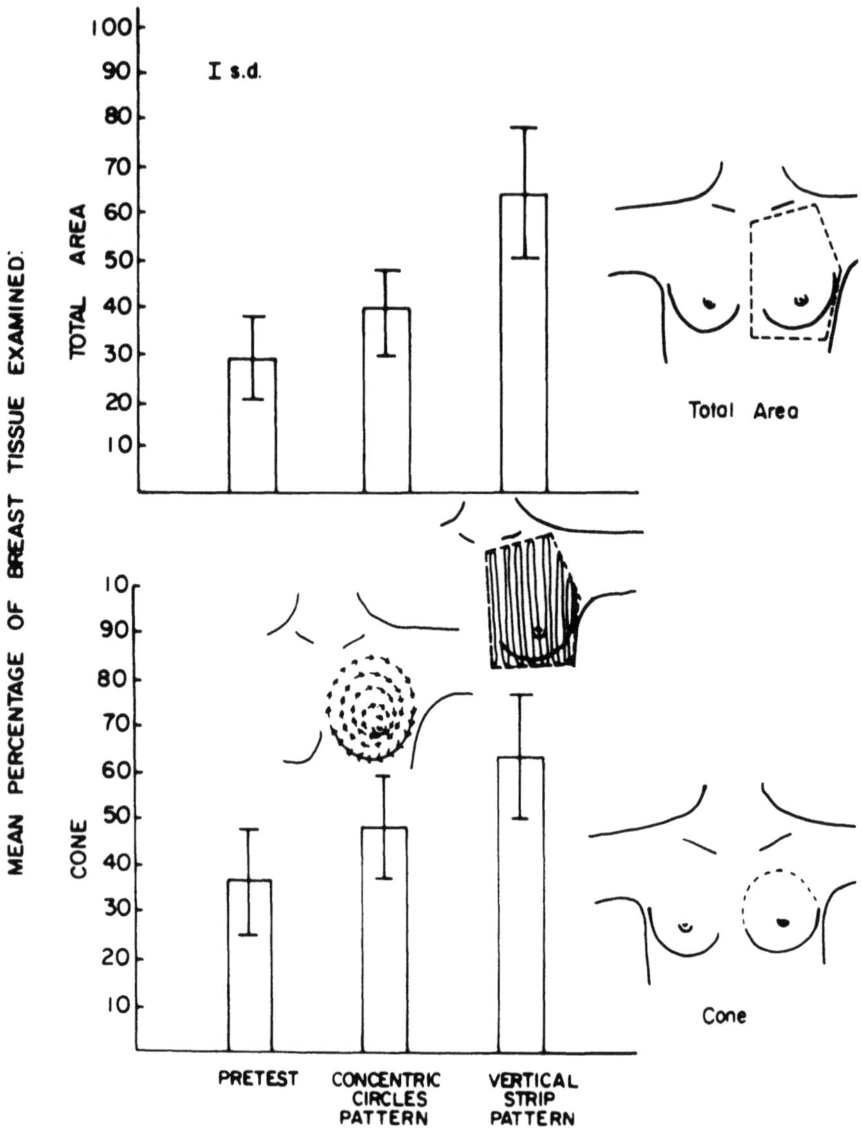

FIG. 13.10. Comparison of total and conical breast area examined before and after concentric circle and vertical strip search pattern training (from Saunders et al., 1986). Reproduced with the permission of the American Cancer Society.

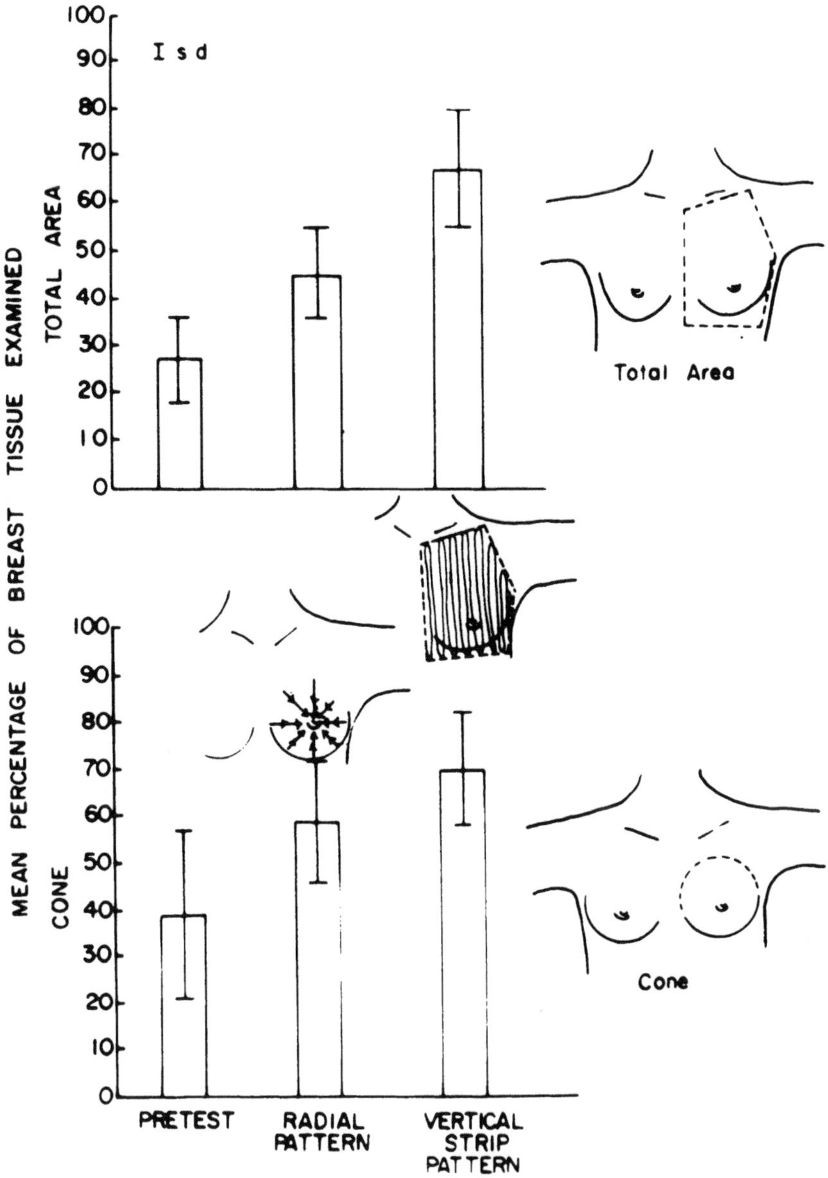

FIG. 13.11. Comparison of total and conical breast area examined before and after radial spoke and vertical strip search pattern training (from Saunders et al., 1986). Reproduced with the permission of the American Cancer Society.

sons involving the VS pattern, however, yielded t-values greater than 5.0 ($P < 0.01$).

Validation and Dissemination

The experiment just described concluded the basic research phase of the entire programme. What had emerged was a technology for teaching breast self-examination that differed from conventional practice in several important respects. It includes:

1. A life-like model of the human breast that simulates real tissue firmness and nodularity in addition to containing lumps of varying size, firmness, depth and moveability.
2. A technique of palpation that requires the use of the middle three fingers of one hand, the flats (rather than the tips) of the fingers, small circular motions, and differentiated pressures.
3. A training procedure that simultaneously involves the simulator and the trainee's own tissue, guaranteeing validity of the final performance while minimising the likelihood of false positive responding.
4. A system of direct measurement that provides both trainer and trainee with objective documentation and feedback and permits standards of proficiency to be established.

The ultimate validation of this technology will be measured in terms of small cancers detected and lives prolonged or saved. The intermediate problem concerns the transfer of the technology to mass application with minimal dilution of its quality. Each of the four features mentioned above is critical to the effectiveness of the skill provided and each requires stringent standards of quality assurance in either manufacture or delivery.

In order to ensure that the technology is transferred properly, the innovators have elected to do it themselves. The tactics involved have been described elsewhere (Pennypacker, 1986) and will not be elaborated upon here. Suffice it to say that should the reader encounter the name "Mamma-Care" in an advertisement or in the office of a health care provider anywhere in the world, he or she can be assured that the experiment is still in progress.

ACKNOWLEDGEMENTS

The research reported here was supported in part by Grant No. CA-20791 from the National Cancer Institute.

REFERENCES

Adams, C. K., Hall, D. C., Pennypacker, H. S., Goldstein, M. K., Hench, L. L., Madden, M. C., Stein, G. H., & Catania, A. C. (1976). Lump detection in simulated human breasts. *Perception and Psychophysics*, *20*, 163–167.

Bailar, J. C. (1977). Screening for early breast cancer: Pros and cons. *Cancer*, *39*, 2783–2795.

Baker, L. H. (1982). Breast cancer detection demonstration project: Five year summary report. *CA*, *32*, 194–225.

Bernard, C. (1957). *An introduction to the study of experimental medicine*. New York: Dover. (Originally published, 1865)

Bloom, H. S., Criswell, E. L., Pennypacker, H. S., Catania, A. C., & Adams, C. A. (1982). Major stimulus dimensions determining detection of simulated breast lesions. *Perception and Psychophysics*, *32*, 251–260.

Boring, E. G. (1942). *Sensation and perception in the history of experimental psychology*. New York: Appleton-Century-Crofts.

Case, C. (Ed.) (1984). *The breast cancer digest*. Bethesda, Md.: National Cancer Institute.

Cole, P. & Austin, H. (1981). Breast self-examination: An adjuvant to early cancer detection. *American Journal of Public Health*, *71*, 572–574.

Fisher, B., Slack, N. H., & Bross, I. (1969). Cancer of the breast: Size of neoplasm and prognosis. *Cancer*, *24*, 1071–1080.

Fisher, B., Bauer, M., Margolese, R. (1985). Five-year results of a randomized clinical trial comparing total mastectomy and segmental mastectomy with or without radiation in the treatment of breast cancer. *New England Journal of Medicine*, *312*, 665–673.

Fletcher, S. M., O'Malley, M. S., & Bunce, L. A. (1985). Physicians' abilities to detect lumps in silicone breast models. *Journal of the American Medical Asociation*, *253*, 2224–2228.

Foster, R. S., Lang, S. P., & Costanza, M. C. (1978). Breast self-examination practices and breast cancer stage. *New England Journal of Medicine*, *299*, 265–270.

Haagensen, C. (1971). *Diseases of the breast*. Philadelphia: W. B. Saunders.

Hall, D. C., Goldstein, M. K., & Stein, G. H. (1977). Progress in manual breast examination. *Cancer*, *40*, 364–370.

Hall, D. C., Adams, C. K., Stein, G. H., Goldstein, M. K., Stephenson, H. S., & Pennypacker, H. S. (1980). Improved detection of human breast lesions following experimental training. *Cancer*, *46*, 408–414.

Henderson, I. & Canellos, G. (1980). Cancer of the breast: The past decade. *New England Journal of Medicine*, *302*, 17–30.

Hicks, M. J., Davis, J. R., & Layton, J. M. (1979). Sensitivity of mammography and physical examination of the breast for detecting breast cancer. *Journal of the American Medical Association*, *242*, 2080–2083.

Huguley, C. M. & Brown, R. L. (1981). The value of breast self-examination. *Cancer*, *47*, 989–995.

Johnston, J. M. & Pennypacker, H. S. (1980). *Strategies and tactics of human behavioral research*. Hillsdale, N.J.: Lawrence Erlbaum Associates Inc.

Madden, M. C., Hench, L. L., Hall, D. C., Pennypacker, H . S., Adams, C. A., Goldstein, M. K., & Stein, G. H. (1978). Development of a model human breast with tumors for use in teaching breast examination. *Journal of Bioengineering*, *2*, 427–435.

Moore, F. D. (1978). Breast self-examination (editorial). *New England Journal of Medicine*, *299*, 304.

Moskowitz, M. (1983). Screening for breast cancer: How effective are our tests? A critical review. *CA*, *33*, 26–39.

Neelakantan, P., Criswell, E. L., Pennypacker, H. S., & Goldstein, M. K. (1981). Experimental comparison of breast self-examination training procedures. Paper presented to the meeting of the Association for Behavior Analysis, Milwaukee, May.

O'Malley, M. S. & Fletcher, S. W. (1987). Screening for breast cancer with breast self-examination: A critical review. *Journal of the American Medical Association*, *257*, 2197–2203.

Pennypacker, H. S. (1986). The challenge of technology transfer: Buying in without selling out. *Behavior Analyst*, *9*, 147–156.

Pennypacker, H. S., Neelakantan, P., Bloom, H. S., Criswell, E. L., & Goldstein, M. K. (1981). The effects of selected training procedures on acquisition and maintenance of skill in detecting simulated breast cancer. Paper presented to the meeting of the Association for Behavior Analysis, Milwaukee, May.

Phillips, A. J. (Ed.) (1974). *Cancer detection*. UICC Monograph Series, Vol. 4, 2nd edn. New York: Springer-Verlag.

Saunders, K. J., Neelakantan, P., Criswell, E. L., Bloom, H. S., & Pennypacker, H. S. (1982). An experimental analysis of the response components of breast self-examination. Paper presented to the meeting of the Association for Behavior Analysis, Milkwaukee, May.

Saunders, K. J., Pilgrim, C. A., & Pennypacker, H. S. (1986). Improved proficiency of search in breast self-examination. *Cancer*, 58, 2531–2537.

Shapiro, S. (1977). Evidence on screening for breast cancer on a randomized trial. *Cancer*, *39* (suppl.), 2772–2782.

Sidman, M. (1960). *Tactics of scientific research*. New York: Basic Books.

Silberner, J. (1988). How to beat breast cancer. *U.S. News and World Report*, *105 (2)*, 52–61.

Silverberg, E. & Lubera, J. (1988). Cancer statistics, 1988. *CA*, *38*, 5–22.

Skinner, B. F. (1956). A case history in scientific method. *American Psychologist*, *11*, 221–233.

Skinner, B. F. (1985). The shame of American education. *American Psychologist*, *39*, 947–954.

Spence, W. (1988). *Educational products catalogue*, pp. 44–48. Waco, Tx.: Health Edco Inc.

Strax, P. (1984). Mass screening for control of breast cancer. *Cancer*, *53*, 665–670.

Veronisi, U., Saccozzi, R., & Del Vecchio, M. (1981). Comparing radical mastectomy with quadrantectomy, axillary dissection, and radiotherapy in patients with small cancers of the breast. *New England Journal of Medicine*, *305*, 6–11.

Yamada, H. & Williams, F. (Eds) (1970). *Strength of biological materials*. Baltimore: Williams and Wilkins.

V CONCLUSION

14 Behaviour, Past and Future

Marc N. Richelle
Laboratory of Experimental Psychology, University of Liège, Liège, Belgium

The present volume has the word *behaviour* in its title, as had also the international scientific meeting at which the papers that make its content were originally delivered. As can be seen from the table of contents, the word is taken here in a very broad sense, that is intended to attract readers of genuine intellectual curiosity who are open to the ideas of those working in other domains or with other theoretical approaches. It is unusual, indeed, that topics as diversified as chronobiology and chronopsychology, language, rational thinking, and behavioural medicine are treated together, as in this volume. Such variety reflects deliberate choices: to maintain links between our knowledge of animal behaviour and of human behaviour; to give basic research and applications the place they deserve in a fruitful interaction; to appeal to various traditions that throw light on current issues; and to encourage contact between behavioural analysis and other fields of science, while addressing crucial debates in contemporary psychology concerning the subject matter of our science, the methods appropriate to its study, and the significance of the epistemological crisis it is often said to undergo.

THE BEHAVIOUR OF ORGANISMS AT FIFTY

By the time the Second European Meeting of the Experimental Analysis of Behaviour took place in Liège in 1988, 75 years had elapsed since Watson's (1913) manifesto was published and served as a catalyst to ideas that were waiting for paradigmatic crystallisation. Also, exactly 50 years had elapsed since another major work appeared, authored by B. F. Skinner with the title *The behavior of organisms* (1938). In his first book, Skinner laid the foundations for the empirical and theoretical work he has pursued since then, which in the laboratory has come to be known as the experimental analysis of behaviour, and in the clinic, school and ever-widening fields has come to be called the applied analysis of behaviour.

Criticisms of Skinner's approach have been numerous, and have been occasionally virulent. They seem to some to have eventually succeeded in relegating Skinnerian behaviourism to the past, even perhaps to the past errors of scientific psychology. Even Skinner (1987) sometimes seems to have resigned himself to the exclusion of behaviour from the field of psychology, an exclusion that is a major tenet of some brands of cognitivism.

The behavior of organisms is certainly not daily reading for contemporary students of psychology. One reason is that so many books have been published since then that convey attractively updated contemporary views of science. Moreover, students are probably not urged by their teachers to read the classical works of psychology at all. Were they to venture a glance through *The behaviour of organisms* for a first time, many young psychologists today would probably be surprised to discover the book was about "the original 'spontaneous' activity of the organism" (as opposed to behaviour elicited by stimuli); that the author, who had limited himself to the analysis of the behaviour of laboratory animals, was none the less aware of specific issues raised by human behaviour, and that he viewed verbal behaviour as the only source of differences between rat and man ("aside from enormous differences of complexity"); that the word "cognition" appears in that 50-year-old book, not with a view to denying that it refers to something important, but to oppose an essentially mentalistic approach to cognitive phenomena. They would also discover empirical data on drug action on behaviour, and a 50-page chapter on temporal discrimination which was written when very few people were interested in the psychology of time and chronobiology was an esoteric science. The book indeed foreshadowed, half a century ago, many important topics that are discussed in the present volume.

There can be no question about the seminal value of *The behavior of organisms*, evidenced by the widespread influence gained by its author in the decades following its publication. However, in the last 20 years or so things seem to have changed drastically, and one is led to ask, as Skinner (1987) himself asked recently, "Whatever happened to psychology as the science of behavior?", or, as was asked at the Second European Meeting on the Experimental Analysis of Behaviour in Liège of a panel of psychologists from a dozen countries, "Is there a future for behaviour in psychology?"

I shall here try to answer the first question in a different way from

Skinner, and I shall answer the second question in a way that is intended to reflect and integrate some of the very contradictory views which were expressed by the international panel at the conference (though without claiming to give each view the weight accorded in that discussion).

FROM BEHAVIOUR TO COGNITION, AND BACK TO ACTION

To answer the first question—Whatever happened to psychology as the science of behaviour?—one can look at what psychologists do, or one can listen to what they say. If the latter strategy is adopted, one will surely be struck by the fact that many psychologists today seem to have banned the word "behaviour" from their talk. It has given place to "cognition" or some other item of the same lexical class. But looking at what psychologists *do*, one can observe that they are indeed still dealing most of the time with behaviour. What they had eliminated is not behaviour but "behaviourism". One should perhaps not mind too much about that. Skinner (1963) himself expected the death of behaviourism in his paper celebrating the 50th anniversary of Watson's manifesto: "Behaviorism, as we know it, will eventually die—not because of its failure, but because of its success." To a large extent, what is done today under the cognitivist flag is clearly of the same stuff as was done 30 years ago under the behaviourist banner. Skinner was emphasising this when he wrote in 1984, "Most of what is called cognitive science is work that was carried on in more or less the same way before that magical word was added." Animal psychophysics, which owes its very development to operant techniques, is a typical case of progress in making accessible previously inaccessible phenomena, and it is quite logical that, after having first objectively studied animals' "sensations" (themselves formally thought of as unapproachable, as being part of an inner world, even by scientists as confident of experimental methods as Claude Bernard), animal psychophysics would turn to more complex issues, as it demonstrated in animals phenomena relevant to after-images (Williams, 1974) and mental rotations (Holland & Delius, 1982). It does not matter whether those who now investigate animal psychophysics label themselves as behaviour analysts or not, provided that they continue to produce new data and new theoretical insights. These are all benefits for psychologists whatever their affiliation to a school of thought. As pointed out by Skinner (1984, p. 282) again: "Many of the facts, and even of the principles, that psychologists have discovered when they may have thought they were discovering something else are useful."

Another still more striking case is to be found in developmental psycholinguistics, where the formal Chomskian approach has been generally abandoned for an interactionist approach characterising pragmatics, which is not far removed from Skinner's earlier emphasis on the "global verbal episode". Few, if any, contemporary psycholinguists make explicit reference to Skinner's pioneering work, just as few specialists of computer-assisted learning today mention Skinner's teaching machines, the principles of which they are nevertheless applying. Such neglects have a number of reasons, reflecting mainly perhaps the sociology of science, which we may here leave to historians of psychology to analyse.

Thus, if we put aside the polemical aspects of the question and observe dispassionately psychological science as it is *done*, "behaviourism" may be dead but "behaviour" is certainly flourishing. However, the shift of emphasis from behaviour to cognition means much more than that to many cognitivists. They would insist that they no longer study behaviour as before, for itself as it were, but as a tool of studying something more important. An extreme stand is to view behaviour as an indicator of internal representations. Progress in the study of these representations, presumably of a non-behavioural nature, will eventually lead to our giving up behaviour completely, because it will no longer be a necessary stage in dealing with the inner cognitive system. This conception has exerted great seduction on psychologists over the last 20 years or so, with the mind appearing to recover its scientific dignity and the philosophical approaches to the study of mind (including those specifically termed "philosophy of mind") regaining much territory previously lost to empirical psychology. But, fascinated by the mind, psychology has now lost *action* (as it has also lost *emotion*, but this is another story), which had been viewed as the source of what we call mind. Cognition, as it is often conceptualised today, is in an empty space, a refined representational machine with no active output.

Is such a view to be regarded as an irreversible step in the development of psychology, and more generally of so-called cognitive science? Clearly, it is not. It has never been so for those who have been interested in the study of movement proper, but such interests have not really shaped the recent evolution of cognitivism. More significantly, it is no longer so for several outstanding figures in the field even of cognitive science. For example, Varela (1989; see also Maturana & Varela, 1986) expresses his dissatisfaction with the current state of affairs in cognitive science (including its recent connectionist versions), and he shows how essential dimensions are still missing. He is led to bring action back into the picture, with some qualifications, under the term *enaction*. A detailed and critical discussion of his view would not fit in this short presentation. The thrust of it can be captured by pinpointing a few elements. Varela clearly emphasises that his conception is "a criticism of the use of the concept of representation in cognitive sciences and technologies since only a predefined world can be represented". His perspective is concerned with "giving the concept of action prevalence over the concept of representation". Varela argues that representations, as the term is used by most cognitivists, imply a predefined world of which they are merely a cognitive conversion; actions are but byproducts of representations. He reinstates the historical (phylogenic, ontogenic and cultural) dimension of knowledge—a rehabilitation that is also to some extent inherent in connectionism. The brain is now conceived of as an organ that "constructs worlds" rather than reflects them. In a polar map that shows how various thinkers can be located in relation to traditional cognitivism and to the theory of emergence and enaction which Varela is advocating, one finds Piaget closest to Varela's ideas, one step removed from more traditional cognitivism as exemplified by Neisser in psychology, by Chomsky and Fodor in linguistics and epistemology, and by Hubel and Wiesel in neurobiology. The point here is not to suggest that Varela's and similar views are only resurgences of behaviourism. Current so-called cognitive science obviously addresses different issues, and uses a different language: Science does not come back to earlier stages. What is clear, however, is that the recent shift in emphasis in cognitive science from representation to action implies a reintegration of behaviour in its own right, and it makes it impossible to view behaviour as merely a potentially dispensable indicator of representations. It drives us to a redefinition of representations that looks for their origin in the interaction of organisms with their environment: at the level of the species through evolutionary mechanisms, at the level of the individual through learning, and at the level of culture through historical emergence and the selection of cultural features. Skinner has himself, of course, repeatedly emphasised these three levels of functional analysis of behaviour–environment interactions.

BEHAVIOUR, BEHAVIOURISM AND THE WILL OF GOD

In the above I have given priority to the issue of behaviour as confronted by cognitive science. This has also been a recurrent theme in the debate on the question "Is there a future for behaviour in psychology?" Feelings about the question at issue, as discussed by the panel of experts at the Liège Conference, are clearly influenced by the geographic context in which people live and by the kinds of activities in which they are engaged. There appear to be countries (Brazil seems to be an example) where psychology is still easily defined as the science of behaviour, if not by all psychologists at least by a large enough group to comfort them in the idea that no dramatic change is taking place. A similar feeling is clearly experienced by people who are involved in fields of application in which practices derived from the experimental analysis of behaviour have been shown to be effective and continue to develop successfully, apart from some epistemological turbulences. The same is true of people who are engaged in basic behavioural research in fields such as behavioural pharmacology or psychophysiology, in which the use of behavioural techniques remains unquestioned.

The situation is quite different for those in basic experimental psychology in an academic context, however, who might stand to suffer from the disrepute into which behaviour has fallen, to the point that access to grants or other Manna is subordinated to a cognitive shibboleth! Maintaining that behaviour is still the main thing for psychology could possibly even mean taking the risk of excluding oneself from the contemporary scientific community. The risk is all the more real when "behaviour" is obstinately confused with "behaviourism" and behaviourism is in turn interpreted merely as an unfortunate mishap of American psychology. This has been, and is still, a widely held view, mainly in Europe. It has been expressed again recently by Voneche (1987), who contends that "the success of Skinner's views in spite of all their logical pitfalls" is to be accounted for by "their adherence to a set of American values that are largely exported by the government of the USA along with other goods". He points to a few features of American culture supposedly transparent in Skinner's writings, such as the taste for simplistic disjunctive discourse (the cult of *versus*: nature *versus* nurture, facts *versus* speculation, etc.); the cult of facts; the consensus about the basic goodness of American society. Elaborating further his socio-historical interpretation, he eventually establishes a cause–effect relationship between the ideology of puritanism, rooted in Calvinism, and Skinner's conceptions: "The mere description of one's own successes and failures (trials and errors, or contingencies of reinforcement) is a better controller and predictor of God's election than any other type of explanation. What better illustration for his theology, could my next-door neighbour on the rue Calvin, John Calvin, imagine than a Skinner box!" How cognitive psychology could possibly emerge in such a social context is a question that Voneche solves by happily appealing to the regenerating effect of importing European ideas, especially Piaget's, to the Western side of the Atlantic.

Voneche's paper is typical of a certain kind of misreading of Skinner's writings, indulging in a strange amalgam of straw-man destruction and cultural egocentrism. I have discussed him here at some length because his sort of neo-Weberian explanation was echoed by a participant in the debate at the Liège Conference, who explained behaviourism as a by-product of puritan ethics which, it was claimed, never really penetrated the intellectual tradition of Western Europe. It was suggested that the success of behaviourism in the USA was linked with the Protestants' willingness to prepare on earth the kingdom of God.

Social determinants of scientific theories and practices are now recognised, but it is also recognised that they are very difficult to decipher. Explanations in terms of one single factor, be it economics, religion, philosophy, climate, etc., are almost certainly inadequate, over-simplifying, and moreover suspect when they involve national, cultural or continental stereotypes.

THE FLIGHT TO PHYSIOLOGY REVISITED

Most participants in the debate in the Conference at Liège had interpreted the question about the future of behaviour in psychology in terms of behaviour versus cognition, as might be expected from the Zeitgeist. A more classic opposition comes to mind, though curiously enough it came on that occasion only to the mind of one person, namely *behaviour* versus *physiological events*. The rapid progress of neurosciences might give some support to the view that turning away from behaviour to neurobiology is not, as it might have seemed earlier, a "flight from the (behavioural) laboratory" to some more appealing and recognised scientific practice, but a real taking-over of the task previously attempted by psychology with crude and approximate methods by a full-fledged science with increasing mastery of the internal machinery that produces behaviour.

This way of stating the issue does not correctly reflect the state of the art, however. Behaviour is surely one of those things which neurosciences are about. There is no way to understand brain functions, in so far as they control the interaction between the organism and its environment, except by including behaviour in the analysis. And, conversely, limiting one's research to behaviour cannot be a matter of principle, and is less than before a matter of convenience: When multiple refined tools are at hand that enable us to track sensory processes and motor control inside the nervous system, why stay at the threshold, either outside or inside the organism? An integrated approach is what is called for and indeed is what is actually practised by many, whatever the respective parts of neural and behavioural techniques and concepts and whatever the subdivision of the task between purely behavioural and purely neurobiological scientists.

This balanced, integrated approach to brain *and* to behaviour is admittedly not shared by all. Crude ontological reductionism is not rare in neuroscience circles. The belief that percepts and concepts are right there at the tip of their electrodes seems still to attract in many neuroanatomists or neurophysiologists. Paradoxically, they might be comforted in that belief by the tenet of some cognitivists that behaviour is not important, being only a (presumably imperfect) manifestation of what goes on in the head. It is quite logical for those who feel they have good techniques to explore directly the stuff in the head, to dispense with psychology.

There is, however, another paradox. Arguments for psychology—or, more correctly stated, for a science of mind—as an autonomous science come also today from the cognitivist side. Cognitivism (I am tempted to say "*radical* cognitivism") resists the prospect of cognition being dissolved in neural matter. Claims are made for something that is neither behavioural nor neural, that would dominate both. The computer metaphor is helpful at this stage: It gives credibility to the idea that some immaterial entities are controlling brain functions, which in turn subserviently produce behaviours. Analysis at the neural level—*implementation*—is only second (both in significance and in time) to analysis at the cognitive level (*computational* and *representational*, in Marr's sense). This gives cognitive psychology a prominent position, reminding us of Chomsky's contention that language development and use could only be studied after linguistics had completed its enquiry into the nature of language. Fortunately, students of language acquisition have nevertheless been pursuing their observations and experiments, and thanks to them we know more today about language itself. Similarly, we can expect that those dealing directly with neuronal circuits, neurotransmitters, microarchitectures of the brain or plasticity in neural tissues are not about to interrupt their research to wait for computational clarifications. Skinner defended a science of behaviour distinct from neurophysiology on two grounds: (1) Behaviour is one part of the whole organism–environment system, and as such one cannot ignore it; (2) neurophysiology, if it is to progress, needs among other things good behavioural analysis. Cognitivism's claim of autonomy looks like a new dualism. It does not elucidate the supposedly missing link between neural matter and behaviour, but instead restores the idea of the irreducibility of an immaterial mind. It is my bet for the future that, through trial and error (as species, individuals and scientists alike have done for hundreds of years) neurobiology and behaviour analysis will cooperate effectively to give cognition not a soul, but a sense of where it comes from and of what it is used for, a *history* and *actions* to perform.

REFERENCES

Holland, V. P. & Delius, J. P. (1982). Rotational invariance in visual pattern recognition of pigeons and humans. *Science*, *218*, 804–806.

Maturana, H. & Varela, F. J. (1986). *The tree of knowledge: The biological roots of human understanding*. Boston: New Science Library.

Skinner, B. F. (1938). *The behavior of organisms*. New York: Appleton-Century-Crofts.

Skinner, B. F. (1963). Behaviorism at fifty. *Science*, *140*, 951–958.

Skinner, B. F. (1984). Canonical papers of B. F. Skinner: Author's response. *Behavioral and Brain Sciences*, *7*, 473–724.

Skinner, B. F. (1987). Whatever happened to psychology as the science of behavior? *American Psychologist*, *42*, 780–786.

Varela, F. J. (1989). *Les sciences cognitives: Tendances et perspectives*. Paris: Du Seuil.

Voneche, J. J. (1987). An exercise in triviality: The epistemology of radical behaviorism. In S. Modgil & C. Modgil (Eds), *B. F. Skinner: Consensus and controversy*, pp. 69–74. Barcombe: Falmer Press.
Watson, J. B. (1913). Psychology as the behaviorist views it. *Psychological Reviews*, *20*, 158–177.
Williams, J. L. (1974). Evidence of complementary afterimages in the pigeons. *Journal of Experimental Analysis of Behavior*, *21*, 421–424.

Author Index

Subject Index

For Product Safety Concerns and Information please contact our EU representative GPSR@taylorandfrancis.com
Taylor & Francis Verlag GmbH, Kaufingerstraße 24, 80331 München, Germany

www.ingramcontent.com/pod-product-compliance
Ingram Content Group UK Ltd.
Pitfield, Milton Keynes, MK11 3LW, UK
UKHW022004180926
475701UK00003B/180
* 9 7 8 1 1 3 8 8 7 6 9 4 1 *